# Honors Theses in International Theory and Policy

2015

# Honors Theses in International Theory and Policy

Contributors:  Cameron Brown
Skoda Oda
Elizabeth Peabody
Nitya Ramanathan
Leila Wang
Owen (Yun) Wang

Editor:  Scot Macdonald

USC Dornsife, School of International Relations,
University of Southern California
Los Angeles, California
2015

*Honors Theses in International Relations* is a serial publication of the USC Dornsife School of International Relations. For information about obtaining additional copies, please contact the Director, SIR, USC, VKC 330, Los Angeles, CA 90089-0043.

ISBN: 978-0-692-44027-8

Printed in the United States of America

# Contents

# John S. Odell and Nina S. Rathbun – Mentors Par Excellence

This volume of our annual series featuring the Honors theses in the USC School of International Relations owes its existence to many individuals—most of all the students who researched and wrote them, but also the professors, librarians, family and friends who helped in every step along the way. Yet two who deserve special thanks are John Odell and Nina Rathbun, the "founder and future" respectively, of SIR's ambitious and growing honors program.

While earlier luminaries such as Tom Biersteker and Hayward Alker gave much in support of honors research, it was John Odell who some fifteen years ago essentially founded our "modern" honors program. Not only did he create the structure for a rigorous research experience, he also served as adviser to many students who still passionately praise his mentorship. Now emeritus, Odell has returned to teach a graduate research-design seminar, serves as a Senior Fellow at the Centre for International Governance Innovation, and chairs policy roundtables on improving global environmental governance.

Nina Rathbun is SIR's Director of Undergraduate Studies and, for several years, has overseen student recruitment and advising on a wide range of research fellowships—from Boren to Fulbright. It was therefore natural that she would take on honors students, and she has done so with a vengeance. This has consisted, first, of creating a new advanced (300-level, following on our introductory course) research methods class, and then redesigning the entire honor's sequence to make it a more rigorous, competitive, and productive two-semester sequence. Modeled on those at Harvard and Stanford Universities, the new honors program takes the quality of our students' work to new heights.

Congratulations and thanks to Professors Odell and Rathbun, both dedicated advocates of excellence and advisers of commitment and passion.

# Introduction

## *Scot Macdonald*

At first glance the theses contained in this volume do not have a great deal in common. Chinese "soft power," post-conflict Sri Lanka, Japanese pop culture, multinational corporate behavior, Egypt and Tunisia after the "Arab Spring," and immigration in Japan—what could possibly unite these topics? Yet think again and the answer is clear. And it points to how much our world has been transformed over the past 20 years, how many new issues crowd the global agenda and how the "levers" of international influence have changed. In these pages you will not find much on traditional "hard power" politics, though these surely remain important. But what our honors students found most interesting was equally important yet far less studied: the influence of a state's cultural policies, for example, the power of shaming and the necessity of inclusion and reconciliation.

All of the theses in this volume were researched, analyzed and written by students in the Honors Program in the School of International Relations (SIR) at the University of Southern California. The program is designed to provide an opportunity for a structured in-depth study of a topic chosen by the student. Under the supervision of a faculty member who is expert in the student's thesis topic, Honors candidates develop a formal research design, conduct a literature review, apply theories and research methodologies relevant to their study, and author a thesis of publishable quality—as shown by their selection for inclusion in this volume. The breadth of topics covered by the papers in this volume reflects the range of issues facing the international community and the vast reach of international relations as a field, as well as the broad applicability of methodologies taught in international relations to a diverse range of issues. From economic policy and migration to healthcare and human rights, security alliances to participation in international forums, the papers include:

- Cameron Brown's incisive and theoretically sophisticated analysis of the tension between international norms and Chinese behavior in examining the impact of Beijing's "soft power" policies in other East Asian countries.

- Shoko Oda's pioneering study of the conditions—particularly when they include prior crises—that lead local Japanese communities to provide better or worse services to their immigrant communities.

- Elizabeth Peabody's comprehensive investigation of differing traditions, and the crucial role of leadership, in shaping the very different post-uprising paths of the Egyptian and Tunisian militaries.

- Nitya Ramanathan's absorbing analysis of post-conflict Sri Lanka—in light of experience from South Africa, Rwanda, and Northern Ireland—and its sober conclusion that peace without justice may not be long-lived.

- Leila Wang's original survey of Chinese respondents to explore the relationship—judged strong, but not definitive—between consumption of Japanese pop culture products and positive attitudes toward Japan.

- Owen Wang's close analysis of the various types of international suasion that have been applied to multinational corporations (MNCs), finding that political and legal levers are much more effective than activist pressure.

Besides contributing, students in the SIR Honors Program also learned crucial new skills in the areas of writing, research and reasoning, which will help prepare them for future graduate work or for a broad range of professions. Viewed narrowly, learning to conduct original research can be seen as solely suited to becoming a professor or researcher. However, the skills acquired in such intensive independent investigation are crucial to a broad number of fields, including law, business, marketing, writing, government, and healthcare—almost any human endeavor. Applying the scientific method to any problem, regardless of the field, is the most efficient means of developing a better understanding of the problem, and devising solutions. Without science, humankind would still be mired in superstition. With science, we have spread economic prosperity around much of the globe, shrunk the world with the Internet and cheap air travel, reached the moon and sent probes far beyond our solar system. Teaching the scientific method to students today is crucial to solving problems on the edge of our solar system, as well as the multitude of problems we face on earth. Whatever field they plan to pursue, the students in the International Relations Honors Program have shown that they have the skills to analyze problems and develop possible solutions.

# Contributors

**Cameron Brown** is graduating with a major in International Relations and a minor in Economics. He is a member of Phi Beta Kappa who enjoys engaging with issues of international politics in an abstract setting through Model UN, and in a practical setting through policy research. This summer, Cameron is planning on continuing his current position with the Milken Institute or accepting an offer with a government security agency.

**Shoko Oda** is from Saitama, Japan and is graduating with a double major in International Relations and East Asian Area Studies. When not in class, Shoko was an active member of the USC Trojan Marching Band. Upon graduation she will return to Tokyo, where she will work as a reporter for an American newswire.

**Elizabeth Peabody** is from Boston, Massachusetts. She is graduating with a major in International Relations and a double minor in Psychology and Screenwriting, and will be working come June in Washington, D.C. for Raytheon defense contracting in the corporation's Leadership Development Program.

**Nitya Ramanathan** is from Phoenix, Arizona. She became interested in examining the relationship between peace and justice after conducting extensive research on the post-conflict period in Sri Lanka, where her family is from. She also traveled to Rwanda to study the grassroots courts and spent a semester in Northern Ireland examining the reconstruction efforts there. She plans to continue this work in justice by attending law school after graduation.

**Leila Wang** is from Singapore. She holds a double degree in International Relations and Business Administration from USC, and has worked in Singapore, the US and Japan. After graduation she is planning to work for the public sector in Singapore.

**Yun (Owen) Wang** is an Undergraduate at University of Southern California, working towards a degree in International Relations, with a minor in Economics. He is interested in exploring the effects of economic activities and globalization on the structure and development of global society. Topics he has explored range from analyzing China's economic rise to studying foreign direct investment's impact on the Turkish civil conflict. He has interned for Los Angele's Chamber of Commerce and USC's U.S.-China Institute. After graduation, Owen will enter law school.

Editor **Scot Macdonald**, PhD, is a graduate of the SIR doctoral program, as well as the University of British Columbia and the University of Nevada, Reno. He is an adjunct professor at the SIR and has published *Rolling the Iron Dice: Historical Analogies and Decisions to Use Military Force in Regional Contingencies* and *Propaganda and Information Warfare in the Twenty-First Century*, as well as articles in *Diplomacy & Statecraft*, the *Marine Corps Gazette*, the *Fletcher Forum of International Affairs*, and the US Naval Institute's *Proceedings*.

# 1

# Through a Normative Lens:
## The Effect of China's Foreign Policy on its Soft Power

*Cameron Brown*

*This study advances the argument that two behavioral dimensions of China's foreign policy conduct are at the heart of its current soft power trajectory. First, it is hypothesized that the PRC's transgressive acts – or behavior which violates norms - has elicited stigmatization from foreign audiences. Such stigmatization involves the loss of status and appeal for China, signaling a decline in soft power. Second, China's aggressive and/or assertive foreign policy actions are hypothesized to have a similar negative effect on public opinion. When examining East Asian media sources, it is observed that aggressive and transgressive foreign policy conduct co-varies strongly with all systematic declines in foreign perceptions. Additionally, both behavioral characteristics are shown to produce their own unique effects on public sentiment towards China. Transgressive actions cause protracted declines that are followed by a high degree of stigmatizing language, while aggression produces sharper, shorter declines that are characterized by heightened threat perceptions. Collectively, the study illustrates that the aggressive and transgressive character of China's foreign policy is countervailing the state's efforts to increase its soft power.*

Since the turn of the century, scholars have favorably appraised China in light of perceived gains to both its image and influence within East Asia (Kurlantick 2006, Nye 2005, Cho and Jeong 2008). Yet this initial optimism regarding China's soft power future has begun to cool in the wake of Beijing's more recent actions. Studies have documented what is being deemed a decline in foreign perceptions, with scholars like Nye changing their initial favorable assessments of the state's soft power (Nye, 2012). The implicit argument behind these reevaluations is that some aspect of China's behavior or identity is eroding the strength of its appeal abroad, much akin to what happened to American soft power following the Iraq War. Speculation has abounded as to what these factors might be in the Chinese case, but few, if any, recent works have empirically examined any such variables in light of a hypothesized decline. The question then becomes, what factors are responsible for the apparent shifts in China's soft power?

For a state like China to be considered a strong soft power nation, its relevant economic, political, and cultural institutions must be considered attractive (Nye, 2004). This "attraction" is felt by external actors and it encourages the emulation or adoption of sympathetic policies. As such, soft power is a resource which aligns another's interests with one's own (ibid.). Because soft power is primarily derived from attractiveness, individual agents and specific populations have a great deal of agency in determining a state's appeal. These entities are the ones who realize soft power, because it is their experience of attraction that causes them to behave sympathetically towards a foreign state. Therefore, factors which impact foreign audiences are highly salient as determinants of soft power success. Already, the normative beliefs, historic status, and political identity of foreign populations have been identified as factors which impact soft power strength (Kern, 2012. Chiozza, 2004. Nye, 2002). Variables like economic success and foreign aid have also been observed to correlate positively with soft power improvements (Li Zhang, 2010. Jung-Nam Lee, 2008). On the other side, reductions in soft power have been linked to instances where a state is perceived to act unilaterally, violate international norms, or behave aggressively (Chiozza, 2004 and Katazenstein and Keohane, 2006).

In China's case, its soft power appears at the crux of both the aforementioned positive and negative forces. The PRC's material success, soft power campaign, and traditional culture ostensibly grant it a strong appeal with foreign audiences. However, East Asian audiences have begun to question the veracity of Beijing's "peaceful rise" rhetoric because of its recent assertiveness (W. Zhang, 2012). The juxtaposition of the PRC's material ascent and its seemingly unfavorable set of behaviors is therefore a unique intersection of two countervailing forces. The material set of forces ought to bring with it a commensurate rise in Soft Power attraction, but this force is offset by the consequences of China's behavior. This intersection offers scholars an opportunity to assess the relative impact of China's behavior on its soft power. By studying the effects of individual variables, it is possible to determine which of these factors are currently affecting the trajectory of China's image in East Asia. In this context, the following study explores two determinants of soft power and their applicability to the Chinese case. The first is transgressive behavior, or conduct which violates normative standards. The second is conduct that is aggressive, threatening, or that heightens security concerns. More specifically, the study posits that these two behavioral characteristics are the primary catalysts behind systematic declines in public perceptions.

To scrutinize each hypothesis, the study departs from traditional opinion poll metrics in constructing a qualified and temporally sensitive data set. This data set is comprised of opinion articles from regional news sources which act as an analogue for regional perceptions. The language of these articles is the subject of analysis due to its ability to reflect changes in popular sentiment. It represents a qualified metric that has the ability to capture more nuanced shifts in discourse and characterizations of China. These frequently released pieces also display rapid changes in opinion and therefore can depict the immediate effects of behavior on public sentiment. Both factors allow a better visualization of the reactive process by which public opinion responds to social stimulus.

The compiled index of articles is analyzed along two dimensions. First, the data is organized chronologically and is then juxtaposed with a timeline of China's behavior. By analyzing the two in parallel, it is clear when perception changes co-vary with instances of Chinese norm violations or aggression. Examining the presence or absence of covariance is also a means by which the primary hypothesis can be falsified. Random shifts with no clear covariance would weaken the argument that Chinese soft power is affected by the aforementioned determinants. Second, the qualified nature of the data set will be used to determine if foreign discourse stigmatizes China or depicts China as a threat. Stigmatization is an important indicator given that it is a social means by which actors regulate the behavior of transgressive entities and they naturally follow instances of norm-violations (Alder-Nissen, 2014). Thus, the presence of this type of discourse would suggest a causal relationship between China's norm violations and the resulting attitudes. Recording threat perceptions also allows visualization into the effect of aggression or transgression on the security mindset of East Asian audiences.

This method approaches the topic of China's Soft Power from a different angle: its application of a temporally sensitive and qualified measurement system will better illustrate the relationship between China's behavior and its soft power status. It hypothesizes the state's aggressive and transgressive behavior as the root of the putative soft power decline. Through an analysis of media discourse, this study demonstrates that these characteristics do indeed correlate strongly with every instance of perception declines within the past five years. In the Philippines, Singapore, Indonesia, and South Korea, each decline possessed specific characteristics based on whether the catalyzing event was aggressive, transgressive, or both. The shifts in perceptions were also systematic and protracted, thus demonstrating that these aspects of Chinese foreign policy explain a large degree of the systematic fluctuations in public perceptions. While these findings are not unexpected, they do highlight these two factors as the primary catalysts behind sentiment which opposes Beijing's soft power agenda.

## Soft Power and its Determinants

As defined by Nye, a state's soft power is represented in the relative attractiveness of that state's system of governance and identity. This "attraction" is felt by other states which subsequently encourages emulation and increases the influence of the domestic state's agenda (Nye, 2004). Under this conceptualization, Soft Power does not constitute overt influence or direct manipulation, nor does it involve material incentivizing (Tatar, 2010). When applied to real world polities, soft power serves to create a sympathetic ideational environment in which positive sentiments and sympathetic policies are more likely to arise (Nye, 2004). It is therefore a tool used to co-opt the agenda of foreign actors by making them more sympathetic to the domestic state's interests. For the purposes of this paper, soft power is defined as an external manifestation of a state's attractiveness which facilitates the alignment of foreign actors' interests with one's own.

Given the passive manner in which soft power is exercised, it is logical that the sources of soft power are typically not active processes. Cultural strength, political appeal, ideational compatibility, as well as sympathetic foreign policies are the resources most frequently associated with soft power (Kearn, Nye, etc). Yet soft power resources should not be mistaken as a form of persuasive currency or political capital to be cashed in. Rather, it is the appeal of these elements abroad that is the real manifestation of soft power. In fact, the determinants of a state's soft power strength are not solely based on their inherent character, but are instead affected by patterns of foreign interpretation. Each aspect of a country's identity cannot be described as inherently appealing or unattractive. Instead, these soft power resources are filtered through the medium of foreign perceptions. This can explain in part the variance amongst regional reactions to China's government policies, international products, cultural events, and media projections (Zhang, 2010). Differences amongst audiences, as well as the vagaries of the projection itself, are liable to cause variance. The state may attempt to shape the trajectory of foreign opinion by projecting a favorable representation of itself, but agency largely resides with the audience. It is these individuals and populations who receive, and subsequently internalize, information about a state's identity. Foreign attitudes are therefore a critical dimension of soft power analysis because they serve this intermediary role.

The attitudes resulting from this interpretation, positive and negative, are also part of the mechanism by which soft power's effects are realized. While Nye's initial conceptualization does not include such a mechanism, Huang and Ding sought to provide one by tracing the effects of attraction on the public, policy elites, and interest groups. They describe country A's Soft Power resources as inducing a sympathetic shift in the interests of these groups in country B, which subsequently causes these actors to align with the foreign policies, agenda, and guidance of country A (Huang and Ding, 2006). Via country A's attraction, the agenda of foreign states are therefore harmonized with the interests of country A. This attraction is integrated into the decision making process of country B as foreign actors base they decisions on their existing knowledge and perceptions of Country A (Zhang, 233-36).

Here, soft power is largely depicted as dependent upon foreign perceptions. As such, a logical follow-up would be to assume that soft power is also largely affected by any structural forces that govern the assessments of foreign actors. These forces are able to shape actor's assessments by dictating the environment in which interpretation is conducted. This is to say that structural forces (like international norms) are able to frame the way information is received. Norms in particular serve this function by assigning values to specific actions and providing preexisting assessment structures that are overlaid on complex situations.

Thus, it is the contextual sensitivity of soft power which places this agency in the hands of foreign audiences. As a result, those factors which govern the assessments of foreign audiences ought to be highly salient as soft power determinants. The determinants of soft power strength are therefore not exclusive to the state's cultural, political, and ideational appeal. These three areas may represent the foundation of soft power appeal but additional scrutiny must be paid to the context in which these resources are used. The following sections will detail those determinants of soft power identified by prior research. This is followed by a discussion of the salience of these factors in the Chinese case, and on how the soft power declines faced by the PRC may be explained along these lines.

## Shaping the Course of Soft Power Growth

When discussing the determinants of soft power, a large section of the literature has concentrated on ascendant cases in which the material gains of the state have correlated with positive shifts in foreign perceptions (Kurlantzick, 2006.). This form of growth brings with it additional benefits beyond the strictly material realm. Increased economic strength and political visibility lend the state a degree of legitimacy and visibility abroad. Legitimacy improves the image of a state's soft power resources while visibility increases the scope of the audience to which that knowledge is spread. Materially ascendant states have thus been found to enjoy these benefits because their growth brings increased public exposure, favorable reviews regarding their economic system, and improved status in the international community (Zhang, 2010). The resulting uptick in attractiveness, under Nye's definition, represents gains in that state's soft power. Therefore, it is easy to conceptualize material growth as a positive soft power factor. The effects of growth typically lead to commensurate increases in the attractiveness of the state abroad. The general argument underlying these conclusions is that improvements to the strength or appeal of a state's soft power resources have a corresponding impact on that state's agenda-setting ability and passive influence.

However, the opposite occurrence of a soft power reduction is less understood because the mechanisms behind these declines are often unclear. Those studies which have focused on soft power declines primarily focus on how the behavior of a state may adversely affect its soft power appeal. When the state behaves in an undesirable manner, this unsurprisingly has a negative impact on foreign perceptions (Chiozza 2004, Nye 2004). As Nye describes, a state's actions may effectively "squander" its soft power resources by negatively predisposing foreign audiences against the domestic state's agenda (Nye, 2012). Yet it remains difficult to disentangle which aspects of such behavior are behind the subsequent decline. In the PRC's case, its South China Sea conduct is a primary candidate for explaining waning perceptions. However, pinpointing the behavior in question does not demonstrate what aspects of China's multifaceted foreign policy are responsible for changes in foreign perceptions. It could be that aggressive quality of those actions was responsible for altering foreign attitudes. Yet audiences may also change their attitudes due to political motivations, or in response to other social incentives. It is even possible that the change in perceptions occurred independently of the behavior in question and the shift was nothing but coincidence.

Given this issue of disentanglement, it is no surprise that a series of variables are hypothesized to be causally related to soft power declines. On the domestic side, a reduction in the positive efforts of the state like public diplomacy campaigns and foreign aid volume have been identified to weaken foreign appeal (Kurlantzick 2006). At the foreign end, political and ideational discrepancies are considered to play a role in soft power declines. Unilateral policies, hegemonic behavior, hypocritical foreign policies, and unpopular ideological stances have all been found to have some causal relationship with negative perceptions abroad (quote, China cases Katzenstein and Keohane 2006). Lastly, external to direct changes in perceptions, events like economic crisis and foreign policy changes have been speculated to impact the effects of positive sentiments in a foreign country (Tartar, 2010). The state's behavior, the overall circumstances of the international system, and aspects of a state's identity all have the potential to be responsible for the audience's disposition.

Additionally, the level of ideational and normative congruence between two entities may affect bilateral opinions and perceptions. Differences in the identities, normative composition, and institutions of two nations have been found to correlate with increased levels of perceived threat (Daousat, 2011). Yet ideational similarities may not only predict foreign perceptions; they may also be a requisite for soft power success. The degree of normative homogeneity between that individual and another entity may directly indicate whether that individual will be receptive to that entity's appeal (Kearn, 2012). Actors have fewer incentives to behave when there is no shared social system because each state is relatively isolated from the consequences of its actions (Ibid, p 6). These arguments suggest that the *relative* identity of the state – that is the identity of the state compared to that of its peers – plays a crucial role in determining foreign perceptions. The implicit conclusion is that when a state's identity or normative behavior is at odds with its surroundings, this will have a significant impact on foreign perceptions and the efficacy of its soft power use. Daousat and Kearn therefore introduce the very pertinent question of how normative systems impact soft power efficacy by shaping the context in which it is used.

While these systemic factors are certainly important, the identities of foreign populations also predict their propensity to view a state in a negative light. For this reason, it is often difficult to identify factors at the state level that correlate with the propensity to view a state in a negative light. Foreign perceptions were not found to correlate strongly with factors like ideological boundaries or even the national identity (Chiozza, 2004). Rather, singular characteristics may better predict any individual's propensity to express negative sentiments about a particular entity. These factors include regional identity, level of interaction with the host country, economic outlook, exposure to culture, and normative constitution (Linley et al, 2012). This suggests an interesting facet of soft power: the determinants of its success may lie both at the international level and at the domestic level. Again, soft power is shown to be sensitive to variables along multiple dimensions. The activities of the state, its identity relative to the broader environment, and the identities of those with whom it interacts each play a key role in determining soft power efficacy.

Yet such propensity for volatility also stems from the fact that foreign perceptions are often opinionated in nature. Opinions are relatively fluid and perception shifts are a natural reaction to alterations in a state's behavior. Thus, they typically do not reflect a long-term issue for the state in question (Katzenstein and Keohane, 2006). However, these short term declines in foreign perceptions do have the potential to affect the underlying attractiveness of a state should they become persistent. Katzenstein and Keohane argue that an objection to one or more aspects of a state's behavior can evolve into a wholesale opposition to that state's identity despite any pre-existing appreciation its character. Therefore, short-term fluctuations do not represent a problem for a state unless these negative perceptions become entrenched. Should this occur, then a state may face the kind of persistent bias that poses a serious long-term issue for its interests (p 27).

While it is still possible to conceptualize soft power as a discrete resource, defined by positive sentiment and attractiveness, the reality is that the concept is interwoven with a myriad of other determining factors. Given soft power's sensitivity to circumstance and actor identity, the context in which it is realized is of upmost importance to its efficacy. The behavior of the state within this specific context represents a second fkey actor because specific actions are often the catalysts for changes in foreign sentiments. Hence, the literature shows that foreign perceptions are affected simultaneously by environmental factors, the identities of the actors, and the behavior of the state in question. Each of these factors represents a separate determinant of soft power. These factors are both external and separate from the state's image projection strategies. While the literature does not provide a hierarchy of which factors may be the strongest in any particular case, it does outline a litany of options that may be applied to subsequent cases. The following section assesses the applicability of two variables--aggressive bahavior and norm violating or "transgressive" behavoir -- to the Chinese case.

# Assessments of China's Soft Power

The past decades have witnessed an ascendant China that has enjoyed massive increases in its economic strength, political visibility, and influence within the East Asian regions. Given the uptick in China's material standing, most would predict that China ought to enjoy a commensurate increase in its soft power. This was largely the conclusion of the first wave of scholarship detailing China's soft power rise. The mid 2000s saw an enormous volume of work produced on this topic with authors like Joshua Kurlantzick detailing how China's soft power campaign was paying large dividends for the state in East Asia. As of the late 2000s, China's foreign aid programs, involvement in multilateral institutions, and economic integration were viewed as having positive effects on the PRC's appeal abroad (Garrison, 2005. D'Hooghe 2008. CSIS, in Holyk).

However, China's material rise and recent foreign policy decisions seem to have a related, and very different, impact upon foreign perceptions. China represents a case where the rise of the state's material power was directly correlated with a rise in worry over the threat that this ascent poses. The "Rise of China" produced serious concern over whether the PRC represents a threat to regional stability. Some authors have also raised concerns over whether China would functionally integrate itself into the global order or instead seek to revise the status quo in its favor (Beeson, 2013). A second generation of Soft Power publications has argued that China has suffered declines in its soft power in light of these worries and the state's recent assertiveness (Nye, 2012, Kearn 2012). Their arguments have been corroborated by surveys which note that foreign perceptions of China continue to lag behind those of America, indicating that China's appeal remains underdeveloped (Pew, 2013). The data reflects a reality that is very different from the positive sentiment that ought to follow a materially ascendant state. These recent studies suggest that the PRC is increasingly unable to translate its immense material wealth into passive persuasive capabilities and positive sentiment abroad.

In light of China's current status, prior studies suggest two separate conclusions: that China's material success would grant it increasing appeal while its assertiveness would result in a soft power decline. In fact, China appears to be at the crossroads of these two conflicting forces. Its unprecedented economic rise has certainly enhanced China's Soft Power resources by, among other effects, increasing the allure of what has been deemed the "Beijing consensus" economic model (Zhang, 2012). Yet this economic ascent is counterbalanced by an increase in worry over China's behavior and its perceived threat to Asian security. It is not clear which set of forces will prevail, or even if it is possible to determine a decisive outcome.

The dichotomy between these positive and negative influences is reflected in a literature which remains at odds over the strength of China's Soft Power. Discrepancy is evident when juxtaposing studies which utilize similar metrics. Kurlantzick, Cho and Jeong, along with Yanzhong Huang and Sheng Ding have all made favorable assessments of China's Soft Power based on opinion poll data. These conclusions directly contradict the rigorous study conducted by Holyk whose survey data suggested China's image is relatively weak with most of the major powers in East Asia (Holyk, 2010). What this disagreement reveals is the limitations of current methodological approaches. Attention has been devoted to aggregate measurements that are highly useful in commenting on the trajectory and current status of the state's soft power. However, the current manifestation of this approach is not suited to analyzing causal relationships between behavior and public perceptions. Prior research has already concluded that multiple soft power determinants are highly salient. Yet a visualization of their effects is nearly impossible using presently available aggregate data on China. The methodologies of studies like Kurlantzick's and Holyk's are therefore in need of alterations so that research may isolate specific variables and observe their effects. Two dimensions of current methodologies need to be addressed: the lack of temporal sensitivity and the inadequate examination of individual variables affecting China's soft power.

The first area, temporal sensitivity, is the most straightforward. Without a more continuous means of measurement, studies are unable to visualize changes within periods. This is problematic because soft power does not remain static but rather fluctuates with changes in public opinion and foreign perceptions. Therefore, knowledge of current perceptions is useful, but provides little information about the sources of said attitudes. The present reliance on annual survey data has precisely this weakness. Long survey periods, often years in length, prevent researchers from observing variation within these period. As a whole, this leads annual survey data to compile the individual effects of bilateral relations, regional identities, population dynamics, and ideational factors into one representation. Without any kind of disaggregation, drawing causal conclusions from these data sets is exceedingly difficult.

Second, the most widely used measurements of public perceptions are not optimized to depict soft power determinants of their causal effects. The assessments utilized by these studies generally categorize foreign attitudes along positive/negative lines and therefore represent a compiled measurement of these actor's perceptions. As a result, they provide excellent aggregate data but do so at the expense of displaying individual variables which affect China's soft power (Lai, 2012). This focus on metrics may then capture the effects of external variables without explicitly accounting for their presence (Blanchard and Liu, 2012). It is nearly impossible to disentangle the multitude of factors informing any individual's holistic opinion of China, which is the measurement collected by these studies. Visualization could be accomplished via the use of specific survey questions, but such an effort is still lacking from current quantitative approaches. This data therefore has a particularly difficult time with variable differentiation by design. Temporal sensitivity also remains a relevant problem. It is extremely difficult to examine causal relationships without being able to witness chronological change in a certain variable, or see the subsequent effects of that change with clarity. This issue is then exacerbated by measurements structures that are not designed to capture the sources of public opinion.

## Revising the Measurement of Soft Power

The question then becomes, how can researchers visualize soft power in a way that allows the study of its determinants? In the past decade, scholars have grappled with this issue in a variety of ways. Opinion polls, capital flows, quantities of students learning Mandarin, foreign student enrollment, and participation levels in multinational organizations have all been used as proxies for assessing Chinese soft power (Kurlantzick 2006?, Cho and Jeong, Blanchard and Liu 2012, Chin Hao Huang 2012). Other modern studies have evaluated Chinese soft power by tracking the projective capabilities of the state itself as a proxy for the strength of its soft power enhancement apparatus (Liu, and Zhang). Yet from among the variety of methodologies presented by scholars, the use of opinion poll data has arisen as one of the most accepted and widely utilized analogues for soft power.

A select few have taken to using qualitative assessments in order to speculate about soft power's determinants. The best example is the work of Hongying Wang, who proposed a unique model of assessing policy efficacy by examining the degree of similarity between China's projected image and foreign opinions. His data was based on opinion polls but operationalized soft power to include a comprehensive analysis of China's image abroad. This knowledge of the state's image or "brand" contains a wealth of information regarding foreign public's holistic perceptions as well as their attitudes towards discrete sub-categories of the state's character (Van Ham, 2008). The inclusion of this image acts as a reference point against which changes in public opinion may be measured. The more comprehensive the depiction, the more leverage researchers have in examining cause and effect relationships because more subtle changes in perceptions are captured. It is therefore easier to visualize causality because each variable may be traced from its inception to its effect on a *particular* dimension of China's image. A highly qualified presentation such as Wang's is thus able to examine soft power's determinants because it illustrates which aspects of the state's image change in response to certain stimuli.

Since Wang's work in the early 2000s however, the literature moved away from these methods and in favor of less detailed metrics. This trend illustrated the growing interest in the trajectory of China's soft power and the affiliated policy implications, rather than the mechanisms behind any such trajectory. Joshua Kurlantzick offered one of the most popular interpretations of China's rise in his Charm Offensive series of publications. These pieces used opinion poll metrics and similar quantitative metrics to a large degree as evidence of a "soft power rise". Kurlantzick's works cite a variety statistics in his assessment of Chinese soft power including high foreign approval ratings, positive polls in business sectors, declining criticism in East Asian media, and an increased foreign demand for Chinese university enrollment (Kurlantzick, 2007 and Kurlantzick, 2006). This data serves its purpose well in supporting the claims made by Kurlantzick that China's soft power efforts in the mid 2000s had paid dividends for the country. Even without moving beyond a dichotomous "positive or negative" assessment, Kurlantzick is able to demonstrate that regional opinion has shifted in China's favor. Yet this genre of study is left with two profound weaknesses. First, it lacks a comprehensive discussion of the countervailing variables that may or may not have also played a role in shifting regional attitudes. Second, this approach is exposed to the weaknesses that scholars like Wang sought to address. There is no way to disaggregate the image of China into its constituent parts, so it is impossible to determine whether it is even "attractiveness", as opposed to material appeal, that produces the shift in opinions.

Despite the aforementioned limitations of this approach, scholars continue to argue for the relevance of such metrics in conducting large scale analysis and identifying demographic trends. Lee makes a strong case in stating:

> "Although some people view with suspicion any rating of a nation's soft power effectiveness through public opinion surveys, it remains one of the best measures for evaluating a nation's capacity and effective utilization of soft power.

It can provide direct insight into core attitudes towards a country, its strengths and weaknesses as a regional and international leader, and its effectiveness in leveraging soft power assets, as well as giving a general indication of public receptiveness to potential future foreign policy options." (Lee, 2008).

At a macro level, opinion polls are indeed extremely useful for tracking patterns in the attitudes towards China and how these attitudes change in conjunction with international developments. These studies have carefully mapped the Chinese usage of soft power. They have also contributed valuable knowledge of which methods China has used to accomplish its soft power rise. That being said, empirical research has thus far been concerned with the ascension of the PRC's soft power appeal. Discussion of the countervailing effects remains underdeveloped. Instead of purely tracking the course of China's soft power, that trajectory should be understood as the totality of both positive and negative influences on its image.

This is an argument echoed by Blanchard and Liu who raise many of the criticisms that are outlined here. Their review of existing literature draws attention to the lack of focus on soft power determinants in the Chinese case. They conclude that current research collects generalized perceptions about China that limit conclusions to similarly broad depictions of Chinese soft power (Banchard and Liu, 2012). No analysis is thus far present that accurately differentiates amongst the litany of forces acting both positively and negatively on China's soft power trajectory. Current assessments lack any strong predictive potential because they are not designed to visualize the forces motivating change in public perceptions. Thus, the next task for researchers is to identify and empirically assess these individual determinants to better understand the source of foreign perceptions and the mechanisms which cause them to fluctuate.

The literature currently displays a tendency to measure foreign perceptions with aggregate, quantitative measurements. As a result, current data is not designed to analyze the causal factors impacting the strength of China's soft power. It also lacks sensitivity to temporal shifts due to the aggregation of large time periods into singular measurements. This represents a serious issue as the literature lacks a strong understanding of the mechanisms affecting China's soft power trajectory. Yet such an understanding remains a critical component of soft power studies. It may contribute to unraveling the relationship between the PRC's behavior and its image, and therefore may provide the key to understanding the future status of China within East Asia. The next step, to be taken by this study, is to construct a qualified measurement of China's image. Such an approach also needs to retain some form of temporal clarity. The inclusion of these two elements would effectively allow researchers to observe both overt and subtle changes in public perceptions as they vary with China's behavior. Using this as a foundation, the effect of China's conduct on foreign perceptions can be detailed in a comprehensive fashion.

## Drawing Parallels with the US

Before these methods can be utilized to their fullest extent, the most plausible determinants of China's soft power remain to be identified. The literature provides a wealth of discrete possibilities, but testing each would be an arduous or even implausible task. Instead, this study seeks to identify the most plausible candidates based on their applicability to the Chinese case. It will then proceed to analyze these figurative test subjects to determine if they are causally related to changes in public perceptions. The question to be addressed is straightforward: what characteristics of the state's conduct, external to its domestic attempts to improve soft power, best explain changes in its appeal abroad?

When identifying suitable behavioral characteristics, prior cases of soft power decline are an invaluable resource. As such, drawing parallels with these cases is a useful means of establishing the basic hypotheses. Out of these cases, the experience of the US following the Iraq war shares a striking similarity with the current Chinese situation. The US invasion of Iraq and its unilateralism during the early 2000s was followed by a documented surge of negative foreign sentiment, or "Anti-Americanism" (Katzenstein and Keohane, 2006). This downturn in foreign perceptions was linked to the US's unchallenged military might and the "overbearing" role of America in international affairs (Meunier, 2012). Additionally, the unilateral actions and perceived normative violations of the US were seen as strong causal factors for the resulting uptick in negative foreign perceptions (Katzenstein and Keohane, 2006). In this environment, the US's inability to meet international expectations regarding the fulfillment of its responsibilities as a global power also contributed to declining foreign perceptions (Nye 2004). In sum, the aggressive disposition and transgressive behavior of the United States severely affected its soft power by reducing foreign perceptions of America.

Many of the same behavioral characteristics accurately describe China's recent conduct in East Asia. First, China's developments of hard power capabilities and its inscrutable set of intentions have both aroused worry within the security-sensitive region (Kearn, 2012). The effects of this behavior bear resemblance to the negative sentiment engendered by America's military strength, albeit for a different reason. China has also engaged in actions that could be deemed both unilateral and in violation of regional, if not international, norms. Multiple incidents in the South China Sea were transgressive relative to regional norms that prioritize consensus and non-intervention (see Goh, 2000 and Acharya, 2001 and Acharya 2004 on Southeast Asian norms). China's conduct also violates institutionalized agreements like the Declaration of Conduct (DOC) although they are not codified in standing laws.

Additionally, China's propensity to precipitate territorial conflicts has the potential to destabilize East Asian region. This in and of itself may be considered a transgression given that states are expected to maintain the status quo rather than take revisionist or destabilizing stances (Huang, forthcoming). Similarly, most states condemn imperialistic and exploitative actions (Chayes and Chayes, 1996) of the sort that China has been accused of committing. The PRC's situation is therefore similar to the US in two key regards: it has behaved aggressively towards its neighbors and its actions have ostensibly violated both international and regional norms. Given that these variables have previously been identified as key determinants of soft power, their effect on Chinese soft power merits scrutiny.

On the normative side, the social and prescriptive function of norms suggests that transgression ought to influence the perceptions of foreign audiences. East Asia is an environment rich with both regional and international normative institutions which serve to structure many of the systematic interactions of regional entities. However, the presence of such a well-defined normative order may serve a function beyond governing interstate interactions. It is possible that the various East

Asian normative systems may provide an interpretive context in which China's image projections are received. Already, research has suggested that a strong normative system like that of ASEAN is able to homogenize the expectations and perceptions of its constituents (Acharya, 2004). This suggests that the norms may therefore amplify reactions to transgressive acts by both unifying and aggregating actors' responses.

Norms also systematically affect public perceptions by dictating the manner in which audiences respond to certain behaviors. A pervasive normative order puts pressure on states to conform, or at least mimic, the behaviors proscribed by the system (Finnemore and Sikkink 1998 and Cortell and Davis 2001). This elicits specific social reactions in response to violations of these norms. Stigma, shaming, and international disapproval are all natural consequences of norm violations as these are the social forces employed to contain transgressive entities (Alder-Nissen, 2014). Pressure to comply with normative order stems from these forces and subsequently produces incentives to comply with said normative order (Huang, 2014 and Oran Young *effectiveness of international institutions*). The consequence of these social exchanges is that one actor's behavior relative to a specific norm will alter the opinions of other actors in specific and predictable ways.

With this in mind, China should experience some kind of social reprisal for its transgressive actions. More specifically, the state's perceived violations of regional and international norms ought to negatively impact foreign perceptions of the PRC. China's soft power resources are never directly implicated by its transgressive actions, but the social consequences of this behavior still has indirect effects on the perceptions of foreign audiences. This negative shift in sentiments ought to then have a commensurate effect on China's ability to coopt and agenda-set by virtue of a decrease in its attraction. The expectation is that transgressive actions will cause foreign audiences to be less receptive to China and more negatively disposed to the state's interests. When examined in the context of China's putative soft power decline, transgressive conduct represents a strong candidate to explain this phenomenon.

A competing theory drawn from the Anti-American literature is that aggressive or threatening behavior may also explain perception declines. Modern states condemn acts of aggression and exploitation as antiquated attempts to leverage material power (Chayes and Chayes, 1996). It is therefore reasonable to assume that states who precipitate security threats are at risk of raising discontent among foreign audiences. Those that engage in such conduct anyways do so at the risk of compromising their authority and international status (Huang, forthcoming). Any resulting dissatisfaction with the state's policy agenda then acts in opposition to the appeal of its political values and popular ideology (Chiozza, 2004 p 165). Acts of aggression therefore represent a second instance in which a state's conduct may have a corollary effect on its soft power.

Threatening behavior and transgressive behavior are hypothesized to negatively affect public perceptions. In both cases, public perceptions represent the medium between the state's conduct and changes to its soft power abroad. There are two plausible alternatives to these hypotheses. The first possibility is that soft power is unaffected by either variable but instead fluctuates independently. This would suggest that an omitted variable is responsible for the shifts and neither aggressive nor transgressive behavior are sufficient to explain observable trends. The second alternate is that there are no systematic trends in public perceptions whatsoever and that all fluctuations are random. The four hypotheses are as follows:

H I: Normative violations are followed by changes in soft power.
H II: Threats to national security are followed by changes in soft power.
H III: Soft power shifts are independent of both aggressive and transgressive conduct.
H IV: Changes in perceptions are random and do not correspond to any set of behaviors.

## Tracking Fluctuations in Public Perceptions

Having identified potential external determinants of China's soft power, the study of these variables must be approached in a manner that accurately captures their effects while mitigating the impact of omitted or external factors. Current approval poll data from sources like Pew or Asiabarometer would not be apt as they do not capture sufficient within period variance. This fact coupled with their inability to distinguish the sources of regional sentiments makes them an ill fit for this study. A different measurement is therefore needed which incorporates both the character of foreign perceptions and provides the temporal sensitivity necessary to isolate specific events. Yet the data must remain tethered to foreign perceptions as these attitudes and sentiments are the key intermediaries between a state's Soft Power resources and actual political effects abroad (Huang and Ding, 2006). Foreign perceptions remain as an accurate proxy for soft power strength. It is the manner in which these attitudes are assessed that will then be revised. This study will implement the revised measurement to analyze perceptions in the Philippines, Singapore, Indonesia, and South Korea respectively.

To this end, foreign perceptions are approximated by examining the PRC's characterization in foreign media. News articles and their internal discourse serve as analogues for foreign perceptions. Media sources have long been shown to be highly useful indicators of perceptions. The media as a body tends to have a strong influence on domestic policy makers and diplomats (Cohen,1963 and Davidson, 1974). The informative role played by the media therefore indicates that news articles often correlate with the attitudes of these key individuals. From the perceptive of the more general public, the media is also closely intertwined with domestic attitudes because of the agenda setting function it serves (Dearing and Rogers, 1996). Dearing and Rogers argue that the media may serve to direct public opinion by making certain issues salient at any given time. Therefore, newspapers and other media are good indicators of the public's attitudes both because they serve both an informative role and because they serve this agenda setting function (Zhang, 2010). It must be acknowledged that the news media is not perfectly representative of the public given that informed, educated individuals are the most likely to consume these sources. However, the media still serves as a strong indicator of regional opinion as long as the underrepresented demographics do not deviate substantially from those who comprise the newspaper's readership.

These characteristics demonstrate that media discourse ought to closely parallel public perceptions. Zhang reaffirms this argument in stating that the perceptions of China represented in esteemed newspapers were indicative of mainstream opinion because of these papers' high readership, volume of distribution, and credibility (Zhang, 2010). The focus on top publications helps alleviate the problem of external validity to a degree as it connects the interests of the publishers and authors with that of a larger population of citizens. To achieve a similar effect, this study prioritized the selection of articles based on the readership base of the newspaper in which they were published.

In the Philippines case, the majority of articles were drawn from the Philippine Daily Inquirer and the Philippine Star. These English language publications are the first and second ranked newspapers by readership respectively according to the Nielsen Media Index (PDI Keeps Big Lead in Readership). Additionally, some articles were drawn from the Manila Times which is the longest current circulating newspaper in the Philippines. Singaporean articles were taken primarily from the Straits Times, which is the largest Singaporean newspaper by readership according to the 2013 Nielsen Media Index Report (Straits Times holds steady as most-read daily). In both Singapore and the Philippines, English is the language in which the top publications are written, so no translation is necessary.

As for Indonesia, articles were drawn primarily from the Jakarta Post and supplemented by articles from the Jakarta Globe. The Jakarta post is the largest English language paper in circulation, with a daily readership of 40,000 according to Multimedia Inc (Multimedia website, Indonesia). The Jakarta Globe is less established given its recent inception, and its articles are more likely to possess localized or readership bias. Articles from the globe comprise roughly a quarter of the sample, so whatever biases do exist are constrained to a small section of the data. Yet both represent a relatively smaller portion of total newspaper readership given that English is not the dominant language in which media sources are published.

For South Korea, publications are primarily in Korean as opposed to English. Newspapers were again chosen based on their readership and their provision of an English language version. The newspapers chosen were the Chosun Ilbo, Joongang Daily, The Korea Herald, and the Korea Times. The Chosun Ilbo, as the newspaper with top readership in Korea, represents nearly 50% of the sample articles for South Korea. According to their website, articles written by their staff are directly translated into English for their online newspaper from which the data was taken. Their circulation base represents nearly 2 million daily readers. The remaining 3 newspapers were the top 3 daily English language publications in South Korea comprising a readership of roughly 100,000 in 2009 according to the Korean Audit Bureau of Circulations (Korea Herald far Ahead in English Paper Circulation, 2010). The Joongang Daily is also a translated version of its sister publication which is in Korean, while the remaining two papers are exclusively in English.

The issue with this approach hinges on its reliance on English language publications. The authors writing to an English speaking audience almost certainly have different prerogatives than authors writing to a general native populace. This is less of an issue in the Philippines and Singapore given that their top papers are published directly in English. Therefore, The Straits Times, Philippine Daily Inquirer, and the Philippine Star are published in English and are simultaneously the papers with the largest readership base. The dominance of English journalism reduces the likelihood that authors are writing to a specific, English speaking population and are suggests that they are instead catering to a general readership base. This ought to improve the function of the analogue between these authors' perceptions and that of the general populace. However, South Korea and Indonesia are a different story. Only Korean sources from Joongang and the Chosun Ilbo are translated directly from their Korean counterparts. Many opinion articles from the remaining publications are written by ex-patriots and journalists from foreign papers.

To mitigate the bias of selecting writers who are less representative of local populations, this study only selected articles written by native authors, staff writers for domestic publications, and individuals working for domestic universities or governments for all the articles studied. The intent of this limitation is to ensure that the selected authors are actually representative of domestic sentiment and are not outlets for foreign opinion. While some bias associated with the English language may persist, the use of a consistent language does assist the study by homogenizing the results. Discursive comparisons become much easier when using English as a medium. It serves as an effective intermediary because analysis may focus on specific labels, characterizations, and metaphors that persist across the entirety of the data set.

In selecting articles, only opinion pieces were selected as these provide the best data on public perceptions. The data set is comprised of articles labeled opinion, editorial, op-ed, column, and viewpoint in which the article served as a platform for the author's expression. Such pieces include a wealth of the descriptive language and characterizations that are the subject of analysis. A focus on these sources also exposes the study to the biases of the authors themselves who are less limited by journalistic objectivity when writing opinion pieces. However, these biases may in fact be relevant as evidence of the subject's perceptions. Objective representations are not the target of analysis. Rather, systematic departures from objectivity provide the best evidence as to the opinions and sentiments of the writers. These articles are helpful in that they capture a nuanced description of the author's attitude towards China, but are also harmful in that the motivations for these characterizations may remain unclear. The data set also includes multiple authors from multiple news sources to control for the slant of any one paper or the political agenda of an individual author.

Articles were first selected based on whether they discussed China, or presented opinions that described China's nature and intentions. From the selected pieces, the language, labels, metaphors, and characterizations used to describe China were recorded. Roughly 50 article were coded for South Korea and the Philippines each from mid 2009 until October of 2014. Another 40 were compiled collectively for Singapore and Indonesia whose discourse is analyzed in tandem. This sample represents a nearly exhaustive compilation of the articles fulfilling the requisite categories. The opinion, editorial, column, and op-ed archives for each of the listed papers were checked individually for relevant articles, and nearly every piece fulfilling these qualifications were included. Both the coding and the label tracking were done prior to chronological organization in order to blind the researcher to confirmation bias. Articles were recorded in a random order, and were not ordered and analyzed chronologically until the coding work was finished. A select few articles, numbering roughly 15 distributed across the cases, were coded after the data was organized to more recent publications were added.

Beyond recording the discursive qualities of the articles, a secondary score was also assigned to each article that recorded the threat level ascribed to China. If an article did not identify China as a threat or described it as peaceful, it received a "no threat" rating. If an article described China's behavior as potentially threatening, or a risk for that state's security, then was coded as "potential threat". If an article discretely identified China as an immediate threat to that nation's security, interests, or residents then the article was coded as "threat".

## Case Selection and Falsification

In terms of case selection, the rationale behind choosing the four states is linked to their respective relationships with the three hypotheses. Each possesses a unique set of circumstances in regards to the presence of Chinese norm violations and aggressive behavior. Individually, they are critical in testing different aspects of the hypothesis and displaying whether shifts in perceptions were explained by any of the hypothesized factors. In the Philippines, China's recent behavior may be described as both aggressive and transgressive. That state represents a perfect opportunity to test the null hypothesis. If perceptions do not decline after specific instances of norm violations and acts of aggression, then such behaviors are not likely determinants of its soft power. The Philippines effectively serves as a means of validating that the two variables chosen can explain most, if not all, of the variance in public perceptions. Similar conclusions have been made regarding the US's soft power decline, but they must be re-analyzed in the context of China and its actions.

Indonesia and Singapore were chosen for a similar purpose. The two states will be discussed jointly as their environment is relatively similar for the purposes of this study. Both nations represent cases in which Chinese bilateral aggression is absent. Thus, they represent a means of differentiating the effects of China's norm violations versus its aggressive behavior. Given that the two states share a common normative framework with the Philippines, China's behavior towards Manila ought to also be perceived as transgressive by both Singapore and Indonesian audiences. If the primary hypothesis is indeed correct, discourse ought to be relatively low despite the stable nature of bilateral relations. The primary hypothesis predicts that the common normative environment of East Asia ought to induce common reactions amongst ASEAN states regardless of their individual levels of bilateral conflict with Beijing. This should subsequently produce negative discursive trends in both Indonesia and Singapore given China's transgressive behavior relative to regional norms. However, a lack of accessible newspaper data prevents the visualization of long term temporal change. To address this in part, discourse is compared with that from the Philippines to observe commonalities and to check for the presence of similar negative trends. The argumentative character of the pieces as a whole is also examined to determine if authors explicitly identify certain aspects of China's behavior as the rationale behind their opinions.

Lastly, South Korea represents a case in which the normative environment is not clear. As will be discussed later, it appears as if China was held to strong behavioral standards that were violated on multiple occasions. Yet these violations cannot be conclusively labeled as norms given their undocumented nature. Instead, the South Korean case is intended to illustrate whether or not there are inherent differences in the discursive shifts following various types of behavior. The bilateral events of import in the South Korean case are varied in nature. Some, as mentioned above, ostensibly possess a normative dimension while others like the ADIZ announcement represent more immediate security threats. Assuming that China's behavior does systematically impact foreign perceptions, the differentiation of the two remaining hypotheses indicates that different conduct ought to produce different responses. South Korea will therefore qualitatively illustrate the disparity, or similarity, of discursive reactions to issues of immediate security versus those connected to the public's expectations. The presence of threatening behavior is a means of testing H2, but the South Korean case also illustrates the salience of specific discursive characteristics and their connection to specific types of conduct.

## Measuring the Effect of Aggression and Transgression on Foreign Perceptions

Two primary measurements are used to assess the causal relationships between specific variables and discernable perception shifts. The first is co-variance. Upon completing data collection, articles were organized chronologically to identify temporal trends in public perceptions. This chronological organization is paired with a depiction of major events in bilateral relations. The observation of interest is whether perceptions changes correlate with specific behaviors and what discursive characteristics define these perception changes. Essentially, the discursive shifts in the sample will be juxtaposed with a timeline of China's conduct to determine what events were followed by negative perception shifts and which events – transgressive or otherwise - produced the greatest changes.

This study will also employ a supplementary method to better augment the study of discursive shifts. So far, the temporal approach provides evidence as to whether negative perceptions co-vary with transgressive behavior. However, to further isolate the effects of normative violations, the character of regional discourse might provide invaluable clues. Alder-Nissen's recent work provides critical insight into the fact that actor's respond in a specific manner when confronted by a norm-violating entity. Social agents will respond by stigmatizing transgressive entities via the use of labels that illustrate social differences, employ stereotypes, isolate the transgressive actor, and rationalizing exclusionary behavior (Alder Nissen, p 147). These elements of stigmatization are common social responses to acts of transgression and therefore ought to consistently characterize discourse related to said transgression. Therefore the presence of stigmatic language represents another means by which the two hypothesis may be differentiated. These characteristics also help to falsify the primary hypothesis. If non-transgressive behavior is the source of perception declines, then stigmatic language should not characterize discourse to a large degree. In the case of China, regional discourse will be analyzed for the presence of stigmatic traits.

The end measurement system of this study will consist of two parts. A decline in foreign perceptions will be attributed to China's normative transgressions or threatening conduct if it: 1) was proceeded by an identifiable instance of these behaviors and 2) displayed the discursive qualities (threat perceptions and stigmatization) associated with each type of conduct. Should these conditions not be fulfilled when examining the data set, then H1 and H2 will be rejected. If no clear relationship is evident between events and discourse, then this will support the null that China's soft power image is static relative to its conduct.

An operationalization of Soft Power along these lines serves multiple purposes. An analysis of the media's representation of China provides the requisite temporal sensitivity demanded by this study. Articles are published daily and are therefore able to rapidly codify any shifts in perception. The character of the media's portrayal directly before and after key events provides one of the most reactive and illustrative manifestations of regional opinion. Also, the intimate connection between regional attitudes and the media's stance suggests that the media's characterizations ought to co-vary with those of the general population. Regional news sources will therefore capture the kind of perception shifts that are hypothesized to follow normative violations and aggressive behavior.

It may be argued that a negative media reaction to China's more unsavory behavior is axiomatic. However, this study seeks to differentiate amongst different styles of reactions, and subsequently construct a comprehensive understanding of the character, duration, and trajectory of perception shifts. Media sources therefore provide the qualitative data needed to track nuanced perception shifts. This understanding allows analysis into the argumentation, metaphors, labels, and discourse of regional media. When compiled, such data can illustrate discursive characteristics like stigmatization to better characterize any shifts in perception. The result is a measurement system which can qualitatively and temporally observe how foreign audiences respond to instances of both Chinese aggression and transgression.

## Discursive trends in the Philippines, Indonesia, Singapore, and South Korea

Recently, maps of the South China Sea are possessed of an ever increasing number of overlapping boundaries, shaded areas, and contradicting claims. Underneath all this colored ink lies a series of historical disputes that are highly grounded in the normative order of the region. As China and its Southeastern neighbors interact, they engage within the context of this framework and are subsequently influenced in part by its presence. The normative umbrella created by ASEAN and various multilateral institutions has led many Southeast Asian nations to adopt common, well-defined standards of behavior (Acharya, 2001). This lends the otherwise mundane sovereignty disputes a normative dimension. Actors' expectations stem from their normative constitution, and so these norms therefore underpin their assessments of others. As with most conflicts, there is also a material dimension to the friction. Issues involving territory, governance, and sovereignty are persistent themes and thus implicate the security of involved parties as well.

As stated in H1 and H2, it is argued that instances of transgression and threatening conduct ought to produce discernable shifts in the perceptions of foreign audiences. Within the past five years, multiple instances have occurred in which China displayed one, if not both, of these behavioral characteristics towards its neighbors. In this context, the hypotheses would predict that aggressive behavior should engender perceptions of threat while violations of norms should induce stigmatic reprisal. If these are the primary forces currently determining the state's soft power status, then the presence of either behavior ought to correlate with observable cases of soft power change. In addition, the effects of such behavior should appear to be the strongest, or perhaps the only, force motivating systemic change in perceptions. An examination of these responses to China's conduct will populate the following section.

One additional point of clarification is the manner in which the study will adjudicate between competing normative claims. As in most territorial disputes, each state's perceptions about the validity of their claims are highly influenced by their political agendas. This makes it difficult to disentangle the political, as opposed to the legal or normative, motivations behind any accusation against China. In fact, multiple sources have actually argued that, excluding its 9-dashed line claim, the majority of China's behavior in the SCS is legally permitted under UNCLOS (Ku, 2014). However, the legal validity of a country's actions is not necessarily the sole factor determining whether a set of behaviors is transgressive. Instead, it can be argued that a population's assessments may be rationalized in the framework of their core ideational values (Hurwitz and Peffley, 1990). In China's case, the ambiguous nature of the PRC's behavior may prevent the use of international legal or formal norms, granting added relevancy to the regional norms and values of specific populations (Linley et al, 2012). These regional normative structures may lack the codified character of their international counterparts, but they are no less efficacious in affecting the perceptions of public audiences. Therefore, these implicit norms also demand attention given the attenuated presence of codified, international norms.

Of particular relevance is the regional environment of Asia which needs to be distinguished from the international piece of the equation. Multiple scholars have emphasized that the development of ASEAN and East Asia as a whole was largely paralleled by the establishment of a tight knit normative community (Acharya, 2004). In particular, this was manifested in an "ASEAN way" of conduct that emphasized consensus, non-intervention, and non-confrontation (Goh, 2000 and Soesastro, 1995). Many behaviors, including the use of force and aggressive confrontation, may therefore be understood as transgressive actions despite the fact that they may not violate any explicit international norms. The East Asian area in general is characterized by its own set of regional norms that possess their own behavioral standards quite apart from those expressed in international settings. For these reasons, the study of bilateral relations will adjudicate whether an act was a normative violation based on whether it deviated from documented norms like the DOC, implicit regional expectations related to the ASEAN way, and international norms. This approach distinguishes a norm based on its relevance to a given domestic population.

## Philippines

The first case ought to be one of the easiest for H1 and H2 given that China has both violated regional norms and behaved aggressively towards the Philippines. For all intents and purposes, discourse should vary systematically given the impact of such conflicts. Yet it is still necessary to empirically demonstrate that perceptions are indeed fluctuating around instances of these behaviors. Prior scholarship has demonstrated these factors to be of import in other instances of soft power declines, and this section will test these conclusions in the context of the PRC's modern foreign policy actions. Changes in discourse, stigmatization, and threat perceptions should all parallel China's conduct if H1 and H2 are to be validated.

The current Sino-Filipino relationship can be described as rocky at best given that competing bilateral claims have come to a head multiple times in the past decade. These disputes have already had a substantial effect on Filipino perceptions of the PRC. The discovery of China's military apparatus on the Mischief Reef in 1995 fostered the public perception that China's words were no more than platitudes and that its real interests were expansionary in nature (Pablo-Baviera, 2002). Despite China's attempts to mitigate tensions, the Philippines has continued its shrill condemnation of China's actions in recent years as breaches of international law and as acts of "bullying" (see Peaceful Rise? & What is China's Intention in the region?). Even along economic lines, there has been a history of threat perceptions in Filipino attitudes as they faced a rising China in the strategic aftermath of the post-Cold War environment (Zhao, 2012). Directly prior to beginning of this study, the Philippine's protests were again manifest in their 2009 protest of China's "9-dashed line" to the UN and their vocal support of the US's efforts to prioritize the use of international law in the SCS.

Yet despite the obvious tensions that these incidents stir up, public perceptions of China were actually not overly negative in the Philippines by the late 2000s. Asiabarometer survey data in 2007 actually reported public approval of China at 57%, while only a small minority of 15% found China's influence to be negative. The Chicago Council on Global Affairs also reported positive, and rising, Filipino attitudes towards China in a comprehensive 2007 survey. Both studies seem to implicitly support the conclusion that the Filipino public was not completely negatively disposed towards China, and that some optimism persisted that China would behave as a responsible stakeholder in the international system (Morada, 2009). Therefore, it did not appear as if China's actions had thus far done any long term damage to Filipino attitudes despite repeated confrontations as of the survey periods in 2007 and 2008. It is from this relative baseline that discursive analysis will begin.

*Initial Environment and Perceptions before 2011*

The media's representation of China throughout 2009 until early 2011 is most accurately described as cautious, yet admiring. On the one hand, authors acknowledged the Philippine's dependence upon China and the future issues that this may raise (Converging Interests: Hanoi and Manila Confront Leviathan). However, this was coupled with a grudging respect for China's economic structure, as multiple authors cited the power and respectability of the Chinese system (Why are Chinese Entrepreneurs successful? & In the Long Run, China will win). The prevalence of both attitudes even within singular articles suggests that perceptions had not yet been polarized. Judgments remained fairly objective and did not significantly criticize China's character or its practices. In fact, articles did not begrudge China's self-identification as a responsible global power and frequently argued for a positive outlook on bilateral cooperation (Aid and Corruption). Lastly, discourse took on no discernable negative slant during the period even despite potentially disruptive events like China's 2009 submission to the UN of its "9-dashed-line" claim. While the Filipino government was shrill in its protests of Beijing's actions, public discourse largely did not mirror this outrage.

As a corollary, stigmatizing language and threat perceptions were understandably absent given that China was not shamed, excluded, or negatively labeled in any of the articles prior to 2011. The presence of concerned rhetoric coupled with the absence of stigmatizing language illustrates that these are indeed independent aspects of the discourse. While the rise of China remained a source of concern amongst Filipino authors, audiences did not utilize stigmatizing language in the absence of any transgressions. Secondly, these concerns were not tied to any kind of threat perceptions. Of those articles which did cite concern, this worry was never translated into arguments stating that China posed a distinct threat to Filipino security. The most worried of the articles only noted that China's actions had the potential to be destabilizing. On the whole, the discursive environment between 2009 and early 2011 was not strictly positive, but neither was it negative. This in itself is a relatively strange conclusion given historic bilateral tensions over territorial disputes in the SCS, but it does support the conclusions drawn from the 2008 and 2007 survey data.

*Reed Bank incident: March 2011*

The Reed Bank incident in March of 2011 drastically changed the discursive landscape and was the first bilateral event to have a significant impact on public perceptions. The event itself occurred as the PRC sought to exercise their sovereignty claim to the territorial waters around the Reed Bank by turning away a Philippine's survey ship attempting to prospect for natural resources. Reed Bank is located amidst the controversial Spratly islands, whose close proximity to the Filipino mainland and historic ambiguity made them a flashpoint in bilateral relations. While the confrontation was minor, its social effect was magnified due to its symbolic nature. The implicit significance of the event was that China appeared to be asserting its sovereign claim to disputed territory despite continued uncertainty over ownership. The Aquino administration responded rapidly by upgrading its military presence and by submitting a complaint to the United Nations (Zhao, 2012).

While discourse had thus far not matched the rhetoric of the Filipino government, the two harmonized to a greater degree in the wake of the Reed Bank confrontation. Prominent Filipino legislator and Inquirer columnist Walden Bello described the Chinese actions as demonstrating a disregard for both the UN Convention on the Law of the Sea (UNCLOS) and international principles (Why China has to climb down on the Spratlys issue). This led him to conclude that China is an aggressive state whose actions encourage the perception that it is an "arrogant military hegemon". Bello was not alone in his use of such language. All but one of the ten articles from the subsequent year identified China's actions as norm-breaking and transgressive. Emerging from this common argumentative foundation was the depiction of China as a "neighborhood bully", which appeared in more than half of the articles between March of 2011 and April of 2012. Additionally, other examples noted China's "imperious" attitude and the hypocrisy evident in its "words-actions-mismatch" (Power asymmetry in the South China Sea).

The post-Reed Bank period was the first instance in which such stigmatizing language appeared in the Philippines case. The language of Bello and others illustrates a near uniformity of the perception that China was acting in both a transgressive and aggressive manner. This lent their writing a consistency which utilized common forms of shaming. The widespread use of the term "neighborhood bully" is exemplary of this kind of behavior. Each part of the label highlights the transgressive aspect of China's actions. The "bully" label brings with it a host of attendant associations related to the low-brow and brutish nature associated with bullies. A bully, by nature, earns their derogatory title due to repeated breaches of the rules governing social interaction. The Filipino authors are very clear on this point as they cite China's breaches of international principles as justification for the title (see Historical right and legal title). The use of "neighbor" also adds a communal appeal by broadening the scope of the exchange beyond the bilateral level. The result is a multifaceted term that both highlights China's perceived aggression and engenders solidarity amongst the community that is being "bullied".

However, the normative dimension of the incident bears clarification. In the eyes of the writers, the Reed Bank incident was identified as a deliberate use of force by China. This assumption was the foundation for multiple claims that Beijing's actions were in violation of UNCLOS and international principles. Expressing wholeheartedly that China's claim is without grounds, Filipino authors argued that China utilized its strength to enforce an illegitimate claim instead of proceeding through international arbitration measures. For these authors, the transgressive element was not only the claim itself, but also the strong-armed manner in which China leveraged its greater size over the Philippines. Therefore, the aggressive character of the act was a perceived violation of proper conduct. This reaction is consistent with the normative character of Southeast Asia in which non-confrontation and consensus are considered paramount values (Goh, 2000). Perceptions of China's transgression therefore stemmed from China's handling of the issue, where the state seemingly leveraged its strength to circumvent international arbitration and legal process. In the data itself, China's aggression was represented a material threat to the Philippine's sovereign territory as well as a breach of standards of conduct. Perceptions changed sharply as levels of stigmatization and threat perceptions rose bstantially. As transgressive behavior and aggression are intertwined in this case, both H1 and H2 are supported.

*Scarborough Shoal: April 2012*

The second major discernable shift in discourse occurred after the Scarborough Shoal incident in April of 2012. Zhao describes the incident as similar in nature to the Reed Bank incident in that sovereignty issues on both sides elicited strong reactions:

> "The standoff grew out of a confrontation in which the Chinese government vessels blocked a Philippines naval ship from arresting Chinese fishermen accused of illegally harvesting coral and poaching sharks in the disputed waters. Both China and the Philippines used the incident to more boldly assert their sovereignty over the area. China took the opportunity to normalize its claims of sovereignty over the South China Sea area, while Manila used the showdown to spark nationalist fervor and internationalize the issue to draw the US, Japan and ASEAN into the dispute to counter China's growing strength.7" (In Zhao, 2012).

Like Reed Bank, Scarborough is presented as a sovereign concern at heart. This aspect of the issue makes it very similar to Reed Bank in a symbolic sense. In both cases, the PRC acted upon a territorial claim that was perceived to be illegitimate. Leaving the actual validity of this claim aside, the sovereignty aspect of the issue injects a normative element into the equation because of the behavioral and legal expectations that surround such issues.

While the Philippines is hardly blameless, China again demonstrated a confrontational manner in asserting its sovereignty claim via the blockade of Filipino ships. Thus, transgression and aggression remained closely linked. The presence of both behavioral characteristics would then suggest that public perceptions ought to follow a trajectory similar to the post-Reed Bank environment, albeit from a lower starting point. H1 would predict a continuation or strengthening of stigmatizing language and threat perceptions. H2 would predict a period of heightened threat perceptions immediately following the event.

The evidence supporting these predictions is fairly strong as discourse retained both its negative character and stigmatizing slant throughout the next year and a half. Authors continued to describe China as behaving in violation of international protocol, utilizing the same language as well as legal arguments from the post-Reed Bank period. While the overall frequency of condemning articles decreased, their structure was remarkably similar. The most common method of argumentation highlighted the violations China committed and followed these criticisms with derogatory language like "bully", "bellicose", "haughty", and "rogue state" (Understanding China & Why China Why & The Call to Boycott China's products & China, A Rogue State?). Nearly three quarters of the articles from the subsequent year utilized the similar language which shamed or degraded China.

Following the initial incident at Reed bank, threat perceptions spiked but then returned to a lower, constant state. The leap that did occur was short-lived as it dissipated after a few months. However, the first few months following the Scarborough confrontation saw some of the highest levels of worry expressed by Filipino authors in the duration of the study. Disregarding this initial reactionary period, the articles did not focus on the security dimension of China's behavior nor did they express serious concern regarding the immediate possibility of a military conflict. While authors did note the potential threat posed by China, the primary discursive characteristics were those of shaming and stigmatization. This was the dominant manifestation of heightened bilateral tensions from 2009 and 2013. This pattern illustrates that changes in threat perceptions appear to be more short term than those related to stigmatic attitudes. Such a conclusion will be further examined in subsequent sections. Overall, both the short-term spike in threat perceptions and the long-term persistence of China's stigmatization support H1 and H2.

*Mid 2013 until September 2014*

The discursive trends identified above persisted until the end of 2013 when threat perceptions began to elevate past their previous lows. Beginning in May of 2013, articles began to more often cite China as a threat to both regional stability and domestic security. For the first time since 2009, articles with titles like "Chinese National Security threats" began to appear. Such pieces were topically centered on the strategic threat posed by a rising China and the policy moves the Philippines could take to mitigate this threat. This trend accelerated in late 2013 and early 2014 as almost 80% of articles specifically labeled China as a threat between November of 2013 and April of 2014.

Yet this rise in threat perceptions during was not followed by the increasing stigmatization of China. Authors assumed an alarmist stance as they frequently highlighted China's military presence, economic might, and recent assertiveness as signs of danger. However, these attitudes carried with them no inherent pejorative labels of the PRC. The distinction between stigmatizing and threat may appear small but it is evident in the author's descriptive approach. Pieces from the 2013 and 2014 periods typically did not devote a significant amount of time to detailing China's violations or arguing for why China's behavior was transgressive. While this was a common trait of earlier pieces, the majority of articles following 2013 were dedicated to detailing the manner in which China challenged Filipino security and the ways in which the state may respond. This was not to say that stigmatization was absent, only that the security oriented language began to dominate the discourse. The thematic labeling of China did persist but in a weaker state. Labels like "bully" and "bellicose" continued to appear but these behavioral characteristics were utilized as evidence of China's aggressive trajectory (see Prepare for China pt 2 & Chinese national security threats).

Moving into mid to late 2014, the presence of these threat perceptions declined and discourse reassumed a relatively stable, if stigmatic, character. As threat perceptions began to dissipate, caution rather than outright alarm re-emerged as the dominant attitude. In the wake of this apparent calming, stigmatizing again assumed a central, if slightly diminished, role. The practices of the Chinese government received the most criticism as this form of "statecraft" was depicted as being at odds with the approaches of other East Asian governments (China practices statecraft, Philippines practices public diplomacy). This illustrative disconnect represented a reemergence of one of the earlier discursive themes in which China was identified as isolated or differentiated from the rest of the East Asian "neighborhood". Such a disconnect was most evident in articles which cited China's "imperial" disposition. At the conclusion of the study, articles commonly noted what was described as a domineering and self-centered attitude. These descriptions also harkened back to earlier arguments regarding China's bullying tendencies (see China's economic militarization & Is China becoming a superpower? & Row with China may derail Asian growth).

Conclusions

The Filipino case as a whole presents strong evidence for both primary hypotheses. Perceptions varied significant following Chinese acts of transgression of those that threatened national security. Additionally, perceptions did indeed vary systematically with behavior. While the Philippine case does not differentiate between the effects of transgressive versus aggressive conduct, events like the Scarborough School and Reed bank were demonstrated to have serious repercussions for the PRC's image. As such, China's soft power was not shown to be immune to the effects of its behavior. These sets of behaviors were correlated with stigmatic language, heightened threat perceptions, and declining public perceptions. The Filipino case is therefore an empirical presentation of the systematic and long term perception declines which follow China's "bullying" and transgressive conduct. It demonstrates that China's soft power, despite initially being favorable, was extremely sensitive to these behaviors.

However, instances of transgression or aggression did not correlate directly with every instance of perception decline. Only two out of the three shifts correlated with instances of normative violations and assertion by China. The shift in late 2013 until early 2014 was not preceded by any major bilateral event. It is possible that this rise in threat perceptions represented the cumulative effect of earlier events, but it is not possible to say for certain without additional evidence. What can be said is that the two earlier declines were the most protracted and displayed high degrees of stigmatizing language. Threat perceptions also spiked consistently with instances of aggression. In contrast, the decline in 2013 was not as lengthy, nor was it as severe in terms of the strength of criticism leveled against China.

The fact that discourse then reassumed its stigmatic character also suggests a persistence of these negative sentiments despite some variance in perceptions. These negative sentiments demonstrated the important of external determinants of soft power. Factors quite removed from the state's image projection strategies were shown to have systematic, negative effects on foreign perceptions that involved shaming, threat perceptions, status loss, and the stigmatization of China.

## Indonesia and Singapore

One lingering issue with the Philippines case is that the Reed Bank and Scarborough incidents witnessed the concurrence of China's transgressive and aggressive behavior. In order to differentiate the predictions of H1 and H2, this study will examine the discourse of states that do not currently have territorial disputes with China to control for the effects of these disputes on domestic perceptions. Here, it is hypothesized that China's transgressive behavior in the South China Sea will still have detrimental effects on its Soft Power within Indonesia and Singapore, who share similar sets of norms with the Philippines. Both states are key members of ASEAN and are involved regional participants. Their high level of institutional integration ought to align their normative constitution with that of their neighbors and produce similar reactions to China's transgressive actions, regardless of the level of bilateral tensions. If H1 holds, discourse in Indonesia and Singapore should display discursive commonalities with the Philippines and similarly high levels of stigmatization.

As of September 2014, Indonesia and Singapore were not formal claimant states in the ongoing South China Sea dispute. Each has had relatively minor spats with China. For Indonesia, China's newer 9-dashed line is seen as overlapping waters that Jakarta has claimed as its own, producing tensions with Indonesia's National Defense Force (TNI) (Keck, 2014). However, this tension has caused no major conflict as of yet due to both sides' careful handling of the issue and Indonesia's unwillingness to legally formalize the dispute (China must avoid destabilizing the region). Even in the wake of the Natuna Issue, the Indonesian foreign minister explicitly stated that, "there is no territorial dispute between Indonesia and China" (South China Sea: Is Jakarta No longer neutral?). Singapore as well remains individually removed from the disputes as a non-claimant. However, it has been active as a supporter negotiating for the establishment of a binding Code of Conduct in the SCS (Might not Right in the SCS).

As such, Indonesia and Singapore remain somewhat peripheral to the ongoing conflict over the South China Sea. However, both states are highly integrated members of ASEAN and its attendant normative structure. Prominent scholars like Acharya describe this common normative framework in East Asia as producing significant, shared behavioral expectations (Acharya, 2001 and Acharya, 2004). Therefore, events that are considered normative breaches by the Philippines are likely to be assessed in a similar manner by audiences in Indonesia. More specifically, China's unilateral behavior, violations of the DOC, and aggression towards the Philippines and Vietnam should be interpreted as transgressive by Indonesian and Singaporean writers. If H1 holds, perceptions ought to display characteristics of stigmatization despite the absence of sovereignty disputes and other sources of bilateral tensions.

Articles from 2012 until September of 2014 will be analyzed for the presence of these characteristics.

The weakness of this approach is that the lack of strong data prior to 2012 prevents the observance of an antecedent period. As such, it is difficult to observe the reactions of Indonesian and Singaporean audiences to the actual events in question and whether these events produced perception changes. Instead, the study will examine the discursive characteristics of the articles and their rhetoric commonalities with the Philippines. Each of these assessments acts as an indicator. Should authors behave in similar ways, use similar language, and explicitly identify China's norm violations as the source of their negativity, then this will be taken as evidence that Indonesian and Singaporean are responding in the same way that Filipino authors did. H1 will therefore be supported if these authors stigmatize China while commonly identifying China's transgressive conduct as the reason for doing so.

While imperfect, the results from Singapore and Indonesia are sufficiently clear. This is because all aspects of discourse in these states reflect the predicted outcomes. Discourse was highly similar to the Filipino data. The same behavior was identified as transgressive and many of the same labels were applied to China's conduct. Common argumentative themes were also present, as China was isolated and shamed in similar ways across all three states. Discourse from Singapore and Indonesia was also distinct in that authors consistently highlighted China's behavior as transgressive while remaining highly positive about bilateral relations. This indicates that it is not bilateral tensions motivating the author's negative perceptions. The Indonesia and Singapore cases therefore demonstrate that transgressive behavior, in the absence of material threats, can still incite negative, stigmatic discourse.

*Public Perceptions between late 2012 and September 2014*

H1 is largely successful in predicting the discursive character of articles from both Singapore and Indonesia. These pieces employed many of the same labels and discursive characteristics evident in the Philippines, albeit less frequently. Pieces citing China's "bellicose" nature and "bullying" strategy remained present in both states (see El Indio: A Chinese Dilemma & Maritime Disputes call for SE Asian Input). Additionally, a wealth of articles took to generally describing China as an aggressive entity whose actions represented material threats to national security (see China Must avoid Destabilizing the Region). Less frequent but still relevant labels were depictions of China as "coercive", "provocative", "insincere", and "self- serving" (Perception of America as 'Weak' Is Making Asia Uneasy & Caution amidst positives of China's Asian push & China's calculated coercive moves & Interesting Times in East Asia & Asia Infrastructure Development Bank: A Gift Horse from China). Themes of China's juvenile nature remained present as well. Authors argued that China still needed to meet the expectations of the international community by behaving in more, "mature and sensible ways" (A reminder for China).

A common variant was the description of China's actions as unilateral. The PRC's deviation from international protocol and lack of multilateral support were provided as reasoning for this criticism (Facing China's claim & China's calculated coercive moves). The argumentative stance is reminiscent of the Filipino case in that both sets of authors justified their use of negative labels in the context of transgressions. As a whole, Singaporean and Indonesian articles were less homogenous than those from the Philippines, but this was largely due to a diverse use of negative labels and criticisms rather than a lack of them. These labels also displayed the striking discursive and stigmatic parallels between the three ASEAN states.

However, Singaporean and Indonesian articles were less overtly critical than their Filipino counterparts. It is thus more difficult to draw conclusions from the language of the articles alone. That being said, an examination of the arguments and their implicit critiques reveals a cohesive tendency to indirectly stigmatize China. Instead of personally condemning the PRC, authors narrated events in a way that cast the PRC as contradictory. A frequent occurrence was the juxtaposition of China's peaceful message with the character of its behavior on the ground. Authors would summarize this discrepancy by making statements like: "[China's] image of a 'friendly elephant'…. fails to manifest in the case of South China Sea disputes" (ASEAN's procrastination in the SCS). Writers also focused on China's irrationality. A common refrain was that the PRC's South China Sea policy was a "March of Folly" in which the state's actions were contrary to self-interest (El Indio: A march of folly). This approach ostensibly preserved the objectivity of the writer, but still functioned to highlight the insincerity of China's platitudes.

The underlying argumentative claim was that China's decision to violate the DOC and refusal to integrate with the ASEAN framework were fundamentally at odds with its rhetorical message. One senior writer for the Straits Times curtly summarized these sentiments:

> "… if the Chinese were to pause to think, Asean states acted out of anxiety, not just about the sheer size and might of China that they cannot hope to match, but also over Chinese actions on the ground that were contradictory to their stated intentions of goodwill and peaceful cooperation." – (Goh Sui Noi, 2014)

While this approach does not directly involve name calling and labeling, the focus on hypocrisy represented a more subtle form of stigmatization. Instead of making personalized claims, authors would argue that the image of China as "inflexible and assertive" was a product of its transgressive actions over the Mischief Reef, Taiwan Missile Crisis, and its violations of the DOC (ASEAN procrastination in the SCS). Authors therefore made a rational case for stigmatization, arguing that China's behavior would logically engender mistrust and criticism in East Asia.

All of the attention devoted to China's contradictions showed the state to be a deviant actor whose behavior was at odds with the standards of the region. Descriptions of contradiction and hypocrisy have strong negative connotations, and authors are able to project these negative qualities back onto the state itself without engaging in personal criticism. As Alder-Nissen describes, linking an actor to such negative characteristics creates, "a rationale… for devaluing, rejecting, and physically excluding the stigmatized" (Alder- Nissen, p 147). While the authors never personally invest themselves in arguing against China, their frequent depictions of Beijing's hypocrisy effectively display the state as an illogical and transgressive entity. While authors less frequently employed negative labels (perhaps for political reasons), they instead implied that China was compromising the stability of the region through its non-compliance with regional standards. In this way, they labeled China as a perpetrator of sorts, whose transgressions were the source of regional tensions. These judgments lent their arguments a normative weight, as authors displayed restraint but still engaged in stigmatization in an indirect fashion.

Topically, China's transgressions relative to ASEAN's norms were the primary source of negative sentiments. Beyond critiquing the maritime disputes with the Philippines, China's placement of its oil rig near Vietnam was described as, "inconsistent with international law" and in "disregard [of] Beijing's pledge to fully and effectively implement the DOC" (China sending mixed signals to ASEAN). Authors were quick to surmise that the East Asian region is, "haunted by China's pattern of assertiveness in managing the territorial disputes in which it is involved" (ASEAN's Procrastination in the SCS). As a body, the negative labels cited earlier were used in a similar manner to reference such aberrant behavior. Singaporean Minister Lee Hsien Loong neatly packaged these sentiments in an address that alluded to China, stating that SCS claimants must respect international principles and that "might is not right" in resolving disputes (Singapore PM, Might not right in SCS).

Yet these strong criticisms occurred in an environment where bilateral relations were characterized positively. Sino-Indonesian and Sino-Singaporean relations were not points of contention for the authors, whose focus remained at the regional level. Those that did reference bilateral relations did so in a calm manner that did not display any signs of serious grievances. The juxtaposition between criticism and optimism was present even within singular articles. In such cases, China was described as behaving with an "aggressiveness unprecedented since Indonesia's independence". Yet the two nations were concomitantly referenced as "good neighbors and good friends" (China must avoid destabilizing the region). Other examples tended to provide a favorable review of China's ascent but would still critique the state for not behaving, "like it is invested in the international system or satisfied with the territorial status quo" (Caution amidst positives of China's Asian push).

This duality shows that negative perceptions were not produced by bilateral tensions or security threats. Indonesian and Singaporean discourse strongly display elements of stigmatization despite the absence of China's assertiveness in bilateral relations. No major sovereignty issues were present, nor was public opinion negatively disposed to China in each of these cases. In fact, many of the most critical articles also referenced strong bilateral ties and expressed optimism for continuing positive relations. This would suggest that H1 correctly predicts soft power swings in the wake of normative transgressions. However, the data does not differentiate between potential alternative sources of these sentiments because of its lack of antecedent period. It therefore must rely on the topical and argumentative content of the articles. In that regard, each of these areas strongly identifies China's transgressions as the source of negative perceptions. Those pieces which assumed a critical tone almost universally cited Chinas unilateral behavior, violation of the DOC, and aggressiveness as justification for the negative attitudes they subsequently expressed.

## South Korea

The case of South Korea may represent one of the hardest cases to test H1, and is therefore a good candidate for falsification. Instead of possessing a well-defined normative environment, Northeast Asia is a region devoid of such a cohesive community. Northeast Asian states possess little, if any, institutional or normative connections relative to the highly integrated environment of East Asia. Therefore, the lack of a strong regional normative environment ought to weaken the cohesion of authors given the absence of an institution for the diffusion and enforcement of specific behavioral norms. A secondary problem is the issue of identifying relevant international norms in the first place. As will be demonstrated, certain dimensions of China's behavior appear to be transgressive but this alone is not enough to identify the norms which were violated.

If the normative environment of South Korea is indeed weak, then H2 would predict that China's threatening behavior is the primary variable affecting shifts in soft power. Yet increasing the burden on H2 in the South Korean case is the absence of major territorial disputes and a low degree of bilateral tension relative to states like the Philippines. Korea and China lack major territorial disputes and those that have arose have thus far been minor (Suk-Hee, 2012). Like Indonesia and Singapore, South Koreans are therefore unlikely be display any prejudices related to ongoing disputes or perceive themselves as victimized by China. Evidence of stigmatizing language should also remain absent if normative transgressions are not a factor impacting Korean public opinion.

As will be shown, South Korea represents a challenge for both H1 and H2 as the first major perception decline was not followed by any easily identifiable instance of transgression or aggression. The normative element of the event is difficult to identify given the absence of well-defined norms. The events themselves, the Cheonan sinking and the Yeonpyong Island shelling, both had security ramifications for South Korea as well. China displayed a reluctance to punish the North, which implied that the North could carry out similar destructive acts without fear of reprisal. However, a case can be made that neither transgression nor aggression are the best descriptions of China's conduct. The most prevalent criticism of China that emerged instead was that China was not behaving according to its "international responsibility" in letting North Korea run rampant. Therefore, this perception decline in particular remains somewhat unexplained by either H1 or H2 under the limits of this study.

Still, a discursive analysis of South Korea reveals the fundamental differences amongst individual perception shifts. The case is therefore able to display the relationship between the catalyzing behavior and the character of the perception shift that follows. Events like China's ADIZ announcement have immediate security ramifications and produce sharp rises in threat perceptions. Yet these events do not correlate with stigmatic language. Stigmatic discourse instead appeared most strongly in the wake of China's lenient treatment of North Korea after the Cheonan and Yeonpyeong incidents. The normative significance of China's leniency remains unclear, but South Korean authors fiercely make the case that China did not behave responsibly given its status as a great power. This failure to meet expectations likely has normative implications but it cannot be categorized as transgressive because the norms in question are not well understood. The next section tracks the perception shifts which followed very disparate events: China's quiescence towards North Korea in the wake of the Cheonan and Yeonpyong incidents, and the PRC's announcement of its ADIZ extension. The South Korean case study will use the model of the Philippines in which perceptions will be tracked across a 5 year period to display their co-variance with bilateral events and the presence or absence of stigmatizing language.

*South Korean Perceptions in the Late 2000s*

Preexisting perceptions of China prior to the sample period are difficult to ascertain in a qualified manner, but attitudes may be approximated using poll studies. As a baseline, the Pew Global Attitudes Survey places South Korean attitudes towards China at 41% favorable in 2009, representing a seven point decline from their 48% favorable rating of China in 2008 (Pew Global Attitudes, 2009). This rating represents a relatively middle of the pack disposition as it is much higher than Japan's 14% rating, yet lower than Pakistan's 84% majority. The lack of a clear majority also suggests the conclusion that Koreans were not systematically predisposed towards or against the PRC despite minor historic disputes like the ones over the Koguryo region.

To unpack these ratings, Chung provides a summary of Korean perceptions regarding China during the late 2000s:

> "if [positive] sentiments are not necessarily stable or constantly reproduced— i.e., interrupted abruptly by certain incidents—we may conceive of South Koreans' favorable views of China as "wishful expectations" they have that are driven partly by their strategic instinct to utilize their large neighbor as a counterweight to other regional powers like Japan, and partly by their disenchantment with the United States... Many recent signs suggest that South Korea's positive views of China are by no means fixed." (Chung, 2009 p 471).

South Korean perceptions of China are understandably described as volatile. South Korea may be understood to have a relatively favorable disposition towards China on account of its economic and cultural ties, yet it is implied that this may be offset by behaviorally induced tensions. On the one hand, China's engagement in the six-party talks and its "strategic cooperative partnership" with South Korea may represent sources of positive sentiments. On the other, China's handling of North Korean defectors, aspects of its stance towards the North, and the debacle of its historical claim on the Koguryo region have served to engender worry over the intentions of the state (Chung, 2009). Thus, South Korea's approval ratings of China reflect bifurcated perceptions, leaving South Korea at a relative middle ground of positive and negative sentiment at the end of the 2000s.

Prior to 2010, a limited sampling of articles suggest that sentiment in South Korea was a mix of cautious admiration and worry over the effects of China's economic rise. While not distinctly positive, the articles describing China were certainly not negative, nor did they depict China as a threat to South Korean security: no article from prior to March of 2010 explicitly identified China as such a threat. A second unifying features of the articles before the Cheonan sinking is the common identification of China's ascendency and the ensuing worry over this trend. China's economic development was described warily as multiple authors cautioned against viewing China's ascent optimistically (How will China's Ascendency affect Asian Nations? & Why We should Worry about a Chinese Global takeover). Using language like "China has woken", these articles prescribed increasing engagement and smart diplomacy as a means of mitigating any bilateral friction that might arise from the PRC's development

(China's Renewed Naval Might Heralds Increased Competition).

Descriptions of China itself displayed a similar uncertainty over the net benefits of having such a giant neighbor. Frequent tags included "superpower", "giant", and "ascendant", further displaying the relevance of China's rise in its neighbor's discourse. While these were the most frequently used descriptors of the PRC, China was also identified as being contradictory, as having a "forked tongue" (China must say where it stands on N. Korea rocket launch). Usage of negative labels like these was not common however. A majority of authors instead turned to behavioral standards or calls for responsible actions as a means of qualifying their analysis of the PRC. These articles expressed worry over China's rise in an indirect fashion, using moralistic language and urging caution as supplements to their analysis. Aggregate opinion therefore did not display any signs of being distinctly critical. Worry was certainly present but it did not necessarily manifest itself in a large volume of negative labels of China. However, it must be noted that the small number of articles and lack of consistent language in this period prevents discourse analysis from being truly revelatory. What this brief overview does seem to verify is the bifurcated theme of Korea's public perceptions. The PRC's material success was depicted as a double edged sword whose benefits may also carry certain costs.

*The Cheonan Sinking and Yeonpyeong Island Shelling*

Taking this snapshot of South Korean perceptions as a starting point, matters changed significantly following the Cheonan sinking. This change began in a political fashion with the assumption of the South Korean government and its military forces that the North was responsible for the attack. The South Korean media then collectively adopted a "monotone chorus" which condemned the North as the perpetrator (Kim, 2011). The event subsequently sparked latent tensions, weakened belief in a communal East Asia, and made it exceedingly difficult to achieve consensus in dealing with the North (ibid). As these effect played out, the disruption caused by the sinking placed increasing power in the hands of entities with the ability to affect change (ibid). China, as one of the nations with the strongest ties to the North, therefore came under heavy pressure from the international community for its lack of action. The Yeonpyeong Island Shelling in November of 2010 further increased international demand for China to take steps. However, China remained fairly supportive of the North, only issuing sporadic platitudes in response.

As expected, the demand for China to act against the North was a consistent theme in the articles following the event. Yet despite the seeming universality of this stance, the character of post-Cheonan discourse was not significantly different from the language used prior to the sinking. Like in 2009, the persistent argumentative line was a call for responsible action on the part of Beijing. Those pieces directly following the sinking assumed a familiar, patronizing tone towards China but ratcheted up the calls for responsibility. The oft repeated claim was that China's actions were not befitting those of a great power (China must stop protecting North Korea & China Should come off the fence). Authors also juxtaposed the firm responses of the US with the quiescence of the PRC as a means to highlight that China was not behaving as an international power should. The logic of these articles strengthened the argumentative line of the pieces appearing before the Cheonan incident. Authors demanded that China ought to behave in a certain way because of its position in the international system and were highly critical of China's continued passive stance. Out of the twelve articles between March 2010 and June of 2011, fully eight of them employed a similar argument.

This assertiveness on the part of the authors was also manifested in their depictions of the PRC. Following the event, authors adopted new characterizations of China that reflected its failure to meet expectations. The most common of these new labels were representations of China as juvenile. Multiple articles described China as immature, even going so far as describing China as a "typical adolescent" because of its ambivalence towards its perceived international responsibility (China's New swagger could lead to isolation & China must stop protecting North Korea). Other articles argued that China's response demonstrated it to be moody, clumsy, hypocritical and brutish. The rhetoric of these articles implicitly suggests that China lags behind a standard unrelated to its unquestioned material growth. Each term carries its own implication that a different aspect of China's character is underdeveloped or weak relative to its peers. Of critical import is the fact that these descriptions were not limited to articles related to the Cheonan sinking, the DPRK's behavior, or China's response. These descriptions of China were not only consistent, but persisted across a range of topics and scenarios. Examples in which these labels appeared including fishing incidents, the awarding of Nobel prizes, and China's economic condition. While the character of arguments in these pieces are similar to those from before the sinking, perceptions did appear to coalesce into a more consistent and common manner of referencing the PRC.

While a majority of authors expressed some form of concern regarding China's behavior, perceptions of whether China represented a threat to Korea remained relatively static. In fact, 40% of articles prior to the sinking identified China as a potential threat, while 42% following the sinking maintained a similar stance. Rhetorically, the authors employed stronger language in their depictions of China but this was only followed by a minor increase in their presentation of China as a threat to South Korean security. The largest change in terms of therat perceptions came as authors more consistently saw China as a future, or possible, threat to South Korea, The fact that the PRC appeared unwilling to sanction the North suggested that it would do little to prevent further attacks to South Korean territory.

The Cheonan sinking therefore appeared to have a polarizing effect rather than an exclusively negative one. Criticisms of China became stronger and more persistent, but they also retained the same character as the criticisms from before the incident. Rather than alter the discourse in a significant fashion, the Cheonan sinking seemed to give increased relevance and appeal to arguments calling or China to take a more "responsible" position towards the North. This is evidenced by the fact that more than half of the articles in the year and a half after the Cheonan sinking appealed to China's responsibility as a great power.

Despite the minor increase in threat perceptions, discourse did display the characteristics of stigmatizing behavior. Not only was China labeled in a derogatory manner, the calls for responsibility were utilized in a way that isolated China from the rest of the international system. Describing China in a juvenile manner implicitly compares China against figuratively superior, or more mature, entities. Articles even explicitly identify the US as the "role model" against which the immature China is referenced (China's bullying serves nobody's interests). This comparison simultaneously shames Beijing for not behaving appropriately, and differentiates it from the metaphorically "senior" states. As a result, the PRC is depicted as isolated from world order based on its underdevelopment and lack of compliance with international norms or responsibilities.

The discursive landscape of South Korea in the wake of the Cheonan also exhibited striking parallels with that of East Asia. Language critiquing China's bullying behavior and "Middle Kingdom", or self-centered attitude began to appear in increasing volume during this period (Insecurity drives Chinas bullying & China's bullying serves nobody's interests). Despite the vastly different contexts, criticism of China's bullying practices remained a consistent theme. This is particularly interesting for Korea given that there were no major instances of bilateral exchanges that would justify such language. Instead, Korea authors tended to adopt China's regional actions as justifications for their assessments. In this manner, their behavior was very similar to that of Indonesian and Singaporean authors. The articles which assigned the most scathing labels were most often topically centered on China's failure to constrain the North, its policies towards Japan and East Asia, and its perceived shirking of international obligations. Therefore, the discursive character of the articles were not the only similarities amongst the Korean and East Asian articles. The stigmatization of China for its regional, as opposed to bilateral, activities was a second persistent theme.

*June 2011 until October of 2013*

The two major issues of import in bilateral relations between early 2011 and late 2013 were the South Korean coast guard murder in 2011 and the minor dispute over Socotra Rock in 2012 (Suk-Hee, 2012?). Neither event was a direct act of transgression nor did China engage in aggressive or threatening actions. In this context, H1 and H2 would suggest that perceptions of China ought to remain fairly stable or actually improve in the absence of these behaviors. Opinion poll data and prior research tentatively suggests that this may be the case. The East Asia Institute-Asia Research Institute (EAI – ARI) reported that Korean perceptions of China remained ambivalent in late 2011, reflecting the continued divide in public opinion over China's rise and the instability that it may bring (Suk-Hee, 2012). Yet of interest to this study is whether this ambivalence is a departure from previous periods or an improvement.

On this front, perceptions from mid-2011 to late 2013 remained fairly consistent - that is to say low - relative to the opinions expressed in the months following the Cheonan and Yongpyeon incidents. However, the defining characteristic of this period was the further increase in the consistency and prevalence of certain discursive labels. Starting in late 2011, perceptions began to crystallize into common statements that were assertive than those of prior pieces. This is first manifested in the manner by which articles addressed China. Instead of using China's actions as a platform for criticism and constructive recommendation, articles began to characterize China using security-oriented language. One particular example cites China's non-adherence with diplomatic protocol as a threat to Korean security. The author argues that South Korea would be at the mercy of its larger neighbor should China abandon international principles and norms (Lack of Principles Leads to Poor diplomacy). This style of argument represented a common phenomenon by which authors strengthened the character of previously made judgments. Articles from early 2011 until late 2013 moved away from making behavioral prescriptions based on standards of appropriate behavior as was common before.

The product of this trend was an increasingly propensity for authors to use China's behavior as rationalization for their disparaging, shaming, and derogatory language (see China must abide humanitarian principles & Lack of principles leads to poor diplomacy & China's true muscle & China's bullying serves noones interests). Authors did continue to cite the need for responsibility on the part of China but these arguments were fewer and farther between, as only four out of the sixteen articles referenced China's responsibility or global duties. This type of logic was not absent, but it was instead subsumed into stronger language which was often condemning, and not constructive. Rather than call for responsible action, articles were more likely to detail China's deviance from international protocols and use this as a cause for alarm, rather than proscribing engagement. The growing number of these articles suggests that Korean perceptions may have begun to coalesce into more uniformly negative attitudes.

As for the character of South Korean discourse, articles continued to utilize stigmatizing language and labels. The most common discursive trend during the period centered on what was deemed "Neo- Sinocentrism" by one editor (China's historical claims strain ties). Such discourse captures both the self-absorption and the breaches of international protocol that constituted many prior criticisms of China's behavior. Use of this specific term was not widespread, but a majority of China's detractors adopted similar language which condemned China for flaunting the rules of the international system. As examples, the disconnect between China's behavior and the standards of international conduct was cited as justification for the use of labels like "discourteous", "crude", and "threatening" (The threat of China's Aircraft Carrier & Chinese military Chief's rudeness). Beijing's diplomatic program, its radiation leak cover-up, and fishing confrontations were other instances where such language was employed. This reflected arguments made in articles from 2010 that characterized the PRC as "isolated" from the international community and as an "unwelcome guest" because of its disregard for international standards (China's new swagger could lead to isolation). A majority of articles utilized such language at all stages from mid 2011 until late 2013 with no major exceptional periods. The progression of these perceptions further reinforces the idea that public opinion began to coalesce in the wake of the Cheonan and Yeonpyeong incidents.

In this context, the dimension of stigmatization that deals with the figurative separation of an "us" from a "them" is of particular relevance. Articles which referenced China's position in the international system often did so by identifying China as an entity whose behavior separated or removed it from that community (see China must observe sanctions). Specifically, China was excluded from consideration as a "great power" on multiple occasions because of its non-compliant attitude.

Discursive labels also provide evidence for this trend as the afore-mentioned articles reference China as "isolated", and "separate" from the rest of Asian states. Again however, it must be noted that there are almost certainly political and personal motivation behind the use of these labels. With this caveat in mind, the descriptive tone assumed of articles from mid 2011 until late 2013 did display characteristics of stigmatization in a manner which emphasized the disconnect between China's behavior and the proscriptions of international expectations. This disconnect was then linked to portrayals of China as out of sync with other states that share similar levels of material success.

The persistence of this type of language reinforces an earlier observed trend. Stigmatizing language and the attitudes it embodies appear to be relatively long-term. The discursive attitudes catalyzed by China's treatment of the North appear to have lasting consequences for the state even years down the road. Amidst the articles stigmatizing China for its more current offences, authors would often harken back to China's treatment of the North as evidence of its transgressive disposition. These attitudes can be traced back to the Cheonan sinking and appear to have set in motion certain perceptions that only crystalized with time.

*ADIZ extension: November 2013*

In late 2013, China announced that it was extending its Air Defense Identification Zone (ADIZ) in the East China Sea. Despite China's prior statements regarding its intent to control airspace, the move caused an uproar in the international community. Previous wariness in the region was intensified as the move was interpreted as indicative of further assertiveness from Beijing. However, as far as transgressive behavior is concerned, the extension of the ADIZ is not in violation of any explicit norms or international laws. As Dr. Yilmaz argues:

> "An ADIZ can be analogous to a warning zone in which any aircraft that enters the prescribed zone is identified and monitored. In this respect, it is neither a no-flight zone nor an extension of a state's sovereign airspace. Essentially, an ADIZ still constitutes international airspace and it is not a binding agreement recognized by international law. Hence, from a legal perspective, it neither reinforces nor impinges on claims of sovereignty. Furthermore, an ADIZ does not restrict the right of any aircraft to fly within its boundaries; it simply requires them to maintain contact with the ADIZ-holding state and to provide flight data. Ever since its adoption by the US in the aftermath of the Second World War, a number of countries have enforced an ADIZ, including Japan, South Korea, Vietnam, Russia and Canada." (Yilmaz, 2014).

China declaration may have been provocative but that is not to say that it was transgressive. There are few, if any, international norms or expectations associated with such behavior. China's actions therefore may threaten or worry its neighbors but these sentiments were induced in a manner that did not involve transgressive acts.

The ADIZ incident is therefore differentiated from the Cheonan and Yeonpyeong incidents in this critical aspect: China was not expected to act in a certain way. Instead, its behavior constituted an immediate material threat to South Korea. The articles following the period reinforce this differentiation. Writers dealing with the ADIZ did not cite behavioral standards as cause for their criticisms, but rather confined their analysis to the security implications of Beijing's move. Whereas articles from 2011 and 2012 explicitly identified that China violated certain norms, the most critical pieces from late 2013 and early 2014 only went so far as to describe Beijing's declaration as "unilateral" and in violation of the "principles of friendship... and cooperation" (China's neighbor diplomacy illusion). In this light, the ADIZ extension is a perfect candidate for the falsification of H1. In the absence of an explicit or perceived normative violation, China's ADIZ extension ought to not inspire an increase in stigmatic language. Instead, H2 would predict only a spike in threat perceptions, without any corresponding stigmatic dialogue.

In period following the announcement, discourse shows a sharp decline for the first 3 to 4 months but then a steady improvement with no retrenchment of negative opinion. Proceeding in a sequential manner, the articles immediately following the ADIZ announcement consistently identified China as a threat. November 2013 to March of 2014 was the only period in which this occurred with any consistency. Half of the articles in the four months following the event labelled China as a security threat to South Korea, thus displaying a security-oriented perspective that was absent in prior articles. China's "Middle-Kingdom psyche", "Sino-Centric" actions, and "unilateral" approach to international affairs represented the most common labels (China's Neighbor Diplomacy illusion & "China time" is fast). However, the first two terms were already widely used prior to the ADIZ extension. Only "unilateral" represented a significant deviation from prior patterns.

Interestingly enough, the vitriol of these articles dissipated rapidly and actually improved over the remainder of the period. Throughout mid to late 2014, attempts by authors to shame and alienate China were notably infrequent despite the fact that such a polarizing event had just transpired. Authors instead showed a tendency to revert back to the advisory position that was assumed earlier. The common method of argumentation was for an author to make an assessment of the PRC's current policies and then use this analysis to make policy recommendations. Using the piece entitled "China's growing menace" as an example, the editorial begins by noting the increasing defense budgets in the Asia Pacific, the dubious nature of China's budget reports, and Beijing's "assertiveness" in handling regional issues. These observations were then used as a platform for the author to recommend a comprehensive strengthening of South Korea's military and a hardening of its policy line. Notably absent from the equation is a condemnation of China based on its character or behavior.

This relative discursive improvement is also evidenced by the fact that "Sino-centric" criticisms dropped precipitously in 2014. Only one article raised a critique of China's worldview on the basis of its "old tributary" mentality. The strong assertions regarding the threat that China poses became nearly non-existent by March 2014 and remained absent until September 2014. Articles instead returned to the speculative worrying that characterized the periods of relative calm in Sino-Korean relations. The constructive approach appeared resurgent during 2014 as nearly half of the articles implemented such a strategy. This paradigm shift was strongly tied to a reduction in stigmatic characteristics. Criticisms and tension still persisted, but articles turned their focus to the domestic consequences of international events. They cited China's behavior only as a reference and did not do so as a means of highlighting the state's failings.

The fact that most articles were constructive rather than critical represents a significant change from the months immediately following the ADIZ announcement. Instead of maintaining a persistently negative standpoint, discourse appears to have recovered in China's favor. China's assertiveness and dubious level of responsibility were still noted in mid to late 2014, but these factors were depicted as political challenges and not as security threats. Such a difference is subtle, but it depicts the reemergence of sentiments that these challenges can be addressed successfully. This constructive disposition therefore indicates that perceptions during the latter portion of 2014 had improved relative to both the period preceding the ADIZ extension, and the period directly following it. The degree of this discursive "recovery" and the rate at which sentiments improved were both distinct features of the post-ADIZ discourse.

The South Korean response to the ADIZ announcement supports H2's prediction that such events ought to be followed by negative sentiment and the appearance of threat perceptions. Yet the ADIZ event is also unique in that this event occurred long after the last instance of transgression. Without a galvanizing instance of transgression within the past year, the strength of stigmatization slackened noticeably. Even immediately after the ADIZ announcement, the discursive focus was on security implications and not condemnation. Stigmatic discourse then fell even further in the next 6 months despite the initial uptick in threat perceptions. Ironically, this verifies the assumptions of H1. Stigmatic language – the systematic shaming and labeling of China – is shown to be intimately linked with instances of transgression. While such events may inspire such discourse for periods of more than a year, this language does appear to weaken if no further instances of transgression occur.

Conclusions

The South Korean case strongly supports H2 as all three events that affected South Korean security (the Cheonan sinking, Yeonpyeong shelling, and the ADIZ extension) were followed by declines in perceptions of China. Yet the case also raises lingering questions over whether China violated some form of implicit norm in its quiescent treatment of the North in 2010. If the authors are to be believed, negative perceptions from this period were largely a product of China's failure to behave according to its status as a great power. They argued that China's status as a "great power" ought to necessitate a more active and responsible position towards the North (China should come off the Fence & China must stop protecting NK). Yet writings from the period also reflect the intangibility of this "responsibility" to act. South Korean authors did not cite commonly upheld conventions or international laws as justifications that demanded Chinese action.

Overall, China's behavior towards the North was not all that different from its peers, although its persistent silence may have been unique. What differentiated China's position was that it undeniably possessed the greatest leverage over the North due to its diplomatic and economic connections. But the case still lacks any sort of codified or explicit norms associated with this "great power responsibility" that the authors allude to. As such, China's subsequent ambivalence can only be characterized as transgressive relative to these intangible expectations. There is also a question of whether the claims made by authors were genuine or politically motivated. In either case, it remains a possibility that norms were indeed violated. This would theoretically support H1, especially witnessing the uptick in stigmatization in 2010, but it cannot be concluded as such under the limitations of this study.

However, several interesting takeaways remain from the South Korean case. The first is that South Korea offers a clear depiction of the different discursive effects that follow security related issues versus those that follow perceived violations of behavioral expectations. On the one hand, discourse following the ADIZ event contained a multitude of articles describing China as a threat but a relatively smaller number utilizing stigmatizing language. These articles were topically focused on the implications of the PRC's actions and not on critiquing the state's behavior. This directly contrasts the period following the Cheonan and Yeonpyeong incidents. This period was unique in that the discourse isolated, shamed, and negatively labeled China but was not overly focused on the security dimension of China's actions. Additionally, discourse recovered after the initial three to four month dip in late 2013, whereas perceptions remained low for nearly three years beginning in 2010. It therefore appears that both threat perceptions and stigmatic language may exist in relative isolation from one another and are dependent upon a different set of circumstances and behaviors. The takeaway from these differing effects is that security threats alone are insufficient when explaining perception shifts. While they capture short-term trends in sentiments, many of the long-term trends instead match the patterns witnessed in Southeast Asia where transgressive behavior set off a cascade of stigmatization and the entrenchment of certain labels.

## The Character of China's Image

Finally, the most common discursive labels from across the data are presented here in order of their prevalence. The five major "families" of labels represent language that was present in each of the cases and occurred with regular frequency. Less frequently used labels, of which there were many, are not included here.

1) "Superpower"- China's size was typically the first characteristic highlighted by authors. Yet the issue of the PRC's ascension did not always carry with it a negative connotation. Its immense size was referenced as both a boon and a source of contention. However, references to the state's "superpower" status were made in reference to its material power alone. In fact, its material wealth was often used as a standard to demonstrate the relative underdevelopment of other aspects of China's statehood.

2) "The Bully" – Using the analogy of a local neighborhood to represent East Asia, author's depicted China as an aggressor towards its neighbors and community. They cite the PRC's transgressive actions as a misuse of its material power and as demonstrative of a disregard for normative frameworks. Taken to its extreme, the label suggests that most of China's aggressiveness is bravado and its material success has not been successfully translated into international status.

3) "Middle Kingdom Complex" – This historical term was used to characterize the Sino-centrism apparent in Chinese foreign policy. Referencing the Middle Kingdom in which China practiced its tributary system, authors argued that the state's current actions represented the state's reversion to a world view in which its neighbors and the larger community of Asia was again peripheral

to China's interests.

    4)       "Two-faced China" – the state is criticized for its apparent double standards regarding issues of sovereignty and legality. This phrase's use often stems from China taking whichever stance suits it best in regards to international laws and principles. Many regional powers expect China to be a "status quo" power and to uphold these standards instead.

    5)       "Responsible Power" – This term was most evident in South Korean discourse but it also underwrote many of the criticisms made by Southeast Asian nations. China's perceived refusal to uphold the status quo and engage with the international community were depicted as irresponsible and juvenile behavior. This was correlated with language depicting China as selfish for not making contributions that were commensurate with its level of wealth.

## Conclusions

This study observes that China's transgressive behavior and threatening conduct are key determinants of the PRC's soft power in Asia. Every major shift in perceptions within the last 5 years was prefaced by some combination of such behavior. Korean, Singaporean, Indonesian, and Filipino authors were all highly sensitive to the appropriateness of China's actions, and whether these actions violated norms. In accordance with H1 and H2, these correlations suggest that transgression and threatening conduct are indeed some of the primary forces currently detracting from China's appeal. Additionally, the consequences of China's transgressions were not synonymous with the effect of its threatening conduct. Norm violating behavior elicited prolonged periods of negative discourse in which China was stigmatized consistently while events that heightened security concerns produced sharper, yet fairly short, dips in public perceptions. Those acts that had immediate security implications raised threat perceptions but, in the absence of transgression, did not necessarily witness a strengthening of discourse which shamed, labeled, and otherwise criticized China. This differentiation highlights that both behaviors affect soft power to differing degrees.

In the end, both H1 and H2 are supported by the results. However, the magnitude of each effect merits further study. Authors were not liable to dwell on aggressive acts for long periods of time, nor did "threatening" behavior elicit protracted shifts. Rather, long-term perception declines were consistently characterized by stigmatization and explicit criticisms of China's norm violating behavior. These stigmatic shifts may even represent a worse status loss for China than the appearance of threat perceptions. Negative sentiment seemed to become entrenched after repeated normative infractions. It did not dissipate quickly as did stigmatic discourse but rather became more consistent until altered by another set of catalyzing events. The increased usage of labels like "bully" and "Middle Kingdom mentality" demonstrate how stigmatic opinion coalesces around specific characterizations that, when popularized, assume a momentum of their own. Thus, it seems plausible that China's transgressions have a greater impact on the state's soft power given that stigmatic shifts were the most severe in terms of magnitude and duration.

These systematic shifts also highlight the causal mechanism by which normative transgressions elicited specific social responses. At the simplest level, Beijing's transgressive actions are in discord with regional actor's expectations. This dissonance motivates actors to shame, label, and otherwise criticize China in accordance with the norms to which they subscribe. Alder-Nissen, who repurposed Goffman's work on stigmatization, expands on the logic behind this behavior. Both authors detail how stigmatization develops via an actor's recognition that another entity's behavior is, "incongruous with our stereotype of what a given actor should be" (Goffman and Alder-Nissen p 145). Cognizance of that difference leads actors to engage in shaming and other practices which realize such an incongruity. When applied to states, the disparity between a given norm and transgressive actions creates the same sort of discordance identified by Goffman. In essence, the state's transgressive actions are dissonant with the public's expectations. This leads foreign audiences to engage in stigmatization and, as demonstrated in this study, leads to a decline in soft power.

However, norms may also have a secondary social effect. Due to their homogenizing effect on the expectations of large populations, this study observed that norms seemed to amplify the negative effects of transgressive conduct at the national level. The presence of norms appears to jumpstart a kind of positive feedback mechanism. State-level or regional norms systematize the expectations of a population. In the wake of a norm violation, the public's reactions are thus harmonized due to their common subscription to these standards. This is illustrated clearly in the data set as authors increasingly addressed China in strikingly similar ways across topics, publications, and even states in the months after a transgression. The homogenization effect appears to then facilitate the diffusion of popular sentiment. A widespread, yet similar, response crystalizes certain perceptions, popularizes others, and appears to reify many characterizations of the transgressive entity in the eyes of the public.

Amplification emerges as a product of the scale at which these reactions occur. Instead of remaining a series of individualized or localized perception shifts, the social response is collectivized at a national level. Norms in effect enhance what would otherwise be a diffuse social response by systematizing the expectations, and reactions, of populations. A strong normative environment can therefore reduce the centrifugal force of disparate opinions by standardizing the reactions of large populations to specific events. The social resistance that individuals face when adopting any critical position appears inversely proportional to the amount of people holding a similar belief. While not explicitly tested here, this social homogenization offers a plausible explanation for both the duration and consistency of perception declines following acts of transgression.

Given the magnitude of these effects, the issue then becomes, what effect will these soft power patterns have on the foreign policy future of both China and its neighbors? In the short run, the observations of this study are unable to visualize the effect of perception shifts on foreign policy abroad. It remains for future research to analyze how behavior-induced soft power declines have or have not affected the creation of sympathetic policy. Yet from a theoretical standpoint, soft power implicitly offers its own mechanism by which attractiveness impacts domestic decision-making. The immediate consequence of a fall in soft power is a commensurate fall in China's ability to coopt and agenda set within East Asia. China's decision makers, if cognizant of this shift, will subsequently modify their policies to reflect the reduced efficacy of cooptation strategies.

Assuming Chinese leaders are indeed aware of these soft power shifts and their cause, the state may be incentivized to rely less heavily on its agenda setting abilities because of their reduced efficacy.

As a result, material strategies and even coercion may become more attractive relative to methods of cooptation. The fundamental reason for this is that the state places its comprehensive national interests as its highest priority. Alone, this is not atypical state behavior. The issue is that China's pursuit of these interests, which include the unification of Taiwan and China's sovereignty claims in the South China Sea, is unyielding. Because the state's pursuit of its goals remains undiminished, this soft power decline may only cause China to switch tactics rather than incentivizing the state to rectify its behavior. The corollary to this observation is that alternate political methods are then made more attractive by comparison. The suggested argument is that, when pursuing its interests in a threatening or transgressive manner, China is more and more incentivized to rely upon material means of pursuing its interests because its soft power resources decline over time.

Yet again, there is an oppositional force that counters this trend. This study has shown that threatening or aggressive acts engender negative sentiments because they precipitate threat perceptions and violate widely held norms. Therefore, any move in a more assertive direction would only further derail China's ability to agenda-set and potentially assume a leadership role in East Asia. This directly parallels what happened to America during and after the Iraq War. The US's commitment to its unilateral course heightened, and then entrenched, Anti-American sentiment abroad (Katzenstein and Keohane, 2006. Chiozza, 2009). After witnessing the duration of the soft power decline that followed, China must think carefully before proceeding any further with its current course. Transgressive avenues may seem more efficacious, but they come with an implicit cost. The real decision then, is whether China values its interests in the South China Sea more than the long-term efficacy of its agenda-setting power. Beijing stands to gain economically fecund territory but at the cost of a huge set-back to its leadership goals.

The consequences of China's current behavior have already affected its recent relations with states like the Philippines and Singapore. In these cases, soft power has been forced to take a backseat role. Instead of being used as a tool to foster a sympathetic political environment, China's soft power has been employed as a form of form damage control. Attractiveness counterbalances the negative sentiment engendered by assertive actions, while that same appeal increases the validity of China's rhetorical self-defenses in the eyes of the public. Soft power allows China to pursue its agenda with attenuated consequences, but it is a poor use of these resources. The innate function of soft power is to encourage sympathetic policy changes abroad. However, these foreign states, when facing a transgressive and threatening entity, are unlikely to do anything more sympathetic than dampen their retaliatory measures.

China, for all its leadership aspirations, is therefore taking the pash of most resistance to reach its goals. On the one hand, its territorial interests are at odds with the stabilizing presence expected of regional leaders. However, the contradiction is deeper than this. The real issue is the tension between China's interests and normative order of East Asia. China appears unwilling or perhaps unable to conduct its national strategies within the confines of the existing regional order. This study highlights China's repeated failure to operate within these confines and the tension that this produces. Substantial resistance to China's agenda also illustrates that the PRC currently lacks the political capital and requisite attractiveness to fully alter the system. Yet the solution to this predicament is exactly what China has thus far failed to do. Reconciliation lies with the integration, or more likely hybridization, of China's foreign policy conduct with the normative order of East Asia. A strong normative community has thus far created incentives for such integration, but the onus to complete the process now lies with China.

# Regional News Sources and Articles

*This list is not an exhaustive compilation of the articles examined, only those explicitly cited.

Philippines:

*Philippine Star*:
"Peaceful Rise?" Editorial. 3/8/2011.
"What is China's Intention in the Region?" Tony Katigbak. 6/26/2013.
"Why are Chinese Entrepreneurs Successful?" Wilson Lee Flores. 2/22/2010.
"In the Long Run, China Will Win" Monico Puentevella. 12/16/2010.
"Aid and Corruption:. Editorial. 9/30/2009.
"Historical Right and Legal Title" Jose Sison. 6/17/2011.
"Is China Becoming a Superpower?" Satur Ocampo. 6/14/2014.


*The Philippine Daily Inquirer:*
"Converging Interests: Hanoi and Manila Confront the Leviathan" Walden Bello. 12/1/2013.
"China has to Climb Down on the Spratlys Issue" Walden Bello. 7/3/2011.
"Power Asymmetry in the South" Aileen Baviera. 12/16/2010.
"Understanding China" Andrea Wong. 7/5/2012.
"Why China Why?" Jose Montelibano. 7/20/2013.
"The Call to Boycott China's products" Randy David. 7/19/2012.
"China, A Rogue State?" Harry Roque. 12/6/2012.
"Prepare for China pt 2" Jose Montelibano.
"Might not Right in the SCS" Associated Press. 6/25/2014.
"PDI keeps Big Lead in newspaper Readership" 2/25/2013.


*The Manila Times:*
"Chinese National Security Threats" Editorial. 2/21/2013.
"China Practices Statecraft, Philippines Practices Public Diplomacy" Yen Makabenta. 5/21/2014.
"China's Economic Militarization" EJ Lopez. 7/13/2014.
"Row with China may Derail Asian Growth" Catherine Valente. 5/22/2014.

Singapore and Indonesia:

*Straits Times:*
"China Can Try Walking in ASEAN States' Shoes" Goh Sui Noi. 9/8/2014.
"Straits Times Holds Steady as most-read Daily" Irene Tham.
"South China Sea: Is Jakarta no Longer Neutral?" Leo Suryadinata. 4/24/2014.
"Maritime Disputes Call for Southeast Asian Input" John Lee. 4/30/2014.
"Caution Amidst Positives of China's Asian Push" Dhruva Jaishankar. 9/17/2014.
"China's Calculated Coercive Moves" Yun Sun. 6/20/2014.
"China Sending Mixed Signals to ASEAN" Nguyen Hung Song. 5/29/2014.

*The Star:*
"Interesting Times in East Asia" Bunn Nagara. 2/9/2014.

*Jakarta Globe:*
"El Indio: A Chinese Dilemma" Jamil Flores. 4/4/2014.
"Perception of America as 'Weak' Is Making Asia Uneasy" Derwin Pereira, Ernest Z. Bower. 4/21/2014.
"Asia Infrastructure Development Bank: A Gift Horse from China" Jamil Flores. 0/26/2014.
"El Indio: A March of Folly" Jamil Flores. 5/18/2014.
"China must Avoid Destabilizing the Region" Andrea Tan. 10/30/2014.
The Jakarta Post:
"A Reminder for China" Editorial. 5/14/2014.
"Facing China's Claim" Editorial. 1/24/2014.
"ASEAN's Procrastination in the SCS" Yeremia Lalisang. 4/30/2013. South Korea:

*Chosun Ilbo:*
"How will China's Ascendency affect Asian Nations?" Park Sung-joon. 3/3/2009.
"Why we should Worry about a Chinese Global Takeover" Kim Ki-hoon. 8/3/2009.
"China's Renewed Naval Might Heralds Increased Competition" Park Doo-shik. 4/27/2009.
"China Must say Where it Stands on North Korea Rocket Launch" Park Sung-joon. 3/20/2009.
"China Must Stop Protecting North Korea" Editorial. 10/10/2010.
"China Should come Off the Fence" Editorial. 5/28/2010.
"China's new Swagger Could Lead to Isolation" Choi Yoo-Sik. 11/10/2010.
"China's Bullying Serves Nobody's Interests" Editorial. 12/23/2010.
"Lack of Principles Leads to Poor diplomacy" Jee Hae-Bum. 11/2/2011.
"China Must Abide Humanitarian Principles" Editorial. 10/16/2011.

*Joongang:*
"The True Muscle of China" Editorial. 8/7/2012.
"China's Historical Claims Strain Ties" Lee Eun-joo. 8/28/2012.
"The Threat of China's Aircraft Carrier" Lee Seok-soo. 7/16/2011.
"Chinese Military Chief's Rudeness Bodes Ill for the Future" Editorial. 7/18/2011.
"China Must Observe Sanctions" Editorial. 7/3/2012.
"China's Neighbor Diplomacy Illusion" Han Woo-Duk. 12/10/2013.
"China Time is Fast" You Sang-chul. 1/16/2014.

*The Korea Herald:*
"China's Growing Menace" Editorial. 3/9/2014.
"Korea Herald Far Ahead in English paper Circulation" Kim Yoon-Mi. 11/29/2010.

# Bibliography

"America's Global Image Remains More Positive than China's". *Pew Center: Global Attitudes Project.* July 18th , 2013.

Acharya, Amitav. *Constructing a Security Community in Southeast Asia: ASEAN and the Problem of Regional Order.* Routledge. 2001

Acharya, Amitav. "How Ideas Spread: Whose Norms Matter? Norm Localization and Institutional Change in Asian Regionalism". *International Organization.* 58.2. 2004. P 239-275

Alder-Nissen, Rebecca. "Stigma Management in International Relations: Transgressive Identities, Norms, and Order in International Society". *International Organization.* 68.1. January 2014. P 143-176.

Beeson, Mark. "Can China Lead?" *Third World Quarterly.* 34.2. 2013. P 233-250.

Blanchard, Jean-Marc and Liu, Fujita. "Thinking Hard About Soft Power: A Review and Critique of the Literature on China and Soft Power". *Asian Perspective.* 36. 2012. Pp 565-589.

Chayes, Abram and Chayes, Antonia. *The New Sovereignty: Compliance with International Regulatory Agreements.* Cambridge: Harvard University Press. 1996. p. 230.

Chiozza, Giacomo. *Anti-Americanism and the American World Order.* The John Hopkins University Press. 2009.

Cho, Young and Jeong, Jong Ho. "China's Soft Power: Discussions, Resources, and Prospects" *Asian Survey.* 48.3. June 2008. P 453-472

Cho, Young Nam and Jeong, Ho Jong. "China's Soft Power: Discussions, Resources, and Prospects". *Asian Survey.* May/June 2008.

Chow, Edward. "China's Soft Power in Developing Regions". *Chinese Soft Power and Its Implications for the United States.* Washington, DC: CSIS Press. 2009.

Chung, Jae Ho. "China's 'Soft' Clash with South Korea". *Asian Survey.* 49.3. May/June 2009. P 468-483.

Chung, Jae Ho. *Between Ally and Partner: Korea-China Relations and the United States.* New York: Columbia University Press. 2007.

Cohen, Bernard. *The Press and Foreign Policy.* Princeton, NJ: Princeton University Press, 1993.

Cortell, Andrew and Davis, James. "Understanding the Domestic Impact of International Norms: A Research Agenda". *International Studies Review.* 2.1. 2000. P 65-87.

Dearing, James and Rogers, Everett. *Agenda-setting.* Thousand Oaks, CA: Sage. 1996.

D'Hooghe, Ingrid. "Into High Gear: China's Public Diplomacy". *The Hague Journal of Diplomacy.* 3. March 2008. P 37-61.

Ding, Sheng. "Branding a Rising China: An Analysis of Beijing's National Image Management in the Age of China's Rise". *Journal of Asian and African Studies*46.3. June, 2011. p 293-306

Ding, Sheng. "*The Dragon's Hidden Wings: How China rises with its Soft Power*". Lanham : Lexington Books. 2008.

Falk, Hartig. "Confucius Institutes and the Rise of China". *Journal of Chinese Political Science.* 17.1. March 2012. P 53-76.

Finnemore, Martha and Sikkink, Kathryn. "International Norm Dynamics and Political Change". *Internatinoal Organization.* 52.4. 1998. P 887 – 917.

G. John Ikenberry, "American Hegemony and East Asian Order". *Australian Journal of International*

*Affairs*. 58.3 September 2004. P 353–367.

Garrison, Jean. "China's Prudent Cultivation of 'Soft' Power and Implications for U.S. Policy is East Asia". *Asian Affairs*. 32. Spring 2005. P 25-30.

Goh, Gillian. "The 'ASEAN Way': Non-Intervention and ASEAN's Role in Conflict Management". *Stanford Journal of East Asian Affairs*. 3.1. Spring 2003. P 113-118

Han Suk-Hee. "South Korea Seeks to Balance Relations with the US". *Council on Foreign Relations*. November 2012.

Hongying Wang, "National Image building and Chinese foreign policy". *China: An International Journal*. March 2003. P 46-72.

Huang, Chin-Hao. "China's Soft Power in East Asia: A Quest for Status and Influence?". *National Bureau of Asian Research*. January 2013.

Huang, Yanzhong, and Ding, Sheng. "Dragon's Underbelly: An Analysis of China's Soft Power". *East Asia*. 23. December, 2006. p 22-44.

Hurwitz, Jon and Peffley, Mark and Seligson, Mitchell. "Foreign Policy Belief Systems in Comparative Perspective: The United States and Costa Rica". *International Studies Quarterly*. 37.3. 1993. P 245-270

Katzenstein, Peter J and Keohane, Robert O. "Anti-Americanisms". *Policy Review*. 139. Oct/Nov 2006. P 25-37.

Kearn, David. "A Hard Case for Soft Power: China's Rise and Security in East Asia". Presented at *International Political Science Association*. Madrid, 2012.

Keck, Zachary. "China's Newest Maritime Dispute". The Diplomat. 3/20/2014. Thediplomat.com.

Kim, Mikyoung. "The Cheonan Incident and East Asian Community Debate: North Korea's Place in the Region". *East Asia*. 28.4. 2011. P 275-290.

Ku, Julian. "So how is China Reacting to the Philippines Arbitration Submission? Not Very Well". *Opino Juris*. 2014. http://opiniojuris.org

Kurlantzick, Joshua. "China's Charm: Implications of Chinese Soft Power". *Carnegie Endowment for International Peace*. June 2006.

Kurlantzick, Joshua. "China's Soft Power in Africa". *Soft Power: China's Emerging Strategy in International Politics*. 2011

Kurlantzick, Joshua. *Charm Offensive: How China's Soft Power is Transforming the World*. New Haven: Yale University Press. 2007.

Lai, Hongying. "Introduction". *China's Soft Power and International Relations*. Routledge, 2012.

Lee, Jung-Nam. "The Rise of China and Soft Power: China's Soft Power Influence in Korea." *China Review*. 8.1. 2008. Pp 127-154.

Linley, Et al. "Whose afraid of the Dragon? Asian Mass Publics' Perceptions of China's Influence". *Japanese Journal of Political Science*. 13.4. 2012. p 501-523

Liu, Youling. "External Communication as a Vehicle for Disseminating Soft Power: A Study of China's Efforts to Strengthen its Cultural Soft Power in the Era of Globalization". *UMI Dissertation Publishing*. March 2012.

Maqsudul, Hasan Nuri and Billah, Mustansar. *Rising soft power of South Korea. Pakistan Observer*. Islamabad. Jan 12, 2012

Meunier, Sophie. "The Dog that did not Bark: Anti-Americanism and the 2008 Financial Crisis in

Europe". *Review of International Political Economy*. 20.1. March 2012. P 1-25.

Morada, Noel. "The Rise of China and Regional Responses: A Philippine Perspective". *The rise of China: Responses from Southeast Asia and Japan*. National Institute for Defense Studies. 2009. (pp. 111-136)

Nye, Joseph. "The Rise of China's Soft Power". *Wall Street Journal Asia*. December 29, 2005.

—— "China's SP deficit". *Wall Street Journal*. May 8, 2012.

—— "Public Diplomacy and Soft Power". *Annals of the American Academy of Political and Social Science*. 616. March 2008. P 94-109.

—— "The Decline of America's Soft Power". *Foreign Affairs* 83.3. May, 2004. p 16-20.

—— *Soft Power: The Means to Success in World Politics*. New York: Public Affairs. 2004.

Ortuoste, Maria. "The Philippines in the South China Sea: Out of Time, Out of Options?" *Southeast Asian Affairs*. 2013. p 240-253

Phillips Davison. "News Media and International Negotiation". *The Public Opinion Quarterly*. 38.2. 1974. 174-191.

San Pablo-Baviera, Aileen. "Perceptions of a China Threat: A Philippines Perspective". *The China Threat: Perceptions, Myths and Reality*. New York: Routledge. 2002. p.252

Serafettin Yilmaz. "China's ADIZ in the East China Sea". E-International Relations. January 8, 2014. http://www.e-ir.info

Soesastro, Hadi, ed., "ASEAN in a Changed Regional and International Political Economy". *Centre for Strategic and International Studies*. 1995. iii-ix

Szczudlik-Tatar, Justyna. Soft Power in China's Foreign Policy". *The Polish Quarterly of International Affairs*. 19.3 2010. P 45-68

Van Ham, Peter. "Place Branding: The State of the Art". *Annals of the American Academy of Political and Social Science. 616. March 2008. P 126-149*

Zhang, Li. "The Rise of China: Media Perception and Implications for International Politics". *Journal of Contemporary China*. Match 2010. p 233-254.

Zhang, Wanfa. "Has China started to bear its teeth? China's Tapping of Soft Power Revisited". *Asian Perspective*. 36.4. October/December 2012. P 615-639

Zhao, Hong. "Sino-Filipino Relations: Moving Beyond the South China Sea Dispute?" *The Journal of East Asian Affairs*. 26.2. Fall 2012

Zheng, Yongnian and Zhang, Chi. "Soft power and Chinese Soft Power". *China's Soft Power and International Relations*. Routledge. 2012.

Zhu, Zhiqun. "China's Warming Relations with South Korea and Australia". *Soft Power: China's Emerging Strategy in International Relations*. 2009. P 185-206.

# 2

# Accommodating the *Nikkei*:
## On the Provision of Services for Brazilian Immigrants by Japanese Local Governments

### Shoko Oda

*This research investigates the characteristics and effectiveness of accommodation services provided by local governments to immigrants in Japan. Certain cities appear to have well-structured services that assist immigrants- specifically Japanese Brazilian immigrants in this study- to become accustomed to their communities. This investigation explores three factors that influence the level of service provision: population of immigrants, nongovernmental organization activities, and historical events related to immigrants. According to this study, these variables are correlated, as one variable alone does not sufficiently explain the level of service provision. Higher population of immigrants does influence the local governments to create accommodation services, but is not sufficient enough of a reason. The occurrence (or lack thereof) of historical crises related to immigrants in the community, in addition to nongovernmental organizations and their relationship to the local government, provide a more comprehensive view of why certain local governments in Japan have succeeded in providing higher level of service than other local governments.*

## Part 1: Introductions, Literature Review, and Methodology

Population decline is not a particularly new phenomenon for Japan; in fact, steady population decline is quite visible in the society. While it was the norm for Japanese families to have several children during the post-WWII baby-boom era, single-child families have become ubiquitous in the Japanese society today. Critics around the world have recently discussed why young adults in Japan are getting married less and having few children of their own. The population decline in Japan is no longer an issue solely debated among the domestic sphere—it is a popular subject of discussion among international critics, scholars, and journalists interested in Japan's population dilemma.

These scholars, journalists, and critics today debate frequently about what policies the Japanese government should adopt in order to halt population decline and uphold their agining labor force. While some debate about the need to provide more support for women to be able to work and have a family at home, others have turned to perhaps the more controversial alternative to alleviating population decline: immigration.

As a highly homogenous nation, Japan has historically eschewed allowing immigrants to enter its borders. But due to decline in population and labor force with no signs of improvement, the Japanese government must now make decisions on whether or not to prescribe immigration as a way to alleviate its demographic woes. Moreover, it is not only the government that must reevaluate its attitudes toward immigration— common Japanese people must also reconsider their negative attitudes towards immigrants. Xenophobia continues to exist in parts of the Japanese society, impeding a working immigration policy from taking root. Yet the society can no longer continue to ignore the population issue. With labor-intensive construction plans looming over Japan for Tokyo Olympics in 2020, immigration is no longer a subject that can be avoided.

This study hopes to shed light into Japan's current stance on immigration, both at the national and local government level. Though the state itself has avoided creating a working immigration policy, immigration services are more actively provided at the local level. The investigation of immigration at a local, grassroot level provides the state government with some lessons that can be taken away, as the country continues to be plagued by population woes.

Research Design

As a result of industrial boom that occurred between the 1980s and 90s coupled with labor shortage, the Japanese national government reformed its immigration law in 1990 to allow immigration of foreigners with Japanese ancestry, known as Nikkeis. This increased the population of South American Nikkeis- namely from Brazil- who found employment in the industrial manufacturing sector. However, the Japanese national government failed to provide adequate services for these immigrants and to this day has not established an official immigration policy. Instead, local governments have stepped forward to provide services for these immigrants, with variation in levels of service provision across the cities. Regional variation has implications ranging from how immigrants are treated to the attitude and perceptions- often negative - that the local Japanese residents have towards immigrants. This brings to question what forces these local governments to provide higher levels of services. In this study, I investigate the role of local Japanese governments in immigrant service provision, as well as the factors that influence them to provide these services. Why are some local governments better at providing services, and what is the most influential factor in determining the level of service provision?

Literatures about immigrants in Japan discuss the issue at a national level, often exploring the reasons behind the lack of an official, national immigration policy (Tsuda, 2006; Papademetriou and Hamilton, 2000). However, Tsuda (2006) claims that local governments are actively responding to the immigrants' needs today. Tsuda addresses several reasons why the local governments have become proactive in providing services, such as the need to prevent tensions from rising between the locals and immigrants, as well as the lobbying effects of NGOs and activists. If the national government has failed to establish an official immigration policy, what factors are pressuring local governments to assume the role of providing services for the immigrants, a responsibility traditionally reserved for the state? The following literatures do not answer the inquiry directly, but nonetheless provide causal mechanisms for working hypotheses.

Pluralist literatures examine the role of group interest on policymaking. Nincic (1999) introduces the assumptive and enumerative approaches to explain how national interests are formed. The assumptive approach, as Krasner (1978) argues, considers interests to be inherent within the state (Krasner, 1978; Nincic, 1999). On the contrary, Latham (1952) sides with the enumerative approach, which builds off of the pluralist argument that state interests are aggregated by various interest groups. Baskin (1970) adds to the pluralist argument, arguing that the lobbying success of these groups depends on their size, intensity of activity, and mobilization methods. Baskin (1970) also argues that individuals who hold cross-membership among various groups weaken the power of groups on policymaking. The pluralist functional argument would expect a gradual increase in the number of immigrants in Japan to also increase the presence of immigrant groups and organizations bound by common interest; if these groups have an adequate level of activity, resources, and techniques to mobilize pressure and face little to no competition from other groups, they would be capable of influencing the local governments to provide more services for the immigrants.

Literatures explaining the impact of NGOs on policymaking provide analysis of the conditions in which NGOs are most likely to form and how they push for interests. Keck and Sikkink's (2002) explanation of advocacy networks argues that groups aim to influence decision makers by utilizing information, calling upon powerful symbols to advocate for a cause, manipulating other actors to join in their cause, and holding those with authority accountable for their actions. While their arguments lean toward explaining how advocacy networks operate transnationally, Keck and Sikkink (2002) explain specific methods that the domestic NGOs use to push for their interest. Channels between groups and the Japanese national government are more or less hampered by the lack of a formal immigration policy; this indicates the need for local NGOs to come together so that best practices are shared and interests are more strongly propagated to the target audience (Keck and Sikkink, 2002; Skjelsbaek, 1971).

Birkland (1998) examines the role of "focusing events" on policymaking; sudden-occurring events- when made visible and deemed threatening by actors such as the media and interest groups- act as powerful symbols, impacting agenda-setting and policymaking. To play an effective role, these focusing events must be supported by well-structured policy domains and interest groups that utilize the event as a symbol to advocate for their cause (Birkland 1998; Baumgartner and Jones, 1993). This mechanism expects interest groups to deploy sudden incidents- such as clashes between local Japanese residents and immigrants- as a sign to urge local governments to consider the needs of the immigrants. Though group actors play a role in this particular mechanism as in the pluralist argument, the two must be examined separately; the pluralist argument traces the long-term effect of immigrant population shift on policymaking, while focusing events examine the immediate changes in attitudes towards an issue after crises that impact both the Japanese and immigrant communities.

From these literatures, I formulate hypotheses to investigate these factors that affect local governments' level of service provision: demand from the immigrant population, the role and influence of NGOs, and occurrence of focusing events. In addition to examining these variables in isolation, I analyze the potential interdependence among these factors, as the aforementioned literatures hint that these variables are related. I then select several Japanese cities at random for sample selection, and categorize them in accordance to variation in total immigration population (categorized as low or high) and total population of Brazilian nikkeis (also categorized as low or high). Among these randomly selected cities, I analyze three cases with variation in levels of service provision for further explanation.

This study collects data for the dependent variable based on family resemblance structure definition of the concept of immigrant inclusiveness—to what extent the governments include the needs of immigrants into the services that they provide. This study measures the independent variables based on the following indicators; based on the percentage of foreign immigrants, I give immigrant population demand for each city an ordinal rank of low, medium, or high. I give an ordinal value of low or high for levels of NGO influence, depending on the total number of NGOs within the city, number of groups working to improve the needs of the immigrants, and whether or not these groups appear to be active in providing services. I also investigate for focusing events, by examining whether or not each city has experienced an incident capable of influencing the local government in the past. This study also examines the details of local government services to ordinally rank the city's level of service provision as low or high.

I then investigate three cities to analyze the role of independent variables as well as their interdependency. This study qualitatively analyzes provision of services using pattern matching, within-case analysis, and process tracing. Pattern matching assesses whether causal mechanisms for each of the factors correlate with the expected outcomes of the hypotheses. I create a timeline of changes in each city's immigrant population, service provision, NGO activities, and focusing events for cross-sectional and longitudinal analysis. I also conduct interviews with local government officials and activists to process trace the services to reveal the causal mechanisms behind service provision. By examining how service provision developed overtime from the 1990s to today, I evaluate the potential correlation across cities and connections to the independent variables. I utilize resources from city government websites, documents, statistical data, as well as interviews with local government officials and NGO leaders to provide a better understanding of mechanisms behind immigrant service provision.

While it is difficult to pinpoint the direct cause of variance in levels of service provision, analysis of the independent variables offers some explanation behind why certain cities have a higher provision of services than others. This study found that increase in immigrant population and a strong NGO groups do influence the levels of service provision. However, these variables are interdependent, and rarely make an impact on the dependent variable alone. An increase in immigrant population leads to increased opportunities for focusing events from taking place. These also influence the development of NGO sectors that deal with the relevant issue. However, the influence of NGOs depends heavily on the strength of its relationship with the local government. Moreover, focusing events do not necessary lead to higher levels of service provision, but act more as a catalyst that encourages the city government to reassess its current services and policies. Ultimately, these factors collaboratively influence the local governments to join a nation-wide coalition dedicated to working with immigrant issues; however, whether or not membership in such coalition improves the service provision is debatable.

Literature Review

What factors influence Japanese local government's level of immigrant service provision? Though there are literatures written about Japan's current dilemmas with its lack of national immigration policy, there are few written specifically about how Japanese local cities are responding to the issue, as the role of local governments have been largely left out of the discussion (Tsuda, 2006; Kondo, 2002; Papademetriou and Hamilton, 2000). However, literatures written about local Japanese governments and their response to immigration provide some clues to what may influence the variation in levels of service provision among the cities.

Tsuda (2006) mentions several reasons why local governments are actively engaging with the immigrant community to provide them with services. He argues that local governments are, out of sheer necessity, forced to actively promote immigration services in order to prevent social repercussions from occurring; local governments are mainly concerned about the growing rift between local Japanese and immigrant residents, which may evolve into a serious conflict. In addition, Tsuda offers alternative reasons such as pressures from nongovernmental organizations and interest groups that lobby local governments for rights and services (Tsuda, 2006; Komai, 2001).

If the national government failed to create a nation-wide immigration policy, what is influencing these local governments to fill the void of the state? While the causal mechanisms behind levels of service provision by local governments are rather complex with no definitive answer, the following literatures help to form relevant hypotheses based on theories about pluralism, nongovernmental organizations, and focusing events.

*National Interest, Pluralism, and Policymaking*

Scholars have long debated about the definition of national interest and how it translates into national policies. Nincic (1999) provides a general overview of two contrasting approaches to national interest, which he labels as the assumptive and enumerative approach (Nincic, 1999, 31). The assumptive approach, influenced by realist and neo-realist theories, stresses the anarchic nature of the international society and views national interest as strictly inherent within the state. Because state interest lies in security, national interest naturally focuses on national security (Nincic, 1999, 35). The assumptive approach does not consider group interests to be part of national interest. Stephen Krasner's (1978) discussion of national interest also falls under the assumptive approach, negating the role of group and individual interests in the formulation of national interest. As Krasner notes, "it is a fundamental error to equate the goal of the state with the summation of the desires of specific individuals or groups." (Krasner, 1978; Nincic, 1999). According to Krasner, specific policies tied to national interest must only include national objectives that are pursued on a long-term basis.

The enumerative approach differs from the assumptive approach as it argues national interest to be an aggregated product of group and individual interests. The enumerative approach designates objectives that define national interest, allowing enumeration of "society's basic normative order and the health of the economy" to also be included in national interest among other goals specific to the society (Nincic, 1999, 43). The enumerative approach lacks the comprehensive definition of national interest for states (Nincic, 1999, 44). This approach, unlike the assumptive approach, allows room for group and individual interests to be taken into account. As these different approaches explicate, national interest is an empirical question examined in this study by analyzing the interest of local city governments in regards to immigration services.

Latham (1952) offers two contrasting approaches to defining group interest and political processes: the utilitarian and pluralist views. According to Latham, the utilitarian approach simplifies the actors involved in political issues down to individuals and the state, disregarding the role of all other actors and groups (Latham, 1952, 378). On the contrary, the pluralist approach stresses the existence of group units bound by loyalty and shared interest (Latham, 1952, 379). Groups, according to pluralists, are the most powerful organized actors in a political community and exist for individuals to belong to fulfill their own personal needs (Latham, 1952, 383).

Based on the American political and socioeconomic life, Baskin (1970) adds to the pluralist theory by including the following five propositions. First, the rapid pace of change in today's modern world has forced the government to "penetrate" into the society while encouraging individuals to cooperate on shared interests. Such developments have increased the "tendency of organized interest to turn to government for aid and cooperation… to secure their own private purpose in society" (Baskin, 1970, 73). Second, public policy is the result of opposing group forces colliding to seek "access to public authority" for the purposes of achieving their own security and interests (Baskin, 1970, 74). Third, the success of these groups' influence over the government depends on their size, intensity of activity, and lobbying techniques. Fourth, overlapping membership across different organizations weakens the groups' influence as their interests may clash with those of other groups that the members have cross-membership in. Lastly, pluralists reject the idea that "public interest" is static (Baskin, 1970, 73-77). Baskin's (1970) propositions describe the conditions that enable interest groups to successfully influence the decision-making processes in a pluralist society.

Koff's (2006) analysis of immigration in Italy serves as a specific demonstration of how pluralist arguments can explain creation of immigrant services and policies. Koff (2006) analyzes the influence of industrial sector make-up on formation of immigrant services and policies in Italy, and argues that the efforts to integrate immigrants into the local community do not necessarily reflect the region's public opinion. Rather, immigrant integration efforts are influenced by structural factors, such as political institutions and the sectoral make-up of the region's economy (Koff, 2006, 173). Koff (2006) argues that while the Italian public's sign of hospitality and acceptance of immigrants may allow local governments to create and promote immigration services and policies, the two are not necessarily correlated (Koff, 2006, 195). Instead, much of the immigration policy in Italy follows "utilitarian logic". Though anti-immigrant political parties have the strongest approval rating in Northeastern Italy, local governments there actively promote immigration integration policies and services because heavy industry sector accounts for majority of the Northeast's economic growth. This makes it necessary for the local governments to promote immigration where cheap, foreign labor is needed in the industrial sector (Koff, 2006). Koff's (2006) analysis of Italy's immigration policy and its regional variation demonstrates the possibility that the industrial sector make-up of the locality influences levels of service provision. A region with a large economic sector that utilizes foreign labor (such as the heavy industries in Italy's case) would urge the local governments to provide more immigrant services as foreign labor force increases within the sector. This suggests that local Japanese governments are motivated to provide more services if there is a high population demand from the Brazilian immigrants who are employed in a sector viable to the community's economy. Because the majority of Brazilian immigrants are employed in the manufacturing sector after the immigration law revision of 1990, Japanese localities with a large industrial sector is expected to have higher levels of service provision.

Nincic's (1999) explanation of the assumptive and enumerative approaches in addition to Latham (1952)'s analysis of utilitarian and pluralist views provide a structure for this research to test whether or not pluralism explains the decisions of local Japanese government to create necessary immigrant services. If local Japanese governments support the enumerative approach, then the governments would take into consideration a wider range of interest and allow various groups to participate in decision-making. Baskin (1970)'s pluralist propositions explain conditions that help interest groups successfully lobby for their interests, such as the number or size of the group. According to his proposition, as the organizations bound together by loyalty and interest increase in number, their presence and opportunities to lobby the local government would also increase. Moreover, Koff's (2006) analysis illustrates how pluralist theory and sectoral arguments explain the formation of immigrant integration policies and services. Nincic (1999), Krasner (1978), Latham (1952), Baskin (1970), and Koff (2006) all explicate theories behind national interest, group interest, and policymaking on a larger scale to provide structure for studying the effect of population demand from the Brazilian immigrants on government service provision.

*Role of Nongovernmental Organizations (NGOs) On Policymaking*

Similarly to the pluralist argument, Shipper (2008) and Walzer's (1992) analysis of nongovernmental organizations argues that the Japanese government utilizes the enumerative approach in decision-making. Shipper (2008) and Walzer (1992) argue that the interaction between the variety of activists and NGOs lead to policy changes and improve the quality of democracy in the state. Shipper (2008) analyzes the interaction between NGOs and Japanese local governments through what he calls associative activism, defined as local actors seeking to initiate change via local activities, which indirectly challenge the broader, national-level policies (Shipper, 2008, 11). Shipper explains associative activism as cooperation among activists, NGOs and local governments to create new institutions and structures that address certain issues (Shipper, 2008, 11). Associative activism brings together a variety of individuals, such as legal foreigners, government officials, and immigrant right activists, allowing for innovative policy recommendations to be presented to the national government (Shipper, 2008, 155). This, in turn, leads to a potentially new and improved form of democratic governance in Japan (Shipper, 2008. 155). Shipper's study on the role of NGOs and local Japanese governments connects back to the pluralist arguments. Associative activism by actors from the nongovernmental sector suggests that the local Japanese governments may define national interest via pluralist, enumerative approach. It also demonstrates how cooperation between nongovernmental organizations and activists brings forth change for the immigrant community while influencing national-level policies and services.

Pluralism, according to Skjelsbaek (1971) is a condition that allows for the development and participation of NGOs in the society. Skjelsbaek (1971) argues that nations with a high degree of technological and economic development are more likely to allow the development of a wide range of interest groups (Skjelsbaek, 1971, 433). Moreover, pluralistic societies are more likely to have a variety of interest groups that lobby the government at various levels (Skjelsbaek, 1971, 434). Lastly, Skjelsbaek argues that nongovernmental organizations in pluralistic societies with high levels of technological and economic development are likely to increase in size. In fact, he cites Japan as an example of a society with conditions that enabled the growth of the NGO sector. In 1964, Japan already ranked 16th in terms of representation by NGOs with 611 organizations. Skjelsbaek's (1971) explanation provides a mechanism for explaining the continued growth of a vibrant nongovernmental organization community in Japan, which is a possible cause of variance in level of service provision at the local level. Most importantly, Skjelsbaek's (1971) arguments reveal the relationship between pluralism, interest groups, and policymaking, indicating how these various factors influence each other's roles within the society.

However, contrary to Skjelsbaek's (1971) explanation, some scholars argue that the Japanese civil society still lacks the vibrancy found in countries like the US. Due to its history with the developmental state model, the Japanese government continues to exert some influence over the civil society sector (Pekkanen, 2004, 369). Haddad (2007), Pekkanen (2004), and Shipper (2006) argue that while the Japanese civil society is strong in terms of "traditional organizations", it lacks the number and strength of issue-oriented "advocacy organizations". Traditional civic organizations in Japan are defined as groups rooted strongly in the local community, such as neighborhood associations. These groups aim to uphold the welfare of the community, often cooperating with the local government (Haddad, 2007, 418). On the other hand, advocacy-style organizations are characterized by their independence from bureaucratic influence, as well as their focus on solving and lobbying for specific issues (Haddad, 2007, 417). Thus, Japanese civil society today has what Pekkanen (2004) calls a "dual civil society" structure (Pekkanen, 2004, 366). Traditional organizations rooted in local communities continue to be strengthened and influenced by the government (Haddad, 2007; Pekkanen, 2004; Shipper, 2006). While these groups receive preferential treatment, the government regulates issue-oriented organizations due to concerns that they may eventually undermine governmental authority (Pekkanen, 2004; Shipper, 2006). The dual civil society structure provides an explanation of why there may be a lack of influence by the NGOs in regards to immigrant issues. If Japanese civil society operates under the dual model, then we would expect to see a lack of lobbying efforts by the very few advocacy-based groups. Moreover, traditional organizations may be the actors that pay attention to immigration-related issues in their community and, along with the government, contribute to provision of services. On the other hand, if the local government has little to no interest in providing for the immigrants in their community, these traditional organizations contribute very little to the cause.

While Keck and Sikkink's (1999) analysis of advocacy networks focuses largely on international organizations that work cross-borders, they also cite examples of domestic organizations and how they lobby for interests. According to Keck and Sikkink, advocacy networks utilize information, call upon powerful symbols and other actors, and hold particular actors accountable to push for their interests (Keck and Sikkink, 1999, 91-95). If channels between groups concerned about a specific domestic issue (such as immigration in this study) and the national government are hampered (as in

Japan where the state has failed to create an immigration policy), then there is a reason to believe that these groups will turn to the local-level government for solutions. This leads to potential mechanisms behind how nongovernmental organizations affect the local governments' policymaking to create immigration services. If nongovernmental organizations influence levels of service provision by the local governments, there would be a vibrant NGO community within localities interacting with one another, sharing information and best practices, deploying powerful symbols (such as focusing events) to their advantage, and lobbying the local governments to consider the issues surrounding the immigrants.

Scholars, however, disagree over whether or not these NGOs improve the quality of democracy in a nation (Shipper, 2008; Walzer, 1992). Shipper analyzes the recent roles of NGOs in Japan and their relationship with the local governments in advocating for immigrant human rights. Through investigation of immigrants in the US, Shipper (2008) and Walzer (1992) both claim that foreigners do participate in a variety of nongovernmental organizations in forms like cultural and religious associations, as well as homeland language schools. While these organizations serve as a platform for new American immigrants to "reinvigorate" civil society and democracy, scholars like Hammar (1990) found that immigrants are less likely than native locals to participate in civil and political societies of their host country. These contrasting viewpoints indicate the characteristics of successful NGOs that make an impact on the local government. If immigrants are less likely to be active in the local Japanese civil society and politics, then we would expect to see more activity among NGOs operated by Japanese locals motivated by either altruism or self-interest. Most importantly, these local Japanese residents and immigrants may differ on the services and accommodations that they wish to advocate for, creating a possible impeding effect on service provision. These are the factors that are considered when analyzing nongovernmental organizations later on in this study.

Following the question of whether or not the local residents and immigrants advocate for similar services, Lim's (2006) analysis of how immigrants gained more rights in South Korea provides an example of how cooperation between local and immigrant residents leads to a national policy change. According to Lim (2006), transnational migrant workers successfully rallied for more rights via network of NGOs in Korea (Lim, 2006, 237). In this particular case, nongovernmental organizations played a key role in expanding the rights of immigrants. These NGOs not only included the participation of locals interested in the issue, but also the immigrants themselves. While it may not be applicable to other states, this particular case demonstrates an example of policy changes taking place as a result of overlapping interests between the locals and immigrants. While Hammar (1990) notes that immigrants are less likely to participate in civil and political society of their host countries, Lim's (2006) case argues otherwise, as local and immigrants with similar interests managed to influence policymakers together. This case suggests the importance of considering both interests of locals and immigrants, as well as the extent to which activism by immigrants themselves impact the local governments. Local Japanese citizens concerned about issues surrounding the immigrant community may participate in political activism aimed at improving the livelihood of the immigrants; yet activism from the affected immigrant community itself may be necessary for policy change to occur at the local and national level.

While the aforementioned scholars demonstrate ways in which NGOs support immigrant service provision and policy changes, Agrela and Dietz (2006) offer a case in which NGOs actually hinder the process of service provision by the local governments. Regional governments in Spain have undergone "nongovernmentalization" of policies, as immigrant integration policies have become largely a NGO-led responsibility. On the contrary, the Spanish government's efforts to control immigrants from entering Spain (much like Japan) and NGO-led efforts to integrate more immigrants into their communities contradict one another, thus weakening the advocacy effect of the NGOs (Agrela and Dietz, 2006, 222). Agrela and Dietz (2006) demonstrate the consequences of having powerful nongovernmental organizations that contradict the national immigration policy (Agrela and Dietz, 2006, 206). At times, influential NGOs that have been delegated tasks by the local governments conflict with the official policies of the state, which weakens the overall success of the immigration services and integration policies. If policies differ at different levels of the government, and if such policies are met with independent and influential nongovernmental organizations, there may be contradictions between what the state promotes and what the NGO advocate for. The case here represents the implications of delegating certain governmental tasks to nongovernmental organizations, which must be analyzed in this research—some local governments in Japan delegate their responsibilities to the NGOs and work collaboratively with them, while some may not rely on NGOs at all and even conflict with the interests of the organizations.

*Historical Focusing Events and Policymaking*

Key historical events and incidents may significantly influence decision-making and agenda setting. Birkland (1998) argues that there is an important relationship between focusing events and how certain policies are formed. Birkland defines a focusing event as:

> "…An event that is sudden; relatively uncommon; can be reasonably defined as harmful or revealing the possibility of potentially greater future harms; has harms that are concentrated in a particular geographical area or community of interest; and that is known to policy makers and the public simultaneously"(Birkland, 1998, 54).

According to Birkland (1998), these events, including both natural disasters and large-scale anthropological accidents like nuclear disasters, influence agenda setting and decision-making within the government.

According to Baumgartner and Jones (1993), greater attention to an issue usually leads to more negative assessments of the current policies in place. Upon the occurrence of focusing events, pressures against the current policies it will increase, leading to changes in topic of discussion and attitudes toward certain policies (Birkland, 1998; Baumgartner and Jones, 1993). However, the degree to which these policies are influenced depends on multiple factors. The pressures against current policies depend on the "visibility" and "tangibility" of harms done by the focusing event, which can vary depending on factors such as media coverage (Birkland, 1998, 72). The organizational structure and the cohesiveness of groups interested in the issue also play a role in pressuring current policies (Birkland, 1998, 57). Moreover, focusing events that are related to issues with "reasonably well organized policy domains" prove to be more effective at influencing the agenda (Birkland, 1998, 72). Nonetheless, group efforts in policy domains are critical, for these organizations and coalitions increase the "likelihood of more influential and powerful actors entering the conflict on the side of policy change" (Schattschenier, 1960/1975; Birkland, 1998, 55).

Birkland's explanations of focusing events explain reasons behind policy changes that occur immediately after sudden incidents, such as demonstrations, protests, and major court cases. If such crises are considered threatening by NGOs and other advocacy groups, they would encourage the Japanese local governments to reexamine the issue, potentially leading to a reassessment of policies and services related to the immigrant community. Under Birkland's explanations, there should be a reevaluation of immigrant service provision following the occurrence of focusing events. The issue lies in determining the characteristics of focusing events that urge local governments to provide higher levels of service—for example, the incident must induce a sense of threat, be visible to the public via actors such as the media, and be propagated by well-structured interest groups. These are just some of the factors that must be kept in mind when determining if an incident can be considered as a focusing event.

Despite such questions, Birkland's study not only provides an understanding of how critical events and incidents can impact policy-making, but also coincides with the role of nongovernmental organizations. Birkland's arguments indicate that while historical events alone may not influence policymakers to enact change within their system, external actors such as NGOs have the capacity to lobby for change. However, Birkland notes that these groups must be "reasonably well organized" to be effective at agenda setting and decision-making. While the pluralist argument also examines the role of these groups, analysis between pluralism and focusing events must be separate; pluralist arguments examine the long-term effects of population change on policy, while focusing events analyze the immediate changes in policy after a particular event. Birkland's arguments question to what extent do focusing events alone influence policymakers, and how "reasonably well organized" interest groups can turn certain incidents into attention-grabbing focusing events.

The following literatures in varying fields of study may not completely answer the complexity of Japanese local governments' efforts in creating immigrant services. However, they nonetheless assist to formulate the hypotheses for this research study.

Methodology:

The literatures provide relevant hypotheses to explain the variance in levels of service provision. This study analyzes the impact of the following independent variables on the dependent variable of level of service provision: demand from immigrant population, influence of NGO groups, and occurrence of focusing events. High demand from the immigrant population will influence the local governments to provide higher levels of services. Cities with active NGOs dedicated to dealing with issues surrounding the immigrant population will have higher provision of services, as these groups will lobby the city governments to do so. Lastly, occurrences of focusing events will influence the local governments to increase its level of service provision. I also evaluate the interdependence among these hypotheses as well as a null hypothesis that there is very little variance among the level of service provision. Lastly, I also analyze the role of an intervening variable—membership in a nation-wide committee of Japanese cities with high population of immigrants.

I randomly select 39 Japanese cities based on variations in total immigration population (categorized as low or high) and total population of Brazilian Nikkeis (also categorized as low or high). Of the 39 cities selected, 27 are members of the nation-wide committee of high immigrant population cities in order to evaluate the potential influence that the committee has over service provision; the rest are selected at random. Total immigration population for a city is deemed as "high" if it is ranked among the top 100 Japanese cities with most immigrant population. If the city is not ranked within the top 100, it is deemed as "low". Total population of Brazilian Japanese immigrants is determined as "high" for a city if Brazilian Japanese are the majority of the demographic make-up of immigrant population—if not, it is deemed as "low".

I collect and analyze the data values of independent and dependent variables for each of these cities. Indicators for the three hypotheses determine the level of population demand, role of NGOs on service provision, and occurrence of focusing events. Indicators that determine the level of population demand are the percentage of total immigrants and percentage of Brazilian immigrants within each city's immigrant population. Total immigrant population is deemed high when the total immigration population is higher than 3% of the total population, medium if between 2 and 3%, and low if below 2%. This scaling standard reflects the results of mid-level data analysis, which indicate that the majority of cities known for their high population of immigrants have roughly 3% of its population composed by foreign immigrants. Role of NGOs on service provision is categorized as low or high, depending on indicators like total number of NGOs registered by the city, the number of organizations specifically related to immigrant services, and the information that they present on their websites. Because of the difficulty in discerning medium from high levels of provision of service, NGO influence is categorized as either high or low. Lastly, I examine each city for crisis events- such as mass riots, protests, and incidents deemed violent by the local government and mass media- to check for presence of focusing events. At the mid-level data analysis of 39 cities, these three independent variables are pattern matched to see if they correlate with varied levels of service provision. I examine to see if interdependency among these variables can explain the variations in dependent variables. High population demand would increase the risk of crisis events from taking place, while it would increase the interest of the public to create NGO groups dealing with immigrant issues as well. Occurrence of focusing events may contribute to increase in NGO activity interested in solving issues surrounding the immigrant community. Thus, interdependence among these variables may explain the variance in levels of service provision. On the other hand, level of dependent variable is determined via the family resemblance structure definition of the concept of immigrant inclusiveness—to what extent the governments include the needs of immigrants in their community into the services that they provide.

Figure 1: 39 Cities categorized based on total immigrant population and total Brazilian population levels

| | | Level of Total Brazilian Immigrant Population (City, (Prefecture)) | |
|---|---|---|---|
| | | **High** | **Low** |
| Level of Total Immigrant Population (City (Prefecture)) | **Low** | Oogaki (Gifu), Soja (Okayama) Minokamo (Gifu), Takaoka (Toyama) Fuji (Shizuoka), Echizen (Fukui) Kakegawa (Shizuoka) Izumo (Shimane) Fukuroi (Shizuoka), Inabe (Mie) Kosai (Shizuoka), Kikugawa (Shizuoka), Iga (Mie) Nagahama (Shiga), Koka (Shiga) Aisho (Shiga) | Ueta (Nagano), Iida (Nagano) Sapporo (Hokkaido), Aomori (Aomori) Morioka (Iwate) |
| | **High** | Isesaki (Gunma), Okasaki (Aichi) Oota (Gunma), Oizumi (Gunma) Hamamatsu (Shizuoka) Iwata (Shizuoka), Toyohashi (Aichi), Kameyama (Mie), Toyota (Aichi), Komaki (Aichi) Tsu (Mie), Yokkaichi (Mie) Suzuka (Mie), Kani (Gifu) | Ichihara (Chiba), Joto Ward (Osaka) Ukyo (Kyoto), Aoba Ward, Sendai (Miyagi) |

Among the 39 cities, I analyze three cities with variation in level of service provision using within-case analysis and process tracing: Toyota, Hamamatsu, and Kameyama. I chose Toyota, a city with high level of service provision, for its past experience with a crisis suitable for the analysis of the role of focusing events. I then compare Toyota along with Hamamatsu, yet another city with high service provision. Hamamatsu, however, lacks the occurrence of a focusing event and demonstrates a strong and vibrant NGO community necessary for the analysis of the role of NGOs. Lastly, I study Kameyama as an outlier city, as it has low levels of service provision and NGO activity despite high immigrant population demand.

This qualitative study thus employs pattern matching, within-case analysis, and process tracing to determine the influence of the independent variables on level of service provision. Pattern matching at mid-level data enables the examination of each causal mechanism for correlation to the dependent variable as well as the timing expected by the hypothesis. Within-case analysis allows the three aforementioned cities to be process traced, which will reveal the causal mechanisms behind the provision of services. To organize information and data for process tracing, timeline of changes in total and Brazilian immigrant population, dates and order of services created by the government and NGOs, and historical focusing events is constructed for cross-sectional and longitudinal analysis. Using these timelines as a resource, I interview local government officials to investigate the historical background of immigrants in their area, as well as the reason and timing behind the creation of specific immigration services. I also interview local NGO activists to examine their role in service provision, as well as to examine the relationship between city governments and local NGOs in terms of immigration issues. Documents explaining the cities' historical background with immigrants, the services they provide, and statistical data about population change are gathered mainly from city and national governments and local NGO group websites. These documents help to create the timeline needed for process tracing. Interviews conducted with local city government officials and NGO leaders also help to organize the construction of timelines for the study. By examining the development of services overtime from the 1990s to today, potential correlation across cities and relationships between independent variables is evaluated as well.

# Part 1 Works Cited

Baskin, Darryl. "American Pluralism: Theory, Practice, and Ideology." *The Journal of Politics* 32.01 (1970): 71. Web.

Baumgartner, Frank, and Bryan D. Jones "Agenda and Instability in American Politics." Chicago: University of Chicago Press, 1993.

Birkland, Thomas A. "Focusing Events, Mobilization, and Agenda Setting. *Journal of Public Policy* 18.1 (1998): 53-74.

"Life as Dekkasseguis: The Brazilian Community in Japan." *FOCUS: Asia-Pacific* 58 (Dec. 2009): 5-8. Print.

Dietz, Gunther and Belen Agrela. "Nongovernmental versus Governmental Actors? Multilevel Governance and Immigrant Integration Policy in Spain." *Local Citizenship in Recent Countries of Immigration: Japan in Comparative Perspective*. Edited by Tateyuki Tsuda. Lanham, MD: Lexington, 2006.

Haddad, Mary Alice. "Transformation of Japan's Civil Society Landscape." *Journal of East Asian Studies* 7.3 (2007): 413-37.

Haig, Kenneth. "Demographic Change and Immigration Policy in Japan." Japan Moves Forward: Views from the U.S.-Japan Network for the Future. Mansfieldfdn.org. The Maureen and Mike Mansfield Foundation.

Hammar, Tomas. *Democracy and the Nation State: Aliens, Denizens, and Citizens in a World of International Migration*. Aldershot, Hants, England: Avebury, 1990. Print.

Jain, Purnendra. *Japan's Subnational Governments in International Affairs*. London: Routledge, 2005. Print.

"Japan's Experiment in Ethnic Immigration." Asiancenturyinstitute.com. Asian Century Institute, 13 Feb. 2013.

Keck, Margaret E., and Kathryn Sikkink. "Transnational Advocacy Networks in International and Regional Politics." *International Social Science Journal* 51.159 (1999): 89-101.

Krasner, Stephen D. *Defending the National Interest: Raw Materials Investments and U.S. Foreign Policy*. Princeton, NJ: Princeton UP, 1978.

Koff, Harlan. "Does Hospitality Translate into Integration? Subnational Variations of Italian Responses to Immigration." *Local Citizenship in Recent Countries of Immigration: Japan in Comparative Perspective*. Edited by Tateyuki Tsuda. Lanham, MD: Lexington, 2006.

Komai, Hiroshi. *Foreign Migrants in Contemporary Japan*. Melbourne: Trans Pacific, 2001. Print.

Kondo, Atsushi. "Development of Immigration Policy in Japan." *Asia and Pacific Migration Journal* 11.4 (2002): 415-36. Web.

Latham, Earl. "The Group Basis of Politics: Notes for a Theory." *The American Political Science Review* 46.2 (1952): 376-97.

Lim, Timothy C. "NGOs, Transnational Migrants, and the Promotion of Rights in South Korea." *Local Citizenship in Recent Countries of Immigration: Japan in Comparative Perspective*. Edited by Tateyuki Tsuda. Lanham, MD: Lexington, 2006. Print.

Nincic, Miroslav. "The National Interest and Its Interpretation." *The Review of Politics* 61.01 (1999): 29-55. Pg. 41.

Pak, Katherine T. "Cities and Local Citizenship in Japan: Overcoming Nationality?" *Local Citizenship in Recent Countries of Immigration: Japan in Comparative Perspective*. Edited by Tateyuki Tsuda. Lanham, MD: Lexington, 2006.

Papademetriou, Demetrios G., and Kimberly A. Hamilton. *Reinventing Japan: Immigration's Role in Shaping Japan's Future*. Washington, D.C.: Carnegie Endowment for International Peace: Distributed by Brookings Institution, 2000.

Pekkanen, Robert. "After the Developmental State: Civil Society in Japan." *Journal of East Asian Studies* 4.3 Special Issue (2004): 363-88.

Schattschneider, Elmer E. *The Semisovereign People*. Hinsdale, Ill.: Dryden, 1960/1975. Print.

Shipper, Apichai W. *Fighting for Foreigners: Immigration and Its Impact on Japanese Democracy*. Ithaca: Cornell UP, 2008.

Shipper, Apichai W. "Foreigners and Civil Society in Japan." *Pacific Affairs* 79.2 (2006): 269-89.

Skjelsbaek, Kjell. "The Growth of International Nongovernmental Organization in the Twentieth Century." *International Organization*. 25.3 (1971): 420-42.

Tsuda, Takeyuki. "Localities and the Struggle for Immigrant Rights." *Local Citizenship in Recent Countries of Immigration: Japan in Comparative Perspective*. Edited by Tateyuki Tsuda. Lanham, MD: Lexington, 2006.

Walzer, Michael. *What It Means to Be an American*. New York: Marsilio, 1992. Print.

## Part 2: Mid-Level Data: Analysis on Correlations Among Variables

Analysis of the effect of three independent variables on service provision demonstrates strong inter-dependency amongst the independent variables, as well as a potential role of an intervening variable.

Population Demand

Figure 1: Cities categorized based on ordinal levels of population demand versus levels of immigrant service provision

| | | Dependent Variable- Level of Service Provision (City, (Prefecture)) | |
|---|---|---|---|
| | | **High** | **Low** |
| **Independent Variables- Population Demand (City, (Prefecture))** | **High** | Minokamo (Gifu), Fukuroi (Shizuoka), Kosai (Shizuoka), Kikugawa (Shizuoka), Aishocho (Shiga), Echizen (Fukui), Isesaki (Gunma), Oota (Gunma), Iwata (Shizuoka), Toyohashi (Aichi), Toyota (Aichi), Komaki (Aichi), Suzuka (Mie), Kani (Gifu) | Kameyama (Mie), Iga (Mie) |
| | **Medium** | Oogaki (Gifu), Kakegawa (Shizuoka), Nagahama (Shiga), Hamamatsu (Shizuoka), Tsu (Mie), Yokkaichi (Mie), Okasaki (Aichi) | Koka (Shiga), Inabe (Mie), Ueta (Nagano), Ukyo (Kyoto), Joto (Osaka) |
| | **Low** | Soja (Okayama), Takaoka (Toyama), Oizumi (Gunma) | Fuji (Shizuoka), Iida (Nagano), Izumo (Shimane), Sapporo (Hokkaido), Aomori (Aomori), Morioka (Aomori), Ichihara (Chiba), Sendai (Miyagi) |

Figure 1 demonstrates the categorization of 39 random cities based on ordinal levels of population demand versus ordinal levels of service provision by the city governments. The data reveals a strong correlation between high population demand (more than 3% share of registered foreign residents in the city) and high provision of services. Many of these cities are found in places like Gifu,

Shizuoka, Gunma, and Aichi Prefectures.

Brazilian Japanese immigrants are not evenly distributed throughout Japan, as majority of them live in regions with a large industrial and manufacturing sector (Tsuda, 2003, 99). Majority of the recent Brazilian Japanese immigrants- called "newcomers" by the local Japanese governments- are employed in the manufacturing sector, living in cities where prominent, multinational manufacturers and factories are located. There is a high concentration of newcomer immigrants in Aichi Prefecture, Shizuoka Prefecture, and the Tomo region of Gunma Prefecture. Cities in Aichi Prefecture like Toyohashi, Toyota, Komaki, and Okasaki host a large concentration of newcomer immigrants as a result of major manufacturing companies headquartered in these regions. Aichi Prefecture is responsible for about 40% of the national output of transportation equipment and machinery shipment, making it a key industrial region of Japan (Regional Information: Aichi, Web). The prefecture is home to companies like the Toyota Motor Corporation, located in the city of Toyota, which hired Brazilian immigrants during the industrial boom of the 1980s. Similarly, cities in Shizuoka Prefecture like Fukuroi, Kosai, Kikugawa, and Hamamatsu are homes to corporations like Yamaha, Suzuki, and Honda (Regional Information: Shizuoka, Web). Cities of Oizumi and Oota in Gunma Prefecture are also known for their heavy industry sector that makes up 30% of the prefecture's total production. Corporations such as Fuji Heavy Industries and smaller-scale manufacturers are located in the cities of Oizumi and Oota (Regional Information: Gunma, Web).

As a result of industrial boom and immigration law revision of 1990, population of foreign residents- in particular the Brazilian Nikkei immigrants- increased during the 1980s and 90s in these regions. As a result, labor shortage became an issue. Because of domestic labor source shortage, Japanese corporations were forced to search for alternative sources of labor (Papademetriou and Hamilton, 2000, 11). However, the Immigration Control and Refugee Recognition Act (ICRRA) historically operated under the policy of prohibiting unskilled workers from immigrating, only allowing legal immigration of skilled workers for a temporary period (Tsuda, 2006, 13). Therefore, the Ministry of Justice, responsible for managing the ICRRA, fashioned "side-door" exceptions that enabled legal immigration of unskilled workers into Japan "under visa categories officially intended for other purposes" (Tsuda, 2006, 14). One of such policies was allowing legal immigration of those with Japanese ancestry, known as Nikkeis, to reside and work in Japan temporarily (Calazans, 2013).

Revision of the ICRRA created guidelines that allowed the Nikkeis to obtain visa more easily. Visa requirements for second-generation Nikkeis were simplified so that they could obtain a visa so long as they prove their Japanese ancestry (Tsuda, 2003, 93). Third generation Nikkeis were also included in a new visa category known as the teijyusha, or long-term resident category. This particular visa freed them from all restrictions in seeking employment and residing in Japan for up to 6 months, with indefinite opportunities to renew their visa so long as their personal records were clean (Tsuda, 2003, 93). Concurrently, an economic crisis hit Brazil, which naturally encouraged Brazilian Nikkeis to migrate to Japan for higher-paying jobs in their ancestral homelands (Tsuda, 2003, 91).

Increase in the newcomer immigrant population after 1990 is quite remarkable. Between 1998 and 2008, legal Brazilian Nikkeis that migrated to Japan increased roughly by 41%, while Peruvian

Nikkei immigrants (fifth in rank for countries of origin among Japan's foreign residents) increased by about 45%. In 2008, about 2,217,000 registered foreign residents, roughly about 1.7% of the total population, lived in Japan; of these, 372,305 Brazilian and Peruvians made up about 17% of the foreign population (Kitawaki, Web).

Figure 1 shows a strong correlation between high Brazilian immigrant population and high level of service provision. Data from Figure 1 reveals that the majority of foreign residents in cities categorized under high level of services are Brazilian, regardless of ordinal level in population demand. Though cities of Soja, Takaoka, and Oizumi are categorized under low population demand (less than 2% of city population are foreign residents), they nonetheless provide high level of services for their Brazilian majority. This indicates evidence of correlation between population demand from newcomer immigrants (as opposed to "oldcomer" immigrants like Chinese and Korean immigrants that have been living in Japan since WWII era) and level of services provided by the city government. The functional argument appears strong in explaining the relationship between population demand and the dependent variable.

Role of Nongovernmental/Nonprofit Organizations: Figure 3: Cities categorized based on ordinal level of role of NPOs (nonprofit organizations) in immigrant service provision versus ordinal levels of immigrant service provision

| | | Dependent Variable- Level of Service Provision (City, (Prefecture)) | |
| | | High | Low |
|---|---|---|---|
| **Independent Variable- Influence of NPOs (City, (Prefecture))** | **High** | Oogaki (Gifu), Minokamo (Gifu), Kakegawa (Shizuoka) Fukuroi (Shizuoka), Kosai (Shizuoka), Kikugawa (Shizuoka), Nagahama (Shiga), Takaoka (Toyama), Echizen (Fukui). Isesaki (Gunma), Oota (Gunma), Hamamatsu (Shizuoka), Iwata (Shizuoka), Toyohashi (Aichi), Toyota (Aichi), Komaki (Aichi), Suzuka (Mie), Kani (Gifu) Yokkaichi (Mie) | Sendai (Miyagi) |
| | **Low** | Aishocho (Shiga), Soja (Okayama), Oizumi (Gunma), Tsu (Mie), Okasaki (Aichi) | Fuji (Shizuoka), Kameyama (Mie), Iga (Mie) Koka (Shiga) Izumo (Shimane) Inabe (Mie) Ueta (Nagano) Iida (Nagano), Sapporo (Hokkaido), Aomori (Aomori), Morioka (Iwate), Ichihara (Chiba) |

Characteristics unique to the Japanese NGO sector must be discussed before analyzing the role of NGOs on levels of service provision. While the American society defines NGOs as nongovernmental organizations, Japanese society refers to them as NPOs, or non-profit organizations. In retrospect, NGOs and NPOs are different entities; nongovernmental organizations are unaffiliated with state agencies, while the term "nonprofit" only indicate the organizations' stance on profitability, not its affiliation with the government. However, the Japanese definition of NGOs and NPOs vary from the one used to define the American NGO sector. The Japanese approaches to NGOs define the term as addressing "global issues such as development concerns" (Takao, 2001, 296). On the other hand, Japanese definition of nongovernmental organizations vision it as "service organizations that deal directly with clients or beneficiaries", while NPOs are defined as "self-help-oriented membership organizations". As Takao notes, there seems to be some overlap in definitions of NGOs and NPOs in the Japanese civil society sector. For the purposes of this study, we will refer to the groups as NPOs.

As discussed earlier, literatures claim that Japanese civil society has a dual structure (Pekkanen, 2004, 366). Japanese civil society has a strong base of what Haddad (2007) calls the "traditional organizations", rooted primarily in the local communities. Traditional organizations, such as neighborhood associations, often focus on upholding the welfare of the community with assistance from the local governments (Haddad, 2007, 418). In the past, Japan's developmental state model regulated the creation and participation of issue-oriented advocacy groups due to concerns that lobbying efforts may eventually undermine governmental power (Haddad, 2007, 418). However, revision of the NPO Law in 1998 eased regulations and financial requirements for smaller civil society organizations to gain legal status (Pekkanen, 2004, 376). This revision not only increased the size of civil society sector in Japan, but also increased the participation of advocacy groups focused on specific issues, rather than groups upholding local welfare. This particularly unique feature of the Japanese dual civil society is important in understanding the extent to which NPOs function independently of bureaucratic influence; such understanding can also potentially explain the lack of participation by NPO organizations in alleviating issues surrounding the immigrant community.

Determining the ordinal level of NPO influence faced several challenges. First, accurately determining the total number of registered NPOs in each of the cities proved to be difficult. In order to gather such data, I utilized the Japanese Cabinet Office database to investigate information such as the total number of registered NPOs. However, the Cabinet Office data often did not match with the data provided by the local government sources, making it difficult to estimate the accurate number of NPOs. Thus, it was unreliable to use the number of organizations in each of the cities to determine the ordinal level of NPO influence. Furthermore, it is quite possible that cities with very few active NPOs may provide a higher levels of services compared to cities with multiple organizations that are not as active in provision of services. Rather than simply relying on quantitative data, it was necessary to qualitatively assess the influence of NPOs on service provision

Cities with medium to high immigrant population had varying levels of NPO influence in their locality. However, majority of these cities had at least one, specific organization working to accommodate the immigrants and foster multicultural coexistence in their localities. These organizations, called kokusai koryuu kai or literally translated as international associations, are at the helm of providing services and programs that bring locals and immigrants together. All 24 cities categorized under high level of service provision (regardless of ordinal level of NPO influence) had an international association specific to their cities. While some cities have smaller non-profit organizations that advocate for immigrant issues and interests, these international associations have a higher status as a koeki zaidan hojin, loosely translated as incorporated public interest corporations. These organizations function like charitable foundations. Earning such status in Japan requires a formal approval by the prefectural governor, and if operating across different prefectures, it requires one of the central government agencies' approvals (Yamamoto, 1998, 3-4). Establishing these foundations thus require more effort and acknowledgement by the government, which legitimizes its role among the local city governments and the public. Hence, majority of these international associations work closely with local governments to provide services and accommodations for the immigrants.

The types of services that these international association foundations and smaller NPOs provide are similar across all cities. Services related to language classes, translation, and education support for grade school students appear to make up the majority of these organizations' work. Local Japanese volunteers, who often receive Portuguese lessons from these international associations and NPOs, are the prominent providers of Japanese language classes for Brazilian immigrants. Moreover, international associations are often appointed by their respective city governments to carry out these services. For example, volunteers from these international associations are appointed by the local governments to provide language classes for immigrant students enrolled in local public schools, sometimes working at schools as language assistants. These NPOs and international association foundations also hold various workshops on educating immigrants about Japanese cultural norms, laws, and welfare benefits that they can earn from the state. Volunteers often hold consultation booths with Portuguese translators for immigrants to visit and consult about any concerns that they have. Despite the NPO efforts to provide immigrants with these services, evidence demonstrates that NPOs alone are unlikely to have an effective influence over levels of service provision. The role of NPOs and its correlation to other independent variables will be analyzed explicitly later in this study.

Presence of a Historical Focusing Event

Investigating focusing events that may have influenced the local governments to reassess its level of service provision was difficult, as there were no meticulous archives that kept documents and articles related to these events. Much of the articles written about the Brazilian immigrants were related to smaller crimes not nearly influential enough to be considered a focusing event. However, Fukuroi in Shizuoka Prefecture and Toyota and Komaki in Aichi Prefecture are cited frequently in secondary literatures as cities that have experienced crises that affected both the local and immigrant residents. As mentioned before, these cities are located in the industrial regions of Japan that attracted a large population of Brazilian Japanese immigrants during the 1990s. As population of such Nikkei immigrants increased, various issues surfaced between the Japanese locals and immigrants, increasing the tension between the two sides and ultimately resulting in the following incidents (Tsuda, 2003, 139).

Figure 2: Cities categorized based on presence of historical focusing event versus ordinal levels of immigrant service provision

| | | Dependent Variable- Level of Service Provision (City, (Prefecture)) | |
|---|---|---|---|
| | | High | Low |
| Independent Variable- Presence of Focusing Event (City, (Prefecture)) | Yes | Fukuroi (Shizuoka), Toyota (Aichi), Komaki (Aichi) | |
| | No | Oogaki (Gifu), Minokamo (Gifu), Kakegawa (Shizuoka), Kikugawa (Shizuoka), Naga-hama (Shiga), Aishocho (Shiga), Soja (Okayama), Takaoka (Toyama), Echizen (Fukui), Isesaki (Gunma), Oota (Gunma), Oizumi (Gunma), Hamamatsu (Shi-zuoka), Iwata (Shizuoka), Toyohashi (Aichi), Tsu (Mie), Yokkaichi (Mie), Suzuka (Mie), Kani (Gifu), Okasaki (Aichi) | Kameyama (Mie), Iga (Mie), Fuji (Shizuoka), Koka (Shiga), Inabe (Mie), Ueta (Nagano), Iida (Nagano), Sapporo (Nagano), Aomori (Ao-mori), Morioka (Aomori), Ichihara (Chiba), Ukyo (Kyoto), Joto (Osaka), Izumo (Shimane), Inabe (Mie), Sen-dai (Miyagi) |

A Brazilian immigrant in Fukuroi, Shizuoka Prefecture experienced what many scholars, jour-nalists, and fellow Brazilian immigrants criticized as a violation of human rights. In April of 2006, major Japanese national newspapers Yomiuri Shimbun and Asahi Shimbun reported that a Brazilian-Japanese immigrant was denied the right to purchase a plot of land in Fukuroi (The Yomiuri Shimbun,

29 June 2007). According to the reports, the immigrant male originally planned to purchase land via a Japanese real estate agency. The CEO of the agency informed the local Japanese neighborhood association, which pleaded the real estate agency to reject the Brazilian's request. The association was primarily concerned about the consequences of allowing a foreigner into their neighborhood. In May of 2006, the Brazilian-Japanese male reported the incident to the Shizuoka Prefecture District Legal Affairs Bureau, arguing that such act violated his human rights. After investigations, the District Legal Affairs Bureau determined that the real estate agency did in fact violate his human rights and access to basic housing needs (The Yomiuri Shimbun, 29 June 2007). The Legal Affairs Bureau officially charged and warned both the real estate agency and local neighborhood association to "refrain from causing similar issues in the future" (The Yomiuri Shimbun, 29 June 2007). This incident was widely covered by mass media outlets of all levels, including both large-scale national newspapers (such as the Yomiuri Shimbun) and smaller local media. Local newspapers published articles that criticized the incident and encouraged the local residents to discuss how xenophobic attitudes among the local communities can be eradicated (Shizuoka Shimbun, 30 June 2007).

Another serious human rights offense against the Brazilian immigrants was the murder of a Brazilian Japanese teenage boy in Komaki, Aichi Prefecture. 14-year old Herculano Reiko Lukosevicius was beaten to death in 1997 by a group of Japanese males, some of who belonged in local gangs (de Carvalho, 198, 2003). According to the reports, a group of Japanese males, angry and "out to get any Brazilian for revenge", attacked Lukosevicius and other fellow Brazilians one night (The Japan Times, 2 March 1998). While Lukosevicius' friends managed to escape, he was captured and beaten to death by the Japanese males (The Japan Times, 2 March 1998). Four 19 and 18 year olds were arrested and indicted; one Japanese male, aged 19 at the time, was eventually sentenced to five years in prison in 1998 (Sankei Shimbun, 9 July 1998). Lukosevicius' death left a strong memory on Komaki city's Brazilian community. Soon after the incident, local Brazilian employment agencies began to distribute flyers advising Brazilian immigrants to not loiter the streets at night and to be aware of their surroundings (The Japan Times, 2 March 1998). Similarly to the incident in Fukuroi city, the incident urged the local Japanese community to debate how to eradiate mistreatment of Brazilian immigrants in their neighborhoods.

But perhaps the most notorious of these crises may be the Homi Public Housing Complex riots in Toyota, Aichi Prefecture. As population of Brazilian immigrants increased in Toyota, population of foreign residents in a popular, public housing complex known as the Homi Complex increased as well. Such demographic shift within the housing complex heightened tensions between the Japanese and Brazilian residents. Brazilian immigrants, unaware of Japanese cultural norms and rules, were often accused of excessive noise for playing their music too loudly at home. Immigrants who were unaware of meticulous procedures that went into garbage disposal were also accused of illegal garbage dumping. Violence eventually broke out at the Complex, with robberies, arson, group threats, and violence occurring between the Japanese and Brazilian residents (Komai, 2001,133). Situation exacerbated to the point that a local, right wing nationalist group began a campaign to evict the Brazilians from the Complex. Local police forces were eventually deployed to the Complex to prevent further outbreak of violence (Tsuda, 2003, 139). This particular incident at the Homi Complex is widely cited by secondary sources as an example of xenophobia in the Japanese community. Most importantly, documents provided by the Toyota city government also reveal how the incident impacted the level of service provision in Toyota. The Homi Public Housing Complex case will be analyzed later as an example of a significant focusing event that influenced the local government to reevaluate and increase its provision of services.

Correlation Among Independent Variables

Study shows that the three independent variables are strongly interdependent and correlate to one another. Pairs of independent variables seem to operate in sync, as it appears rare that these variables influence levels of service provision on its own.

*Correlation Between Population Demand and Presence of Focusing Events*

There is some correlation between population demand and presence of focusing events, as the three cities with focusing event experience are all categorized under high population demand and high levels of service provision. Increase in immigrant population in the following cities increased the chances of disputes from occurring between the local Japanese and immigrant residents. As implied from the human rights violation in Fukuroi, the Japanese public does not generally view the Brazilian immigrants positively, as xenophobic attitudes are still prevalent in the society. Many fear that an increase in immigrant population would jeopardize the security of the local community. For example, the city of Toyota conducted an opinion poll on local Japanese residents in 2009, asking questions regarding the foreign immigrants that have settled in Toyota. Out of 1673 local Japanese residents that participated in the survey, 26.5% majority expressed that foreign immigrants "are undesirable" residents of the city as they may "jeopardize the community's safety" (Toyota International Affairs Division, 2013, 24). 26.4% believed that the tensions between the local Japanese and foreign immigrants arose as a result of cultural and normative differences between the two sides. 56.3% of the Japanese wished that the immigrants "learn to respect Japanese cultural norms and relevant laws" (Toyota International Affairs Division, 2013, 25). However, when asked about what Japanese local residents themselves can do to accept the immigrants as fellow residents of the community, overwhelmingly majority of 20.1% expressed that they "would rather not interact with the immigrants in the first place". Despite having one of the largest Brazilian immigrant populations in the nation, local Japanese residents in Toyota do not necessarily have positive attitudes towards the immigrants. Underlying xenophobic attitudes continue to exist today even after the surge of Brazilian immigrants has begun to establish their livelihood in Toyota. Due to such sentiments among the local Japanese residents, population increase may contribute to a rise in tension and violence between the two groups, resulting in severe crises that are considered as focusing events.

Figure 4: Cities categorized based on ordinal levels of population demand versus levels of immigrant service provision in consideration to occurrence of focusing event; Bold and Capitalized - has experienced focusing event

| | | Dependent Variable- Level of Service Provision (City, (Prefecture)) | |
|---|---|---|---|
| | | High | Low |
| Independent Variables- Population Demand (City, (Prefecture)) | High | Minokamo (Gifu), **FUKUROI (SHIZUOKA),** Kosai (Shizuoka), Kikugawa (Shizuoka), Aishocho (Shiga), Echizen (Fukui), Isesaki (Gunma), Oota (Gunma), Iwata (Shizuoka), Toyohashi (Aichi), **TOYOTA (AICHI), KOMAKI (AICHI),** Suzuka (Mie), Kani (Gifu) | Kameyama (Mie), Iga (Mie) |
| | Medium | Oogaki (Gifu), Kakegawa (Shizuoka), Nagahama (Shiga), Hamamatsu (Shizuoka), Tsu (Mie), Yokkaichi (Mie), Okasaki (Aichi) | Koka (Shiga), Inabe (Mie), Ueta (Nagano), Ukyo (Kyoto), Joto (Osaka) |
| | Low | Soja (Okayama), Takaoka (Toyama), Oizumi (Gunma) | Fuji (Shizuoka), Iida (Nagano), Izumo (Shimane), Sapporo (Hokkaido), Aomori (Aomori), Morioka (Aomori), Ichihara (Chiba), Sendai (Miyagi) |

*Correlation Between Population Demand and NPO Influence*

Figure 5: Cities categorized based on ordinal level of role of NPOs in immigrant service provision versus ordinal levels of immigrant service provision in consideration with level of population demand

| | | Dependent Variable- Level of Service Provision (City, (Prefecture)) | |
|---|---|---|---|
| | | High | Low |
| Independent Variable- Influence of NPO (City, (Prefecture)) | High | *Oogaki (Gifu)*, **Minokamo (Gifu)**, *Kakegawa (Shizuoka)* **Fukuroi (Shizuoka), Kosai (Shizuoka), Kikugawa (Shizuoka)**, *Nagahama (Shiga)*, <u>Takaoka (Toyama)</u>, **Echizen (Fukui)**. **Isesaki (Gunma), Oota (Gunma)**, *Hamamatsu (Shizuoka)*, **Iwata (Shizuoka), Toyohashi (Aichi), Toyota (Aichi), Komaki (Aichi, Suzuka (Mie), Kani (Gifu)** *Yokkaichi (Mie)* | Sendai (Miyagi) |
| | Low | Aishocho (Shiga), Soja (Okayama), Oizumi (Gunma), Tsu (Mie), Okasaki (Aichi) | Fuji (Shizuoka), Kameyama (Mie), Iga (Mie) Koka (Shiga) Izumo (Shimane), Inabe (Mie) Ueta (Nagano) Iida (Nagano), Sapporo (Hokkaido), Aomori (Aomori), Morioka (Iwate), Ichihara (Chiba) |

Legend: Bold - high level of population demand
Italicized- medium level of population demand
Underlined- low level of population demand

Population demand by Brazilian newcomers appears to correlate with the level of influence that NPOs have in each city's provision of services. Of the 19 cities categorized under ordinally high level of NPO influence and high level of service provision, 13 are also categorized under high level of population demand. Five are categorized under medium level of population demand, while one is categorized as low. As seen from the data, high population demand coincides with high level of influence by the NPOs. On the contrary, many cities categorized as low in population demand were not only categorized as low in influence of NPOs, but also in level of service provision as well. On the other hand, it is interesting to see Kameyama and Iga of Mie Prefecture be categorized under low NPO influence and low service provision despite their high population demand. Kameyama will be analyzed later in the study as an outlier in the data.

*Correlation Between NPO Influence and Presence of Focusing Events*

As indicated by Figure 6, focusing events have some influence over the level of NPO influence in cities that have experienced a crisis. Focusing events may encourage not only the local government to reassess its services and accommodation for immigrants, but also the local NPO community and international association foundations to reevaluate their roles in providing services. Toyota's Homi Complex is an obvious example of NPOs increasing their service provision after occurrence of a focusing event. This case will be discussed later in the study to analyze the effect of focusing events on formulation of immigrant services and the NPO sector.

Figure 6: Cities categorized based on ordinal level of role of NPOs in immigrant service provision versus ordinal levels of immigrant service provision in consideration with occurrence of focusing events

| | | Dependent Variable- Level of Service Provision (City, (Prefecture)) | |
|---|---|---|---|
| | | High | Low |
| Independent Variable- Influence of NPO (City, (Prefecture)) | High | Oogaki (Gifu), Minokamo (Gifu), Kakegawa (Shizuoka) **FUKUROI** (Shizuoka), Kosai (Shizuoka), Kikugawa (Shizuoka), Nagahama (Shiga), Takaoka (Toyama), Echizen (Fukui). Isesaki (Gunma), Oota (Gunma), Hamamatsu (Shizuoka), Iwata (Shizuoka), Toyohashi (Aichi), **TOYOTA** (Aichi), **KOMAKI** (Aichi), Suzuka (Mie), Kani (Gifu) Yokkaichi (Mie) | Sendai (Miyagi) |

| | Low | Aishocho (Shiga), Soja (Okayama), Oizumi (Gunma), Tsu (Mie), Okasaki (Aichi) | Fuji (Shizuoka), Kameyama (Mie), Iga (Mie) Koka (Shiga) Izumo (Shimane), Inabe (Mie) Ueta (Nagano) Iida (Nagano), Sapporo (Hokkaido), Aomori (Aomori), Morioka (Iwate), Ichihara (Chiba) |
|---|---|---|---|
| | | | |

Legend: Bold and capitalized - occurrence of focusing event

Correlation with the Intervening Variable

As an intervening variable, membership in a nation-wide coalition of cities with large immigrant population appears to correlate with the three independent variables.

The coalition, known as Gaikokujin shuju toshi kaigi or the Committee for Localities with Concentrated Foreign Population (CLCFP), is a nation-wide coalition composed of 26 cities that have a large population of foreign immigrants in their locality, majority of which are Brazilian. Founded in 2001, the first coalition meeting took place in Hamamatsu with the creation of Hamamatsu Declaration (Hamamatsu Sengen). The Declaration, created by the original 13 member cities, officially established the CLCFP and urged the national government to reassess policies relevant to immigrants (such as healthcare programs) while improving the conditions of the communities that they live in. The Declaration urged the government to reconsider current immigrant registration procedures and establish better language assistance system for immigrant children in local public schools (Committee for Localities with Concentrated Foreign Population, 2012). So far, the coalition has met 11 times to discuss issues surrounding their immigrant community and to share best practices. Most importantly, the CLCFP has also continued to petition to the prefectural and national government for revisions and creation of policies relevant to immigrant population (Tsuda, 2006, 68).

There is a strong correlation between the intervening variable and population demand and focusing events based on the timing of relevant events. As written in the introduction of the Hamamatsu Declaration, the founding 13 cities wished to foster a better multicultural community for both the local Japanese and newcomer immigrants (Hamamatsu Declaration, 2001). Among the three cities that have experienced focusing events, Toyota is the only one that has been a member of the coalition since its foundation (Toyota International Affairs Division, 2013, 17). But because Toyota's Homi Complex incident was widely covered by the media, occurrence of such crisis may have influenced the creation of this coalition and may have encouraged other cities to join. On the other hand, Fukuroi and Komaki cities have also witnessed human rights violations against Brazilian immigrants in their locality, but both did not join the coalition until much later in 2007. This demonstrates that while there is some correlation between the timing when Toyota joined the coalition and when the riots took place at Homi Complex, focusing events may need to be severe or violent enough before it can influence cities to join the CLCFP. Moreover, the riots at Homi Public Housing Complex and the subsequent decision to join the CLCFP may have played a larger role in elevating the level of service provision in Toyota. The relationship between the CLCFP and the independent variables will be discussed further in the study, when services in Toyota, Hamamatsu, and Kameyama are process traced.

# Part 2 Works Cited

"Burajiru-jin Tennyu Wo Kyohi, "jinken shinpan" to Houmukyoku Ga Setsuji, Fukuroi No Jichikai Ni= Shizuoka." (Brazilian rejected from move-in, human rights violation, Legal Bureau warns Fukuroi local neighborhood association= Shizuoka) *The Yomiuri Shimbun*, 29 June 2007. Factiva. Web.

Calazans, Erika. "Life as Dekkasseguis: The Brazilian Community in Japan." Hurights.or.jp. Asia-Pacific Human Rights Center, Dec. 2009. Web.

"Choueki 5-nen no hanketsu, Nikkei shounen shuugeki no hikoku Ni, Nagoya chisai." (Sentenced 5 years for attacking Nikkei boy by Nagoya District Court) *Sankei Shimbun*, 9 July 1998. Factiva. Web.

"Dai jizai = Gaikokujin okotowari." (Dai Jizai Column = Rejecting foreigners) *Shizuoka Shimbun*, 30 June 2007. Factiva. Web.

De Carvalho, Daniela. "Nikkei Communities in Japan." *Global Japan: The Experience of Japan's New Immigrant and Overseas Communities*. London: Routledge Curzon, 2003. 195-208. Print.

Haddad, Mary Alice. "Transformation of Japan's Civil Society Landscape." *Journal of East Asian Studies* 7.3 (2007): 413-37. Print.

"Hamamatsu Sengen." (Hamamatsu Declaration) Http://www.shujutoshi.jp/. Gaikokujin Shuju Toshi Kaigi (Committee for Localities with Concentrated Foreign Population), 19 Oct. 2001. Web.

Kitawaki, Yasuyuki. "A Japanese Approach to Municipal Diversity Management: The Case Of Hamamatsu City." Coe.int. Council of Europe. Web.

Komai, Hiroshi. *Foreign Migrants in Contemporary Japan*. Melbourne: Trans Pacific, 2001. Print.

"Koremade no katsudo to nagare." (History of activities from past to today) Http://www.shujutoshi.jp/. Gaikokujin Shuju Toshi Kaigi (Committee for Localities with Concentrated Foreign Population), 1 Apr. 2012. Web.

Papademetriou, Demetrios G., and Kimberly A. Hamilton. *Reinventing Japan: Immigration's Role in Shaping Japan's Future*. Washington, D.C.: Carnegie Endowment for International Peace: Distributed by Brookings Institution, 2000. Print.

"Parents Cope with Slaying of Japanese-Brazilian Son." www.japantimes.co.jp. *The Japan Times*, 2 Mar. 1998. Web.

Pekkanen, Robert. "After the Developmental State: Civil Society in Japan." *Journal of East Asian Studies* 4.3 Special Issue (2004): 363-88. Print.

"Regional Information: Aichi." Investing in Japan. Japan External Trade Organization, July 2013. Web.

"Regional Information: Gunma." Investing in Japan. Japan External Trade Organization, July 2013. Web.

"Regional Information: Shizuoka." Investing in Japan. Japan External Trade Organization, July 2013. Web.

Takao, Yasuo. "The Rise Of The "third Sector" In Japan." *Asian Survey* 41.2 (2001): 290-309. Web.

"Toyota-shi No Kokusaika: Genjou to Torikumi." (Toyota City's Internationalization: OnPresent State and Initiatives) Toyota International Affairs Division, 2013. Print.

Tsuda, Takeyuki. *Local Citizenship in Recent Countries of Immigration: Japan in Comparative Perspective*. Lanham, MD: Lexington, 2006. Print.

Tsuda, Takeyuki. *Strangers in the Ethnic Homeland: Japanese Brazilian Return Migration in Transnational Perspective*. New York: Columbia UP, 2003. Print.

Yamamoto, Tadashi. *The Nonprofit Sector in Japan*. Manchester, UK: Manchester UP, 1998. Print.

# Part 3: Process Tracing Results:
## Analysis on Cities of Toyota, Hamamatsu, and Kameyama

Results of Process Tracing on Three Cities

In order to investigate the causal mechanisms behind the varying levels of service provision, three cities were process traced. I chose to investigate the development of service provision in Toyota from Aichi Prefecture, Hamamatsu from Shizuoka Prefecture, and Kameyama from Mie Prefecture. All three cities have a high concentration of Brazilian immigrants, while immigrants in these cities are employed in similar key industries and are of similar socioeconomic status. While Toyota and Hamamatsu have a high level of service provision, Kameyama has a low level of service provision despite having a high population demand.

It is difficult to determine the direct source of variance in levels of service provision based on analysis of the role of population demand, NPOs, and focusing events. This is particularly due to the fact that these variables are interdependent, influencing each other's outcomes. However, process tracing reveals several key points. First, it is clear that an increase in the newcomer immigrant population plays a significant role in urging the city government to increase its service provision, as seen primarily in Hamamatsu. Second, NPOs play a significant role in providing basic services for immigrants in the community; however, comparison of NPO developments in Hamamatsu and Kameyama indicate that these NPOs do not often fare well when left to operate alone. Relationships with the city governments influence the degree to which these NPOs can provide services for the immigrants. Lastly, analysis of focusing event in Toyota reveal that such events serve as a catalyst to encourage the city governments to provide higher level of services for their immigrants. In addition, focusing events contribute the development of NPOs concerned about issues affecting the immigrants in their community.

Ultimately, the development of immigrant services influences the Japanese local governments to join a nation-wide committee, known as the Committee for Localities with a Concentrated Foreign Population (CLCFP). However, whether or not joining such national-level committee improves the level of service provision is debatable as seen from the analysis of service provision in Kameyama.

Background on Hamamatsu, Toyota, and Kameyama

Hamamatsu, Shizuoka Prefecture, is an industrial city with one of the largest population of Brazilian Nikkei immigrants in Japan. Automobile and motorcycle companies like Suzuki, Yamaha, and Honda are headquartered in Hamamatsu (Regional Information: Shizuoka, Web). In 2009, about 32,000 registered foreign residents lived in the city, making up about 3.95% of the total population (Hamamatsu Statistics, Web). Population of Brazilians has significantly dropped since the financial crisis in 2008 and the earthquake disaster in 2011, as unemployment rates and natural disaster urged many Brazilian immigrants to repatriate back to their home country. Nonetheless, Hamamatsu continues to host a large population of Brazilian immigrants in Japan (Hamamatsu International Affairs Division, 2014, 9). As of January 2014, of the 21,327 foreign immigrants that compose 2.63% of the city's population,

44.5% were Brazilian (Ministry of Internal Affairs and Communications, Web).

Similarly to Hamamatsu, the city of Toyota in Aichi Prefecture also hosts a large population of Brazilian immigrants. Home of the famous Japanese automaker Toyota, 3.09% of the city's population as of January 2014 are registered immigrants, with 40.6% of them being Brazilian (Ministry of Internal Affairs and Communications, Web). Likewise, majority of these Brazilians work in the manufacturing sector. Contrary to Hamamatsu and Kameyama, Toyota experienced a crisis that occurred as a result of tensions between the immigrants and local Japanese residents, which will be discussed later in detail. Years after the event, Toyota has developed high provision of services comparable to Hamamatsu; both cities are also often cited as case studies in other secondary sources related to Japanese immigration policies.

The city of Kameyama is located in Mie Prefecture, yet another region known for its industrial manufacturing sector. Kameyama is home of the Sharp Corporation, an electronic manufacturer that produces high-quality LCD televisions. Corporations like Sharp in Kameyama attracted Brazilian immigrants after the immigration law revision of 1990 (Kameyama Local Industry Basic Plan, 2012, 2-3). Kameyama continues to have a high share of foreign residents among its population. Roughly 3.45% of its population are foreign immigrants, with 52% of them coming from Brazil (Ministry of Internal Affairs and Communications, Web). Yet contrary to Hamamatsu and Toyota, Kameyama's service provision remains low despite having high population demand.

As indicated by the aforementioned descriptions, these three cities hold constant the ordinal level of immigrants and Brazilian population in their localities, the socioeconomic status of the Brazilian immigrants, and the industrial sector that these Brazilians are employed in. Process-tracing results reveal the underlying mechanisms behind population demand, NPOs, and focusing events on the levels of immigrant service provision.

Effect of Population Demand

Numerical values of Brazilian population in these 3 cities illustrate a different image that allows for a better comparison of population demand. As indicated by the data above, populations of Brazilians between 1991 and 2012 in the three cities differ significantly. Hamamatsu leads with population peaking at about 19,000 people in 2008, before the financial crisis forced many Brazilians to repatriate. Toyota's Brazilian immigrant population peaked on the same year, but only at about 8,000. Kameyama, on the other hand, peaked in 2006 with about 1,500 Brazilian immigrants. The data demonstrates that the population of Brazilian immigrants in Hamamatsu has historically been the largest among these three cities. Though the Brazilian immigrants in these cities are employed in similar industries and are of similar socioeconomic statuses, there is a difference in the absolute size of the Brazilian population among the three cities. This gap may explain, to a certain extent, the variance in levels of service provision. Kameyama, which has a low level of service provision, undoubtedly has the smallest Brazilian immigrant population among the three cities. On the other hand, Hamamatsu and Toyota both have high levels of services, despite Hamamatsu's significantly larger population of immigrants. In order to analyze the reason why these cities have comparable level of service provision despite population size difference, I process trace the timeline of events for activities within the city government, NPO sector, and focusing events. Figure 1: Population of Brazilian Residents in Hamamatsu, Toyota, and Kameyama, 1991-2012

| Year | Hamamatsu | Toyota | Kameyama |
|------|-----------|--------|----------|
| 1991 | 4,072 | 2,646 | 194 |
| 1992 | 6,132 | 3,448 | 342 |
| 1993 | 6,489 | 3,358 | 431 |
| 1994 | 5,920 | 2,933 | 429 |
| 1995 | 6,527 | 3,129 | 488 |
| 1996 | 7,279 | 3,806 | 698 |
| 1997 | 8,136 | 4,976 | 802 |
| 1998 | 10,086 | 4,972 | 908 |
| 1999 | 9,969 | 4,613 | 917 |
| 2000 | 10,789 | 5,074 | 944 |
| 2001 | 11,716 | 5,883 | 1,160 |
| 2002 | 12,111 | 6,065 | 1,206 |
| 2003 | 13,363 | 6,270 | 1,262 |
| 2004 | 13,270 | 6,497 | 1,447 |
| 2005 | 14,377 | 7,006 | 1,648 |
| 2006 | 18,548 | 7,343 | 1,560 |
| 2007 | 19,267 | 7,753 | 1,118 |
| 2008 | 19,461 | 7,917 | 1,279 |
| 2009 | 18,247 | 7,264 | 1,419 |
| 2010 | 14,959 | 6,663 | 1,336 |
| 2011 | 13,447 | 6,152 | 1,109 |
| 2012 | 12,268 | 6,062 | 870 |

Sources: Hamamatsu- Hamamatsu Foundation for International Communication and Exchanges; Toyota- "Toyota-shi No Kokusaika: Genjou to Torikumi." (Toyota City's Internationalization: On Present State and Initiatives) Toyota International Affairs Division, 2013. Prints; and Kameyama- "Kameyama Shisei Jouhou- Jinkou." (Kameyama City Information- Population) Kameyama City Government, Web.

## Timeline of Events for Toyota:

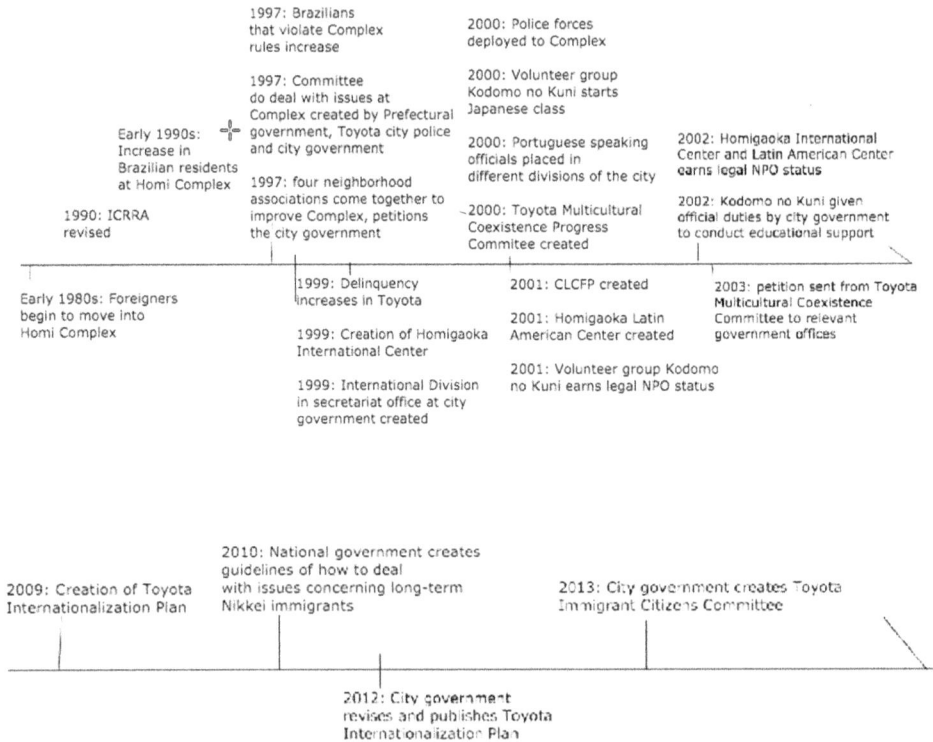

1997: Brazilians that violate Complex rules increase

1997: Committee do deal with issues at Complex created by Prefectural government, Toyota city police and city government

Early 1990s: Increase in Brazilian residents at Homi Complex

1997: four neighborhood associations come together to improve Complex, petitions the city government

1990: ICRRA revised

2000: Police forces deployed to Complex

2000: Volunteer group Kodomo no Kuni starts Japanese class

2000: Portuguese speaking officials placed in different divisions of the city

2000: Toyota Multicultural Coexistence Progress Committee created

2002: Homigaoka International Center and Latin American Center earns legal NPO status

2002: Kodomo no Kuni given official duties by city government to conduct educational support

Early 1980s: Foreigners begin to move into Homi Complex

1999: Delinquency increases in Toyota

1999: Creation of Homigaoka International Center

1999: International Division in secretariat office at city government created

2001: CLCFP created

2001: Homigaoka Latin American Center created

2001: Volunteer group Kodomo no Kuni earns legal NPO status

2003: petition sent from Toyota Multicultural Coexistence Committee to relevant government offices

2009: Creation of Toyota Internationalization Plan

2010: National government creates guidelines of how to deal with issues concerning long-term Nikkei immigrants

2013: City government creates Toyota Immigrant Citizens Committee

2012: City government revises and publishes Toyota Internationalization Plan

## Timeline of Events for Hamamatsu:

1992: Ministry of Internal Affairs and Communication appoints Hamamtsu to be project city for community internationalization program

1992: Hamamatsu government creates Hamamatsu International Cultural Exchange Center, left to HICE to be managed

1990: ICRRA revised

2000: Foreign Residents Council informally created

1982: HICE founded

1983: HICE starts Japanese language classes

1991: Hamamatsu International Affairs Organization earns foundation status, starts a consultation window

1995: Cultural Affairs Bureau appoints Hamamatsu to be model city for Japanese Language Learning System Initiatives Project

2001: CLCFP founded with Hamamatsu Declaration

2010: Hamamatsu Foreign Resident Study Support Center created by city government, left under HICE authority

2002:Hamamatsu Multicultural Coexistence Vision Plan made

2013: Hamamatsu Multicultural Coexistence City Vision Plan created

2008: Financial Crisis, leads to unemployment of many Brazilians

2012: Creation of Multicultural Coexistence Plan Council created

2014: Hamamatsu Internationalization Strategy Plan created

2008: Foreign Residents Council created officially by city government

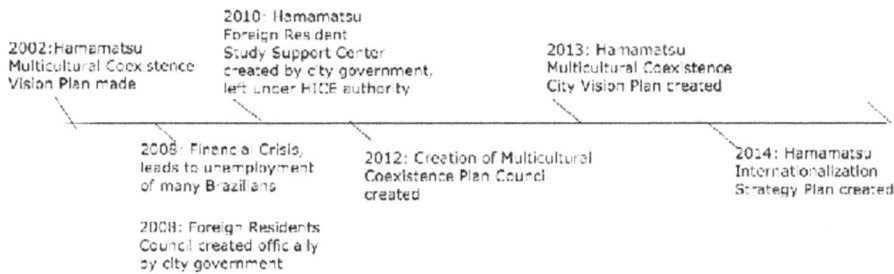

Timeline of Events for Kameyama:

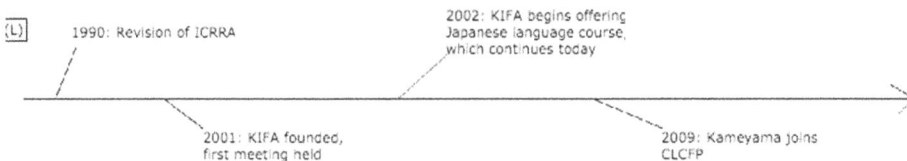

(L)    1990: Revision of ICRRA

2002: KIFA begins offering Japanese language course, which continues today

2001: KIFA founded, first meeting held

2009: Kameyama joins CLCFP

## Role of Local NPOs

*Development of Service Provision by Local NPOs*

Patterns of NPO development in Hamamatsu, Toyota, and Kameyama vary; Compared to Toyota and Kameyama, Hamamatsu demonstrates an evidence of earlier developments in NPO sector working to resolve immigration issues. Kameyama, on the other hand, continues to lack a strong NPO sector even today. Much of the NPO groups in Toyota were founded immediately after the focusing event, which will be discussed in detail later.

One of the difficulties in obtaining relevant data about the local NPOs was seeking out activists who were willing to be interviewed to explain more about their organizations; because the local governments delegate duties to many of these NPOs, activists often advised me to contact the local governments instead, rather than engaging in the interview themselves. However, analysis of prominent NPOs responsible for providing immigrant services in Hamamatsu, Kameyama, and Toyota indicates that NPOs play a significant role in setting the framework necessary for local governments to develop a structured service provision guideline. Differences between NPOs in Hamamatsu, Toyota and Kameyama indicate that NPOs alone do not effectively provide services, as the relationships that these groups have with the local governments ultimately influence the level of service provision. Lastly, the delayed development of NPOs in Toyota reveals a possible relationship between the role of focusing events and NPOs.

According to Hamamatsu International Affairs Division official Kouki Furuhashi, Hamamatsu Foundation for International Communications and Exchanges- known by the local government as HICE- provides majority of the services for immigrants in Hamamatsu (Furuhashi, 22 July 2014). From the Hamamatsu government's perspective, HICE is considered a nongovernmental NPO foundation, operated by individuals from the private sector. However, HICE staff Erika Suzuki claims that while the organization is nonprofit and nongovernmental in nature, the history behind HICE's development reveals connections to the local government as well as the national government. First and foremost, HICE was not privately founded; the organization was founded in 1982 through funding from the Hamamatsu Chamber of Commerce and the city of Hamamatsu as one of the earliest NPOs in the city to work with immigrant issues (Suzuki, 22 July 2014). Furuhashi believes that the development of HICE started in early 1980s, as large multinational industries brought foreign laborers into the community. HICE quickly grew to provide Japanese language lessons for these immigrants in 1983, and by 1991 offered consultation services (Outline of HICE's Development, Web). The local government also played a role in developing HICE, when it created the Hamamatsu Intercultural Center in 1992. The Intercultural Center became a one-stop location for immigrants to access a wide range of services, and along with this facility the city also opened the Hamamatsu Foreign Resident Study Support Center in 2010 (Furuhashi, 22 July 2014). The Study Support Center provided language and cultural education for both local Japanese and immigrant residents. Later on, the city government left the operations of both facilities under HICE's authority. As Suzuki notes, HICE is a nonprofit, nongovernmental organization; however, the organization has historically worked with the city government in providing highly effective services. HICE exemplifies a case where NPOs serve as extension of the city government, providing immigrants with services on behalf of the government.

On the contrary, Kameyama lacks the strength of local NPOs found in Hamamatsu; Kameyama has an inactive NPO sector in the field of immigrant issues, with only one organization dedicated to improving the lives of local immigrants in the area. The Kameyama International Friend Association, or KIFA, is perhaps the only organization within the city that provides activities and services to improve the relationship between Japanese locals and immigrants. Yoshio Tanaka, the founder and head of KIFA, offered some background on the history behind KIFA and its activities. According to Tanaka, KIFA was founded in 2001 following a city-wide meeting among local residents, who expressed interest in creating an international affairs association to allow for interaction among the local residents and immigrants (Tanaka, 16 November 2014). Tanaka claims that prior to 2001, Kameyama had no specific organizations dedicated to serving the needs of the immigrants (Tanaka, 16 November 2014). KIFA was thus privately established based on the interests of local residents and activists, who wanted to address the issues surfacing from increase in population of immigrants (Tanaka, 16 November 2014). Such historical background differs significantly from that of HICE, which was founded with partial funding from the Hamamatsu city government. While it has similar missions, goals, and activities as HICE does, KIFA was founded strictly via private individuals, and remains independent from bureaucratic influence, as they have not been officially appointed by the city government to carry out specific programs and services.

As mentioned before, KIFA provides services similar to those given by HICE in Hamamatsu; KIFA has conducted cultural exchange events and programs to bring local Japanese and immigrants together, as well as workshops and classes for immigrants on topics like Japanese language, welfare, health, and education systems in Japan (Birth of KIFA, Web). KIFA has translated crucial documents related to Japanese social welfare programs into Portuguese, giving Brazilian newcomers access to information on how they can receive certain benefits from the state. Most importantly, Tanaka believes that KIFA's Japanese language classes for immigrants have continued to this day because of local government support. KIFA receives partial support from the city government for its Japanese language classes, as it provides a location large enough to hold classes and subsidizes transportation fees for Japanese language instructors (Tanaka, 16 November 2014).

Comparison of NPOs in Hamamatsu and Kameyama demonstrate the extent to which the local government's relationship to the NPO sector shapes the development of service provision by the NPOs. While KIFA's language lesson program receives partial funding from the city government, KIFA has yet to be officially appointed by the city government to carry out specific services for the immigrants. On the contrary, HICE in Hamamatsu has a strong relationship with the city government, as the two work collaboratively to provide services for the immigrant population. Such relationship (or lack thereof) between the local city government and NPOs influence the extent to which accommodations and services for the newcomer immigrants are made available; comparison of Hamamatsu's HICE and Kameyama's KIFA reveal the variance in levels of service provision that can be expected depending on NPOs' relationship with the city governments, as well as the difficulties that NPOs experience when left to operate on their own.

On the other hand, NPO groups in Toyota were established within years after violent riots that took place during the late 1990s. Among one of the earlier NPO groups founded to serve the interest of the immigrants was the Homigaoka International Exchange Center, which continues to work to improve the conditions in the Brazilian community at Homi Complex. In 2002, the organization was officially recognized as a legal NPO by the local government, and by 2004 was appointed by the city government to carry out programs that would engage foreign residents in local community building (Toyota International Affairs Division, 2014, 13). The Toyota city government also appointed various other NPOs to provide services such as language classes, immigrant children support systems in schools, and multicultural community development programs. Though they collaborate with the local government, NPOs in Toyota are still nongovernmental, founded privately by activists themselves. While Toyota's NPOs were founded privately like KIFA, the relationship that they have with the local government matches more closely to that of HICE and the Hamamatsu government. Like HICE, these vibrant NPOs in Toyota provide high levels of service to immigrants with the support of the local Toyota government.

Yet the most notable difference between Hamamatsu and Toyota's development of NPOs is that Toyota's NPOs were influenced largely by a violent crisis that occurred in Toyota. In addition to nongovernmental structures, development in local government structures are also concentrated with the years of the crisis occurring in Toyota, while Hamamatsu had developed both nongovernmental and governmental structures much earlier than Toyota. This particular focusing event magnified the need for not only local individuals to take interest in the issue and create NPO organizations, but also the local governments to create necessary structures within the city government to address the issue.

Role of Focusing Events

Toyota's lack of governmental and NPO structure for provision of immigrants services may explain why the city experienced a large-scale, violent crisis that took place in a public housing complex. While Hamamatsu had a structured NPO during the 1980s, Toyota did not until later in the 1990s. Known as the Homi Public Housing Complex incident, this focusing event urged the Toyota city government to consider establishing committees dedicated to creating solutions to issues surrounding the immigrant community, while also encouraging the creation of NPOs.

Home for Immigrants: The Homi Public Housing Complex in Toyota

Clashes between the local Japanese and Brazilian residents took place at a large, housing complex known as the Homi Public Housing Complex. The housing complex opened its doors for local residents in 1978, and by early 1980s admitted foreign residents. The number of foreign residents- especially among the newcomer Brazilian immigrants- began to increase steadily during the late 1980s, and as a result the demographic makeup at Homi Complex began to shift significantly. Brazilian immigrants found their residence at Homi Danchi via employment brokers, establishing a small yet concentrated Brazilian community at Homi Complex (Komai, 2001, 133). Foreign residents made up 31.8% of the population at Homi in 2000, and by 2008 the number swelled to 48.8% (Toyota International Affairs Division, 2013, 7).

Tensions between the local Japanese citizens and Brazilian residents in Homi Complex increased between 1997 and 1999 as disputes over improper garbage disposal, excessive noise from the Brazilian residents, and other issues surmounted. Group threats, robberies, and arson ensued between the two sides, resulting in a violent clash between right-wing Japanese nationalists and Brazilian residents in 1999 as Japanese nationalists campaigned to evict Brazilians from the Complex (Tsuda, 2003, 139). The tension between the two sides prompted deployment of police forces into the Complex, shedding light on the severity of schism between the local Japanese and the newcomer immigrants (Tsuda, 2003, 140).

The Effect of Focusing Events (or Lack of) in Toyota, Hamamatsu, and Kameyama:

Unlike Kameyama, Toyota and Hamamatsu both have high levels of service provision today, with both nongovernmental and governmental sectors contributing to the provision of services. Yet when compared to Hamamatsu, Toyota's development in service provision is much more concentrated within the immediate years following the crisis at Homi Complex, while Hamamatsu's services developed more organically. Process tracing results of Toyota was made possible through extensive local government documents in addition to personal interviews conducted with city government officials. Keiko Aoki of Toyota's International Affairs Division provided explanations behind specific service developments. Though there are limitations on the extent to which mechanisms can be revealed from these interviews, documents and interviews from a city official provide evidence that these services were created as a result of the Homi riots. Toyota's experience with the conflict had a catalytic effect on the development of both city government and NPO-led immigrant service provisions. Such focusing event in Toyota forced the city government to develop the necessary accommodations within a short period of time rather than developing it naturally over a span of time as Hamamatsu had done.

As demonstrated by the timeline, Toyota's development in immigrant service provision took place after the crisis at Homi Public Housing Complex. Tensions between Japanese locals and Brazilian immigrant residents began to arise around 1997 and climaxed during 1999 to 2000, when violence between young Brazilian immigrants and Japanese right-wing nationalists prompted the deployment of police forces. Toyota city government's International Affairs division, now responsible for organizing programs and services for immigrants in the community, was created as a part of the secretarial division in 1999. The city government established the Internationalization Plan Committee on the same year, composed strictly of city government officials from relevant division in order to address the issues surrounding the immigrant community (Aoki, 8 July 2014). Aoki believes that the creation of these local government structures occurred around this particular time period as a result of "increase in Brazilian newcomer population"; however, such explanation based on population demand is insufficient in explaining the mechanisms behind Toyota's development in service provision. Toyota's immigrant population- especially among the newcomer Brazilians- had been on the rise since 1990. Increase in the newcomer immigrant population during the riots at Homi Complex is no different from population growth that occurred before 1999. Aoki denies that the Homi Complex riots was the most important triggering factor that forced Toyota to reevaluate issues related to immigrants—but timeline of service development proves otherwise, as much of the government structures and NPO groups were established immediately following the focusing event at Homi Complex.

Following the founding of International Affairs Division and the Internationalization Plan Committee, the Toyota city government established the Multicultural Coexistence Plan Council a year later, hoping to incorporate not only city government officials but also individuals from the public sector for a much-needed service provision structure. According to Aoki, this council was created as issues among the immigrant community- including the one at Homi Complex- demonstrated an urgent need for governmental intervention and solutions (Aoki, 8 July 2014). Unlike the Internationalization Plan Committee, this council consists of local Japanese residents from the private and public sector, including the police, NPOs, leaders of local neighborhood associations, heads of Brazilian association, individuals from multinational corporations, and hospitals. At first, the council operated under a narrow set of goals, as their primary purpose was to swiftly deal with the issues present at Homi Complex and the surrounding community. The council continues to meet annually to discuss possible solutions to issues regarding newcomer immigrants. Aoki notes that while the council in the past were much more focused on providing solutions and services to the immigrant community, it has taken on a different goal today. The Council today aims to create a framework that would allow foreign residents to collaborate directly with the Japanese locals in creating a multicultural community (Aoki, 8 July 2014).

After the establishment of these committees operated by local Japanese residents, the city of

Toyota established the Foreign Residents Council in 2013. This council, made up of 10 individuals from eight different nationalities, was established to gain opinion from foreigners and to allow them to participate in local decision-making. According to Aoki, the Foreign Residents Council is much more entrepreneurial, as the council focuses on designing new ways and methods to creating an immigrant-friendly city, rather than working to solve present issues. The creation of the Foreign Residents Council is yet another effort by the city government to bring both the local and immigrant residents together to create a better multicultural community (Aoki, 8 July 2014).

"It's incomparable how much things have changed since the clashes occurred at Homi," says Aoki. As she mentions in the interview, the aforementioned council provided a much-needed platform for local Japanese residents concerned about immigrants to discuss issues and create solutions. While she gives credit to the creation of Multicultural Coexistence Plan Council, Aoki also believes that the Japanese locals gradually became accustomed to having immigrants in their community. "But unfortunately, there are some people out in the public today that hasn't forgotten about the incident in 1990s and still cannot see foreign immigrants in a positive light," says Aoki. Such sentiments were evident even in public polls, conducted by the city of Toyota in 2009 and discussed in the earlier chapter. Aoki's comments and the poll results reveal the long-lasting historical memory of Homi Complex on the Toyota public and local government, connoting the severity of the issue.

On the contrary, the timing of Hamamatsu's service provision development differs significantly from Toyota's. Like Toyota, Hamamatsu has an International Affairs Division within the city government, along with its own Multicultural Coexistence Plan Council and Foreign Residents Council—yet these structures were established much earlier compared to Toyota. In 2000, Hamamatsu founded its Foreign Residents Council with foreign residents as members, while establishing its Multicultural Coexistence Plan Council, composed of Japanese locals from various sectors, in 2013. According to city official Kouki Furuhashi, the founding of the Multicultural Coexistence Plan Council accompanied the creation of the Hamamatsu Multicultural Coexistence Vision Plan in 2013 (Furuhashi, 22 July 2014). The plan, much like Toyota's, created a set of goals and guidelines for Hamamatsu to pursue between the years of 2013 and 2017 in order to create a better, multicultural community (Hamamatsu Multicultural Coexistence Vision, 2013). As Furuhashi assumed in the interview, the Foreign Residents Council was established earlier in 2000 as a way to inquire foreign residents about issues surrounding their community, so that the city government could create potential solutions. Furuhashi notes that the Foreign Residents Council at first viewed the immigrants as temporary residents, believing that they would only require minimal support. However, as immigrants began to seek long-term residence in Hamamatsu, it became necessary to consult the local Japanese residents on how locals and immigrants together can create a multicultural community (Furuhashi, 22 July 2014). Hamamatsu's Multicultural Coexistence Plan Council was a way to engage Japanese locals in various sectors, and ask for their understanding and support in creating a better community for both locals and immigrants. As Furuhashi explained, establishing a solid committee allowed for the creation of specific guidelines not only for the city government to follow, but also for other related sectors to refer to as well.

The difference between Toyota and Hamamatsu' Councils is an interesting point that reveals the relationship between provision of services to occurrence of focusing events. For Toyota, which experienced a violent focusing event, establishing a committee led by Japanese locals was necessary to alleviate tensions between the immigrants and the Japanese locals. This appears appropriate when considering that the majority of residents in Toyota are Japanese locals; the government must thus cater primarily to their concerns and needs. On the contrary, Hamamatsu naturally sought the opinion and demands of immigrants themselves before establishing a committee of Japanese locals interested in discussing how to create a multicultural community. Neither Aoki nor Furuhashi were able to offer concrete evidence and historical background behind the order in which these committees were created in their respective cities. However, focusing event may have forced Toyota to seek the opinions, solution ideas, and approval of the predominant Japanese constituents before consulting immigrants for new ideas. Hamamatsu had less urgency in consulting the local Japanese residents; instead, the city first inquired the immigrants for their opinions and views on what services they needed, leading to an organic development of services by both the NPOs and the local government.

While Toyota's service provision development is concentrated within few years after the crisis at Homi Complex, Hamamatsu had been developing its accommodations much earlier. This may explain why the national government was attracted to utilizing Hamamatsu as a "model" city for other cities to follow. In 1992, the Ministry of Home Affairs (now Ministry of Internal Affairs and Communications) chose Hamamatsu as a participant for Cities for Progressing International Exchange Project (Hamamatsu International Affairs Division, 2014, 19). In addition, the Japanese Agency for Cultural Affairs selected Hamamatsu as a participant city for an experimental program to create better, Japanese language classes (Hamamatsu International Affairs Division 2014, 19). Specific documents related to these national programs were unavailable; however, Furuhashi offered several potential reasons that Hamamatsu was selected for such programs. First, Furuhashi believes that Hamamatsu was chosen because of its status as a prominent industrial city, which brought foreign workers from various nationalities even before the immigration law revision in 1990. Furuhashi also believes that having foreigners as a visible part of the Hamamatsu community naturally directed the national government to appoint the city as a project participant. In addition, Furuhashi notes that the 1995 project on developing a Japanese language program coincided with a point in time when Hamamatsu government was collaborating with various other municipalities to develop a better Japanese language program for immigrants; this, he believes, may have led the national Agency for Cultural Affairs to choose Hamamatsu as a model city for experimental project (Furuhashi, 22 July 2014).

The chance to participate in these national programs may have played a role in how service provisions in Hamamatsu were developed much earlier compared to Toyota; this may also explain why the city was able to prevent an outbreak of serious crises. Though the national agencies and ministries did not directly contribute to the level of service provision, appointment into these experimental programs may have given Hamamatsu the incentive to develop immigrant services earlier on in the 90s, while Toyota did not have the motivation until the incident at Homi Housing Complex.

In conclusion, comparative analysis between Toyota and Kameyama does not reveal a direct causality between focusing events and local government provision of services. In addition, these cases cannot generalize for other cities with high population of Brazilian immigrants developed their immigrant services. Despite differences in how related committees and services were developed, both cities today have high levels of service provision, hinting that focusing events alone may not be the only variable responsible for increasing government attention to immigrant issues. Moreover, the case in Hamamatsu demonstrates that occurrence of focusing events is not a necessity for a city to create immigrant service provision systems. However, the timing in development of local government actions within Toyota indicate that, to a certain degree, crisis at events do influence the local government to direct its attention towards issues related to the immigrants. Based on comparison of how various Councils were established in Toyota and Hamamatsu, focusing events magnify the urgency of establishing a structure that would oversee provision of services for immigrants.

The Effect of Service Provision

*On the Committee for Localities with a Concentrated Foreign Population (CLCFP)*

While population demand, NPO influence, and presence of focusing events have varied influence over level of service provision, they also encourage Japanese cities to join a nation-wide committee dedicated to responding to immigrant issues. There is evidence that the creation of CLCFP, or the Committee for Localities with a Concentrated Foreign Population, emerged along with steady increase of Brazilian immigrants, magnified by the increase in issues affecting the immigrant community. Population demand and issues of various intensity- from miniscule, everyday incidents to the violence at Homi Complex- influenced cities to create and join this committee.

Aoki refers to the creation of CLCFP as a reaction to lack of proper services by the city governments, along with the rising tension between the immigrants and local residents. The CLCFP, as discussed earlier in the study, was founded in 2001 to bring localities with high population of immigrants together so that they may share best practices, release reports on research, and petition the national government to resolve issues related to immigration. As for Toyota, the city "joined several other cities in creating CLCFP to let the national government know that there was a lack of proper infrastructure dealing with immigrants," (Aoki, 8 July 2014). As Aoki notes, the national government did not have a proper immigration policy prior to the revision of ICRRA; thus, both the national and local governments were unprepared when an influx of immigrants moved into these localities. This urged the local governments to establish the CLCFP as a forum to voice their opinions to the national government.

Today, the CLCFP serves as a forum that allows city governments to not only discuss issues surrounding their immigrant community and share best practices, but also to lobby the national government know of how these cities with large population of immigrants are fairing. On certain years, CLCFP compiled comprehensive reports and petitions to present to the prefectural and national governments. Perhaps the most notable of these documents is the one created at the time of CLCFP's foundation in 2001, which was followed by the formulation of several documents including the Hamamatsu Declaration and Proposal. These documents officially established the CLCFP, but also petitioned the state government to improve school environment for immigrant children, social welfare and benefits, work environment, and the immigrant resident registration procedures. These Proposals were published in 2001, and were delivered directly to several national level ministries including Internal Affairs and Communication, Justice, Foreign Affairs, and Health Labour and Welfare (Hamamatsu Declaration, 2001). In addition to the Hamamatsu Declaration, the CLCFP has continued to release series of declarations, reports, and proposals to the national government over the course of years.

The national government's response to these reports and petitions by the local governments vary. The national government responded to these documents in 2006 with the creation of research committee on multicultural coexistence programs, led by the Ministry of Internal Affairs and Communications. The research committee released its first report on the same year, prompting national government to regard immigrants as long-term residents, rather than laborers temporarily living in Japan for work (Ministry of Internal Affairs and Communications, March 2006, Web). This particular action strongly matches the multiple proposals filed by local governments via CLCFP, which notes the increase in newcomer Brazilian immigrants seeking long-term residence in Japan. In addition, the report suggests that certain social welfare and educational programs should be improved. The same research committee filed reports of similar kind in 2010 and 2012, indicating a gradual increase in level of interest that national government agencies have over what had historically been dealt primarily by the local governments.

However, Aoki notes that these state actions are not enough to aid local governments accommodate immigrants. Aoki comments that the local governments to this day are still at the forefront of managing immigrant issues in Japan (Aoki, 8 July 2014). In addition, the effectiveness of these reports filed by the Ministry of Internal Affairs and Communications is questionable, as it provides limited advices for city governments. The reports do not mandate local governments to take any course of action. Most importantly, while it encourages the prefectural governments to support their cities improve the living situations of immigrants, it does not urge the national government to take any course of action regarding formulation of an actual immigration policy. While national ministries and agencies may have increased attention and interest to immigrant issues, the state government itself continues to display no interest in creating a working immigration policy, thus limiting the effect of the intervening variable on the level of national government involvement in immigrant service provision.

In addition, the continued lack of governmental structure and NPO groups demonstrates the limited ability of the organization in increasing the level of services among these localities. Kameyama joined the CLCFP in 2009, yet the city does not have an actual guideline for provision of immigrant services. While cities like Hamamatsu and Toyota are also members of CLCFP, Kameyama has yet to indicate any progress with its own service provision structure. City government official Ms. Kitagawa of Kameyama city government's Social Harmony Promotions Section recognizes how Kameyama has failed to improve immigrant service provision. Kameyama lacks the division of city government dedicated solely to working with immigrants in their community; instead, the city government has the Social Harmony Promotions Section. This division works with issues not only related to the immigrant community, but also with various other societal inequalities, such as gender inequality in the Kameyama community. According to Kitagawa, volatility in Kameyama's immigrant population may influence why guidelines for service provision have yet to be created in Kameyama. Kitagawa claims that a large population of immigrants in Kameyama does not seek long-term residency in the city (Kitagawa, 19 November 2014). This is due to the fact that many immigrants migrate to Kameyama for temporary job training at the industrial factories based in the city. Thus, these immigrants do not necessarily seek long-term residency, as they repatriate back to their country after training period. However, Kameyama's immigrant population has been steadily increasing over the last decade, making Kitagawa's argument is insufficient in explaining the reason why the city to this day lacks services for its immigrant population. Though it is a member of the CLCFP since 2009, Kameyama has made very little progress in developing a provision framework. From such case, it becomes difficult to determine the effectiveness of CLCFP as an organization to improve the quality of service provision among member cities. It will be interesting to see if Kameyama's service provision will improve in the future, and if so, what factors will influence it to do so. Whether or not Kameyama will progress or remain stagnant in service provision is an interesting topic for future studies.

# Part 3 Works Cited

Aoki, Keiko. "Interview with Toyota International Affairs Division Official." Personal Interview. 8 July 2014.

"Tabunka Kyousei no Suishin ni Kansuru Kenkyuu Kai." (On the Research Committee for Multicultural Coexistance Initiatives." Ministry of Internal Affairs and Communications, March 2006. Web.

Furuhashi, Kouki. "Interview with Hamamatsu International Affairs Division Official." Personal interview. 22 July 2014.

"Hamamatsu Ni Tsuiteno Data/Toukei." (Hamamatsu Statistics) www.hi-hice.jp. Hamamatsu Foundation for International Communications and Exchanges. Web.

"Heisei 26 nendo Hamamatsu-shi no Kokusaika Shisaku no Gaiyou." (2014 Hamamatsu Internationalization Plan Outline) Hamamatsu International Affairs Division, April 2014. Print.

"HICE no Gaiyou." (Outline of HICE's Development) www.hi-hice.jp/aboutus/outline.html. Hamamatsu Foundation for International Communications and Exchanges. Web.

"Kameyama Chiiki Sangyoo Kasseika Kihon Keikaku." (Kameyama Local Industry Basic Plan) City of Kameyama, 2012. Web.

"Kameyama Shisei Jouhou- Jinkou." (Kameyama City Information- Population) Kameyama City Government, Web. "KIFA Tanjoo." (Birth of KIFA) Kameyama International Friendship Association, 2006. Web.

Kitagawa. "Interview with Kameyama City Official." Phone interview. 19 November 2014.

Komai, Hiroshi. *Foreign Migrants in Contemporary Japan*. Melbourne: Trans Pacific, 2001. Print.

"Regional Information: Shizuoka." Investing in Japan. Japan External Trade Organization, July 2013. Web. 26 Oct. 2014.

"Registered Foreign Residents Statistics." Portal Site of Official Statistics of Japan. Ministry of Internal Affairs and Communications, 2013. Web.

Suzuki, Erika. "Interview with HICE Staff." Personal interview. 22 July 2014.

Tanaka, Yoshio. "Interview with KIFA Staff." Email interview. 16 November 2014.

"Toyota-shi No Kokusaika: Genjou to Torikumi." (Toyota City's Internationalization: On Present State and Initiatives) Toyota International Affairs Division, 2013. Print.

Tsuda, Takeyuki. *Strangers in the Ethnic Homeland: Japanese Brazilian Return Migration in Transnational Perspective*. New York: Columbia UP, 2003. Print.

# Part 4: Conclusion and Future Studies

Analysis of population demand, influence of NPOs, and focusing events reveal that one variable alone cannot influence the local government from providing high level of service for its immigrant population. These variables are interdependent, influencing one another in a chain of relationships that lead to influence on the local government. In addition, this particular study sheds light on several interesting points not only about Japan's population and immigrant dilemma, but also how the Japanese civil society sector functions, as well as the potential implications of the immigrant issue on Japan's future.

Overall, pluralist arguments explained the reasons behind local governments' motivation for providing services to its immigrant communities. As population of immigrants in the community increase, local governments are inclined to pay more attention to the needs of such group, and thus provide services that would enable immigrants to settle into the local community. However, population alone cannot explain what incentivizes these local governments from providing services. It is with the role of other factors, such as the NPO sector and historical memories related to immigrants, that motivates the local government to direct its attention to immigrant issues. Pluralist explanations are simply too general and insufficient to explain the causes of service provision among the Japanese local governments.

This study reveals that historical memories in forms of focusing events serve as a catalyst in increasing the level of service provision by the local governments. Population demand influences the chances of focusing events from occurring. As the case in Toyota indicates, growth in immigrant population increases the risks of such crises from occurring in communities, especially when the city government and the local community is not structurally and psychologically prepared to accommodate an influx of immigrants. On the other hand, occurrence of these events, when coupled with immigrant population growth, incentivizes the local governments to pay greater attention to the immigrant community's needs.

Focusing events, however, have long-lasting consequences that may impede future developments in establishing a stable immigration policy. While these events do encourage local governments to provide necessary services and incorporate the needs of the immigrant community, it nonetheless imprints negative, xenophobic attitudes into the minds of the Japanese public. As seen from the analysis of poll results in Toyota, focusing events influence local Japanese residents to eschew interacting with foreigners. While crises events provide a catalyst for higher level of services to be brought to the immigrant community, it is an issue that the city governments would obviously not want to experience as immigrant population increase in their community. In addition, focusing events provide the state government with important lessons for the future. When considering immigration as an alternative to increasing population and labor force, the Japanese national government must recognize that any influx of immigrants into its highly homogenous state is likely to invoke negative attitudes from the local community; moreover, the state government must first be sure that services and policies in these localities are developed extensively before immigrants begin to reside in these communities.

Perhaps the most interesting point of this study is the role of NPOs and Japanese civil society in advocating for immigrant issues. Highly effective NPOs are at the center of service provision among cities with high level of service provision. As seen in Toyota and Hamamatsu, these NPOs work hand-in-hand with the local government, who at times delegate majority of the responsibilities to these organizations. It is this particular relationship with the local government that makes a significant impact on the city's level of immigrant services.

This research reveals several characteristics unique to Japanese civil society sector. First, Japanese NPOs fail to fit the definition of advocacy groups that Keck and Sikkink utilize. Such model, often used to characterize NGOs in countries like the US, does not accurately explain with how Japanese NPOs function. From this research it is clear that Japanese NPOs that deal with immigrant issues do not necessarily advocate or lobby the governmental sector for a particular change. Through the process of contacting NPOs and asking them to interview for this research, it became evident that these NPOs were not like advocacy groups that seek public attention, support, and utilize them to lobby the government for change. These organizations were rather reluctant and eschewed interviews altogether; often times, NPOs that had close ties with the local government advised that the interview be directed to the local officials instead. Japanese NPOs working with immigrant issues appear to function predominantly as an extension of the local government; while they fulfill the responsibility of giving immigrants the access to services, lack of advocacy by the Japanese NPOs have implications on whether or not a stable immigration policy can be established at the local and national level. If the current NPOs do not actively advocate or lobby the local and national government to change their policies, what actors or organizations would take on such advocacy roles? Does such attitude among the NPOs exist in other issue-related fields, or is this primarily found in groups dealing with immigration issues, simply because it is a controversial topic that Japan has avoided for so long? Are there cultural and historical reasons to why Japanese civil society sector functions in a way that these organizations are not necessarily free of bureaucratic influence? While explanations behind these questions were touched upon in throughout this study, deeper investigation into these concerns in future research may improve the understanding of the role that the Japanese civil sector has on the immigrant community, as well as the potential impact that it has on the future of policymaking in the field of immigration.

Another point of interest that should be investigated in future studies is the role of the nation-wide coalition CLCFP. While its role as a coalition for local cities to discuss issues related to immigration were discussed in this study, further research on the CLCFP may shed light on how the coalition may be the key factor to influence the future course of Japanese immigration policy. Will the CLCFP activities, petitions and reports be successful in the future in influencing the national government to establish an official immigration policy? The effectiveness of the CLCFP on the national government is an interesting future subject of study.

Nonetheless, it is clear that local governments are at the helm of interacting with immigrant communities, working to accommodate for their needs and integrating them to the local Japanese community. The national government should refer to methods that these local governments and NPOs utilize to integrate immigrants into their community, especially as immigration is becoming increasingly necessary for the Japanese society and economy. The national government should also refer to these local efforts to learn and understand the key issues that immigrants face in Japan, the critical services that they need to be able to work and contribute to the local economy, and how cultural differences between the local Japanese residents and immigrants can be mitigated to foster mutual understanding and tolerance. Examples from local community efforts in accommodating immigrants will provide the national government with information and cases necessary to create a stable and working immigration policy.

As mentioned briefly in the introduction, immigration is a topic that Japan can no longer avoid. With Tokyo Olympics 2020 in sight, Japan is under pressure to build and establish solid infrastructure system that would enable Tokyo to host millions from around the globe. One of the concerns debated among the Japanese society is the cost and labor force necessary to build these infrastructures by the time of the Olympic Games. Many are concerned that with a steadily graying and declining labor force, Japan would not finish these architectural projects in time for the Games. Without a larger labor force, Tokyo would not be prepared to host the Olympics—but as mentioned throughout this research, current Japanese policies do not allow legal immigration of unskilled workers. It appears that Tokyo's future goals and ambitions as a host city for 2020 Olympic Games will be the catalyst necessary to initiate discussions about immigration among the Japanese government and public. Perhaps the national government will look to establishing a formal immigration policy—and perhaps it will refer to its local counterparts for example and advice on the services and accommodations necessary for the state to smoothly integrate immigrations into the country.

## Acknowledgements

I could not have finished this work without the support of USC Dornsife College and its generous funding programs, which my study abroad and research in Japan possible. A heartfelt thank you to Professors Robert English, Nina Rathbun and Saori Katada at the SIR. Their patience and guidance has been integral from the drafting of the proposal to the last drafts of the thesis. They've showed me how stimulating and wonderful the academic community can be, and made me a little tougher too. Thank you to my fellow 2014 Honors Program students for all their support. All of you are some of the brightest, hard-working and humorous people I know—I'm blessed to have learned so much from all of you. To my friends at USC who were patient with me during my hectic semester, thank you. Special thanks to my roommates Sara, April and Anokhy for being supportive listeners, and waking me up when I fell asleep at my desk writing. Last but not least, to my parents, for giving me the freedom to do everything that I've wanted to do and always supporting me 100 percent. Without you I wouldn't be who I am today. All the great opportunities I've had in my life are because of you two. Thank you and I love you both.

# 3

# Tunisian and Egyptian Military Intervention

# in the Arab Uprisings and Post-Uprising State Transitions

*Elizabeth Peabody*

*In the winter and spring of 2011, a string of popular uprisings termed the Arab Spring swept across the states of the Middle East and North Africa region, protesting decades of authoritarian, repressive rule. Two of these popular uprisings, those in Tunisia and Egypt, succeeded in removing the authoritarian ruler – Ben Ali and Mubarak, respectively – from power. In both cases, the military institution played an essential role in the success of the uprising, refusing the regime leaders' directives to fire on the people. After the uprisings, however, the Tunisian military retreated to its barracks while the Egyptian military inserted itself into the lead role in the political transition. This thesis examines the historical factors that determine the role of military intervention in the state uprisings and post-uprising political transitions, focusing primarily on the catalytic role of the relationship between the military and leader.*

In a wave of popular dissent protesting decades of authoritarian rule, the string of uprisings termed the Arab Spring swept across many of the countries of the Middle East and North Africa region (MENA) beginning in the winter and spring of 2011. Since then, many scholars have questioned why some of the Arab uprisings were successful in overturning the regime in power while others were not. The study of these questions have focused primarily on the role of the populace - unemployed youth populations and the prevalence of social media – in the uprisings, but in MENA, another major determinant of a popular uprising's success in overthrowing the authoritarian regime leadership was the intervention by the state's military. In many cases, the militaries in the Arab countries of the MENA region fill prominent roles in the states' societies and government hierarchies. In the 2011 uprisings, the military's decision to intervene either on the side of the regime leadership or that of the popular uprising largely determined whether the regime would topple or retain power.

This thesis explores the historical factors that determine the role of a military's intervention in a popular uprising and, if the uprising is successful, the state's subsequent post-uprising political transitions. Few scholars have examined the role of the military institutions in the Arab uprisings. By studying the cases of Tunisia and Egypt and their militaries' roles in each respective uprising and post-uprising transition, we can critically analyze the factors that determine how a state will emerge from an uprising as a result of its military. For both countries, the absence of military action in the 2011 uprisings was a precondition for regime change. After the uprisings occurred and the authoritarian regimes were overturned, however, the paths of the two countries diverged. Why did these two militaries, similar in many respects, intervene differently in state politics after the authoritarian regime leaders in their country had been removed? How did the pre-existing characteristics of these two militaries affect their intervention and lead their respective countries in two directions: in Tunisia, towards democracy, and in Egypt, towards military-based authoritarian rule?

While very few scholars have analyzed the role of military intervention in the Arab uprisings, the general literature of military intervention in governmental politics is relatively substantial, especially after regional waves of military intervention in state politics that occurred throughout the 20th century. Many countries in Latin America, for example, experienced such a wave in the 1960's and 1970's. As a result of these regional waves, scholars have already extensively examined factors that explain military intervention in state transitions. The cornerstone theories of this body of literature began with Samuel Huntington's thesis (1957) that higher levels of professionalization in Third World militaries would transition a military's focus to an apolitical concentration on national defense. In contrast, Alfred Stepan (1971) argued that a professionalized military would instead play a moderating role in the state until a satisfactory government could be created. This type of moderating military would then step down from political affairs when a new civilian government was elected.

But the Latin American wave of military intervention undermined Stepan and Huntington's theories, and promoted other theories to explain the observed phenomena. O'Donnell's bureaucratic authoritarianism theory (1978) describes military intervention as a result of a Third World country's frustration in attempting to overcome developmental barriers to capitalism, and, specifically, the military's role as the protective institution of the distressed middle class in such situations. Finer (1962) proposed evaluating the level of the military's political intrusion based on its relationship with various civilian elements of society, such as police forces and constitutional channels, on a scale from influence to blackmail to complete displacement of those civilian elements. In many ways building off of Finer's theories, Stepan (1988) revised his cornerstone theory to better explain the variation in military intervention by outlining "military prerogatives" in political intrusion – focusing on numerous factors, including the military's constitutional role in the political system and its relationship with the government and police forces – where the military assumes that its societal role grants it the right to intervene in politics for the protection of the country. Zagorski's national security doctrine theory (1992) described military intervention through a different lens. For him, the common training and educational experience of Third World militaries in Cold War tactics by global powers (an example of military-military relationships for soft power purposes), and learning to focus more on internal security, made them more likely to intervene in governmental politics to retain control over this security. Most recently, Farcau (1996) pointed out that the above theories focus too much on the military as an institution. He proposes that a focus on factional interests within inter-military cliques is a better way to understand military intervention.

This extensive body of literature points to a wealth of possible military factors that could be useful in explaining the decisions of the militaries in the Tunisian and Egyptian cases. This thesis draws from the above literature and examines certain factors of the military that affected decision-making during and after 2011, focusing especially on the historical precedents of the military and its relationship with the regime leadership, the regime's security apparatus, and civilian institutions. This focus includes factors such as the constitutional constraints on the militaries in constitutions prior to the uprisings, control of the military by the regime, use of the military in past wars, revolutions, and international cooperation, the relationship of the military with the police forces, the societal image of the military and public perception of the institution, and class conflict and factional disputes within the military itself.

In assessing these theories, this thesis employs a qualitative study that utilizes two central research methods: cross-case comparisons between Tunisia and Egypt and within-case process tracing that examines the affect of the above described military characteristics on decision-making and involvement in post-conflict political transitions. Process tracing allows me to examine for each case the causal mechanisms affecting each factor of the military, its decision-making, and involvement, as well as the combination of factors that together form the military's defining characteristics. This method allows me to evaluate whether events unfolded consistently with the logic of theory and determine in which ways events are unique to the specific situation. Employing a path dependent argument, such as historical precedents of the militaries' experiences pre-2011, allows me to analyze how contingent events and practices created institutional patterns that in turn formed the military's nature and led to its intervention in the uprising and in state politics. Cross-case comparisons, meanwhile, highlight the differences in military characteristics between the two chosen cases and show how these differences in military history and relationship with the state may have led to the different outcomes experienced.

I measure the above-mentioned variables by looking at class conflict within the military and I examine the precedence of factional disputes within the military institution prior to the uprising and how these factional interactions affected the military's relationship with the state. For constitutional constraints, versions of the state constitution prior to the uprisings show the level to which the military was constricted by regime politics. Control of the regime by the military can be measured through authoritarian leader-military leader relationships and commands. Prior intervention of the military in the past involves examining the number and extent of prior wars, revolutions, coups, and international cooperation efforts. The relationship of the military with the police forces and mukhabarat can be measured in instances of one institution imposing or attempting to impose control, constraints, or violence on the other. Finally, the societal image of the military can be measured through public opinion, reactions of the populace to military actions and leaders, and the interaction of the civilian conscripts and the officer corps. I am not evaluating the military's role against other factors to explain the state transitions in Tunisia and Egypt. Instead, I argue that the military's lack of intervention in a popular conflict is a precondition for regime change, and that the military is a critical factor in political transitions and the state's ability to transition to civilian-controlled democracy.

## Literature Review

In the last three years, a diverse body of literature has developed that examines the factors leading to the Arab uprisings. Various scholars try to explain the unexpectedness of the uprisings and the apparent durability of the authoritarian regimes that have controlled the states in the region for the last half-century; theories of revolution and democratization try to explain the rapidity and spread of the uprisings throughout the Arab regimes. However, the existing literature attempting to explain the causes of the Arab uprisings focuses primarily on the various roles of the populace in social change. As will be described below, scholars examining the social structures of Arab authoritarian-ruled countries before the uprisings deemed them "weak societies" because of the society's inability or unwillingness to challenge the authoritarian government, but cite certain catalysts that can inspire the society to act – such as the success of an uprising in a different country. Another common theory highlights the "youth bulge" in the Middle East – the large proportion of the population in the region under 30 years of age – and this age group's knowledge of technology/social media as a catalyst behind the causes of the uprisings. In this vein of literature, the role of the military is deemed at most secondary to other social factors.

Though not an academic source, the first documented analysis of the factors behind the Arab uprisings was The Economist's "Shoe-Thrower Index" from February of 2011. After observing the first month of the uprisings in Tunisia and Egypt, the Index attempted to predict the location of the next Arab uprising by listing possible determinants of instability, such as the percentage of youth population under 25, the length of time the government retained power, GDP per person, censorship of media, and level of corruption and lack of democracy (The Economist, 2011). Only a month after the Arab uprisings had begun in Tunisia, the article inspired scholars of the region, so accustomed to the robustness of the authoritarian Arab regimes, to begin studying the unexpected phenomena that were occurring.

John Pollack (2011) focuses particularly on the youth bulge in Tunisia and Egypt and cites the secret organization Takriz – a pro-revolutionary "cyber think-tank" based in Tunisia – as the primary catalyst in inspiring the youth of Tunisia to come together to form the uprising. As young people are more likely to be proficient in technology and social media – and the elderly authoritarian governments not so much – this group of society was able to mobilize in a way that other groups in the past were not. Nordas & Davenport (2013) also focused on the role of the youth population: the idea that authoritarian governments are aware of the existence of the disproportionate amount of young people within their borders and will specifically target government oppression towards that group. However, in the case of the Arab uprisings, the youth population had a weapon – the knowledge of technology that Pollack speaks of – that the government was not able to fully keep in check. Clarke (2014) focused her study on civil society as a whole, not simply the youth bulge. She asserted that the uprising in Egypt was primarily the result of societal groups – once "weak" and unwilling or unable to challenge the legitimacy of the regime – that were inspired by the success of Tunisia's uprising. These groups consequently brokered a reconfiguration of Egyptian social networks that better assisted the society as a whole to more cohesively work together towards removing Mubarak's regime.

The Arab Spring literature's focus on civil society, youth populations, and technology – together, the role of the populace – identifies the people as a primary cause of the uprisings. However, looking at the pattern of successes and failures of the uprisings across the Middle East, it is clear that only considering the various effects of civil society on the uprisings is not sufficient in determining whether the uprising would succeed. In Tunisia and Egypt, as will be demonstrated in this thesis, the military played a differential role in both the 2011 uprising and the political transition that followed.

In both cases, as mentioned previously, the military institution chose to ignore the regime's command to fire on the people. The role of the military in the uprising, and the choice to side with either the populace or the regime, must be considered when evaluating the potential success of an uprising. From there, the role of the military institution in the political transition post-uprising – whether the military intervenes in politics or removes itself from them – also determines the long-term success of the uprising and the transition from authoritarian rule to democracy. Considering the importance of these decisions, I will explore the factors behind the military's choice of intervention in the uprising and post-uprising political transitions. The literature on military intervention in state transitions is extensive, and, while in many cases it may refer to the militaries of other regions, it will be important to apply these theories to the military institutions of the MENA region.

Military Intervention in State Uprisings

The militaries in the Arab countries of the MENA region are highly professionalized institutions that fill prominent roles in the states' societies and government hierarchies. As a result, a major factor behind the success in overthrowing the regime and subsequent democratic transition is the level of intervention of the state's military. In 2011, the military's decision to intervene largely determined whether the regime leader would retain or lose power. While few scholars focus on military intervention during the string of Arab uprisings in 2011, as well as the civil-military factors that led to this intervention, there is an extensive literature on military intervention in other regions from which I can draw.

The literature on military intervention in governmental politics is substantial, explaining regional waves of military intervention in state politics that occurred throughout the 20th century. To better understand military intervention in the state transitions during the Arab uprisings, as well as the decision-making of the military institutions, it is helpful to first examine the body of literature explaining military intervention in another region that experienced a wave of transition: Latin America. Many countries in Latin America experienced such a wave in the 1960's and 1970's. This wave of military intervention in politics caused a surge in scholars studying the phenomenon. Over time, a substantial body of literature seeking to explain military intervention began to emerge.

The cornerstone of the literature on military intervention in state politics was Samuel Huntington's The Soldier and the State (1957). Huntington asserted that increasing the level of professionalism of the militaries in Third World countries would eliminate the "illegal intervention" of the military in governmental politics. In Latin America, for example, what had been disorganized, "armed mobs" of political dissenters in the nineteenth century became professionalized militaries in the twentieth century. Huntington hypothesized that such professionalization would force the officer corps to focus solely on military matters and avoid intervening in state politics, much like the American and British militaries had done. The military institution, in order to be effective, was required to separate itself from the civilian society and their politics in order for modernized development to occur.

The common critique of Huntington's theory was that it applied mostly to established democracies, rather than transitioning regimes (Barany, 2012). How do we explain the level of military influence, or the range of behavior within military actions that fall between a coup d'état and full compliance with a civilian government? Such measurement is inherently difficult because of the complexity of the potential cases and the range of factors that could affect the military institution's decision to intervene in state transitions. In an attempt to describe civil-military relations across all manners of government structures, Finer (1962) explained a military's political intrusion based on its relationship with various civilian elements of society, and categorized these relationships with civilian elements on a scale ranging between slight influence of the military on civilian institutions, to blackmail of those institutions, to the displacement of those institutions. While Finer's strategy measured military intervention, a critique of his measurement suggests that it does not take into account other factors influencing the military outside of civilian institutions, such as the military's own inner factions and politics. In describing a military institution's relationship with the governing regime and civil society, more specific theories – and less generalization – became more of the standard.

The first major example of this type of theory was Alfred Stepan (1971), who, in his exploration of military decision-making for intervention in state politics and uprisings, suggested that militaries in developing Third World countries tend to conform to the idea of the "moderator principle." In this model, the militaries are highly professionalized, deeply respected institutions within the state. As a result, the military institution is "wooed" by political actors and groups in order to achieve some level of governmental legitimacy. Whenever a political group or actor came to power that had not deferred its interests to the military institution and was therefore not acceptable to govern from the military's perspective, it would be the military's role to step in and govern – for a short period of time – until new elections could be had. In essence, the basic goal of a "moderating military" was simply to fix a political situation that had overstepped the military's control, and then quickly return to its own business of national defense. (As described by Farcau in his critique of Stepan in The Transition to Democracy in Latin America (1996)).

What Stepan's moderator principle does not explain are the instances when the military does not limit itself to solely a moderating role. In many cases in the Latin American wave, as well as other cases around the world, the military that originally saw itself as simply the moderator would overstep its bounds and postpone elections and civilian rule until changes could be made to better the state's society – essentially taking control of society until it could be improved by what the military deemed to be its own advanced outlook. The Latin American wave of state transitions in the 1960's and 1970's illustrated this point perfectly: the militaries of the region undertook "the running of the entire society to a degree never before observed" (Farcau, 1996). These events undermined Stepan's and Huntington's theories, instead promoting other theories to explain these phenomena: what Stepan (1973) now called "the new professionalism" (and what Zagorski (1992) later termed "national security doctrine theory").

Stepan (1973) argued that the new focus on internal security and national development would lead inevitably to an expansion of the military's role in the state. But Stepan added that another variable in the state system also played a role in allowing the military to assume this role. A weak civilian government, for example, would not be able to provide and supervise the development process as well as the military – now a stronger institution with the new professionalism – might have believed it could provide. As a result, weaker governments provided greater tendencies for the military to intervene in state politics and impose their own idea of how the state should develop. A version of this theory could be applied to the events in Egypt following the 2011 uprising: the Egyptian military, powerful and professionalized, was able to insert itself into the leading political role, monitor an alliance with the Muslim Brotherhood political party, and remove the elected government when the military felt it was too singularly focused to account for its own interests and the general interests of Egypt.

In a similar vein, Guillermo O'Donnell (1978) also explored why a military might deem itself more qualified to run the government than the government itself. Responding to the modernization theory that a state's economic development would lead to democracy, O'Donnell argued that such developing Third World economies might hit barriers towards further, more First World-like development. In the state society's struggle to overcome these barriers, the middle class would find itself increasingly overburdened with taxes while the smaller, minority capitalist class endeavored to push society even further towards economic prosperity enjoyed by more developed countries. Such societal conflict would in turn lead to frustration within the governing body, and leaders of the military would believe it to be the best qualified institution to intervene in government affairs and restructure society to better assist the majority middle class – from whence many of the military's officers and conscripts came. The theory hypothesizes that the struggle of the middle class in an increasingly capitalism-driven, Third World society would inspire the military to act on the behalf of the middle class. In the MENA region, especially in Tunisia and to some extent in Egypt, the military institution did in fact intervene militarily or in negotiations on behalf of the middle class – though there may have been other motives for intervention as well – in order to protect the interests of the greater populace. And while these two countries are not of the Third World, their reasons for intervention are similar to the events in Latin American instances.

With the Cold War mentality and the rise of communism, state governments were forced to focus equally on enemies from within the state as from the outside. National security doctrine, Zagorski (1992) argued, was the adaptation of militaries and governments to the change in the nature of warfare from total war (the concept of states fighting only other states) to the new "unconventional" warfare. Such an approach was encouraged and taught by the United States to its Third World allied countries – especially in Latin America, as the US wanted to ensure that its southern flank was protected from the spread of communism. To solidify this goal, the US military held joint training exercises and warfare instruction in the Latin American countries, supposedly "teaching" their Cold War doctrine to the militaries. As a result, the now-highly trained militaries began to view themselves as most advanced aspects of their countries' society, and therefore that the military institution was obligated to ensure national defense through the complete control of society until inner threats could be eliminated. While Zagorski specifically references the case of Latin America in his theory, the idea of military-military relationships between a great power state and a developing country could also apply to the Middle Eastern states during the 20th century, when powers such as France and Britain held mandate power over MENA and in many cases assisted in the training and development of the military institution.

Kiers' 1995 discussion of the importance of a military's culture uses the example of the French army between the two World Wars to illustrate that the choice to pursue a specific doctrine – whether offensive or defensive – is not a calculated response to the external, international environment.

Instead, civilian and military policymakers, who maintain beliefs about how the military should be organized and what its role should be in society, are those who form military doctrine. Military cultures differ widely between countries based on each state's interests and worldview, and are shaped by the institution's responses to constraints set my civilian policymakers. In this way, scholars can understand a military's decision-making by examining the institution's culture as the government shapes it. While Kiers' argument examines the French military – and therefore the military culture of a global power, instead of the smaller Arab states that I examine in this thesis – her focus on the importance of military culture, and the interaction between military culture and the governing regime, can inform discussions of the relationships between the Egyptian and Tunisian leaders and their military counterparts.

Farcau (1996) differs from the above-discussed theories because of their tendency to treat the military as a single entity. To him, these theories rely too heavily on the idea that the military institution represents one common ideology and set of values, and assume that the officers in power adopt common operational codes. As such, these theories do not acknowledge the possibility of individual decision-making within the military institution. Farcau argues that, in understanding the role of the military as an institution, it is essential to also understand the competing goals and values of the individual officers and factions. The actions of factions and individual leaders within the military institution are crucial in determining the course of action taken by the military. This is because such individualistic theories can explain the anomalies that are unaccounted for in the more overarching theories, where the military's decision-making is analyzed as that of a collective body.

Farcau draws much of the ideas relevant to this thesis from the works of Dixon (1976) and Janowitz (1988). Dixon, a trained psychologist, former military officer, and theorist of "the military mind," proposed that the military lifestyle should attract only certain types of people: those who require security and uniformity in their surroundings, appreciate stable structure in their work, and welcome a legal outlet for their aggression. As a result, those officers who are talented enough within the military institution's framework to rise through the ranks will be particularly suited to this lifestyle and these constraints. Therefore, the top officers – the ones who will be making decisions that affect the institution as a whole – are likely to be more aggressive, assertive, and bureaucratic than the average civilian, and are more likely to believe that it is within the military's legal duty to take charge of the state's governmental politics. For Dixon, it is this individual-based mentality that leads to military intervention in politics.

Janowitz (1988) also acknowledges that military figures will naturally have a certain type of ambitious mind, and such people recognize and work within the nature of the hierarchical structure within the military institution. In this case, only a few people occupy the top leadership positions within the military institution, with limited opportunities for sub-leadership. As a result, factions of inferior officers that represent the personal followings and ambitions of these top leaders are quick to develop and, from there, in many cases, eventually materialize into politically driven groups. This is especially the case in militaries whose institutional cultures are highly connected with state politics.

Finally and most recently, Pop-Eleches and Robertson (2014) examine the decision-making of elite players and institutions – such as "specialists in coercion like the military and security forces"

(Pop-Eleches & Robertson, 6) – when confronted with elections in authoritarian regime states. In many authoritarian regimes, including those in the MENA region, state politics are governed primarily by the regime leader, but also by an "incumbent leadership" that creates a political coalition of elite players with a wide range of interests and resources at their disposal. These elite players, argue Pop-Eleches and Robertson, are pivotal in deciding the fate of the regime: as long as they ally themselves with the regime, and the regime continues to make it worth their while to do so, the regime will most easily remain stable. However, if some or all of the elites split from the ruling party, for whatever reason, and form their own opposition movement, the regime's legitimacy is in danger, and the presence of elections in state politics can best provide these opposing elites with a platform to overpower the regime. Depending on the state, some elite groups can be termed pivotal: their participation in the ruling regime determines its ability to retain authoritarian control. This concept of an elite institution directly affecting the regime's authoritarian control is especially useful to keep in mind when examining the authoritarian regimes in MENA – especially states like Tunisia and Egypt, where the militaries both occupied some form of elite role in civil society, and where both militaries eventually were able to depose the ruling regime once the institution's interests defected from those of the ruling party.

Application to the Arab Uprisings in Egypt and Tunisia

The body of literature discussed above was originally intended to describe the circumstances of military intervention in Latin American government transitions in the 1960's and 1970's. Despite the intended regional focus, however, such theories form the base of the overarching body of theory of military intervention. As a result, the theories can be carefully applied to other regions experiencing unrest, and therefore can inform this study's analysis of the factors that explain the Tunisian and Egyptian militaries' choices. According to Grand (2014), the regions of Latin America and MENA had similar historical backgrounds in certain fundamental ways, which can explain why military intervention theories directed towards the Latin American experience could be loosely applied to the cases of the Arab uprisings in MENA. Both regions were shaped by colonialism and then subsequent authoritarian regimes, both regions suffered from state-dominated economies that caused economic inequality, and both regions were "pawns" played by the US and Soviet Union during the Cold War when the superpowers provided their client countries with political, economic, and military support in exchange for ideological allegiance.

Prior to the Arab uprisings, only a few scholars attempted to describe the role of civil-military relations in the authoritarian Arab regimes. Cook (2007) explored the role of the military in the robustness of the authoritarian regimes in Egypt, Algeria, and Turkey. He argues that the military institution's pervasion into the political system of the country is based on the military's desire to retain four "core interests:" economic dominance, control over the state's security and foreign policy, political manipulation, and control over the nationalist narrative in favor of the military institution. This argument suggests the path dependency of informal military control of the civil society since independence; in other words, the military controls the regime and not the other way around. The military institution can therefore remove or replace the regime when it believes its interests are no longer the regime's priority. Cook's argument does not, however, take into account the historical precedents of Arab regimes' numerous strategies to protect themselves from military coups during the latter half of the 20th century, which, as I will argue in this thesis, prevented the military institution from achieving the control that it desired and in many ways led to its intervention in 2011.

In contrast to the idea that the military controls the regime, Brooks (1998) discussed in her cases of Egypt, Syria, and Jordan the regime's use of certain factors to "coup-proof" the regime from potential military coups. She cites as these factors the use of economic patronage, frequent officer purges and co-optation, and the minimization of coalition politics to prevent officer factions within the military institution from taking the initiative to intervene in politics if the regime is not satisfactorily addressing military interests. Quinlivan (1999), though focusing on the cases of Saudi Arabia, Syria, and Iraq, also describes the combination of co-optation, coercion, and control of the military by the regime in longstanding Arab regimes. This body of theory gives more weight to the regime's ability to control the military through various strategies, which seems to better explain the Tunisian and Egyptian militaries' decisions in 2011. If, as Cook suggested, the militaries are able to overthrow the regime whenever it is best for the institution's interests, it could be argued that these militaries would have accomplished this decades before 2011. Instead, as I will argue, the amalgamation of multiple factors – all coming to a head in 2011 – allowed the military to intervene in a way it had not had the opportunity to do before.

What is missing from the already existing analyses of the Arab uprisings, and the void that I hope to help fill, is a detailed comparison analyzing the factors that caused the Tunisian and Egyptian militaries to intervene in the uprising, and the differences in the two institutions that led to their intervention – or lack thereof – in the political transition that followed. Above all, this study seeks to show that military intervention was a necessary, though not sufficient, condition for regime change, and to explain why the paths of the militaries and their roles in post-uprising political transitions diverged. Based on the above theories, and on a thorough examination of other sources specifically regarding the Egyptian and Tunisian cases, I focus on two categories of factors (described below in Table 1) that, when taken together, appear to capture the most important aspects of civil/military relations and military decision-making highlighted in the existing literature: the regime-military relationship and the military culture. Analysis of these six factors also provides the potential to illuminate those most relevant in shaping the outcomes of the 2011 uprisings in MENA, and specifically to explain those uprisings in Tunisia and Egypt.

| Category | Factors within the category |
|---|---|
| Regime/governing institution-military relationship | Regime leader – military relationship |
| | Police/intelligence forces – military relationship |
| | Control by state constitutions |
| | Past military interventions |
| Military culture | Class conflict within the military |
| | Public perception/image of the military |

Table 1: The six factors I will be discussing in this thesis and their organization into the two categories.

The first category of factors, focusing on the relationship between the military and the regime/governing institution, will demonstrate the interaction of the military with civilian institutions such as the police forces and mukhabarat (intelligence forces utilized by the regime); the relationship between the military and the authoritarian leader; the control of the military institution by the state constitutions prior to the 2011 uprising; and the prior interventions by the military in the state wars, coups, or international coalition efforts. The impact of the governing institution on the military will help to explain the formation of the military institution's interests and how those interests were supported or marginalized during the period of authoritarian rule.

The second category of factors focuses on the military culture within the institution and in the state's civil society: for this category, I examine the class conflict within the military institution and the image of the military in the public sphere and public opinion. This category of factors presents the impact of the inner workings of the institution and the effects of the military culture on the interaction with external actors such as the regime and civil society. As there has been so little exploration regarding the role of the military in the Arab uprisings, and because of the timing and close proximity of the events, the overarching goal of this thesis will be to set groundwork for future studies of the region and the ongoing military interventions there.

## Research Methods

Acknowledging that other scholars and fields of study may point to different factors in regards to the effects leading to military intervention in the Arab uprisings, I chose the six factors described above based on an amalgamation of thorough examination of the literature surrounding the Latin American experience, interviews with experts of the region, and extensive research specific to the historical precedence of the militaries in Tunisia and Egypt. To best measure the factors included in the first category regarding regime-military relationship, I will employ an analysis of the critical junctures and the path dependent processes leading to the military's intervention during and after the Arab uprisings.

Path-dependent analysis relies on three basic foundational points regarding the causal mechanisms of the events being studied: one, that the causal processes are highly sensitive to earlier events in the historical process being studied; two, that these early historical events affecting the causal processes are contingent events that are not easily explainable or that fall into normal theory; and three, that the contingent historical events set into motion processes that reflect a particular outcome (Mahoney, 2000). In studying military intervention in the Arab uprisings, especially the cases of Tunisia and Egypt, path-dependent analysis illuminates the causal mechanisms that began with the contingent events that brought about both states' presidential authoritarian era: the 1952 Free Officer coup in Egypt and the 1956 independence agreement in Tunisia. In Egypt, the military institution played an indispensable – if not causal – role in separating the country from British colonial influence and instituting presidential authoritarian rule. Playing such an essential role in Egypt's modern politics allowed the military to maintain a guiding influence in the chain of events following the removal of the monarchy. In Tunisia, meanwhile, the military was marginalized and controlled by the regime immediately following independence, and the regime continued to co-opt the military institution through the remainder of authoritarian rule.

Presented graphically below, the factors that I have identified for scrutiny would suggest that we can measure both categories of factors – the regime-military relationship category and the military culture category – using path-dependent analysis with a focus on the interaction between the two categories. Using the transitions from colonial and monarchical control to presidential authoritarian rule in Tunisia and Egypt in the 1950's as contingent events that set into motion the policies, interactions, and decisions that would determine the military's role in the state for the next sixty years, we can observe which factors most affected each military to act as they did during the 2011 uprisings and in the political transitions that followed.

Table 2 (right) presents each of the six factors to be discussed in this thesis and, in the second column, the indicators that we might expect to see if each of those factors are salient in the national case.

Within the category of factors describing the military's relationship with the governing regime, there are four factors to examine. First, looking at the relationship between the military and the regime leader, I examine the interactions and relationships between the regime leader and the military leaders: how the regime leader co-opted, marginalized, or imprisoned or destroyed military leaders, whether the regime called on the military when needed or instead relied on the police or intelligence forces, whether the leader encouraged or forced the military personnel to remain apolitical, or whether the military retained power over the regime leader, and to what degree – through influence, blackmail, or the ability to overturn the regime. The second factor, closely tied to the regime leader's relationship with the military, is the military's relationship with the police and intelligence sectors. Which branch does the regime leader favor, and subordinate to the other? Is the military ever called upon to subdue police or intelligence forces, or do the intelligence forces marginalize and subdue the military? How do military leaders view the police and intelligence forces?

The third factor examines the control of the military by the state constitutions prior to the 2011 uprisings. For this factor, I assess how the constitutions address the military, the rights the military institution is given, whom the military institution reports to in the government (a civilian or a military leader), the military's right to intervene in the civilian government if needed or try in court those

| Factor | Indicators |
|---|---|
| Regime leader – military relationship | Leader co-opts, coerces, imprisons, etc. the military leaders<br>Leader encouraging or forcing military to remain apolitical/"in the barracks" OR military institution holds power over leader (through blackmail, influence, arms) |
| Police/intelligence – military relationship | Regime leader favors military branch or intelligence branch<br>Military called upon to subdue police forces<br>Military leaders' interactions with the police/intelligence leaders |
| Military presence in state constitutions | Rights given to the military institution<br>Military institution led by civilian or military leader in government<br>Military's rights to intervene in government<br>Military's rights to try civilians in military court |
| Military intervention pre-2011 | Prior military intervention in coups, wars, revolutions, or international coalitions<br>Military chooses to respond to these interventions, or is ordered by leader;<br>Military has specific interests in the conflict & positive outcome of conflict |
| Class conflict within military institution | Prevalence of class conflict as a result of stratification of officers/lower echelons<br>Conscript armies are forced to labor when not in wartime<br>Opportunities for upward mobility within institution<br>Instances of conflict within military based on these class distinctions |
| Public opinion of military; military's image | Positive public opinion of the military (the institution is morally sound and concerned primarily with the interests of the state; it is considered an honor to serve the military)<br>Instances of the military inviting the public to participate in military events<br>Positive reactions from populace when military intervenes in society |

it deems a threat to the institution. Finally, for the fourth factor of the regime/military category, I examine military interventions prior to 2011 in coups, revolutions, wars, or international cooperation conflicts, how the military has responded to these crises, the military institution's specific interests in the conflict, the outcome of the conflict, and whether the military chose to intervene or was ordered to do so.

The second category examines each military's culture within the institution and in the public sphere. Within the institution, I examine the prevalence of class conflict as a result of stratification of conscripts and officers, opportunities for upward mobility, the perception of each class by the rest of the military institution, and instances of conflict within the institution based on these class differences. Regarding the image of the military in the public sphere, I examine public opinion of the military, whether they believed the institution to be morally sound and concerned with the interests of the state, whether it was considered an honor to serve in the military, instances of the military inviting the populace to participate in military cultural events, and the reactions of the populace when the military intervened in some aspect of society.

Using in-depth country case studies, which look first at the case of Egypt and then that of Tunisia, I will explore how the factors described above influenced the military to act as it did in the 2011 uprising and the state transitions that followed. The mechanisms that these factors create present a cycle of events beginning with each country's shift to presidential authoritarianism in the 1950's and continue through the authoritarian era until its end in the 2011 uprisings. In many ways, as will be argued in the cases, the factor that acted as the catalyst for these mechanisms, as well as the emergence of the remaining five factors discussed here, was the regime leader's relationship with the military.

In Egypt, it is the military's crucial and intimate association with the president that ensures the continuity of Egypt's political system (Cook, 73). The president commanded the military, and manipulated, coerced, subordinated and coopted the military institution in order to maintain his power over it. At the same time, however, the president and the military share interests and worldviews and were socialized in the same manner (all four of Egypt's presidents from 1952-2011 were military men). Because of these similar interests, the officer corps repeatedly found that it could influence political events through the president. The president would then need to find new ways to control the military in order to retain power over it. This mutually reinforcing relationship – illustrated below in Figure 1 – determined the military's actions and in many ways created the institution's relationship with the public and the police forces, as well as the military culture and the instances of intervention. The path dependent sequence of events produced by this cycle eventually led the military's interests to align with the popular uprising in 2011, and to refuse the president's order to fire on the people. After the uprising, however, the Egyptian military inserted itself into the lead role in state politics, creating the current military authoritarian government that we can observe today and adding a significant obstacle to Egypt's path to civilian-led democracy.

Figure 1 (next page): PRIOR TO THE UPRISINGS: Reinforcing mechanisms that describe the power struggle cycle between the regime leadership and military institution prior to the 2011 uprising. When the regime is no longer able to respond with coercion, the military will take power from the regime for its own interests and/or the interests of the state.

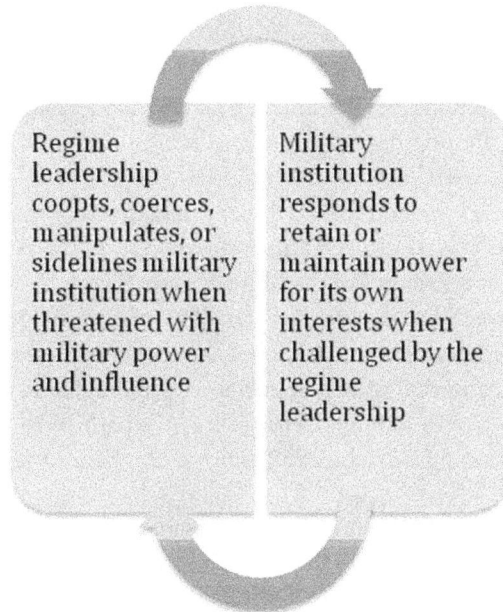

Regime leadership coopts, coerces, manipulates, or sidelines military institution when threatened with military power and influence

Military institution responds to retain or maintain power for its own interests when challenged by the regime leadership

In Tunisia, the president-military relationship also demonstrated the mutually reinforcing cycle displayed in Figure 1, though in a different way. Though one of the two authoritarian era presidents was military educated, both presidents bred the military institution to be entirely apolitical and uninvolved in state politics or economics. As a result, the Tunisian military had no particular loyalty or lack thereof to the regime, but instead focused its efforts on the protection of the Tunisian state and its interests. When the regime leadership threatened the interests of the state or of the people, the military would bargain with the leadership to fix the issues. Both presidents still considered the military a threat to their power, however, and manipulated, coerced, or coopted the institution in ways similar to those of the Egyptian case. By the 2011 uprising, the military's interests aligned with the popular uprisings, and the military ousted Ben Ali. From there, however, the military retreated to the barracks and allowed a civilian government to take over state politics. The military institution's apolitical culture, originally created by the regime leadership, removed the military as an obstacle to civilian-led democracy.

How did two countries with such different regime leader–military relationships lead to such similar outcomes in the Arab uprisings, and what accounted for this discrepancy? Nasser and Bourguiba, the two initial authoritarian leaders in Egypt and Tunisia, respectively, both came to power in environments that allowed them to not only catalyze the independence movement but also to form the military's role in society that would determine its actions and interactions with other state actors. As will be discussed in the case studies, the regime leadership's relationship with the military formed the institution's relationship with the police, and also created its culture by coopting, coercing, and marginalizing the institution in multiple ways throughout the authoritarian period.

The path-dependent argument illustrated above describes the cycle of events that led to military intervention in Tunisia and Egypt in the 2011 uprisings. The reinforcing mechanisms of the regime leader-military relationship can help to illuminate the process we can expect to see if, indeed, the regime leaderships' interactions with the military affected the military's presence in civil and state society and was a causal factor in the military's intervention. Through examining the above processes, and looking at the actions of the individuals and factions within the military and other regime institutions, as well as the populace and the intelligence- and police-based security apparatus, we can evaluate the factors discussed above within each state's society leading up to the Arab uprisings and the salience of each factor in the context of the entire national case. From there, we can reach a further judgment of the factors that were overall the most important in determining what caused each military to first turn against the regime in 2011, and then, as in Egypt, intervene in state politics in the post-uprising transition, or, as in Tunisia, step back to allow civilian democracy to take over. I begin my discussion of these factors with the case of Egypt, but before I delve into critical analysis of the categories of factors described above, it will be important to first highlight the historical events leading to the emergence of the military as a defining actor in Egypt's path from monarchy to independence from the Mubarak regime, beginning with the 1952 coup of the Free Officers.

# The Case of Egypt

Historical Context

The Egyptian military has played an effectual part in the state's political transitions. From British imperial control of the Egyptian monarchy to the start of presidential authoritarian rule, the military and its leaders remained a catalytic force that combined military actions with political influence. It will be the goal of the following case study to describe how the Egyptian military both affected and was affected by the climate and structure of the governing regime, and therefore how the institution's role in Egyptian political and civil society led to its highly involved role in the post-uprising transition in 2011 and beyond. The following historical summary of defining events between the 1952 coup and the 2011 uprising will give contextual background of Egyptian politics and a general discussion of the state's relationship with the military institution. Next, I will explore in greater detail the nature of the regime-military relationship and military culture, and specifically the interaction of these factors and their effect on the military's intervention in the 2011 popular uprising. Finally, I will end this case study examining which of these factors had the greatest impact on the military's intervention.

Barring the Arab uprising in 2011, Egypt's most recent major governmental transition occurred in 1952, when a faction of the military called the Free Officers was responsible for Egypt's coup from monarchy into military-based authoritarian government. In the years leading up to this transition, the military had been forced to sit idle while the British – who had occupied Egypt since 1882 under the pretext of protecting the Egyptian sovereign from his own army – manipulated the young King Farouk, who cooperated in preserving British interests and keeping the army limited in size (Kandil, p. 9). The environment that fostered the creation of the Free Officers therefore primed a sense of patriotism within the founding faction of mid-level officers and caused them to direct their focus on the politics and social stagnation of the country, thereby creating a nationalistic military that was driven to create an Egypt independent from British influence.

On July 23, 1952, the Free Officers, a group of middle-ranking officers within the Egyptian military and led by infantry lieutenant colonel Gamal Abd al-Nasser, seized the leadership of the armed forces by arresting the top generals loyal to King Farouk. The King was powerless without the army, and received no assistance when he appealed to the United States for support (his only possible ally, as his relations with Britain had been strained since a 1942 showdown involving the British rearranging the government to "best avoid Nazism"). U.S. policymakers had consciously decided to apply the national security doctrine policy to Egypt that they had adopted in Latin America: allowing a modernizing coup in Egypt would put an end to political chaos and economic stagnation in the country and would therefore keep it from drifting towards communism. In addition, the Free Officers had shared the plans for the coup with the U.S. Embassy in Cairo prior to taking action, pledging to protect American interests in Egypt. All that remained was for the U.S., which was eager to replace British influence in the region, to keep Britain from intervening. This was not difficult as Britain already disliked King Farouk and was in the process of withdrawing from its colonies. As a result, the Egyptian monarchy ended without much fanfare when Farouk departed Egypt in August of 1952, leaving the Free Officers and the army to govern and rebuild their damaged country.

Aside from the short presidency of Mohammed Naguib, as discussed below, Nasser's control of Egypt over the next two decades would create the dichotomy between the military and the rest of the security apparatus, and set into motion the chain of events that would eventually lead to the military's actions in the 2011 uprising and the transition that followed. According to Kandil, Nasser retained his power through a grand strategy of three pillars: building an entrenched security force, replacing the existing power centers with a new political apparatus, and garnering geopolitical support (22). In terms of creating the security force, Nasser wanted to ensure that a coup similar to the one he had executed with the Free Officers could never occur again and overturn his own regime (El-Houdaiby, 4). A colonel trained and accustomed to manipulating groups of people, Nasser adopted the strategy so often used in authoritarian regimes where "the multiplication of offices provides an extra security measure" (Kandil, 18), spreading the tasks of state governance and security among many actors and offices, minimizing communication among them, and all the while keeping the essential decision-making solely in the hands of the central decision-maker. The "hydra-headed security community" (Kandil, 18) that emerged not only put the power solely in Nasser's hands, however: it also served to elevate Nasser above the influence of the military institution and marginalize the military in the protection of Egypt's national security. Nasser was well on his way to becoming an all-powerful leader.

It is important to remember that, while the military institution was indeed a part of the security apparatus that Nasser created, it was only just that: a part. The web of control that Nasser created stretched far beyond the army: a strategy Nasser utilized on purpose, as mentioned previously, to ensure that a military coup such as that of the Free Officers in 1952 could never happen again. The creation of the Office of the Commander-in-Chief for Political Guidance (OCC) was instrumental to this goal. The organization served as a sort of "political watchdog" over the military that "ferreted out trouble-making officers and ensured the loyalty of the rest through the dispensing of patronage" (Kandil, 22). Nasser, as chief of the OCC, organized the office to eventually include about 65,000 of the original Free Officers (McDermott, 16) and to monitor political views and activities within the military institution so that the officer corps outside of Nasser's trusted groups would be isolated from political and ideological forces. In this way, the military was subordinated and controlled under Nasser's greater security apparatus. Such a security community would affect Egypt's political course for the duration of the century, creating the mukhabarat (intelligence) and police force that would eventually work with the regime leader to control Egypt's politics and assert itself over the military institution.

Nasser controlled the political apparatus in much the same way as the security apparatus. Initially, Nasser's Revolutionary Command Council (RCC) allowed him and the rest of the Free Officers to retain executive authority until a new government could be "elected." In effect, however, only Nasser knew the full list of all of the members of the Free Officer faction, so only he retained control of the group's actions and efforts. Egypt's first official president, Naguib, was another former military man who Nasser had enlisted during the 1952 coup to act as a figurehead, as he was largely beloved by the populace. But while Naguib enjoyed his extensive street popularity, Nasser worked the back channels of the political environment in order to solidify his own power. And while Naguib believed in law, the legitimacy of political groups, democratic procedures, and popularity with the people (Kandil, 27), Nasser worked around the popular influence Naguib garnered with these more democratic ideologies by deepening his security structure, eliminating all opposition political parties and replacing them in 1953 with the Liberation Rally, a loosely organized political platform that eliminated opposition political parties, organized the masses, and established a political organ for Nasserite legitimacy and support - all under a banner which Nasser could watch closely (Perlmutter, 142).

In terms of securing foreign support, Naguib did not actively pursue his political interests in negotiations with the U.S. At this time, the Western powers were not necessarily supportive of Naguib's ideological attachment to democracy: they cared more that Egypt did not fall under the Soviet Union's curtain of communism, and democratic elections might lead to political parties such as the Muslim Brotherhood, with potential Soviet sympathies, winning votes and therefore power. In terms of the dominant foreign policy strategy of the U.S. at this time, American policymakers chose to pursue alliances in the Middle East by encouraging the countries' independence movements from Britain and France and then, once the countries had achieved independence, the U.S would "draw the newly independent nations to its orbit through strategic alliances and economic aid" (Kandil, 23). These strategic alliances were directed towards the actors the U.S. policymakers believed would be most likely to renounce communism. As a result, the U.S. was drawn more towards Nasser's aggressive campaign to build a security state – the reality of which Nasser was sharply aware.

The final catalyst on the path to what would become Egypt's police state was Naguib's inability to create a new, progressive military institution that better fit the demands of the evolving Egyptian society and would centralize the institution's role in global politics and affairs. Naguib was, surprisingly, largely unaware of Nasser's security apparatus that was enveloping Egypt and co-opting or eliminating the influence of many of the previously powerful military officers (Kandil, 29). Even those "army dissidents" who believed in Egypt's path to democracy, and who sided with Naguib because of his clear propensity towards democratic ideals, were unable to overpower Nasser's deeply rooted and widely influential security apparatus when the conflict between Nasser and Naguib finally came to a head in the "military mutiny" of March of 1954, only two years after the 1952 coup.

When the March 1954 crisis was over and the smoke had cleared, Nasser had "won" the government and deposed Naguib from the presidency, taking the position for himself and setting the new regime on its authoritarian trajectory. Despite Naguib's representation of democratic ideals, Nasser's factions and coercive security and intelligence apparatuses were able to outsmart and overpower Naguib's strategies. The triumph of Nasser's security state was mainly due to the military's inability to act quickly in response to political threats (normal in such large institutions with deeply ingrained bureaucratic procedures) while, in contrast, the security institution under Nasser had been built to move quickly, unfalteringly, and effectively (Kandil, 41).

The 1954 military mutiny on the side of Naguib against Nasser ended badly for the former and in triumph for the latter. But the military's clear disloyalty towards Nasser led to the leader's deep distrust of the military institution. In response to the mutiny, Nasser sidelined the military's most influential leaders, except for those he could co-opt into working for the interests of the security apparatus. A few years later, the resounding defeat of the Egyptian military in the 1956 Suez Crisis – mirrored by what many consider to be Nasser's most brilliant political maneuvering – only highlighted the imbalance in power between Nasser's personalized security apparatus and the military. His personal success in the Suez Crisis also showed that Nasser could mobilize civil society and win the populace to his cause – a trait that would serve him well throughout the following years of his regime.

This triumph was not to last forever, though. Nasser began to realize that his subordination of the military to his own security forces and his marginalization of opposition political groups had caused the military to seek power elsewhere: the institution was now beginning to dominate the void in the political arena that the old opposition parties had left. Nasser could not rely forever on the adoration of the public, so he began rebuilding the political arena around his own interests. He formed the National Union (NU) in place of the Liberation Rally, which encouraged the people to "come together occasionally only to express approval of whatever the regime did" (Kandil, 56). Through the NU Nasser created the Arab Socialist Union (ASU), an organization focused on championing freedom (from Western colonialism), socialism, and Arab unity. The ASU was intended to represent the seat of political power in Egypt, and, through its continued machinations – including soliciting widespread popular support and covertly coopting and coercing prominent military leaders who showed signs of opposition – Nasser was able to significantly counterweigh the ability of the military to intervene in state politics. But the fact that Nasser needed to create these coercive institutions in the first place not only highlighted the importance of the military in the control of society, but also that the military leaders were willing and driven – at least to a point – to remain relevant and present in Egyptian politics.

The mass reaction to Nasser's premature death of a heart attack in 1970 showcased the extent of the people's admiration of his leadership and personality. It also highlighted the popular opinion within the government and the military institution that Nasser's vice president, and therefore the new commander in chief, Anwar al-Sadat, was weak and inexperienced. Sadat was a Free Officer, but he had come from one of the least significant sectors of the military – the communications-based signal corps – and he had never physically experienced war. As such, the rest of the military, mainly the officer corps, had deeply distrusted Sadat since even before the 1952 coup. Sadat recognized when he came to power that many regarded him as a "fill-in" until his political opponents could organize themselves. He therefore needed a support base to retain his position, and set about building his popularity with the military so that the opposition groups could not use the institution to carry out a coup (Kandil, 102).

Sadat's control over the military began in earnest with the lead-up to the October 1973 war with Israel. Israel's build-up of military defense lines across the Sinai passes was a dangerous prospect for military leaders, who had long felt that controlling the passes was "one of the few long-standing strategic doctrines in defending Egypt's eastern borders" (Kandil, 115). Sadat was intent on going to war immediately to take back the passes, even though his military generals were adamant that the army did not have the weapons to execute the strategy sufficiently; the war could easily turn defensive if Israel was better prepared than Sadat had bargained for. Sadat was unwilling to listen to other ideas, however: he evicted about 15,000 Soviet arms and weapons experts from Egypt without consulting the military leaders, and, later, when the generals rebelled against Sadat's "hasty" decision-making, he dismissed all who had opposed him in addition to removing more than a hundred high-ranking officers. Sadat's first military purge had begun (El Shazly, 25).

But it was Sadat's signing of the Camp David Accords in 1978, in which he signed a peace treaty with Israel, that in many ways defined Sadat's legacy. Being the first Arab state to recognize Israel would also tighten Egypt's alliance with the hegemonic U.S. and elevate Egypt as a progressive regional leader. But the signing of the Accords directly affected the Egyptian military as well. The existence of a peace treaty with Israel removed Egypt's main enemy, and therefore also removed the military's primary target and raison d'etre. Egypt was no longer participating in the Arab-Israeli conflict, and there were no other international conflicts in which Egypt was involved: other than a brief air skirmish with Libya in 1977, the military no longer had a target on which to focus its war-making abilities. Soon after Sadat signed the Accords, it would become clear that the leader had redefined the role of the Egyptian military – a development that would affect the institution's interests until the 2011 uprising.

After signing the Camp David Accords, Sadat declared that the October 1973 war would be the last Arab-Israeli war, and he set about redesigning the role and the makeup of the military institution to transition away from the traditional military role of national defense. Sadat's policy, dubbed infitah (meaning "opening" in Arabic), allowed the members of the military institution to benefit from economic commissions (Cook, 19). In 1978, he created the National Service Projects Organization (NSPO), which would direct the army's significant manpower towards domestic economic development projects instead of through traditional military activities. These economic development projects would utilize the full extent of the institution's resources and would also provide for the Egyptian state, thus making the military self-sufficient in its employment of both its officers and significant number of conscripts (Kandil, 182). In other words, the military was now forced to "reinvent itself as a primarily economic actor," focusing its resources on economic ventures instead of military ones: fewer military exercises, less focus on weapons acquisition, and little to no focus on potential wars, since no enemies existed outside of Egypt's borders.

Many questioned the motivations behind this shift in military focus, and criticized Sadat for bringing about such a change in what had been the most powerful Arab military in the MENA region. But many high-ranking generals within the military – ironically, those who most benefitted from the economic returns – defended the economic shift, noting that, in an absence of war, the military institution was required to find employment for its conscripts (Kandil, 182). So began the Egyptian military's legacy of deep economic ties to the state that would define the institution through Mubarak's presidency, through the 2011 uprising, and into present day. The new economic role of the military caused many problems within the institution, weakening the military in its traditional role of protecting the state, but also providing it with deeply engrained economic interests that defined its decision-making and its relationship with Egyptian civil society – the implications of which will be discussed in the following sections.

When Hosni Mubarak came to power after Sadat's assassination in 1981, he inherited a military that had been considerably tamed through Nasser's purges (which had effectively removed all politicized officers), Sadat's retiring or cashiering of any officers who were too popular, too loyal to the military, or too resistant to his authority, and the shift of the institution to a more economic focus. Mubarak himself had not been a Free Officer, though he had already graduated from the military academy when the 1952 coup occurred. Unlike Nasser's relationship with Sadat, Mubarak had been deeply distrusted and marginalized by Nasser. Under Sadat's regime, however, Mubarak blossomed: Sadat trusted Mubarak's faithful and quiet temperament, and eventually made him vice president. Once president, though, Mubarak's problems with the military began when he promoted his friend, major general Abd al-Halim Abu Gazala, to the post of field marshal. Mubarak believed Abu Gazala to be an ally, especially as the two men were friends and military-trained colleagues. But, "like everyone else who assumed the top military post in Egypt…Abu Gazala chose the military over political loyalty" (Kandil, 177). Abu Gazala believed that the military's role was primarily to protect Egypt's interests, and he sought to empower the armed forces by raising soldiers wages, forming close-knit alliances with the U.S., and reaching out to the public sphere by highlighting the military institution's and his own religiosity (a move that highly contrasted with Mubarak's strict secularist platform).

Almost immediately after Mubarak came to power and promoted Abu Gazala to field marshal, it was clear that Mubarak's and Abu Gazala's interests diverged once state politics and power were now involved in their decision-making: Abu Gazala repeatedly chose to raise his men's wages, and won over the institution as the military's "savior" (Kandil, 177). Perhaps understandably, Mubarak was threatened by Abu Gazala's devoted following both within and outside the military institution, and deliberately sidelined Gazala's military allies and lowered the military budget (Hashim, 109). But when 17,000 Central Security Force troops (a branch of the intelligence and security apparatus created under Nasser) took to the streets in 1986 to protest abusive treatment and low wages, the army was deployed to quell the riot. Interestingly, Abu Gazala immediately pulled his forces back when Mubarak told him to do so, without bargaining for an increase in the military's political leverage. This, according to Kandil, was the military's last chance under Mubarak to assert any kind of power over the regime, and Abu Gazala failed to do so (179). When his name was slandered by an Israeli newspaper claiming that he had illegally acquired U.S. missile parts, Abu Gazala lost his close ties to the U.S., and Mubarak demoted him in a bid to further depoliticize the armed forces and continue the civilianization of the political process that Sadat had begun (Hashim, 109). Abu Gazala's replacement was tasked with wiping out Abu Gazala's legacy, and minimizing the military's capabilities as much as possible. By 1991, Hussein Tantawi had Abu Gazala's job, and would remain there until 2011.

The Military's Economic "Privilege" Under Mubarak

Before addressing in greater detail the factors that determined the military's decision-making and intervention during and after the 2011 uprisings, it is important to address the economic role of the military during Mubarak's presidency. While Sadat initiated the infitah economic policy, it was under Mubarak, especially during the 1990's, that the military institution's economic dominance within Egypt was largely considered to have reached its peak. The military-economic complex was said to employ one hundred thousand people, and its holdings included a diversified business portfolio that specialized in the construction, land reclamation, agro-industries, and factories for the manufacture of civilian durables and weapons (Kandil, 181). Additionally, high-ranking officers supposedly enjoyed discounted apartments and vacation homes as well as subsidized food and other services. One perspective of the military's economic situation highlights this "golden age of military economic dominance" by underlining the military institution's extensive developmental projects, entrepreneurialism, and "mega-projectism:" the military was willing and able to carry out its own business projects across various sectors of the Egyptian economy (Amar, 23 October 2014). In this way, the military's refusal to protect Mubarak's failing regime in the 2011 uprising and the subsequent political takeover of Egypt's government by the Supreme Council of the Armed Forces (SCAF) could be argued to represent a direct attempt by the military to preserve the economic privileges that had been provided by a leader who, by 2011, was clearly no longer in control of the government (Silverman, 10).

However, despite the image of economic dominance maintained by the Mubarak regime and the military officers close to the president at the time, a closer look at the numbers suggests that, in fact, the military's economic dominance was not as prominent as previously thought. This "economic empire" was "considerably more modest in volume than commonly believed…it has probably shrunk in proportion to a national economy that has grown by more than 3% annually since 2003…although a few generals are rumored to have become rich, the main purpose [behind the military institution's economic activities] of ensuring a separate income stream…is to ameliorate the impact of a rapidly privatizing economy on the living standards of officers" (Sayigh, ft.com). Abu Gazala, for his part, attempted to dissuade the common perception that the military's economic prowess was as considerable as many thought; he highlighted how officers struggled with inflation – their salaries were not as high as perceived – and how the military's subsidized services were not comparable to the "more luxurious standards enjoyed by the members of the Egyptian upper middle class" (Kandil, 182).

Indeed, a look at the numbers (see Table 1) shows that the idea that military spending under Mubarak was high is not, in fact, accurate. The military budget as a proportion of GDP fell from about 20% at the end of Sadat's presidency to 11% at the beginning of Mubarak's leadership – and, finally, down to only about 2% of GDP near the end of Mubarak's regime, despite the boom in Egypt's total GDP. Clearly, the military's economic holdings did not account for an increase in military spending – and, consequently, the perceived economic dominance of the military (Springborg, 22 April 2014). From this perspective, it is easier to see why the military might end its loyalty to Mubarak when the uprising occurred in 2011, and why the institution would take have such an influential role in the governmental transition afterwards. Preserving the institution's own interests, and taking a chance to regain power when it looked as though Mubarak had lost control, would allow the military to retain and even take control of its economic – and political – destiny.

Table 3: Egypt's GDP, Defense expenditure, and defense expenditure as a proportion of GDP throughout the Mubarak regime (Kandil, "Back on Horse," p. 184).

| Year | GDP ($bn) | Defense Expenditure ($bn) | Defense Expenditure / GDP (percent) |
|------|-----------|---------------------------|-------------------------------------|
| 1980 | 17.82 | 3.47 | 19.47 |
| 1985 | 31.75 | 3.71 | 11.68 |
| 1990 | 34.00 | 4.30 | 12.64 |
| 2000 | 92.40 | 2.39 | 2.58 |
| 2005 | 93.20 | 2.75 | 2.96 |
| 2010 | 188.40 | 4.10 | 2.20 |

Application of Factors to the 2011 Uprising

The military's decision in 2011 not to side with Mubarak and capitalist cronyism that formed his regime was, as might be expected, an act intended to enhance the interests of the institution, but it was also "the prime factor in [Mubarak's] relatively quick downfall; had [the military] chosen to take the president's side, the outcome could have been violent" (Hashim, 116-117). The causes behind the military's role in the uprising and the political influence that it imposed on the government afterwards, however, stemmed from the long history of cycles of political marginalization as described in the preceding historical discussion. The Egyptian army had played a powerful role in the evolution of Egyptian politics, and it did retain a strong influence on the regime leadership, as demonstrated by the regime's continuous need to sideline any oppositional military leaders. However, for the most part, the military had been subdued and manipulated by its other two "ruling partners" – the regime leadership and the police forces – for four decades (Cook, 26). The 2011 popular uprising, and Mubarak's and the police forces' clear inability to contain it, allowed the military to defect from the control of the regime leadership. This action not only solidified the military's public image as the savior of the state and of the revolution, but also allowed the military to claim the majority share in shaping and later controlling the political transitions after Mubarak was ousted.

In considering the role of the military in the transition during and after the 2011 uprising, I will first examine the military institution's relationship with the rest of the regime apparatus – the leadership and the security forces – prior to 2011. Because the military played a catalytic role in the formation of independent Egypt back in 1952, the regime-military relationship is perhaps the most essential defining factor of the state's policies and affairs. Before 2011, the military had no formal role in state politics; on paper, it was solely responsible for protecting the country. But while the regime leadership ensures the legality of the formal structure of the Egyptian government in the retention of political control, the informal institutions of state politics – the category under which the military's close ties to the president can be placed – are equally if not more important to the maintenance of the authoritarian regime (Cook, 73). As Steiman notes in his discussion of regime-military relationships in the Arab uprisings,

> "The decision by the military to intervene in protests in the Arab Spring was dependent on the relationship between the military and the regime, which determined whether the military leadership concluded that the ruling regime was worth saving. If the [military] leadership viewed the survival of the regime to be indispensable to the survival of its interests, they chose to use repressive force against the protesters. If the leadership concluded that they could survive the overthrow of the regime, or if they deemed that they would perhaps benefit from the regime's fall, they refrained from using force against the protestors." (In MUFTAH, 29 May 2012)

In other words, the military leadership's decision in Egypt not to comply with Mubarak's command to fire on the people was an act guided by a calculation of the institution's interests, and determined the differential role that the military would play in the uprising and the post-uprising transition. While the military and the regime are united by common roots and ideology, the relationship cannot be understood without an examination of the regime leader's interests once he rose above the membership in the military institution into the presidency, where interests besides that of the military must also be taken into account.

Regime leader – military relationship: Authoritarian regimes have used a variety of institutional means to create a system of checks and balances that controls the military establishment, and ensuring political control over the military institution entails depriving it of both the means and motives to challenge the ruling regime. As a result, authoritarian regime leaders use a combination of inducements and safeguards to give the armed forces a vested interest in the status quo, and to make it difficult for them to conspire against the regime. In authoritarian regimes, such control is usually the result of a highly personalized regime structured around the leader, and an extensive security apparatus separate from the military institution (Brooks, 1998). In Egypt, there is an additional layer of interests that must be taken into account: the military institution educated and trained each of Egypt's presidents. Nasser, Sadat and Mubarak were socialized as officers, and therefore in many ways retained the interests and perspectives of their military counterparts once they reached the presidency.

As discussed in the historical section, the authoritarian leaders in Egypt were all guilty of co-opting or coercing the military institution in order to retain power. However, their actions towards the military are not necessarily dependent on the specific agency of each leader. Instead, the involvement of the military in the cycles of Egypt's political progression was dependent on the structure of the political system – on the interactions of the military institution with the leader and his security apparatus. Nasser ensured that he was the only person with knowledge of all the military and governmental projects and he controlled the politicization of the military; Sadat created the infitah policy from the regional political environment to force the military out of defining militaristic activities and into the economic sector; and Mubarak co-opted the military by restricting its actions through providing it with its own economic "empire." As a result of this cooptation and coercion, as well as each leader's roots within the military institution, the military was constantly forced to evaluate its relationship with the president and adjust its interests accordingly. In 2011, when the regime leadership and its security forces seemed both incapable of and unwilling to quash the popular uprising, the military took a stand against the authoritarian leader in order to preserve its economic interests, but also to appear to the people to be a morally sound institution (Hashim, Part 1, 116). Presenting this image of morality to the public would give the military legitimacy when it attempted to insert itself into a leading political role after the uprising was over.

Before 2011, the Egyptian military's relationship with Hosni Mubarak seemed to outsiders to fit the description of cooptation: Mubarak diverted the military's interests away from politics and into the economic sector by giving the institution access to lucrative land and business deals. However, looking deeper into the Mubarak-military relationship yields different answers to this question, especially when considering the context of the military's self-interest. During the latter two-thirds of Mubarak's regime in the 1990's and early 2000's, it was clear to everyone that the leader was aging. As speculation throughout the media and upper echelons of political society began to spread regarding Mubarak's health and ability to continue running the government, those in physical proximity to the leader noticed a growing paranoia in his character (Pelletreau, 9 August 2014). By the early 2000's, distrustful of the influence of the military institution, which had accumulated a popular following with its economic development projects, Mubarak distanced himself from his military connections and began cultivating a distinct group of civilian crony capitalists within his regime. This group of civilian "businessmen" served as a cushion for Mubarak's son, Gamal, to begin establishing a basis of power and position himself to take over the leadership when his father was no longer able to do so. Gamal had never served in the military, and had instead attended business school in Europe, avoiding the mandatory military service. He had also developed his own economic and political base through his business ventures, and would not be making any alliances with the military institution. Not surprisingly, the military officers were intensely distrustful of Gamal, and realized that if Mubarak were to transfer his power to his son, the military institution would lose its legacy of leverage over the leader that it had enjoyed since Nasser's Free Officers (Pelletreau, 9 August 2014). In this way, Mubarak's clear choice of Gamal as his successor highlighted his distrust of the military: even though he was a military man, he preferred to put the future of the Egyptian leadership in business and capitalism, for the first time removing the military connection from the leadership. It was unclear what the military's role might have become if Gamal had assumed power; as a result, the military may have believed that removing Mubarak in 2011 was simply an act of survival.

Police/intelligence forces – military relationship: This connection between the military and the president cannot be overstated. While during the entire fifty years of authoritarian rule the successive presidents came from the military, it inevitably would become apparent after a few years in power that the military institution – believing the leader to be "one of them" – would attempt align the leader's interests with their own. Without exception, each leader was forced to find some way to take control of the military so as not to lose power. As mentioned above, for Mubarak's presidency, this cooptation of the military was most obvious during the decline of his health. In addition to training Gamal for the leadership role and promoting his crony capitalist class, Mubarak began to focus his efforts on retaining his power through the maintenance of a more extensive security state than that built by Nasser.

In both policymaking and in retaining control of the security apparatus he had built around his authoritarian regime, Mubarak had always relied heavily on two men: Hussein Tantawi, minister of defense since 1991, and Omar Suleiman, director of military intelligence since 1991 and chief of the Egyptian General Intelligence Services (EGIS) since 1993. Mubarak held daily conferences with the two men regarding the state of affairs in Egypt. However, as the speculations surrounding his health multiplied, Mubarak pulled away from Tantawi's military and towards Suleiman, the intelligence apparatus, and Suleiman's control over the police and intelligence forces. Mubarak often played the two men against each other, fostering a deep rivalry (Pelletreau, 9 August 2014). This lack of unity in the governing institutions, and Mubarak's favoritism of the police forces, created a culture of "entrenched institutional tribalism" that became called "Taifas" or "petty kingdoms" (El-Houdaiby, 3), in essence separating the regime – made up of the security forces, the leadership, and the military – into individual groups focused solely on their own interests.

As a result, the decade before the 2011 uprising saw the police grow in influence, at the expense of the once-dominant military, as part of an alliance with a clique of Gamal's business leaders surrounding the Mubarak inner circle (El-Houdaiby, 6). The security strategy of Mubarak and Suleiman's police forces during this time were based on two pillars: the destruction of any political or social opposition movements – which was carried out by coopting unions and political parties – and the encouragement of reformation of any potentially violent movements by minimizing the space for media and reform movements to form. In many regards, this cooptation and marginalization of political opposition was used to control the powerful and respected military officers. Suleiman was easily able to organize his forces around these goals, and the security sector thus enjoyed unrepressed power during the lead-up to the 2011 uprising.

At the height of influence and power, it is surprising that the police forces lost the confrontation against the popular uprising in 2011. At this juncture, the actions of the military defined the outcome: the powers of the army had been brutally repressed in past years through its economic spending and the cooptation and coercion of its leaders, and the military institution was clearly unsatisfied with its role in the regime's politics subordinated underneath that of the police forces. While the police may have been prepared to go to battle with the common masses in 2011, the lack of military support caused them to lose the confrontation. The military had sided with the regime and the police against the people on three occasions – in 1968, 1977 and 1986, to be discussed in greater detail below – but in 2011, the interests of the military, and its subordination by the police forces for the last two decades, was enough to turn the military against the regime leader and its favored security forces and create for itself its own niche in state politics (El-Houdaiby, 1).

Control by state constitutions: Like the military-police relationship, the role of the military in the Egyptian state as dictated by the national constitutions was a factor tightly connected with, if not a part of, the military's relationship with the regime. As mentioned previously, the military institution was to have no formal role in politics, as dictated by the president, who, in every case leading up to 2011, needed to co-opt and control the military institution for the sake of consolidating power. The 1971 Egyptian Constitution, which lasted until the uprising in 2011, clearly stated, "The State shall establish the Armed Forces which shall belong to the people. Their duty shall be to protect the country, and its territorial integrity and security" (Article 180). In addition, "the law" – meaning, in many cases, the imposition of the president's will – would also regulate military courts and "define their competences in the framework of the principles in the Constitution" (Article 183). In this way, the regime not only claimed control of the military's actions in defense of Egypt, it also defined the role of the institution as an informal actor: and therefore not a political actor. At the same time, the police forces were given no such constitutional guidelines: only that their Supreme Commander would be the President of the Republic and that they should undertake the implementation of the duties imposed by the laws and regulations (Article 184).

Viewing the role of the military in the constitution provides on-paper proof of the regime's ability to control the military institution in the period prior to 2011. While scholars of the Egyptian military can study the actions of leading actors during the authoritarian period, it is helpful to see how the "official law" – and, more directly, the will of the leader – dictated the military's actions. As can be expected in authoritarian regimes, the informal actions (interactions, debates, etc.) between the regime leadership, military, or police forces can give a clearer picture of these institutions' true motives; however, the formal constitutions can give an interesting perspective on the official role of these institutions. The role of the constitutions also becomes important when describing the role of the military after the 2011 uprising: a discussion of these events can be found in the following section.

Past military intervention: Another factor that defined the regime-military relationship was military intervention: how and in what situations the military chose or was forced by the regime leader to use force. Egypt's role in regional disputes was determined by its military strength, and the institution even used its sheer size and firepower to make deals with the leadership. During Nasser's presidency, the commander of the armed forces was Nasser's closest friend, Abdel Hakim Amer, who "eschewed military professionalism" and "thought the military could have both political power and military effectiveness" (Hashim, Pt 1, p.70). The problem with Amer's focus on a political/military balance was that it took away from the military's ability to perform military tasks; one result of such politicization was the catastrophic defeat of the Egyptian army by Israel in 1967. The military had become a state within a state: it created propaganda around the "flourishing strength of the institution:" that it was its own autonomous power within the Egyptian state. The five-year occupation of Yemen, in which the Egyptian military lost about 10% of its manpower through death and injury, actually benefitted the officer corps. The government offered such extensive material benefits to soldiers who served that men begged to be allowed to go to Yemen (Hashim, Part One, 71). These benefits under Nasser and Amer's use of the military only created a corrupt class of officers, however. Many of the top officers became rich, and those who did not only looked upon the military in disgust. In reality, however, the military's actual capacity to accomplish "a transformation to a regional powerhouse" was a façade (Hashim, Part One, 70). This was made painfully clear in the brutal loss to Israel in the 1967 war.

But after the 1973 October War, in which Sadat's unwillingness to work with his generals' expertise squandered their advantage over the Israelis, the Egyptian military was not to be used again in international wars. This inaction was largely as a result of Sadat's infitah policies that transitioned the military mass towards an economic focus, and, after 1978, Sadat's treaty with Israel, which effectively removed the possibility of war with Egypt's major international enemy. So began the rivalry between the military and the police/security forces: now both institutions were constrained inside Egypt's borders with a similar desire for control.

The military's intervention in the 1977 Bread Riots was a perfect example of the military intervening when the police forces were unable to do so (Pelletreau, 9 August 2014): a reduction of subsidies on badly needed food products led to the mass protests of thousands of Egypt's poor. When it became clear that the police and security services would not be able to contain the riots, Sadat asked his Minister of Defense, Mohamed Abdel Ghani al-Gamasy, to use the military to intervene and quash the riots. The army had gained the trust of the people after its "honorable" role in the October War, and Gamasy was therefore reluctant to lose this positive image. He made a deal with Sadat: reminding the leader that the political leadership had made a pact after the 1973 war that the army would never be used against the civilian population, Gamasy agreed to use the army to restore order only if Sadat were to re-establish the food subsidies (Hashim, Part One, 73). Gamasy's ability to negotiate with Sadat showed not only the power of the military at this time – Sadat reportedly feared that Gamasy would take over the government after the Bread Riots (Hashim, Part One, 74) – but also its interests and decision-making vis-à-vis the interests of the populace. When it was clear that military's positive public image would help it to gain power against Sadat's marginalizing infitah policies, the military took advantage of the opportunity. This reasoning would become a major part of the military's decision not to intervene on the side of the regime three decades later in 2011.

The second category of factors affecting the Egyptian military's decision-making during and after the 2011 uprising focuses on aspects of the military culture. In many ways, the nature of the military's culture interacts extensively with the factors described previously relating to the regime-military relationship, as well as the consequent formation of the military culture and its relationship with civil society. Likewise, as Amy Holmes noted in her article following the Rabaa Square massacre in August 2013 (to be described in greater detail in the epilogue), "attention has focused too much on analyzing internal aspects of the armed forces, rather than their relationship to society" (Providence Journal). Looking at the relationship between the military and the populace will highlight how and why the military's interests manifested themselves in ways that aligned with those of the populace in 2011.

Class conflict within the military: In Egypt, military service is obligatory for all males between the ages of 18-30 for a period of 18-36 months, with 9 years of required reserve status afterward (Central Intelligence Agency, World Fact Book). The combined forces of the army, navy, and air defense forces had in 2011 a combined strength of about 450,000 soldiers, meaning that there are 190 soldiers for every 10,000 civilians – a disproportionately high percentage when compared with the Egyptian economy and the small percentage of GDP allocated to military spending (Springborg, 22 April 2014).

Even so, the Egyptian military institution as a whole is famously stratified – the possibility of promotion for conscripts or even low-level officers, while not high even in democratic militaries, has been non-existent in Egypt (Springborg, 22 April 2014). Mainly because of the focus on economic "mega-projectism" under Mubarak in the 1990's and early 2000's in which the military needed projects for which to pay its soldiers, the military's conscripts were kept separate from the leading officer body of the military as most of the conscripts were relegated to spend their required years in hard labor projects (Amar, 23 October 2014). For a time, the high-level officers were indifferent to this use of the conscripts because relegating the enormous conscript population to some kind of labor dealt with Egypt's underemployment problems in the 1990's (Pelletreau, 9 August 2014). However, because of this separation from the inner workings of core of the military institution, the conscript population is likely to have different interests than that of the elite officer corps.

In the event of a popular uprising, then, the enormous conscript population would be likely to direct its loyalty not to the military institution but to those the conscripts identify with: the civilian populace. Likewise, conscripts would be entirely unlikely to obey a command from an officer to fire military weapons on their own people (Springborg, 22 April 2014). Even though some of the higher-level officers may have been loyal – or at least indifferent – to Mubarak and his policies prior to 2011, the weight of the general opinion of the mass corps in the army, as well as the orders of the higher level generals, led the rest of the military officers to abandon Mubarak to his fate. Acting otherwise would have led to the fracturing of the institution (as had occurred in Libya and to some extent in Syria). The Egyptian military has always acted primarily for the interests of the institution above all else, and in light of the economic burdens Mubarak had placed on the military in the twilight of his regime, it was clear that preventing any class split within the institution was critical to its retention of power after the 2011 uprising was over (Kandil, 226).

Public perception/image: The army tanks that rolled into downtown Cairo during the Tahrir Square protests in late January of 2011, with soldiers embracing the protestors and assuring them that their cause was legitimate, solidified the image of the military as a savior to the people's causes and best interests. Tied to the tanks were banners that read, "Down with Mubarak!" and the people followed the rolling machines chanting, "The people and the army are one hand!" This image of a united cause between the military institution and the people represented the military's goal of preserving its image as a legitimate and professional institution, removed from political ambitions but willing to take control of the government when it was asked by the people to do so. The image of the military had always been a positive one from the people's perspective: it had included the populace since the 1960's in military parades and events. The military refused to side with the regime against the people – unless a deal was made, as in the Bread Riots, that would eventually help the state in the long run – and its propaganda, which emphasized the institution's power and respect for the Egyptian state, made the military's support of the struggles of the people more visible (regardless of their motives for this support). In this way, the military had always been seen as an ally of Egypt and of the common man, despite the military's strong connection with the regime leadership. The military's actions in 2011, highly publicized and dramatized with the media, not only maintained the military's high level of popularity – it also created a source of political legitimacy when SCAF took power only a month later.

The Egyptian Military's Role Post-2011

After the 2011 uprising, the military was able to insert itself into a much more involved role in state politics; its involvement was welcomed by many of the people with open arms because they already deeply distrusted Mubarak's crony capitalists and other senior ministers and leaders. The following section will describe the effects of the previously described factors on the nature of the military's role in the transition after the 2011 uprising and the removal of Mubarak, and will conclude with the drafting of the January 2014 Egyptian Constitution. A description of the events occurring between January 2014 and the present day can be found in the epilogue.

The leadership of the military played an enormous role in retaining the public trust of the institution in the light of the failure of both the regime leadership and the police forces. Tantawi, as field marshal of the military and declared leader of SCAF, had since 2008 been "skeptical" of the potential for political and economic reform under Mubarak, calling the leader (somewhat hypocritically) "aged and change-resistant" (CNN Wire Staff, 15 February 2011). While the military could in some ways have been equally implicated in the oppression during Mubarak's rule, as it had been coopted continuously by the regime and marginalized by the police forces, Tantawi's position on Mubarak's policies was already clear when the popular uprising began in 2011. In this way, Tantawi and the military managed to sufficiently distance themselves from Mubarak.

The extent of the military's involvement in the uprising and the following transition – claiming to assume a moderating role in the political transition until elections could be held, but in reality controlling most of the process and later removing the elected regime in power – was a direct result of the causal mechanisms that had come from the Free Officer's movement in the 1950's. Without Nasser's Free Officers catalyzing the transition out of monarchy, the resultant highly involved role that the military would play in politics and society for the next sixty years, and the three leaders' consistent control and marginalization of the military institution, the military would not have needed to intervene against the regime as it did in 2011. Removing Mubarak from power allowed the military to gain control over the political transition.

SCAF did not simply remove Mubarak from power, however. Two days after Mubarak's fall, SCAF disbanded the 1971 constitution, called for elections, and formed a constitutional amendment committee – which the military participated in. For a while, it appeared as though the military would simply take over the government completely, but after a year of violence and repression on the part of the military, as well as a series of mass protests, SCAF finally agreed to hold parliamentary and presidential elections. The military's political party ally, the Muslim Brotherhood, emerged victorious from both election – but not before SCAF issued one last declaration that gave the military legislative authority, autonomy from the civilian-elected government, and veto power over the new constitution (Wenig, Washington Institute, 2014). Despite the elections, it appeared that the military was still the most powerful actor in Egypt.

Mohamed Morsi's election to the presidency in 2012 and the Egyptian Muslim Brotherhood's accompanying rise to power was originally the result of a three-way alliance between the military, the remnant police forces, and the Muslim Brotherhood. This unlikely alliance was the result of widespread protests under the interim military government commanded by SCAF following Mubarak's relinquishment of the presidency (El-Houdaiby, 1), causing the military to seek alliances with a civilian party with broad popular appeal. The remnants of the destroyed police forces, meanwhile, was placed under the command of the military, which sought to rehabilitate the police image after decades of playing the role of the unpopular, brutal mukhabarat forces that had oppressed the populace and opposition parties alike.

However, Morsi's civilian government caused the Egyptian military to begin rethinking its alliance with a civilian political party (Rugh, 6 August 2014) when Morsi abrogated the military's autonomy referendum, taking full executive and legislative power from the military for himself. Taking advantage of the popular discontent towards the military, Morsi removed Tantawi from the position of defense secretary and replaced him with General Abdel Fattah al-Sisi, one of Tantawi's protégés. Morsi also purged the top ranks of military, forcing many generals into retirement and replacing them with a younger generation of leaders (Wenig, Washington Institute, 2014).

However, the Brotherhood's drafted constitution of 2012 did, as will be discussed below, allow the military to retain substantial autonomy over its own affairs. But on a broader level, the new constitution did not reflect political consensus opinions. In general, Egyptian politics represent an amalgamation of many religious and ideological differences. A ruling party such as the Brotherhood, which showed little regard for other parties' interests once it was elected into power, was not readily accepted by the masses that had originally voted for Morsi. When the 2012 constitution was drafted, showcasing its very singular interests, many feared a shift into theocracy. Over the next few months after December 2012 constitution was drafted, Morsi and the Brotherhood's popularity sharply declined. Some reports even hinted that Morsi was contemplating removing Sisi in order to stave off a military coup (Wenig, Washington Institute, 2014). As more and more mass protests occurred throughout the spring, it became apparent that Morsi and his government would not last until the next round of elections. As it had done in the opportune moment during the uprising against Mubarak, the military stepped in to once more regain power. SCAF issued an ultimatum demanding that Morsi step down from the presidency, and when he refused, they removed him from power. This time, the civilian population – excluding the Brotherhood's supporters – was largely grateful to the military. As a result of this collective relief and extensive military propaganda, Sisi was not simply hailed as the leader of Egyptian political reform, but as a celebrity idol as well.

As for the military's relationship with the security forces after the 2011 uprisings, the two institutions found that their roles had been entirely reversed: the military finally found itself in command of the disbanded and destroyed police forces. However, it was important to the maintenance of legitimacy to appear as if the two institutions were working together towards reform. The Minister of Interior, Major General Mansour el-Essawy, was intent on reforming the police forces and the image of the police institution, and attempted to co-opt the police force under the military branch and in alliance with the Muslim Brotherhood. Displaying a degree of tolerance towards the police officers attempting to reform themselves showcased the military's patience and open-mindedness, and the efforts it was willing to make to reform the security sector towards the common goal of public security (El Houdaiby, 13).

In regards to the military culture during the post-uprising transitions, the factors of class conflict and public opinion of the military institution reveal some interesting conclusions about the military's consideration of public perception once it is in power. When, in October of 2011, SCAF unleashed a bloody crackdown on Coptic Christian protestors (Steiman, MUFTAH), and later in

August 2013 when the military massacred 817 Muslim Brotherhood supporters in Rabaa Square and placed hundreds more in prison under death sentences, the Egyptian populace initially responded with a general sentiment of shock (Holmes, Providence Journal). These incidents demonstrated that the military was not afraid to utilize its substantial security forces to use violence against civilians if it benefited the institution's interests: a reality that clearly goes against the narrative of partnership and loyalty to the state and the people that the military has always presented. At risk was the highly respected role in society that the military had enjoyed for decades, and that had allowed it to manipulate the public image in its favor.

The way around this reality, and to justify this violence against civilians, was to create a new narrative: one that presented the protesting groups of civilians as terrorists. This was particularly easy to do with the Muslim Brotherhood, which had angered many civilians during its short tenure in control of the presidency, and which other MENA countries were beginning to distrust because of the Brotherhood's highly religious form of political Islam. Before and during the shift in power in the military's favor in 2011, some theorists believed that the more institutionalized the army, the more similar the soldiers were to the protestors in religious, ethnic, and socioeconomic identities, and the less likely the soldiers would be to open fire on civilians (Holmes, Providence Journal; Bellin, 2011). In order to justify military actions against a group of the populace, then, the military created a narrative that separated the protestors from civil society: supporters of the Muslim Brotherhood were not a part of Egyptian society, so therefore were also not a part of the military institution.

However, the violent actions of the military post-2011 after it had seized political power suggests that the military's choice to defect from the regime in 2011 was based solely on the institution's need to regain control over state politics that it had progressively lost over the previous four decades under authoritarian rule. The 2011 popular uprising gave the military an opportunity to take back this control under the umbrella of popular support, but the military's subsequent treatment of the populace demonstrated the institution's lack of commitment to civilian-led democracy. Hence, the Egyptian military's commitment to positive public perception can be viewed as a defining factor only if it happens to work within the military's interests at that time; public opinion is not, in reality, an influential factor in military decision-making unless it can advance the institution's interests, which in this case was focused on political control.

The most concrete way to observe the growing, all-encompassing influence of the military in Egyptian politics after the 2011 uprising is to track the military's growing autonomy as dictated by the changing constitutions. While the 1971 constitution, as discussed previously, marginalized the role of the military under the power of the regime, a significant shift occurred after the 2011 uprising when the military became the trusted ruling institution in Egypt. Some especially marked differences in the new constitutions have given the military an unprecedented amount of control over the governing body.

The first of these changes in the 2012 constitution under Morsi stated that the Defense Minister could be a leader of a key body of the military; but in the 2014 constitution, the Defense Minister now must be a leader of a key body of the military. As such, control of Egypt's defense is the responsibility of a military general, not a civilian, giving the military institution control over its own affairs. The Defense Minister's powers also now encompass the role of the "supreme commander of the armed forces" – a role which used to belong to the president alone – and the army's conscripts would pledge allegiance to the defense minister, not to the president or even the country of Egypt (Springborg, 22 April 2014). Such a direct shift in power towards the Defense Minister demonstrates the military institution's attempts to safeguard its power and its control over its own affairs, regardless of who the president is and which institution he comes from. For now, of course, military-man Sisi is President, and will remain so at least for the four years that make up one presidential term; however, given the recent unrest and civil tensions in the country despite the military's attempts to quash them, the new changes in the constitution give the military the autonomy to retain control over its own forces through the Defense Minister. What is more, given the history of the Egyptian military-trained leaders who eventually were forced to marginalize their own institution in order to retain power, the new constitutional processes secure the military (and its economic and autonomous interests) in the event that it somehow loses its status as the preeminent force in Egyptian politics.

Perhaps even more concerning in human rights terms, the powers of the military institution have extended into civilian affairs (Springborg, 22 April 2014). Beginning with the 2012 constitution, military courts can try any person they believe have committed "crimes that constitute a direct assault against the military." By the 2014 constitution, the Military Court is defined as "an independent judicial body exclusively competent to adjudicate on all crimes pertaining to the Armed Forces" and the members of the Military Court "shall be independent and immune to dismissal" (Article 204). In other words, the military is able to act as an independent institution: it can decide for itself, without any system of checks and balances, whom to identify as enemies of the military, and can try them in military courts with military judges. As such, the military can, and has done already with hundreds of Muslim Brotherhood supporters, imprison anyone they believe to be opposing the military institution (Springborg, 22 April 2014). The censorship of ideas and political dissent can easily be punished by imprisonment or death. The military is therefore using its newfound political power to ensure that it retains control of the government and of any possible rebellion or uprising. While this can easily be seen in the military's actions since 2011, especially in regards to the Muslim Brotherhood, the manifestation of these goals is clearest "on paper" in the recent Egyptian constitutions.

Looking at the amalgamation of factors and the events that formed them, it is clear that the Egyptian military's actions and its role in the post-2011 transition are affected mainly through the influence of the regime leadership since the start of authoritarian rule: the combination of marginalization, cooptation, and coercion of the military by the regime leader formed the military culture and interests that would inspire the institution to intervene in 2011. As Cook described the relationship between the Egyptian military and the regime leader,

> "It is the military's crucial and intimate association with the presidency that ensures the continuity of Egypt's political system…critical though the formal institutions of political control might be, informal institutions are equally, if not more, important to the maintenance of the Egyptian authoritarian regime. The origin of informal institutions lies in precedents from the time of the Free Officers'

coup, which placed the military in an exalted political and social position. Despite the attenuation of the military's prestige [over the years]…the nexus between the president and Egypt's commanders indicates that informal institutions relating to the power of the military establishment endure to this day." (Cook, 74).

Though Cook wrote this analysis in 2007 in reference to Mubarak's relationship with his commanding generals, in some ways his point is still valid today in the context of the military's current control over Egyptian politics. The military's actions during the three years of political transition – 2011-2014 – focus on the institution's political interests and the maintenance of political power. The military's role in Egypt has been politicized since 1952, and yet at the same time so heavily marginalized by the regime leadership that it is unsurprising that the military inserted itself into the lead role of the political transition after 2011.

In the aftermath of the last three years of continued upheaval in Egyptian politics, through the uprising against Mubarak, the elections bringing Morsi into power, the overthrow of Morsi and the crackdown on the Brotherhood, and finally the military's retaking of power, the constant change and turbulence has caused a disruption in the balance of power, because the Egyptian people have "awoken to their own power to take political action" (El-Houdaiby, 2). Sisi's celebrity image, once overpowering and all encompassing throughout Egypt, is beginning to garner suspicion and outrage from the people and the marginalized media. The media, which has so far lost much of its credibility acting as a channel for Sisi's propaganda, is beginning to come under fire for its lack of integrity (Seikaly, 23 October 2014). And after decades under the thumb of authoritarian regime and the success of the 2011 uprising, the Egyptian populace has seen that they can exact change in state politics. It will be the role of the populace and the younger, unbounded generation of the media to temper the military's power in order to achieve politically stable middle ground. In the next case study, I will explore the Tunisian military's involvement in the Tunisian 2011 uprising and the institution's role in the post-uprising transition. Like that of the Egyptian military, the experience of the Tunisian military in the post-independence authoritarian period directly affected the military's role in the transition. Comparing the experiences of the Egyptian military with those of the Tunisian military will offer insights into how the background of a military institution's role in politics – from independence to uprising – can lead to similar institutional decision-making and yet very different actions during a state transition.

## The Case of Tunisia

### Historical Context

Unlike Egypt's transition out of monarchy, Tunisia's quest for independence from its colonial power, France, was not driven by the interests of the military institution. And unlike most of the Arab states in the region, the military was neither an actor nor a catalyst in the transition when Tunisia became an independent state in 1956. Tunisia's path to independence was based on the decision-making of Tunisia's civilian leaders, their political parties, and their relationship with France, and was not supported by or the result of a military-backed coup. In order to understand the path dependency of the evolution of the Tunisian military's role in society, and the effect of this role on the military's intervention in the uprising in 2011 and its relative disappearance from politics afterward, it is important to first explore the historical context of Tunisia's independence movement and the near-sixty years of authoritarian leadership leading up to the 2011 uprising.

Before Tunisian independence in 1956, the dominant political party, the Neo-Destour Party, had advocated a vigorous anti-colonial movement against the French occupation. The Neo-Destour had dominated the political arena since it had eclipsed its predecessor, the Destour Party, in the 1930's (Willis, 2012). Because of its political dominance and range of influence, and therefore its comprehensive reach across Tunisian classes and groups, the Neo-Destour was also a heterogeneous mix of beliefs and ideals. In this way, it was very likely that divisions would eventually occur across this spectrum of beliefs once the common goal of the party – independence – had been achieved.

Not surprisingly, as the possibility for independence loomed, a major break in the Neo-Destour did split the party between its two main leaders: Saleh Ben Youssef, its secretary general, and Habib Bourguiba, the party's president, both of whom had built and retained significant factions of allies and followers within the party. As expected, this rupture was due to the two groups' differing beliefs on how to best negotiate the process of transition from French colonial rule to independence. Ben Youssef was intent on achieving Tunisian independence in the fastest and most secure way possible, even if this meant taking military action against the French colonists; Bourguiba, meanwhile, strongly believed in the merits of retaining close ties with the French, and wished to negotiate Tunisian independence through a "stepping stone process" (Willis, 38). The French, of course, preferred Bourguiba's route, and in 1955 began negotiating an autonomy agreement with the promise of further steps towards full independence down the road. Ben Youssef's Neo-Destour faction, suspicious of French interests in Tunisian "autonomy," openly condemned these agreements, called the Franco-Tunisian Autonomy Conventions, believing them to be an unacceptable compromise that did not give Tunisia the full independence it deserved. It was at this juncture that Bourguiba moved to marginalize and then expel Ben Youssef from Neo-Destour – a feat he easily accomplished – foreshadowing his ability to use and manipulate the party politics for his own political gain.

By 1955, Bourguiba enjoyed full control over Tunisia's ruling party and the independence negotiations with the French. When, in the same year, Ben Youssef's marginalized supporters staged a small insurrection against the ruling party, Bourguiba was able to convince the French to intervene to crush the rebellion. The French appreciation for Bourguiba's moderate position in Tunisia's independence quest made their support for him worthwhile, and, later, also more willing to negotiate with him for independence. When Bourguiba made it clear that, if Tunisia were granted independence, he would retain close military, economic, and cultural ties with France, the colonial power was convinced of the merits of Bourguiba's policies and finally granted Tunisia independence in 1956.

The following decade was marked by Bourguiba's creation of a "presidential monarchy" within Tunisia's political system. He utilized the already existing, well-organized party structure of the Neo-Destour to build a power base around himself, institutionalizing and establishing his own rule over the dominant political party (Willis, 51). For a while, at least, this highly organized bureaucratic structure, which touched all tendrils of the far-reaching Neo-Destour party, provided Bourguiba with extensive popular support and legitimacy during the difficult post-independence years of state-building (Moore, 99-100). However, as Bourguiba's power base solidified into the late 1960's, he eventually dispensed with all formal appearances of the "party politics" and simply took over all high level appointments himself. By the 1970's, the Neo-Destour had changed from a mass popular organization to a "simple piece of bureaucratic machinery for the president to utilize" at his will (Willis, 65).

The decade of the 1970's ushered in an unstable regional and domestic climate for Tunisia, and tested the highly personalized governmental system that Bourguiba had created. It also established the first true test of Bourguiba's system in his marginalization of the military. At this point, the military had become nothing more than "a bureaucratized garrison force" that had not left its barracks for any major conflicts (Ware, 594). The military's almost non-existent role in Tunisian politics was, however, not surprising given the nonviolent way in which Bourguiba had secured independence from France. The Tunisian military was simply not needed to achieve state independence; it was instead the actions of the leadership, and the climate of Tunisian politics under French colonial rule in the 1950's, which brought about the contingent independence moment. From 1956 onward, the causal events outlining the Tunisian military's relationship with the president would in turn affect the military's role in Tunisian society. In this way, the lack of a role in the independence process did define the military's role in Tunisian politics: it would serve to support the regime ideals but not, at least for a time, to challenge them.

This system of subordinated cooperation between the Tunisian military and Bourguiba manifested itself in the waves of Libyan-backed Tunisian social unrest in 1978, 1980, 1981, and 1984 which put strains on the police and intelligence within the Ministry of Interior, and forced the military to send in units to help quell the rioting. And while the army returned immediately to its barracks after each confrontation, their presence in Tunisian society and their involvement in the issues created a slight rise in the political influence of the military leaders (Willis, 95). During this social unrest, when the military was constantly utilized, the military budget began to rise and some military leaders were appointed to positions within the Ministry of Interior. Of course, Bourguiba oversaw all of these promotions, and made many of them only temporary. However, his change in policy towards military leaders, and allowing them into his trusted ministry for the first time in his presidency, was pointed out by his opponents as a sign of his potentially aging mind. The most significant and surprising of these appointments was that of Brigadier General Zine al-Abedine Ben Ali to the post of Director of National Security within the Ministry of Interior. Ben Ali was the first career military man in such a high position within Bourguiba's carefully constructed security apparatus – and he was also the orchestrator of Bourguiba's eventual removal from power three years later in 1987, when Ben Ali had just taken over the post of Prime Minister under Bourguiba.

Ben Ali's coup d'état, which bloodlessly removed Bourguiba from power, was carefully constructed to follow Constitutional guidelines that provided for the removal of a president: seven doctors signed an agreement acknowledging that the aging president was no longer fit to continue his post. Ben Ali, as Prime Minister, then easily inserted himself into the presidency. Many speculated that the timing of Ben Ali's takeover – almost immediately after he was appointed prime minister

– signified his regard for the legality of the removal process, as it was possible that he could have orchestrated a more forceful coup even as early as 1985 with the assistance of the military (Willis, 96). However, Ben Ali did not inform the senior officers of the coup or even meet with them until after he had successfully carried it out – foreshadowing his future continuance of Bourguiba's policies towards the control and marginalization of the military whenever possible.

The initial impression of the Ben Ali regime was that it would be a welcome change to Bourguiba's paternalistic "monarchy" that had repressed opposition movements. From the beginning, Ben Ali assured both the populace and international observers that political liberalization was the priority of his new agenda: a stance that stimulated many scholars to suggest that Tunisia was a prime candidate for a potentially successful democratic transition (Huntington, 287). By 1988, less than a year into Ben Ali's presidency, a law was introduced that improved the status of existing political parties in regards to the then-ruling Neo-Destour party, and even allowed for the creation of new political parties. A few months later, the leaders of these new parties met with Ben Ali and the Neo-Destour leaders to draw up the National Pact, introduced on the first anniversary of Bourguiba's removal from power, that showcased the government's commitment to greater political freedom and multi-party elections (Willis, 129).

The façade of political freedom was not to last long, however. Within two years of Bourguiba's ousting, Ben Ali and his restructured Neo-Destour party, now called the Rassemblement Constitutionnel Democratique (RCD), were clearly reasserting themselves as the dominant ruling party in Tunisia. The 1989 legislative elections boasted the involvement of the newly fledged political opposition parties; yet, after the votes were counted and the parliament seats distributed, the RCD had won every single seat in parliament, even in constituencies where it was clear that opposition parties controlled the majority of the population (Willis, 131). In response to this supposed fraud, the opposition parties tried to create a common front to resist the suddenly clear restrictions on the political system, but were eventually unable to agree on a common strategy about the extent to which they should confront the regime. In addition, many of the opposition parties were fearful of the Islamist movement – called in Tunisia the Ennahda Party – and decided it was in their best interests to side with the regime when the Islamist purges began in the 1990's. When Ben Ali and the RCD began persuading the rest of the opposition parties to abandon their plans to boycott the falsified elections with state subsidies and other benefits, the last hope of political opposition to Ben Ali's regime in Tunisia fell apart. Between coopting the opposition parties, coercing or marginalizing the rest, and banning the Ennahda movement, Ben Ali had successfully removed all potential rivals during the late 1990's and early 2000's. Through this purging, he was then able to form the personalized and paternalistic regime around himself that Bourguiba had made so successful, and spent the remainder of his regime utilizing his extensive security apparatus to impose oppressive control over the Tunisian people, political oppositions, and the military – which he believed could pose a threat to his regime.

Application of Factors to the 2011 Uprising

The self-immolation of Mohammed Boazizi, a struggling, 26-year old college graduate who had been relegated to selling vegetables on the street in a quiet Tunisian town, was the catalyst that set the Arab

Spring in motion. It took only days for the rest of the country to begin protesting the authoritarian government in the name of Boazizi and of the countless youth who were wasting their intelligence, their potential, and their lives in poverty while the upper echelons of the authoritarian government continued to oppress and marginalize the population. While the Tunisian uprising is credited with starting the string of Arab uprisings that spread across the MENA region, the Tunisian military is credited with playing a catalytic role in the eventual success of the Tunisian uprising, as it refused Ben Ali's order to fire on the civilians during the riots. General Rachid Ammar's decision to disobey Ben Ali – as well as Ammar's "strong suggestion" that the leader leave the country – inspired and galvanized the populace and in many ways allowed the uprising to succeed (Willis, 2012). However, unlike the case of Egypt, the failure of the military to back Ben Ali was highlighted by the subsequent withdrawal of the military institution from politics after the uprising had succeeded, with Ammar refusing calls from the populace to assume a position of leadership. The differential role of the military in the post-uprising transition can be explained by factors affecting its involvement in the past. In order to examine why the military did not play a significant role in Tunisia's transition towards democracy, I will examine in the following case how the regime-military relationship and the military culture affected the military's withdrawal from politics after its intervention on the side of the popular uprising in 2011.

In assessing the path dependency of the military's intervention in the 2011 uprising and its subsequent disappearance from state politics, the contingent moment of state independence in 1956 is critical in the construction of the military's political relationship with the regime leadership as well as the military's own culture. More specifically, the situations facing Bourguiba during independence and in the events following Bourguiba's state-building process was the most effectual factor in shaping the military's relationship with the other pillars of Tunisian politics and culture. From the starting point of Bourguiba's decision-making, I will trace the interacting mechanisms between the leadership's formal and informal effect on the military, the military's relationship with police forces and the populace, the military culture, its use in domestic and international interventions, and finally the reasons why the institution acted as it did in 2011 and beyond.

In presenting this case, I will show first how the actions of Bourguiba and Ben Ali set into motion a sequence of causal events that affected and produced the military's nature. As will be argued below, in stark contrast to the Egyptian military and its involvement in state politics and economics, the Tunisian military was immediately and dramatically marginalized by the regime leadership, beginning with independence and lasting until the 2011 uprising. Tunisian independence in 1956 was entirely orchestrated under the civilian leadership of Habib Bourguiba (who had been a lawyer, not a military man as in many cases of Arab authoritarian rule); as a result, there was at the beginning no organic link between the military and the political system (Cook, fp.com). And unlike the Egyptian military, the Tunisian military had no economically reinforcing relationship with the regime, had not faced any major threats or past wars, and was created to be a small, apolitical and less professional military than its counterparts in the region (Pelletreau, 9 August 2014). As a result, the complete lack of political or economic stakes directly affected the military institution's interests in and ability to have any role in Tunisian politics, and encouraged the development of a military mentality directed towards the preservation of order in society – in direct contrast with the Egyptian military, which sparred with the regime leadership to achieve political and/or economic control over the state.

The two Tunisian authoritarian regimes – that of Bourguiba from 1956-1987 and then that of Ben Ali from 1987-2011 – clearly and forcefully defined the role of the military institution within the country, marginalized the military leaders, and created a military that, for a time, had very little – if any – political interest in politics. In this way, the contrast between the institutional evolution since independence of the Tunisian military and that of its Egyptian counterpart can illuminate the patterns of military political interests in the two states' transitions. However, in a similar fashion to the case of the Egyptian military, the role of the Tunisian regime leadership directly affected the military's role in state constitutions and interventions, its relationship with the police force, and its culture, thereby setting into motion a chain of events that would shape the military's role in Tunisian society and politics.

Regime leader – military relationship: The absence of the military institution in Tunisian politics between independence in 1956 and the 2011 uprising is "almost entirely explained" by the attitude and actions of the leadership, and Bourguiba in particular (Willis, 86). From 1956 onward, Bourguiba made the strategic decision to remove the military from all political actions and decision-making. He also wanted to ensure that his commitment of loyalty to the French remained intact, and determined that the best way to ensure both this commitment and his own power structures was to marginalize the military as best he could (and, given his innate ability to manage Neo-Destour and the entire governing apparatus in Tunisia, this was not difficult). First, Bourguiba structured the upper echelons of the military around former members of the French colonial army, creating a loyalist mentality that would retain the relationship with the colonial power (Willis, 86). Part of this process involved the Bourguiba Promotion, a yearly program in which 50 Tunisian military members were sent to France to be trained and educated before returning to Tunisia to begin their careers (Pelletreau, 9 August 2014).

Bourguiba was also aware of the astronomical cost of retaining an army fully outfitted for war; if Tunisia did not have any external enemies, therefore, he could put more funds into more domestically focused aspects of the Tunisian economy, such as health and education (Taylor, 74). He therefore worked hard to ensure good relations with powerful Western states (especially France, but also the United States) on whom he could rely to aid Tunisia in the event of an attack from another state (Willis, 87). By pursuing this strategy, Bourguiba could afford to constrain the Armed Forces and devote more resources to developing the country's economy, avoiding the crippling costs of purchasing external security by pouring funding into the military institution. Indeed, between independence and 1979, the country never spent more than 2% of its GDP on defense (Taylor, 74). Such meager funding kept the Armed Forces small, poorly equipped, and, for the most part, untrained.

Bourguiba also placed a civilian at the head of the Ministry of Defense, and in 1957 officially banned political activity and association for all members and ranks of the military. No military members could vote in elections (even though the elections were effectively non-democratic) or publicly hold any political views. As a result, the Tunisian military was kept shuttered away from politics, in contrast to the Egyptian military, or even those of Algeria and Morocco where military figures played central roles in politics. Senior military leaders were entirely absent from the Tunisian ruling elite, and no generals played any role in civil or political life; the Tunisian military was confined to its barracks, and as a result Tunisian society knew very little about the military institution and its values under Bourguiba's tenure (Willis, 2012).

Bourguiba laid out his reasoning for the marginalization of the military in 1965, explaining that military leaders could not have political opinions like normal citizens because they would become involved in the struggle for power and could use their weapons to impose political solutions of their own choosing (Willis, 2012). Bourguiba had undoubtedly been influenced by the actions of the militaries of other Arab states such as Egypt, Algeria and Morocco in which military leaders had either assumed control of the government or had at least attempted to do so through coups. Ironically, Bourguiba's power was challenged twice by two unsuccessful attempts to remove him from power, both supported by the military (to be discussed in greater detail below). His eventual removal from the presidency was carried out by a military man.

Bourguiba's strict marginalization of the military from the outset set the standard for the military's actions until 2011; in essence, Bourguiba "bred the military to distance itself from politics" (Pelletreau, 9 August 2014). When, in 1979, Defense Minister Abdallah Farhat was found to be including senior military officers in the Neo-Destour annual congress, Bourguiba fired him. However, the heightened use of the military in the 1970's and 1980's did lead to an increased presence of military figures in Bourguiba's security apparatus. This development would in some ways lead to Bourguiba's undoing, because the "blurring of the distinction and personnel between the military and the internal security apparatus [in the Ministry of Interior] deprived Bourguiba of the security that such a separation and rivalry between the two gave him" (Stone, 150). Bourguiba was aging, and his paranoia regarding the loyalty of his power base growing: his appointment of Ben Ali to director of national security was surprising: for the first time, a military man had reached the upper echelons of Bourguiba's extensive, hand picked power pyramid.

When Ben Ali removed Bourguiba in the 1987 bloodless coup, he continued many of his predecessor's strategies of restraining the military. But Ben Ali's past as a military man was unlike those of the Egyptian presidents. He had been educated at the military academy in France where other officers were trained, but his focus had been intelligence and security – he was not schooled in the same manner as most of the high-ranking officers within the Tunisian Armed Forces (TAF). The implications of his focus on security were indicated by his favoritism of the security forces over the military institution. While the military's budget did increase after Ben Ali came to power in 1987, the increase was better explained by Ben Ali's preoccupation with internal security rather than any increased influence of the military leaders because of Ben Ali's military background. Indeed, the police forces' budget under Ben Ali grew much faster than that of the military (Willis, 104).

The military did enjoy a higher public and political profile under Ben Ali than it did under Bourguiba; however, this "did not equate to an effective assumption of power by the military as an institution...rather, these developments were the result of the designs of Ben Ali" (Willis, 104). As a result, the regime that Ben Ali designed would be a highly personalized one – much like Bourguiba's power base – that would revolve around his leadership instead of his relationship with the military. His National Pact of November 1988 followed Bourguiba's policy of explicitly subordinating the military to civilian control and forcing its public and political neutrality. Even Ben Ali's restructuring of Bourguiba's Neo-Destour party into the RCD saw no discussion of the role of the army under the new president: the result of Ben Ali's intention to take full control over the management of the security sectors within his own regime and to minimize the formal role of the military in society. By the mid to late 1990's, most of the senior military officers that Ben Ali had appointed to the Ministry of Interior at the beginning of his presidency had been removed and replaced with loyal civilian personalities. Perhaps even more telling of Ben Ali's preferences was his ensuring that he was never again referred to as "General Ben Ali" – he presented himself always as a civilian leader, portraying his regime as "one lacking any khaki tinge" (Willis, 104).

Police/intelligence forces – military relationship: Creating a strong security force to check the military institution's power is a common form of political restraint that leaders often leverage against the military (Taylor, 76). The rivalry between the TAF and the security forces within the Ministry of Interior was entirely engineered by Bourguiba and then Ben Ali as a way to focus each institution's loyalty towards the leader at the expense of the other, much in the same way that Mubarak pitted Suleiman against Tantawi. But the military was hardly utilized for most of the authoritarian years: the National Police controlled the major cities and the National Guard was used for the numerous counterterrorism operations along Tunisia's borders. And more members of the National Guard than the TAF were sent to assist Egypt during the 1973 Arab-Israeli War (Taylor, 78).

This pyramid-like power structure fit Tunisian politics well. As a result of Bourguiba's and Ben Ali's military alliances and security agreements with great powers such as France and the U.S., and considering the tendency for Arab authoritarian regimes to direct significant efforts towards coopting or coercing any form of political opposition, the focus on domestic security in Tunisia was far greater than that of international security. By 2010, Ben Ali had reallocated funds from the TAF to the National Guard branch of the internal security forces – so much so that the National Guard received 50% more funding than the Tunisian army, navy, and air force received combined. Since independence, the dominance of the police had always been a distinctive feature of the Tunisian security sector – especially "when compared with Egypt, a country where the military has traditionally been a very influential actor" (Ouerghemmi, 4). Many considered this focus on the police forces and the marginalization of the military in favor of the Ministry of Interior "a deliberate act of Ben Ali's" (Ouerghemmi, 4). Ben Ali's security background, his distrust of the military institution after observing its potential for power in other Arab regime states, his focus on removing opposition political groups, and his preoccupation with personalizing and centralizing his regime around himself all created an atmosphere in which the branches of the Ministry of Interior – especially the National Guard – were prioritized over the military institution. He specialized almost exclusively in "matters relating to the maintenance of order and intelligence" which explained Ben Ali's focus of resources and attention on the police, internal security forces and intelligence services – and, as illustrated previously, at the expense of the military.

Ben Ali also used his preferred intelligence and security forces to further control the military. Throughout the early 1990's – when the Islamist movement gathered influence and the governmental crackdown on the groups became more and more brutal – the security forces conducted numerous purges of the military's higher ranks, removing junior and senior officers "suspected" of having Islamist tendencies. These purges were in reality directed solely at removing military leaders who might be threatening to the regime – as a result, senior officers found "their room to manoeuver and activities curtailed and increasingly controlled" by the police (Willis, 2012), resulting not only in a growth of the climate of suspicion within the military institution, but also the heightening of the rivalry between the military and the Ministry of Interior branches.

The extent to which Ben Ali and his security forces curtailed the military during this time was a testament to the paranoia percolating within the regime: the military as an institution had never participated in any anti-regime activity before, nor had it ever actually participated in a coup or coup attempt. Because of its apolitical and marginalized nature, its lack of war experience, and its tendency to stay confined to its barracks, the TAF was not likely to turn against Ben Ali. Instead, the military was further coerced into submission. It was not treated as an equal in the triangular power struggle between the president, the security forces, and the military, and its interests had not been catered to. It was only Ben Ali and his "small circle of cronies" in the Ministry of Interior who seemed to benefit from the corruption of the regime (Steiman, 2012). This fractured, distrustful relationship between the military and the security forces – engineered entirely by Ben Ali – would prove to be the downfall of the regime when the police forces found themselves unable to curtail the 2011 uprising, and suddenly required the help of the military to crush it.

Control by state constitutions: As might be expected, the role of the military as dictated by the Tunisian Constitution was entirely subjugated to the power of the president. Under the Tunisian Constitution of 1959 – the first independent Tunisian constitution, which was executed three years after the French occupation ended – the Tunisian military was under complete control of the President of the Republic, who acted as their Commander-in-Chief (Article 44, 1959 Tunisian Constitution). In addition, the President was also able to appoint high military officials (Article 55, 1959 Tunisian Constitution). In formulating the first constitution in this way, Bourguiba was able to marginalize the military institution as well as control both the actions of the military institution and its leadership. As mentioned previously, Bourguiba's ability to appoint his choice of military officials allowed him to pick those he believed either did not have strong political backgrounds or whose families were prominent supporters of his faction of the Neo-Destour, and could be co-opted to his apolitical military model. In this way, the military had very little formal role as laid out by the country's founding documents.

Past military intervention: The TAF were never considered a military power in the region and performed underwhelmingly whenever they were called into service – which was not often. At the moment of independence in 1956, the army only numbered about 1,600 soldiers, and had to rely on France to help crush Ben Youssef's small rebellion. As mentioned previously, in order to retain the promised connection with France, Bourguiba ensured that military officers would have to be sent to France to be trained, instead of creating military schools within Tunisia. Then, in 1961, the military was upset that the French army would not cease to use its air force base in Bizerte to conduct operations in Algeria; the military attacked the base for a week, and lost about 2,000 soldiers to the French loss of only 13. A small contingent of TAF forces were sent to Egypt to participate in the Arab-Israeli War of 1973, but the units never saw combat. Finally, the air defense units of TAF were completely unable to stop Israeli planes from bombing the Palestinian Liberation Organization's headquarters in Tunis in 1985 (Taylor, 78). Such an underwhelming track record for the TAF signified the lack of international conflict that Tunisia had to face: the majority of the security problems, as seen by the leadership under Bourguiba and then Ben Ali, were confined within the country's borders, and therefore mostly required the services of the security forces.

But the TAF did have two successful missions: both against their own people. Twice during Bourguiba's presidency, in 1978 and then 1984, the army obeyed the president's orders to quash a popular uprising when it became clear that the internal security forces could not do so themselves. In the first instance in 1978, called Black Thursday by Tunisian civilians, the army intervened in overwhelming force in organized protests by some of Tunisia's labor unions. About 40 people were killed. Then, in 1984, in events termed the Tunisian bread riots (which involved ten times the number of protestors as Black Thursday), the combined forces of the army and security forces killed roughly 100 people, wounded about 1,000 and arrested another thousand. In both cases, the TAF was initially unwilling to intervene because it believed its role to be entirely apolitical, and it resented the regime for this reason; however, the military cooperated with the president's order to crush both protests in the hopes that Bourguiba would change his policies to avoid further rioting (Taylor, 79). But policy changes in favor of the popular uprisings never happened: instead, on both occasions the riots were followed by a stronger security crackdown from the Ministry of Interior.

Class conflict within the military: Like Egypt, Tunisia's military was a highly stratified institution in terms of the class divides between the officers and the conscripts. The nature of this class divide was another imposition of Bourguiba's. He had originally selected the top officers based on their loyalty to the Neo-Destour party, mostly to surround himself with allies and form a military force against the Youssefists, who advocated a military-first policy in Tunisia, and the Islamists, who opposed Bourguiba's modernist, progressive social policies (Taylor, 74). Most of these officers came from Tunisia's educated and politically conscious middle class, and belonged to families that made up the country's urban elite. Under Bourguiba's policy of retaining strict ties to France, many of these officers were trained and educated in France and were therefore "bred" to support the French alliance and Bourguiba's policies. However, while he selected these officers based on political loyalty, Bourguiba still disallowed any involvement in politics.

Meanwhile, the TAF also retained a force of conscripts: at least one year of service is mandatory for all Tunisians at the age of 20. Most Tunisians viewed this one mandatory year "a solemn duty for the greater good of the country" because the military tended to have a significant humanitarian focus: conscripts build roads, hospitals, and houses and also farm the land. However, a career in the military apart from the obligatory conscript year was not highly regarded: largely because of the president's ability to promote only those officers who were politically loyal, the Armed Forces was mostly considered a lower-middle-class profession with little chance of any form of social advancement – just as with Egypt's military, where the conscripts were similarly unable to rise through the ranks.

Public perception/image: Because of the military's largely minimalized role in Tunisian society, public knowledge of the military extended only to the barracks. However, even before the military's actions in the 2011 uprising, the Tunisian public respected the Armed Forces. Each year on June 24, Eid al-Jaysh (National Army Day) saw a large turnout of civilians who came to celebrate as the military marched through Tunis with its soldiers and military equipment (Taylor, 78). Tunisians also valued the TAF because it was not part of the Ministry of Interior's "ring of corruption." But the extent of this public respect was mainly directed towards the military's position of authority, humanitarian assistance, and reputation as a national institution – not because of their strength or prowess on the battlefield (Pelletreau, 9 August 2014), which, as described above, was never impressive. Otherwise, the populace had little involvement or experience with the military. In this sense, the public's perception of the military had been largely confined by the regime's restriction of military actions. The Tunisian public had been oppressed and confined by the Ministry of Interior's branches – the police, intelligence, National Guard, and others – while the military had been for the most part largely removed from national issues. But this was all to change in 2011: the public's perception of the military elevated from respectful to adoring when the military became the key actor in the removal of Ben Ali and the 55-year-long authoritarian regime.

The Tunisian Military's Role Post-2011

When General Ammar decided to disobey Ben Ali's order to fire on the popular uprising, the military's role in Tunisian political society would drastically change. Before the uprising, as described previously, the military had been politically weak, had suffered from inadequate funding, was not considered an acceptable path of social mobility, and was effectively sidelined by the Ministry of Interior's numerous security branches. But by playing the key role in the removal of the Ben Ali regime – and being, as General Ammar proclaimed in a much publicized speech, "the guarantor of the country, the people, and the revolution" – the military gained "political muscle, public prestige, bureaucratic autonomy, and priority in resources over the security forces" (Taylor, 78) as well as formidable control over the reform of the security forces. Ammar became a Tunisian hero after the revolution, and the military emerged as the only strong institution left standing. The newly political role of the Tunisian military changed overnight: the refusal to turn against the popular uprising proved crucial to the galvanizing of the populace and the eventual success of the uprising. The military's role in the post-uprising transition, however, would be unclear: would the military be willing and able to fill the power vacuum that had been left by Ben Ali and his now decimated security apparatus?

In 1991, Samuel Huntington identified Tunisia as a prime candidate for future democratization because of its pace of economic growth, its educated middle class and the liberalization measures undertaken in the beginning of Ben Ali's presidency (Huntington, 287). Of course, it turned out that Ben Ali's supposed reforms were short-lived had the opposite effect on Tunisia, and that it was instead the languishing youth population and their social media movement that, 20 years after Huntington's statement, began the spread of uprisings both within the country and the rest of the region. Indeed, of all of the states affected by the Arab uprisings, Tunisia has come the closest – if it has not arrived there already (This thesis examines material up until January 2014; please refer to the epilogue for a discussion of the recent Tunisian elections) – to achieving a successful democratic transition from authoritarian rule. Almost four years after the initial uprisings, Tunisia has enjoyed a mix of factors that increase its chances for democratization. These factors, identified by Maddy-Weitzman in Middle East Quarterly in 2014, included the educated middle class noted above, as well as "a compact, well-defined national identity and collective sense of self" (2) and a tradition of active civil society. More importantly, however, the other factor identified by Maddy-Weitzman was the "small-sized, non-politicized military, whose chief of staff [Ammar] pointedly refused Ben Ali's directive to fire on the protestors, instead acting to control policemen, security and intelligence personnel...[Ammar] also turned aside any suggestion that he and his fellow officers, and not civilians, should assume control of the country" (2).

The military's refusal in 2011 to insert itself as a political leader – at a defining moment when it was both able and encouraged by the populace to do so – allowed civilian political actors to take over. Unlike in Egypt, where the SCAF "temporarily" suspended the constitution in order to remove Mubarak (and later Morsi) from office, the process of transferring power to the civilian population in Tunisia "maintained a greater degree of constitutional legitimacy and continuity during the fashioning of a new order" (Maddy-Weitzman, 4). Even though Tunisia's path to democracy since 2011 has been difficult and, at times, questionable (the initial government leaders belonged to the class of political elite that had governed since independence under Bourguiba and Ben Ali), the military's voluntary lack of intervention in the post-uprising transition allowed the civilian control of the political restructuring process to take root. The instances of authoritarian military regimes taking control of state politics in Latin America were not about to be repeated in Tunisia.

If Ammar had accepted the leadership role, the military institution would have found itself with astronomically more power and responsibility than ever before. It is likely that the TAF would not have been prepared to control and restructure Tunisian political and economic society as well as the now-sidelined Ministry of Interior forces, and that Ammar was aware of this fact when he declined to lead. However, it is the opinion of this thesis that the military's history with the regime leadership and the subsequent formation of the military culture since independence in 1956 predetermined the extent of the military's role in 2011. Ammar's military was and always had been apolitical: its job was to intervene for the good of the country, regardless of the politics involved, and then return to the barracks as it had always done.

As discussed in the introduction to this case, and from analyzing the effects of each factor discussed, the most influential factor – and the catalyzing factor that produced and affected the other five discussed in this thesis – in determining the military's involvement in the Tunisian uprising and the subsequent transition was the relationship between the regime leadership and the military. Bourguiba's marginalization and control of the military – the result of his strategy to "breed" the military into an apolitical actor, as well as Ben Ali's continuation of this strategy, through the causal mechanisms that followed – was essential to the creation of the military culture and motives that led the institution to turn against the regime. Senior military officers had been raised under Bourguiba's ethos of strict political neutrality, and indeed had been aware of this fact when they had chosen a military career. These same leaders had been reluctant to quash the uprisings in the late 1970's and early 1980's, but had been forced to intervene in such political situations anyway. The further marginalization of the military continued when Ben Ali's regime then created in the TAF an environment of resentment against the Islamist purges of the 1990's, and the military leaders had been forced to undergo the humiliating control that the police forces exercised over them.

The causal sequence of events that began with Bourguiba's independence movement and his breeding of the apolitical Tunisian military affected, and in some ways created, the factors that were to eventually lead to the Tunisian military's withdrawal from political society after the 2011 uprising. In terms of the military's relationship with the regime leadership, the president purposefully created the rivalry between the police forces and the military; it built into the constitution the formal role of the military as subservient to the regime, and it forced the military to intervene in international affairs it knew it could not win and domestic ones it did not agree with. In terms of the cultural factors affecting the decision-making, the apolitical nature of the institution built by Bourguiba, coupled with the combination of conscripts loyal to the populace and officers tired of being marginalized, aligned the best interests of the entire military institution with those of the popular uprising.

It is therefore not surprising that the Tunisian military acted against the regime in 2011, nor that General Ammar declined to assume a political role in the transition and appeared to the public only once, ten days after Ben Ali's removal, to assure the people that "the military would not move beyond the role ascribed to it in the constitution." The military had the opportunity to play a pivotal role in determining whether Tunisia would fall back into autocratic rule or become the first Arab democracy, and its removal of this obstacle to democracy allowed civilian political parties to step in a form a government. In many ways, the military as whole benefited from the fall of the Ben Ali regime, which is why it is not surprising that it refused to intervene in the 2011 uprising: officers were persecuted by the police forces and the military was able to create for itself a public persona dedicated to the Tunisian ideals of political freedom and equality, and to the survival of the popular revolution. On a more ideological level, though, the military institution had always supported the interests of Tunisia as a country, including economic and political development, which is why it is not surprising that the TAF stepped away from politics to allow civilians to take over the transition to democracy.

## Conclusion: A Factoral Comparison of the States

As noted throughout this thesis, both the Tunisian and Egyptian militaries refused the regime leaderships' directives to fire on the popular uprisings in 2011. Yet, as described in the previous cases, the events leading these two institutions to the same action were the results of playing entirely different political roles in their countries' societies. These roles most clearly manifested themselves in each military's level of involvement in the political transition after the uprising had succeeded. However, it was the ways in which this role was formed where the TAF's self-removal from politics diverged dramatically from SCAF's full-scale intervention and takeover of the Egyptian political transition. In many ways, the role of each military in the transitions after the 2011 uprisings was largely defined by its connections and interactions with the regime leader at the critical political shift in the 1950's, when both countries transitioned to authoritarian rule. The interactions between the military and the regime's actors – the leadership and the police forces – reinforced and built upon the mechanisms that influenced the militaries to either act in the interests of the institution, as in Egypt, or the interests of both the institution and the state as a whole, as in Tunisia.

As described in Figure 1 (below), this intra-regime power struggle between the regime leadership and the military formed a rivalry between the two actors. In this way, all of the factors discussed in this thesis played some role in the formation of the military institution's interests. When, in 2011, the regime leader and his security forces found themselves no longer able to crush the popular uprising, and could not align their own interests with those of the military through coercion, cooptation, or manipulation, the military was able to overake the regime and remove it from power.

Figure 2: PRIOR TO THE UPRISINGS: Reinforcing mechanisms that describe the power struggle cycle between the regime leadership and military institution prior to the 2011 uprising. When the regime is no longer able to respond with coercion, the military will take power from the regime for its own interests and/or the interests of the state.

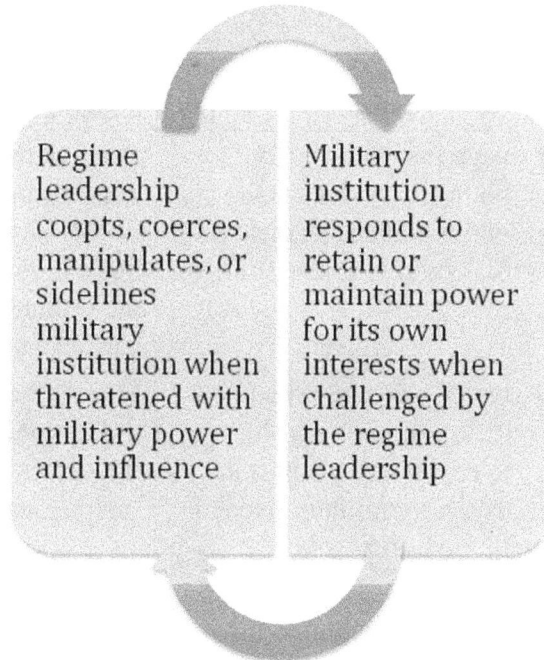

Regime leadership coopts, coerces, manipulates, or sidelines military institution when threatened with military power and influence

Military institution responds to retain or maintain power for its own interests when challenged by the regime leadership

Figure 3: At the risk of oversimplifying the discussion of this thesis, this chart visually compares for the reader the conclusions drawn from each factor and their effects on the military's role during the uprising and in the political transition that followed.

| Factor | Egypt | Tunisia |
|--------|-------|---------|
| **1. Military interests created by the regime leadership** | Economic holdings that had been marginalized under Mubarak led military to act in consideration of its economic interests. | Apolitical agenda focused on maintaining the interests of the Tunisian people and state. No economic holdings. |
| **2. Military-police relationship** | Controlled by regime leader & police forces; 2011 uprising allows military to insert itself into the lead role in politics and reform police image | Military often subordinated under police forces and officers coerced by leader/ police; leading military to insert itself into the uprising when police failed & reform police image |
| **3. Military's popular image** | Popular image boosted by 2011 takeover, but military does not consider public perception once it assumes the lead role in the political transition | Positive but nonexistent relationship with populace boosted by 2011 intervention, but remains static once the military retreats to the barracks afterward |
| **4. Class conflict within the military** | Officer/conscript divide risked splitting the military during the uprising; to ensure the institution did not split, the entire military needed to side with the uprising | Similar class conflict, but did not necessarily play as important a role in decision-making as occurred in Egypt |
| **5. Military's role in state constitutions** | Controlled by leadership in formal constitutions; after assuming lead role in politics, military writes constitutions to ensure its own autonomy and political power | Controlled by leadership in formal constitutions, but after uprising allows civilian leadership to retain command over armed forces |
| **6. Prior interventions** | Reflect leadership's control over the military | Reflect leadership's control over the military, but also show the military's apolitical desire to protect the interests of the Tunisian state |

However, the roles of the two militaries in the transition that followed the 2011 uprisings diverged dramatically. Again, as demonstrated by the country cases, this divergence can be accounted for by the examination of the factors discussed. The Egyptian military took over the lead role in state politics and eventually removed the democratically elected ruling party; meanwhile, the Tunisian military removed itself from politics entirely – despite public desire for the military to lead the new government – and allowed an elected civilian caretaker government to assume the leadership role. For the next three years, despite the elected government's inability to quash violent terrorism, the Tunisian military remained separate from politics and focused its efforts solely on minimizing the violence. Outlined below is a chart roughly comparing the historical factors discussed in this thesis and, organized by country, the conclusions drawn regarding the role of the military in the 2011 uprising and the political transition that followed. The chart is followed by a more in-depth discussed of the comparison of these factors.

The Egyptian military had played a leading role in Egypt's transition out of the monarchy in the 1950's, and had grappled with the military-educated regime leaders in a power struggle throughout the next sixty years of authoritarian rule. Under Nasser, the military was marginalized and coerced under an extensively personalized security apparatus; under Sadat, the same coercive strategies were used, in addition to the infitah policies directed at the military institution that sidelined it into a purely economic, not war-making, actor; and under Mubarak, where the economic focus continued and the military was subordinated under the oppressive police forces. The reinforcing mechanisms of these actions created a cycle between the cooptation, coercion, and manipulation of the military by the regime leadership and the military's actions against the regime. Military leaders were forced to respond to the regime's actions in ways that would best accomplish the interests of the military as a whole, which meant obeying the regime leadership when necessary and creating political opposition when necessary. The military's interests became clear in 2011 when the military intervened against Mubarak in favor of the popular uprising, and proceeded to take over control over state politics.

In examining the effects of each of the factors in the formation of the Egyptian military's interests, we can make the following conclusions: 1) the economic focus built into the military institution by Sadat's infitah policies and Mubarak's continuation of the same, though with significant budgetary controls, led the military to act in protection of its economic interests when Mubarak lost control in 2011; 2) the military-police relationship largely defined the military's intervention in 2011: after years of being controlled by the regime leader and his security forces, the military was able to insert itself into the lead political role during and after the uprising and reform the police forces; 3) the military's popular image was boosted by their role in the 2011 takeover, but the military would not take into account public perception once it had regained power; 4) the class conflict within the military between conscripts and officers placed pressure on the institution to maintain its integrity: it was not within the military's interests to split along class divides during the 2011 uprising, so the entire military opposed Mubarak's regime; 5) the military's role in the formal state constitutions had been controlled by the regime leadership up until 2011, but after the uprising and the military's newly acquired lead role in politics, the military was able to write the new constitutions around consolidating its own autonomy and power; and 6) the military's prior interventions reflected its controlled relationship with the regime leader. This amalgamation of factors and their effects on the military institution brought about the military's role in the uprising and in the political transition that followed.

Meanwhile, in Tunisia, the military had never played a defining role in state politics, and had since independence been marginalized and kept in the barracks, mostly untrained, by the regime leadership. To keep the military removed from politics, Bourguiba and Ben Ali forced the TAF to pursue an entirely apolitical agenda and only utilized it in a few international skirmishes and civilian riots. The TAF was overshadowed and controlled by the police forces, its officers coerced into political subordination, and the institution was for the most part unknown to the Tunisian public. As a result, the TAF's actions in the 2011 uprising allowed the military to claim the role as "the revolution's savior," elevating its image in the eyes of the public while also removing a dictator who no longer supported the goals and best interests of the state. But the military's apolitical nature also left it without the need or ability to take over political control, and therefore military was not a driving force in the political transition.

From the starting point of the apolitical nature of the TAF as defined by the regime leadership, comparisons can be drawn between the TAF and the highly political role of the Egyptian military. The most effectual factors in the Tunisian military case lead us to the following conclusions: 1) unlike the Egyptian military, the Tunisian military had no economic holdings or interests and therefore did not have economically motivated reasons to intervene in 2011; 2) the military-police relationship was, like in Egypt, one that subordinated the military under the security forces and often controlled the military officers, leading the military to insert itself in the uprising when the police failed and take responsibility for revamping the police image; 3) the military's positive but almost nonexistent relationship with the populace was boosted by the military's intervention in 2011 but remained relatively static once the military retreated to the barracks during the subsequent political transition; 4) the class conflict within the Tunisian military was similar to that of the Egyptian military, but did not necessarily play a role in the military's intervention in 2011; 5) the military's role in state constitutions reflects its relationship with the regime leader: controlled and subordinated; 6) the prior interventions of the Tunisian military showcased its lack of power in the international arena, but domestically highlighted the military's apolitical interest in bridging the divide between the interests of the Tunisian people and state.

Comparing the effects of the historical factors in this way, we can observe how the chain of events created by the factors influenced the military to act as it did in 2011 and, from there, how the military's actions led to its role in the political transitions that followed.

In Tunisia the Military refuses regime directive to fire on the popular uprising. The Tunisian military was an uninterested party in politics. General Ammar did not believe it was the military's role to lead, so he stepped aside, thereby removing an obstacle to a democratic transition. A constitution was written, a civilian caretaker government took control affter Ennahda stepped down, and elections were planned for the fall.

In Egypt, the military also refused the regime directive to fire on the popular uprising. The Egyptian military is an interested party in state politics. SCAF moderated elections, then later deposes Morsi and takes over. Therefore, the military added an obstacle to a democratic transition. Sisi was elected under dubious circumstances, a new constitution granted unprecedented rights to SCAF, opposition groups were jailed and executed, leaving the military in control of governance.

In pursuing possible expansions of this research, an examination of military interventions in the other Arab uprisings could extend the discussion beyond a military's choice to side with the popular uprising. Both the Tunisian and Egyptian militaries chose to ignore the regime's directive to fire on the populace, though clearly that decision led to very different interventions in the political transitions that followed. The Tunisian and Egyptian popular uprisings were initially considered the only ones successful in the toppling the authoritative regime; while that point is debatable in Egypt today, where it appears authoritarian rule has been reestablished, much could be illuminated in military intervention theory by examining cases in which the military's interests did not initially align with the popular uprising. In contrast, the other Arab uprisings all led to very different outcomes. Some were entirely unsuccessful and even, in some cases, plunged the state into full-scale war. In some of these cases, the military institution fractured its loyalty between the populace and the regime; other times international military intervention was required, and in other cases the military solely decided to crush the uprising in favor of siding with the regime.

Examining the relationships between the military and the governing regime in other countries affected by the Arab uprisings, and how those relationships and historical factors affected such actions in the uprisings and subsequent transitions or reforms in different ways than occurred in Tunisia and Egypt, would provide insights into an overarching pattern of regime-military relationships. Perhaps more importantly, considering the current instability in many areas of the MENA region, such a comprehensive study of military interventions in post-uprising transitions would illuminate the driving interests of the Arab military institutions, perhaps providing possible strategies for combining the military's interests with those of the civilian population. Such strategies, if studied in more depth and detail, could minimize the effects of military authoritarian rule and maximize the potential for democratic transition and an open political society. The future of many of the countries affected by the 2011 Arab uprisings still remains to be seen, and while Tunisia pushes towards a legitimate democracy, Egyptian civil society progressively loses more human rights and freedoms. The examples created by these two cases, demonstrating the sheer importance of the military institution's actions on the states' political transitions, can provide analogues to analyze and improve the potential for greater political freedoms across the MENA region.

## A Tale of Two Elections: January 2014 to the Present

This study examined military intervention in the 2011 uprisings and in the politics of the state transitions afterwards up until January 2014, when both countries introduced their most recent constitutions. Since then, significant political events have occurred in both countries that are necessary to mention in the context of regional events, though they are not directly examined in the body of this thesis. In both cases, elections have been held. In Egypt, Sisi stepped down from his command of the military only to be "elected" president in June 2014, and has devoted significant efforts to reorganizing SCAF and revamping Egypt's economy by adopting economic policies reminiscent of the "mega-projectism" of the Mubarak era. The control that the military holds over Egyptian politics and media has devolved

Egypt into a military dictatorship. Meanwhile, Tunisia's transition to democracy since 2011 has not been an easy path; however, the military institution has remained on the whole absent from politics. In the last year, the Islamist party Ennahda, elected into the government majority at the end of 2011, responded to harsh criticism by stepping down in favor of a bipartisan caretaker government until a new round of elections could be held (Gall, 29 January 2014). These elections, which pitted Ennahda against secularist old-guard politicians from Ben Ali's regime under the banner of the party Nida Tunis ("Call for Tunisia"), took place in October and November of 2014. The final presidential elections took place just a few days before the completion of this paper, with Nida Tunis' candidate, Beji Caid Essebsi, winning the majority vote. The path to these elections has not been an easy one, yet the current triumph of Essebsi and Nida Tunis in the polls seems to solidify Tunisia as a fully functioning, legitimate democracy (Al Jazeera, 22 December 2014).

Not so in Egypt, where it has become clear that a military dictatorship, and not a democracy, is in control of state politics. In March 2014, Sisi stepped down from the position of field marshal, announcing his candidacy for the Egyptian presidency. Sure enough, two months later, Sisi won the presidential elections with 96% of the vote. While most Egyptians simply did not vote in the elections, it was clear that the numbers had been fixed in some way – and even clearer that voting was pointless. The voting appeared to only be a form of propaganda; it was widely suspected that the military would simply have violently seized power if the people had come out to vote against him (Seikaly, 23 October 2014). President Sisi and his military-backed cabinet had promised to restore stability to the social unrest as well as reform the faltering economy. As of this writing, the economic reform has recovered most of the losses – but at the cost of human rights. Sisi has revamped the energy platform that lost significant support for the Morsi administration, and removed costly energy subsidies that hit the people hard – but trimmed 2.5% off of Egypt's GDP (Wilson, 15 September 2014). In addition, Sisi has instigated the Suez Canal project, which seeks to widen the canal in the next year in order to double the number of ships that can pass through it, dramatically increasing income from the canal.

However, human rights and the freedom of speech have been all but completely taken away. The media has been coopted into pro-Sisi propaganda, and those who do not comply – such as three Al-Jazeera journalists who experienced such treatment in an internationally publicized case – are sentenced to long jail terms without fair trials. Perhaps even more concerning is the treatment of the Muslim Brotherhood – supporters of the former majority political party are labeled as terrorists, thrown in jail by military courts, in some instances sentenced to death in mass numbers, and even massacred such as in the Rabaa Massacre in 2013. Even Dr. Bassem Youssef's famous political satire show, which broadcast throughout the end of Mubarak's regime through Sisi's rise to power, was mysteriously taken off the air in June 2014.

At this point, a year and a half after Morsi was deposed and Egypt has fallen back into military dictatorship, the Egyptian military is powerful enough and retains enough resources to restructure the existing order to better achieve stability within Egypt. However, as can be seen throughout the history of the military's influence on the state, the institution has so far been unwilling to prioritize reforms that could come at the expense of strengthening and safeguarding its own interests. The current lack of parliamentary or judicial oversight on the military is the most direct challenge to democracy: if

Egypt is to achieve legitimate democracy, such as what Tunisia seems to have accomplished within the last year, the military and security forces would need to become subject to civilian authority. Without significant protest and intervention on the part of the populace, it is difficult to see how democracy might formulate. This time, there is no Egyptian military to step in and guarantee the revolution.

# Works Cited

Amar, Paul. "Spotlight on Egypt." Los Angeles: USC Department of Middle East Studies, 23 October 2014.

Al Jazeera, "Essebsi declares victory in Tunisia vote." 22 December 2014.

Associated Press. "Tunisia election results: Nida Tunis wins most seats, sidelining Islamists." *The Guardian* 30 October 2014.

Barany, Zoltan. *The Soldier and the Changing State.* Princeton: Princeton University Press, 2012.

Bellin, Eva. "Reconsidering the Robustness of Authoritarianism in the Middle East: Lessons from the Arab Spring." *Comparative Politics* 44.2 (2012): 127-149.

—. "The Robustness of Authoritarianism in the Middle East: Exceptionalism in Comparative Perspective." *Comparative Politics* 36.2 (2004): 139-157.

Ben Mahfoudh, Haykel. "Security Sector Reform in Tunisia Three Years into the Democratic Transition." *Arab Reform Initiative: Security in Times of Transition* July 2014.

Brooks, Risa. "Political-Military Relations and the Stability of Arab Regimes." Adelphi Paper 324 (1998).

Central Intelligence Agency. "Egypt: Military." June 2014. CIA World Fact Book. 1 November 2014 <https://www.cia.gov/library/publications/the-world-factbook/geos/eg.html>.

Clarke, Killian. "Unexpected Brokers of Mobilization: Contingency and Networks in the Egyptian Uprising." *Comparative Politics* 46.4 (2014): 379-397.

CNN Wire Staff. Egyptian Military: Key Facts. 15 February 2011. 12 October 2014 <http://www.cnn.com/2011/WORLD/africa/02/14/egypt.military.facts/index.html>.

Cook, Steven. *Ruling but Not Governing: The Military and Political Development in Egypt, Algeria, and Turkey.* Baltimore: Johns Hopkins University Press, 2007.

—. "The calculations of Tunisia's military." *Foreign Policy* 20 January 2011.

Dixon, Norman. *On the Psychology of Military Incompetance.* New York: Basic, 1976.

Dunne, Michele & Hamzawy, Amr. "The Ups and Downs of Political Reform in Egypt." *Beyond the Facade: Political Reform in the Arab World.* Ed. Marina & Choucair-Vizoso, Julia Ottawy. Washington, D.C.: Carnegie Endowment for International Peace, 2008.

*Economist, The.* The Shoe Thrower's Index: An Index of Unrest in the Arab World. 9 February 2011. 23 October 2014 <http://www.economist.com/blogs/dailychart/2011/02/daily_chart_arab_unrest_index>.

Egypt: State Information Service. Constitution of the Arab Republic of Egypt, 1971. 5 September 2014 <http://www.sis.gov.eg/En/Templates/Articles/tmpArticles.aspx?CatID=208#.VFpF-4copUR>.

—. Constitution of the Arab Republic of Egypt, 2014. 12 August 2014 <http://www.sis.gov.eg/Newvr/Dustor-en001.pdf>.

El Ouerghemmi, Nadia. "Steps Towards Reconciliation: The Difficult Relationship between the Security Forces and the Population in Tunisia." "The Arab Spring Three Years On". Montreal: World Congress of the International Political Science Association, 2014. 1-20.

El Shazly, Saad. *The Crossing of the Suez.* American Mideast Research, 2003.

El-Houdaiby, Ibrahim. "Changing Alliances and Continuous Oppression: The Rule of Egypt's Security Sector." Arab Reform Initiative June 2014.

Farcau, Bruce. *The Transition to Democracy in Latin America: The Role of the Military.* Westport: Praeger Publishers, 1996.

Finer, Samuel. *The Man on Horseback: The Role of the Military in Politics.* London: Pall Mall, 1962.

Gall, Carlotta. "Islamist Party in Tunisia Hands Power to Caretaker Government." *The New York Times* 29 January 2014.

—. "Runoff Will Decide President of Tunisia." *The New York Times* 25 November 2014.

Grand, Stephen. *Understanding Tahrir Square: What Transitions Elsewhere Can Teach Us About the Prospects for Arab Democracy.* Washington, D.C.: Brookings Institution Press, 2014.

Hashim, Ahmed. "The Egyptian Military, Part One: From the Ottomans Through Sadat." *Middle East Policy* 18.3 (2011): 63-78.

—. "The Egyptian Military, Part Two: From Mubarak Onward." *Middle East Policy* 18.4 (2011): 106-128.

Holmes, Amy Austin. "Why Egypt's military orchestrated a massacre." *The Washington Post* 22 August 2014.

Huntington, Samuel. *Political Order in Changing Societies.* New Haven: Yale University, 1968.

—. *The Soldier and the State.* Cambridge: Harvard University Press, 1957.

—. *The Third Wave: Democratization in the Late Twentieth Century.* Norman: Oklahoma University Press, 1991.

Janowitz, Morris. *Military Institutions and Coercion in the Developing Nations.* Chicago: University of Chicago Press, 1988.

Jebnoun, Noureddine. "In the shadow of power: civil-military relations and the Tunisian popular uprising." *The Journal of North African Studies* 19.3 (2014): 296-316.

Kandil, Hazem. "Back on Horse? The Military Between Two Revolutions." Korany, Baghat & Rabab El-Mahdi. *The Arab Spring in Egypt.* Cairo: The American University in Cairo Press, 2012.

—. *Soldiers, Spies, and Statesmen: Egypt's Road to Revolt.* London: Verso, 2012.

Kier, Elizabeth. "Culture and Military Doctrine: France between the Wars." *International Security* 19.4 (1995): 65-93.

Maddy-Weitzman, Bruce. "Tunisia's Morning After." *Middle East Quarterly* 18.3 (2011).

Mahoney, James. "Path Dependence in Historical Sociology." *Theory and Society* 29.4 (2000): 507-548.

Maswood, Javed & Usha Natarajan. "Democratization and Constitutional Reform in Egypt and Indonesia: Evaluating the Role of the Military." Korany, Baghat & El-Mahdi, Rabab. *Arab Spring in Egypt: Revolution and Beyond.* Cairo: American University in Cairo Press, 2012.

McDermott, Anthony. *Egypt from Nasser to Mubarak: A Flawed Revolution.* London: Croom Helm, 1988.

Moore, Henry Clement. *Tunisia Since Independence: The Dynamics of One-Party Government.* Berkeley: University of California Press, 1965.

Nordas, Ragnhild & Christian Davenport. "Fight the Youth: Youth Bulges and State Repression." *American Journal of Political Science* 57.4 (2013): 926-940.

O'Donnell, Guillermo. "Reflections on the Patterns of Change in the Bureaucratic-Authoritarian State." *Latin American Research Review* 13.1 (1978): 3-38.

Pelletreau, Robert: U.S. Ambassador to Bahrain (1979-1980), Tunisia (1987-1991) and Egypt (1991-1993). Interview. Elizabeth Peabody. 9 August 2014. During his three years in Cairo, Ambassador Pelletreau considered himself to be a friend and confidant of Hosni Mubarak.

Perlmutter, Amos. *Egypt: The Praetorian State.* New Brunswick: Transaction, Inc., 1974.

Pollack, John. "Streetbook: How Egyptian and Tunisian youth hacked the Arab Spring." *Technology Review* 114.5 (2011): 70.

Pop-eleches, Gregor & Graeme Robertson. "After the Revolution: Long-Term Effects of Electoral Revolutions." *Problems of Post-Communism* 61.4 (2014).

Quinlivan, James. "Coup-proofing: Its Practice and Consequences in the Middle East." *International Security* 24.2 (1999): 131-165.

Rugh, William: Ambassador to UAE. Interview. Elizabeth Peabody. 6 August 2014.

Sayigh, Yezid. "Egypt's army looks beyond Mubarak." *Financial Times* 2 February 2011.

Seikaly, Sherene. "Spotlight on Egypt." Los Angeles, USC Department of Middle East Studies, 23 October 2014.

Silverman, David. "The Arab Military in the Arab Spring: Agent of Continuity or Change? A Comparative Analysis of Tunisia, Egypt, Syria, and Libya." New Orleans: American Political Science Association, 2012.

Springborg, Robert. Egyptian Military Elizabeth Peabody. 22 April 2014.

Steiman, Daniel. "Military Decision-Making During the Arab Spring." MUFTAH 29 May 2012.

Stepan, Alfred. *Authoritarian Brazil.* New Haven: Yale University Press, 1973.

—. The Military in Politics: Changing Patterns in Brazil. Princeton: Princeton University Press, 1971.

Stone, Russell. "Tunisia: A Single Party System Holds Change in Abeyance." *Political Elites in Arab North Africa.* Ed. I. W. Zartman. New York: Longman, 1982.

Taylor, William. *Military Responses to the Arab Uprisings and the Future of Civil-Military Relations in the Middle East.* Palgrave MacMillan, 2014.

The Guardian. "The Arab spring: made in Tunisia, broken in Egypt." *The Guardian* 16 January 2014.

Ware, L.B. "Ben Ali's Constitutional Coup in Tunisia." *Middle East Journal* 42.4 (1988).

Wenig, Gilad. "Egypt's New Military Brass." The Washington Institute for Near East Policy 26 March 2014.

Willis, Michael. *Politics and Power in the Maghreb: Algeria, Tunisia and Morocco from Independence to the Arab Spring.* London: C. Hurst & Co. Publishers, Ltd., 2012.

Wilson, Nigel. "100 Days of Sisi: Egypt Economic Recovery Kicks Off, but Human Rights Trampled." *International Business Times* 15 September 2014.

World Intellectual Property Organization. "The Constitution of Tunisia, 1959." Tunis, 1 June 1959.

Zagorski, Paul. *Democracy and National Security: Civil-Military Relations in Latin America.* Boulder: Lynne Rienner Publishers, 1992.

4

# Piecing Ourselves Back Together: Conceptualizing the Relationship between Peace and Justice in Post-Conflict Societies

## Nitya Ramanathan

*Within international relations there is a normative belief that peace and justice exist as a positive, linear relationship. Justice may be sought as redress for crimes, but also as a way of coming to terms with the past and building a new future. The international community, mainly Western in makeup, believes that in order for a country to achieve true peace and reconciliation between the previously warring factions, some sort of justice mechanisms must be put in place. In this paper I looked at the impact of different factors of transitional justice and their achievement in contributing to stability, peace, and reconciliation. Using Northern Ireland, Rwanda, South Africa, and Sri Lanka as examples of various post-conflict states, I examined what are the necessary and sufficient conditions of justice to achieve peace. All four countries have experienced an upheaval in the social, political, and economic spheres and have implemented different mechanisms to deal with the trauma that their respective societies face. An analysis of the cases questioned the relationship between peace and justice to identify if the seemingly linear relationship is universally applicable.*

It was found that in countries such as Rwanda and South Africa that both implemented formal justice structures some sense of peace was created in the short term impact. While South Africa only implemented the formal Truth and Reconciliation Commission, Rwanda went a step further in using its grassroots justice mechanisms, and implementing legislation to unify the differing identities into a singular unit. These extra steps, with the help of international assistance and support have left Rwanda with a more widespread and developed peace, than that of South Africa. In the cases of Northern Ireland and Sri Lanka there has been very little formal justice mechanism components implemented in either country. While the Northern Ireland government has not touched the issue of justice at all, they have allowed the United Kingdom criminal justice system, European Human Rights Court, and grassroots non-governmental organizations to take on the issue. This has led to peaceful society in the sense that there has been no more major outbreaks of fighting between the factions, but Northern Irish society is heavily divided, so much so that when conducting field research in the area, multiple people, both Catholic and Protestant, referred to their community as a 'benign apartheid.' In Sri Lanka there was a commission conducted that looked at the events of the war and its aftermath, but it has been widely condemned as extremely biased toward the government and neglectful of the victims of the war. Other than the Lessons Learned and Reconciliation Commission the Sri Lanka government has made very little steps toward justice, but the country has been at peace for the five years since the end of the war. While the time frame might limit extensive analysis on the impact of justice and peace, it can be hypothesized that the lack of justice in Sri Lanka might impact long term peace in the country. For now it seems that forgetting the war and moving forward with economic development might be the best vehicle of peaceful relations in Sri Lanka.

| Case | GPI | Lund Type | Peace |
|---|---|---|---|
| Rwanda | 137 | Durable | High |
| Northern Ireland | 47 (UK) | Stable | Medium |
| Sri Lanka | 105 | Compelled | High |
| South Africa | 122 | Stable | Medium |

Peace has simply been defined as the absence of war, but a more in depth look at the concept has led to the definition of a peaceful society where citizens are free, prosperous, and unthreatened. In the post-conflict context peace and justice have been inextricably linked as necessary for one another. Scholars have argued that without justice societies cannot create a foundation for democracy, trust, and hope. Justice has now become the precondition for peace because it can make the difference between renewed fighting and long-lasting stability. The UN legitimized this relationship with the 2004 report on transitional justice that stated justice and peace are mutually reinforcing imperatives.

Critiques of the linear relationship between peace and justice cite silence and forgetting as important concepts that must be considered in post-conflict reconstruction. In the aftermath of great upheaval justice and truth telling can rip a society back apart, so these scholars suggest that sometime be taken before attempting these monumental tasks. Silence and forgetting are not necessary mutually exclusive to justice because selectivity of these concepts can shape public memory and opinion. Some societies choose to focus on the future rather than remember the past, binding their citizens together by looking forward toward prosperity and peace. Once a society is stable and the past is distanced from the citizens there is a greater ability to make crimes public without the fear of opening up fresh wounds.

While scholars vocally argue these points, they all agree that maybe in a more distant future, some sort of transitional justice mechanism must be put in place. Transitional justice has been described as the overall field of post-conflict reconstruction, human rights, and international criminal law. Most of the literature focuses on the use of legalism and formalized systems to implement a notion of justice. While justice has been broken down to the three categories of restorative, retributive, and criminal, most of the international community pushes for the retributive and criminal form since these have tangible outcomes and are in line with the traditional western concepts of justice. Most of the formalized legal structures are outcomes of state actors whether domestic or international, making the government and governance structures of importance to justice.

Critics of the legalism and rigid nature of transitional justice expand upon the concept to argue that justice should be understood as a concept that is fluid in who it applies to as well as who are the agents of change. They advocate for the use of victims and survivors in justice mechanisms as well as more grassroots work by non-governmental agencies and individuals. By combining the many theoretical frameworks presented in the literature it is possible to use the existing hypotheses to determine the universality of the linear relationship between peace and justice.

I use a comparative case study analysis to examine the relationship between peace and justice. The dependent variable is the degree of peace that accompanies justice. Indicators of dependent variable include: international ranking (global peace index), lack of violent outbursts between previously warring ethnicities, media freedom. The independent variables that I believe contribute to the expected outcome are factors identified across the three case studies as well as through an analysis of the literature on transitional justice. The variables and their indicators are presented in the following table:

| Independent Variables | Indicators |
| --- | --- |
| Truth and Reconciliation Mechanisms | open spaces for dialogue between previously warring factions |
| Power sharing structures | coalition governments, ethnically represented political parties, equal access to political power for minorities; Identity policies including legislation relating to identity, |
| Identity Legislation | relating to identity, respect for culture and values of minorities |
| Civil Society | human rights organizations, reports, research, local and international |
| International Engagement | UN reports and investigation, diaspora financial and human rights contribution |

Hypotheses:

Pursing justice through official mechanisms leads to higher levels of peace.

Pursuing justice through official mechanisms and grassroots activism leads to higher levels of peace.

Pursuing justice leads to more violence, not peace through a resurgence of violent behavior by previously opposing groups.

I chose Northern Ireland, Rwanda, and Sri Lanka as high level case study analysis and South Africa as mid-level analysis because they provide variation in the independent and dependent variables to evaluate the three hypotheses presented by the literature. They span the range on how conflicts ended, of types of justice schemes implemented in a post-conflict society, changeability on the conflict themselves, and a range of domestic and international assistance, as well as different time frames. While South Africa, Rwanda, and Northern Ireland are almost twenty years into their reconstruction, Sri Lanka is at the beginning of its process- it has only been 5 years since the end of the war. With this variation of case studies, my thesis creates a chronological analysis of transitional justice while providing recommendations for Sri Lanka's future. Variation of the case studies with common variables makes key factors exportable to other countries facing the huge task of reconstruction.

The global normative statement that justice is implicit for peace has led to many post-conflict countries focusing on the idea that they must pursue a certain agenda that has been determined by the western international community. The international community tends to push the ideology of one general solution onto countries that are struggling to define what justice means to them, instead of creating a unique solution molded around the situation of that country. By identifying the more nuanced and detailed elements of the relationship between peace and justice it is possible provide countries in similar situations with alternatives ideas to base their framework of justice.

# Literature Review

## Peace and Justice

Peace and justice are presented as being mutually constructive and justice being a necessary precursor for peace. Peace has been defined at its simplest as the absence of war (Bull 1984, Hobbes 1998) but scholars in the more liberalists and idealist literatures have proposed peace as a state of existence where states and their citizens are 'free, prosperous, and unthreatened' (Richmond 2008, Angell 1910, Posonby 1925). This debate on the definition of peace becomes especially important in the post-conflict context when the relationship between peace and justice is considered. Some scholars believe that peace can only be achieved through justice because it is the only way for victims to get even some sort of equivalency for the crimes done to them (Al Huessin, 2006). Others support this sentiment stating that they are mutually reinforcing concepts because justice is a way to restore "dignity, trust, and hope in a country" (Wierda 2006). Long term, peace can only be sustainable with justice (Teitel, Turner Deconstructing Transitional Justice). When done 'correctly,' justice can make the difference between continued violence and durable peacetime order (Bass, 2000). The widespread acceptance of the linear relationship between peace and justice can arguably be traced to the UN Doctorine in 2004 of the Report of the Secretary-General: The Rule of 7 and Transitional Justice in Conflict and Post-Conflict Societies, UN Doc S/2004/616 which stated that "justice, peace and democracy are not mutually exclusive objectives, but rather mutually reinforcing imperatives." (Sharp 2013)

In contrast, there is a body of literature that argues that peace does not have a positive linear relationship with justice, but rather the lack of justice can often lead to peace. Silence and forgetting, rather than truth and an outpouring of stories, might be better for peace, for the newly instated stability. Silence then can hold a divided society together after it has been torn apart in conflict (Winter, Zeruvabel 2010). Because these societies are so newly stable, remembering the recent past and atrocities can fuel still existing animosities, creating a fertile ground for history to be changed into war slogans and the foundation for dangerous ideology (Rieff 2011). Silence is then imperative for maintaining social order (Renan 1882, Simmel 1906). Some have pointed out that silence is not the lack of an opinion or perspective, but a tool through which victims can "maintain, assert, and enforce" an opinion (Winter, Zeruvabel 2010). Silence does not have to be part of the remembering-forgetting binary, but can shape public memory and occupy an intermediate position on the path to justice and peace (Winter, Zeruvabel 2010). Through forgetting the past a government can bind its citizens together through the fulfillment of a peaceful future (Al Huessin, 2006). Critics of the assumed relationship between peace and justice point out that it is usually only a selective justice and truth that the country chooses to view- not the truth in its entirety or without a frame that works in the favor of the governing party. Amnesties can also be used in a post-conflict society if they offer a simpler peace "without trials or assigning individual criminal responsibility" which might be what that society needs at the moment. Post- World War II Europe provides a positive example for the use of silence and forgetting, because with the exception of Germany after 1968 and one or two other countries, most have forgotten their crimes and have not fallen back into war (Al Huessin, 2006). Scholars tend to agree that at some point, maybe in a more distant future, some sort of transitional justice mechanism must be put in place. While often overlooked, this non-linear perspective and analysis of the relationship between peace and justice is important to consider when creating policy with a nuanced understanding of the situations in post-conflict countries.

Transitional Justice Mechanisms

Transitional justice literature combines post-conflict reconstruction, human rights and international criminal law, and provides nominative recommendations through the shift in values that characterize the transition to peace and stability (McEvoy 2007, Teitel 2000). The field's legitimacy was secured by the UN Secretary General report which defined the term as,

> compris[ing] the full range of processes and mechanisms associated with a society's attempts to come to terms with a legacy of large-scale past abuses, in order to ensure accountability, serve justice and achieve reconciliation. These may include both judicial and non-judicial mechanisms, with differing levels of international involvement (or none at all) and individual prosecutions, reparations, truth-seeking, institutional reform, vetting and dismissals, or a combination thereof (UN 2004).

There is a necessary link between human rights and justice, because transitional justice inculcates universal human rights and establishes it as something that must be protected with violations met with punishment (Turner 2011, Dyzenhaus 2003). Justice has been broken down into three general categories: restorative, retributive, and criminal. Scholars have created a list of seven principles that justice must meet: prosecutions; truth-telling and investigations of past violations; victims' rights; remedies and reparations; vetting, sanctions and administrative measures; memorialization, education and the preservation of historical memory (Bassiouni 2007). These themes are usually distilled into a mechanism such as a Truth and Reconciliation commission in South Africa or the gacaca courts in Rwanda. These tend to combine restorative, retributive, and criminal justice into one space where victims can be heard and perpetrators punished.

While the western community views criminal justice as the most productive category, scholars are more likely to promote restorative justice as a more holistic and beneficial mechanism that allows the victim to tell their whole stories (Dyzenhaus 2003). Most of the literature on transitional justice follows legalism, with a normative belief that law can transcend politics and partisanship (Turner 2008). Holding individuals accountable for crimes committed during conflict can create an atmosphere of justice that pervades an entire country facing the monumental task of post-conflict reconstruction (Sikkink 1995). The international community has been the most vocal in perpetuating legalism through institutions like the International Criminal Court, where leaders are indicted for war crimes or crimes against humanity, as well as the more localized tribunals such as the International Criminal Tribunal for Rwanda (ICTR) or the special court in Sierra Leone. The international community believes that by holding the ones in power accountable it will deter others within the country, as well as in the global context, from committing similar crimes.

This justice cascade has become a commonly pursued course of action for both the international community and individual countries, but critics say that it focuses too heavily on the perpetrators and setting a precedent rather than advocating for the needs of the victims. Legalism, while important, is only one method that should be used to pursue justice in a post-conflict society. Survivor's justice puts the emphasis on the victims, making perpetrators the secondary focus (Mamdani 2001). In this way victims are put in the focus of society and both they and perpetrators must find ways to reconcile.

Scholars such as McEvoy and McGregor propose an alternative, holistic and integrated approach to conceptualizing justice in transition, with three distinct, but inter-related dimensions: legal, reflective and distributive. While legal means has come to dominate the field of transitional justice because of its easy in measurability, some scholars see this as too narrow a lens for the larger amount that is attempting to be accomplished in this field. These narrow lens limits the scholarship and process of theorization of transitional justice (McEvoy 2008). Critical of the traditional view of transitional justice, scholars such as Rajagopal and others from the developing world, have commented that transitional justice practices, policies, and implementation must be broader and deeper in order to fully address the needs of the individuals and the state as a whole.

Those who carry the burden of victimhood and tragedy are not always heard, nor are they the focus of transitional justice in the legalistic sense (McEvoy, McGregor 2008, Rajagopal 2003). Civil society can advocate for the victims who have lost their voice, especially when the political situation in the post-conflict period is adverse to their circumstances. In this way they are the mouthpieces for the victims who are routinely ignored in a legal based mechanism. While non-government organizations, both international and domestic, play the role of monitor and evaluator they also provide legitimacy for the justice mechanisms and actions taken on by the state (Boranie 2000). These scholars state that the use of truth and justice mechanisms is predicated upon the ideology of legalism as the most viable way to deal with justice. Within the truth and justice mechanisms, victims can take back the power ripped from them by the perpetrators during the conflict by participating in a democratic structure that punishes the guilty (Dyzenhaus 2003). These mechanisms offer a space for the truth and allow history to be told in a very public manner (Al Huessin, 2006).

Through these mechanisms states and the international community are obligated to prosecute and punish, and to discover truth (Al Huessin, 2006). Because states and official international bodies such as the UN are focused on the results of court proceedings and tangible evidence of justice, it becomes the responsibility of civil society to make sure that there is a balance when pursuing restorative and retributive forms of justice.

Alternative methods focus on the engagement of civil society with transitional justice. While the general discussion of transitional justice has been focused around the international and national governmental decisions, some suggest that the involvement of civil society is necessary for justice because it provides a different perspective because the growth in the power of civil society, both in the international and domestic context, has a direct connection to the rising global trend of pushing for universal recognition of human rights and democratization, two of the leading links to transitional justice (Sikkink 1998; Risse et at. 1999).

Civil society is well suited to determine the goals of transitional justice within a state, in partnership with that government, as well as help design, implement and monitor the various mechanisms put in place (Crocker 2000). Those engaged in civil society bring knowledge, skills and expertise to the field of transitional justice, components necessary for applying justice to each individual country (van Zyl and Simpson 1996). One of the biggest areas in which civil society participates is the collection of data used by justice mechanisms. Human rights organizations have proved to be very good watchdogs in multiple countries such as Chile and Argentina, and their findings have been used by those national commissions on truth and reconciliation (Bickford 2000). These civil society organizations collect data and facts about what happened during the conflict and can be more unbiased than government organizations that played a role in the conflict itself. The biases of a government structure are diluted when there are power sharing mechanisms put in place to assure the needs of both sides of the conflict. While civil society can play a mediating role, it is ultimately the state that is the biggest actor in post-conflict justice.

A balance of power and the sharing between formerly opposing forces at the end of a conflict can impact the type of justice that is implemented in the aftermath. This balance of power typically translates to the governmental structures that are present in a newly peaceful society. These institutions are functions of the balance of power and directly impact the justice that will be carried out in the post-conflict society (Siffee 1999). Within the transitional justice literature government actors and the international community bear the responsibility of implementing order to achieve a true mechanism of peace. These top-down structures of justice are created without a large amount of input from the local community, who are usually the ones who suffered the most during the conflict. This line of scholars believe that there should be a change in the actors who implement justice.

State implemented justice mechanisms allow politics to play a large role in the decision making of those bodies. Even within a 'democracy,' which is usually the aim after conflict, justice can be manipulated to further the interests of that new government (McGregor, Stanley, Diaz 2008). Governments switch between amnesty and prosecution for their perpetrators depending on what is politically useful at the moment. This situation has been seen in countries like Uganda, Timor Leste, and Colombia, proving that geography and time periods have no impact on the power of political decisions (McGregor, Stanley, Diaz 2008). Because of the power of politics it is usually the victims and survivors who lose the ability to use the justice mechanisms, and they in turn lose faith in the new state agenda.

Because the average citizen suffers the most when political games become the focus of the state, according to scholars like McEvoy, transitional justice must be a grassroots effort as well as a state led one in order to address the needs of all those affected by the conflict and find all levels of perpetrators (McEvoy 2007). The groups and individuals involved in social and political struggles which placed them in the conflict in the first place must be those who are directly involved with the broader framework that justice is incorporated in. Transitional justice was initially narrowly defined as the judicial response to human rights abuses. It was also seen as independent to other ongoing state building activities that operated in a less legal and more political framework (Bell 2009, IJTJ 2007). There has been a push for the normative form of justice to encompass the political elements of the ongoing state as well as fulfill its usual retributive and criminal components.

Some argue that the most significant components of transitional justice are nonprosecution based (Freeman 2010). Allowing citizens of the state, particularly those adversely affected by the violence, the opportunity to have a say in their justice and peace can be done through various ways other than legalism. Through the use of outreach, education, story-telling and mobilization by grassroots organizations such as women's groups, citizens can feel that they have more of an impact on the state reconstruction process (McConnachie, Morison). The distributive aspect is addressed through the use of a more 'tiered' system of justice which encompasses the experience of the local victims and communities (McGregor 2008).

In this field, the victims and survivors of the conflict are themselves agents of change. They stress the need for movements 'from below' to be 'written back into' historical struggles for human rights and social justice and that justice is marked not simply by the deliberation of the major legal institutions or landmark cases but by the individuals and groups involved in social and political struggles which placed them on the political agenda in the first place (Rajagopal 2003). This critique of justice is not in direct contradiction to the traditional concepts of transitional justice but in works in tandem with the existing thought process. The 'from below' perspective is a way of providing a secondary lens in order to see interactions, accommodations, and relationship with institutions and structures 'from above' (Falk 2003).

Pulling from the literature we see legalism as a court mechanism, a definition of legalism that can be extended to the government structure and legislation, civil society involvement, and international involvement as factors of justice in post-conflict reconstruction.

# Methodology

The analysis of these five factors identified from the literature allows the creation of a holistic and thorough picture of justice in the case studies and the identification of peace and stability in each country. Three hypothesis have arisen from the literature in regard to the relationship between peace and justice:

- Pursing justice through official mechanisms leads to higher levels of peace.
- Pursuing justice through official mechanisms and grassroots activism leads to higher levels of peace.
- Power sharing without justice leads to peace and complete power with or without justice leads to peace. (null hypothesis)

Although this thesis uses small-N comparative analysis, the use of the four selected cases allow variation on the dependent variable in terms of the type of justice mechanisms implemented and the level of peace that resulted from these structures. Through the chosen case studies these hypothesis are tested through an examination of the factors drawn from the literature. The cases of South Africa, Rwanda, Northern Ireland, and Sri Lanka are all prominent post-conflict societies that are distinguished from one another by the causes of their conflict, geography, time, culture, political structures, and levels of international engagement, yet they share the similarities of being post-colonial countries that were forced to adapt to their new circumstances in times of turmoil.

A mid-level analysis of South Africa, instead of a full case study is used due to the international recognition of the country as well. South Africa is held up as the international standard for peace and justice but with very little analysis it can be seen that the current day country has very little peace. The 'South Africa Model' is usually referenced in transitional justice even though it has very clear flaws within South Africa itself. The other three cases take a more in depth look at the five factors of justice and their relationship to peace. Rwanda, Sri Lanka, and Northern Ireland all have different types of government structures due to the nature of the end of their respective conflicts (see chart 1), but their versions of justice are not as well-known as the South African model. I have also spent extensive time in each of the three countries conducting informal interviews and making first-hand observations which allows for a deeper look and analysis of these three cases.

| Case | Military Defeat | Peace Treaty | Power Distribution Outcome |
|---|---|---|---|
| Sri Lanka | Yes- The Sri Lankan government defeated the rebel group, the Tamil Tigers | N/A | concentrated in single ethnicity executive branch |
| Rwanda | Yes- The rebel group, the RPF, defeated the Rwandan government | N/A | ethnicity diverse government with powerful executive branch |
| Northern Ireland | N/A | Yes- all political parties, Ireland, and England signed the Good Friday Agreement | five parties share power equally |
| South Africa | N/A | Yes- multi-party talks agreed on interim constitution and non-racial elections are held | multiparty system, but one party holds majority of power |

Pattern matching shows how relevant a variable is to the relationship between peace and justice as well as which variables are important within that relationship. The variables are analyzed within their specific country's context, seeing what legislation was implemented and the human experience that resulted from it. The comparison between cases holds the valuable inferences for the larger field of transitional justice. Within each case the variables are isolated in order to gain better leverage on understanding their impact on peace. The breakdown of each variable into what has been formally written, whether it has been implemented, and the human experience of that implementation are compared to the level of peace within the country. This matching leads to support of one of the three hypotheses stated previously.

For formal justice mechanism, the normative causal relationship, endorsed by the international community, supports the hypothesis that pursing justice through official mechanisms leads to higher levels of peace. It can be seen that the lack of an official mechanism has played some part in creating peace, and that the causal arrow might work in reverse, in that a country might need peace before it approaches justice. Pursuing justice leads to more violence, not peace through a resurgence of violent behavior by previously opposing groups.

Conventional wisdom makes the logical argument that if those who were victimized come into power they will implement justice mechanisms to hold those responsible for violence accountable for their actions. However, this is not always the case because of potential international pressure on a country's government as well the priority of maintaining the balance of power over justice. Power alone does not dictate the type of justice mechanism, and although the type of government that is in power after conflict is certainly an important factor, the actions that governments take are not dependent on their post-conflict structure. The independent variable, power sharing structures, is traced through the cases to determine whether multi-party governments that represent both sides of the conflict or single party structures have a direct impact on justice and peace.

Identity legislation, the third factor of formal justice mechanisms supports hypothesis 1 but in certain cases this legislation does not remove identities, but suppresses and renames them. This does not led to peace within a society but instead leads to the restructuring of the discussion of identity, sometimes in more damaging and harmful way then the original labels. Therefore identity legislation must be looked at from the human experience in order to gain a holistic understanding of its effect on peace in terms of uniting factions or further dividing them.

Civil society engagement and its allowed level of engagement by the government is examined in order to gain some perspective of justice mechanisms outside of the formal structure. This factor differentiates hypothesis 1 from hypothesis 2 by seeing if the involvement of civil society has an effect on peace.

International engagement holds constant at a high level throughout the four cases, but is shown to be a necessary, not sufficient cause of peace. Governments without power sharing benefit from international engagement because this factor can push the regime toward justice mechanisms that would normally not be implemented.

To view details of the factors as they relate to each case study please see Chart 2.

Each variable is broken into three phases. Each variable has associated legislation that is analyzed by what was passed, implemented, and the human experience outcome of the legislation. Verifying what is passed and implemented is done through primary source material of each document, while the human experience is critically analyzed through first-hand observation and informal interviews taken while spending time in Rwanda, Sri Lanka, and Northern Ireland. These accounts are supported by newspaper articles of journalists who have drawn on their first-hand experiences as well.

Although peace is hard to define, this paper will define it not only as the absence of war, conflict, or violence, but also the fear of the aforementioned and the level to which warring factions are incorporated into the new post-conflict state. Peace in each case is measured using an ordinal system of durable, stable, unstable, and compelled, based on Michael S. Lund's Curve of Conflict. In addition, the Global Peace Index is used to provide a secondary look at level of peace within the each country. (see chart 3)

The GPI uses data from ongoing domestic and international conflicts, safety and security in a society, militarization, and economic prosperity. The ranking that the Global Peace Index assigns each country is not completely applicable to this study because it also takes into account external conflicts a state is involved in, while this paper is only looking at the internal structure of a country. The index also looks at the indicators of a country's military build-up which at a high rate are related to a lower level of peace. In recent post-conflict states a high level of militarization is to be expected. For this reason Michael S. Lund's Curve of Conflict categorization of peace will be used in tandem with the Global Peace Index.

| Type of Peace | Desciption |
|---|---|
| Durable (or warm) | involves a high level of reciprocity and cooperation, and the virtual absence of self-defense measures among parties, although it may include their military alliance against a common threat. A 'positive peace' prevails based on shared values, goals, and institutions (e.g. democratic political systems and rule of law), economic interdependence, and a sense of international community. |
| Stable (or Cold) | relationship of wary communication and limited cooperation (e.g. trade) within an overall context of basic order or national stability. Value or goal differences exist and no military cooperation is established, but disputes are generally worked out in nonviolent, more or less predictable ways. The prospect for war is low. |
| Unstable | situation in which tension and suspicion among parties run high, but violence is either absent or only sporadic. A 'negative peace' prevails because although armed force is not deployed [or employed], the parties perceive one another as enemies and maintain deterrent military capabilities... A balance of power may discourage aggression, but crisis and war are still possible. |

The terms- durable, stable, and unstable, give a more clear view of the internal level of peace, especially in post conflict societies. While Lund's definition of peace (see Chart 2) give the most comprehensive view of peace with justice they do not take into account peace that comes with extreme force. Post WWII peace, with the founding of the United Nations, and the passage of the Geneva convention have typically seen peace achieved through diplomacy and compromise, and as such the study of peace and justice has followed this model. The idea that peace can be achieved because the opposing side is completely subdued, has been removed from the literature because it is not seen as part of the international law or the general system anymore.

For this reason Lund's categorization of peace is missing an essential label that falls somewhere between unstable and stable peace. This is not just a hole in Lund's breakdown of peace, but in the scholarship of peace and justice as a whole. This new category, termed 'compelled peace' is a stable but not durable peace that is the result of complete and total military victory of one side of the conflict. In this case 'compelled peace' can be described as 'the virtual absence of self-defense measures among one party, tension and suspicion among parties run high, parties perceive one another as enemies, victor maintains deterrent military capabilities , but violence is absent, there are high level of cooperation between parties, shared goals and institutions, economic interdependence.'

In this case there is high levels of peace, which should not be mistaken for reconciliation, but stability and the unification of a once fractionalized society on some level. This designation re-conceptualizes that relationship between peace and justice, changing it from linear as Lund and the GPI models view it, to a non-linear model that mirrors a parabolic function (see diagram 1).

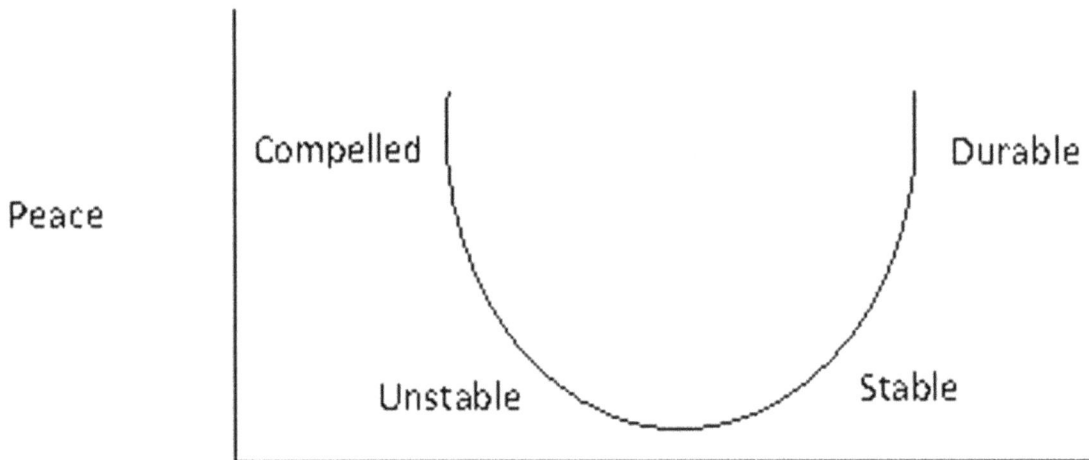

## Rwanda

Rwanda has always been divided into groups but rather than ethnic groups, the terms Hutu and Tutsi referred to a class system. Tutsi denoted a higher stratum of society and was consequently equated to the ruling class, but unlike an ethnic hierarchy, this class system was a fluid power dynamic where the acquisition of cattle would raise social class. Beginning with the Belgian colonization, ID cards were given to all Rwandans classifying them into ethnic groups.[1] They also blatantly favored the elite class of their choosing -- the Tutsis through creating more schools specifically for Tutsis and choosing them for positions of authority. When they left, the Hutu race was determined to take back the power that had been denied to them for many years. With a Hutu power-based ideology, the first President of

Rwanda, Kayibanda, used the resentment toward Tutsis to further his political campaign and caused a huge population of Tutsis to flee from the country. His successor, Habyarimana, used the same fear tactics in the face of an economic downturn, but his actions toward the Tutsis spurred the fight of those Rwandans living as refugees outside their home country. In 1990 the Rwandan Patriotic Front (RPF), comprised mostly of Tutsis, invaded Rwanda from the northern country of Uganda in an effort to protect their rights within Rwanda.[2] This was the perfect opportunity to justify attacks against the Tutsi and Habyarimana, and his regime took full advantage. A war began between the RPF and the Rwandan government and did not end until Habyarimana agreed to sign peace accords with them in Arusha, Tanzania in July of 1993. UN peacekeeping forces, led by Romeo Dalliare, were deployed to oversee the shift in power, but when the President Habyiramana's plane was shot down on April 6, 1994 the violence happened extremely quickly and without anybody to stop it.

Romeo Dalliare describes the Rwandan genocide as "a grab for power,"[3] because it fell within a war between two sides trying to control one country. Like many genocides, war provided a secure cover for the mass atrocities that occurred. In 100 days, it is estimated that up to 1 million people were killed. This number is comprised mostly of Tutsis but many moderate Hutus were killed as well when they refused to participate in the mass slaughter. Women were especially targeted as victims of rape and sexual abuse throughout the country and thousands were displaced and fled to neighboring countries as refugees.[4] Tactics such as roadblocks, radio propaganda, and organized killing events under the guise of work allowed such a large number of people to die in such a short time. The crimes committed by the Hutus in the genocide against the Tutsis were unique in the sense that it was not a government army carrying out the majority of the actions, but the actions of common citizens who killed their fellow Rwandans. The massacres were organized by Hutu militias who were trained by the government, but most of the killing was neighbor on neighbor and even family on family. It was a bloody fight that destroyed almost the entire Rwandan infrastructure and did not end until July of 1994 when the RPF took control of the whole country.

Post-Conflict Reconstruction

*Legal Mechanisms*

After the genocide, the RPF and its leadership had the difficult job of rebuilding a country from nothing. In addition to recovering from the physical destruction, the Rwandan citizens had to regain their faith and trust in the government and their own country. The issue of reconciliation and justice was an immediate one that the government had to deal with for fear of a retributive genocide occurring between the populations. Without any sort of legal system in place, including an estimated 10 lawyers left in the country[5], the Rwandan government had to be creative in the way it would accomplish the goal of justice for its people. Because of the massive scale of the genocide, as exemplified by the large number of perpetrators, the government could not use a traditional Western approach to justice. Lacking any means, Gacaca seemed like the best way to reconcile people with the past and each other, and with an estimated "100,000-125,000 Rwandans awaiting trial in overcrowded prisons,"[6] a solution needed to be found quickly. As defined by the Rwandan government, "In order to expedite the delivery of justice, the Rwandan Government has returned to the traditional Gacaca Court system.

The local Gacaca courts, meaning 'justice on the grass,' combine traditional local justice with modern jurisprudence, with the aim of achieving truth, justice, and reconciliation. Upon its completion, it will have been the most thorough process in bringing the rank and file of genocide to justice. Over 100,000 inmates have been indicted for crimes of genocide."[7] Though a more community-service based system, as opposed to the Western punishment system, many Rwandans were tried for their crimes of genocide and taken through the Gacaca system. While the Gacaca system has many issues, including electing judges that were genociders themselves and a lack of formal punishments, it did attempt to hold those responsible for the acts of violence, accountable for their actions.

The international community also wanted to make sure that justice was upheld, and did so through the creation of the International Criminal Tribunal for Rwanda, held in Arusha, Tanzania. UN Resolution 955, passed in 1994 declared

"Decides hereby, having received the request of the Government of Rwanda (S/1994/1115), to establish an international tribunal for the sole purpose of prosecuting persons responsible for genocide and other serious violations of international humanitarian law committed in the territory of Rwanda and Rwandan citizens responsible for genocide and other such violations committed in the territory of neighbouring States, between 1 January 1994 and 31 December 1994 and to this end to adopt the Statute of the International Criminal Tribunal for Rwanda."[8]

The International Criminal Tribunal was set up to hold the highest government officials accountable for their actions. This was widely considered a precedent setting trial, in that it was one of the first international trials to be set up. But by the Rwandan community the trial was seen as too distant and removed from their own lives and sense of justice and reconciliation. The trial was seen to have issues of its own such as its lack of prosecutions of the RPF membership, who were suspect of massacring Hutu civilians during the takeover of the country.[9] It has been hypothesized that the lack of RPF prosecutions is due to the international community's guilt of having done nothing to stop the genocide themselves.[10]

*Power Sharing Government Structures*

On July 19th, 1994, the RPF took Kigali and established the Government of National Unity. This new government was based on the principles of the Arusha Accords which established a power sharing government with both Hutus and Tutsis, and included previously existing political parties, excluding the Hutu Power party which was responsible for the genocide (Mouvement Révolutionnaire Nationale pour le Développement—MRND). The five parties included in the new Unity governmment were the Liberal Party (PL), the Social Democratic Party (PSD), the Christian Democratic Party (PDC), and the Republican Democratic Movement (MDR), the Islamic Party (PDI), the Socialist Party (PSR), and the Democratic Union for Rwandese People (UDPR), and the Rwandese Patriotic Army (RPA).[11] Following the genocide, the position of President was occupied by Pasteur Bizimungu, a Hutu, and the position of vice-president was occupied by Paul Kagame, the military leader of the RPF. While the parties were all allotted a specific number of representatives based as the Arusha Accords, in reality the RPF , which represents the majority of the Tutsi community, has occupied more than their allotted spaces within the government. The RPF has expanded its power and reach throughout the government through the rhetoric of a family, suspected coercion and threantening tactics.[12] This includes the position of the Presidency, which has been held by Paul Kagame since 2000. Although Kagame has been accused of expressing authoritarian tendencies, he has used his position to promote justice and reconciliation for both the Hutus and the Tutsis. In his speech made during the 20th anniversary of the genocide in 2014 he stated,

> "After 1994, everything was a priority and our people were completely broken. But we made three fundamental choices that guide us to this day. One — we chose to stay together. When the refugees came home — we were choosing to be together. When we released genocide suspects in anticipation of Gacaca — we were choosing to be together. When we passed an inclusive constitution that transcends politics based on division and entrenched the rights of women as full partners in nation-building, for the first time — we were choosing to be together. When we extended comprehensive new education and health benefits to all our citizens — we were choosing to be together."[13]

This speech is representative of the Rwandan government in that the idea and philosophy of 'One Rwanda' has been pushed heavily through media campaigns.

*Identity Legislation*

The RPF led, new Rwandan government made the abolishment of ethnicity and ID cards one of its first steps on the agenda for rebuilding the country.[14] This had an incredibly meaningful impact in that ethnicity was no longer a defining characteristic within Rwandan society, at least in name. While it has created an environment in which people no longer refer to themselves as Hutu or Tutsi but as Rwandan, it has also created new terms that are used as synonyms for ethnic labels. For example, when saying victim is it most likely one is talk about a Tutsi and the same assumption is used for perpetrator and Hutu. Overall the move to abolish ethnicity is seen as positive but it has created an atmosphere in which people cannot talk about their identity in regards to this characteristic.

After the genocide the newly created Rwandan government was careful to draft a constitution that included justice at its core. The preamble of the Rwandan constitution states,
"(2)resolved to fight the ideology of genocide and all its manifestations and to eradicate ethnic, regional and any other form of divisions;
(4) Emphasizing on the necessity to strengthen and promote national unity and reconciliation which were seriously shaken by the genocide against the Tutsi and its consequences;
(5) Conscious that peace and unity of Rwandans constitute the essential basis for national economic development and social progress."[15]
This is furthered in Chapter II of the constitution where the Fundamental Principles in Article 9 are stated as, "The State of Rwanda commits itself to conform to the following fundamental principles and to promote and enforce the respect thereof:
(1) fighting the ideology of genocide and all its manifestations
(2) eradication of ethnic, regional and other divisions and promotion of national unity."[16]

In title II on the Fundamental Human Rights and Rights and Duties of the Citizen, Chapter 1: Fundamental Human Rights, Article 11 it is stated that,

> "All Rwandans are born and remain free and equal in rights and duties. Discrimination of whatever kind based on, inter alia, ethnic origin, tribe, clan, colour, sex, region, social origin, religion or faith, opinion, economic status, culture, language, social status, physical or mental disability or any other form of discrimination is prohibited and punishable by Law."[17]

The law that punishes those for discrimination is Law No 47/2001 of December 2001 instituting punishment for offences of discrimination and sectarianism, which provides for penalties to be imposed on people for divisionism, a poorly-defined term often used interchangeably with sectarianism, meaning: "the use of any speech, written statement, or action that divides people, that is likely to spark conflicts among people, or that causes an uprising which might degenerate into strife among people based on discrimination."[18] The government was sure to define 'divisionism' within the law as

> "Any person who makes public any speech, writing, pictures or images or any symbols or radio airwaves, television, in a meeting or public place, with the aim of discriminating [against] people or sowing sectarianism [divisionism] among them is sentenced to between one year and five years of imprisonment and fined between five hundred thousand (500,000) [US $1000] and two million (2,000,000) [US $4,000] Rwandan francs or only one of these two sanctions."[19]

While this law seems to be working to create a safe space for all Rwandans the government has been criticized by many human rights groups to use divisionism to keep all dissention down from political and individual opposition.[20] Further legislation such as the 2008 domestic law against genocide ideology- Law no. 18/2008 the Law Relating to the Punishment of the Crime of Genocide Ideology adopted on July 23, 2008- has been cited as being used to quell opposition to the ruling party, instead of creating the intended safe space for all the victims of the genocide.[21]

The Rwandan government institutionalized justice with the creation of the National Unity and Reconciliation Commission (NURC) in 1999. Parliamentarian Law no. 03/99 of 12 March 1999 legislated the creation of the National Unity and Reconciliation Commission (NURC) with the directive to, 'organize and oversee national public debates aiming at promoting national unity and reconciliation of Rwandan people.'"[22] This is seen as a long-term plan to work toward and justice for those who were victimized during the genocide, but more so a move toward reconciliation and unity for the whole country. Overall the Rwandan government has made great strides to implement justice on a country-wide level, but the consequences of the legislation that have been passed are seen as less favorable by some including NGOs and the international community.

*Civil Society*

Civil society is controlled by the Rwandan government through the Law Governing the organization and functioning of National Non governmental organizations (Law No. 04/12), which was adopted in February 2012. Many of the organizations society advocated for the return of the Rwandans who had been stateless since 1959 and lived in foreign countries such as Uganda, Tanzania, Burundi, and the Democratic Republic of Congo. Notably there was an emergence of dynamic women's groups and associations in all sectors of civil society, particularly at the national and regional levels. These groups have been particularly active in supporting the Gacaca justice initiatives, lobbying for assistance and justice for widows, orphans, and other vulnerable groups in Rwandan society; and providing credit for women's associations engaged in economic activities.[23] The government has created other platforms in which to engage local organizations such as the Joint Action Development Forum, which serves as a forum for districts' development activities, Civil Society Platform, which is a government led initiative. Engagement between CSOs and the government continues to improve, and CSOs have set up networks to maintain engagement with the government on citizen welfare issues.[24] Despite these efforts, challenges and weaknesses continue to hamper CSO advocacy. CSOs do not generally have the resources and skills to conduct surveys and other research needed to conduct evidence-based advocacy. Furthermore, although there has been some progress over the past few years, information sharing, coordination, and networking among CSOs are not yet sufficient. Another weakness in CSO advocacy is that CSOs do not fully involve constituents in their efforts.[25] An analysis of the role of civil society in Rwanda has rated its impact as moderate[26], but it is important to note that the impact of civil society is completely regulated by the government. As long as the government is favorable toward civil society, they are allowed to continue their work in justice.

International Engagement

Rwanda has been called the "Donor Darling"[27] There are two main viewpoints that the international community take when looking at the Rwandan government: that the government is doing great job and the international community should follow its lead, and that the government is manipulating the international community through guilt of their in-action during the genocide. A highly placed manager of a North American foreign aid agency: 'if you are going to understand what is happening in Rwanda today, you have to understand genocide and the enduring consequences of genocide. It permeates, affects, and influences human behavior so totally that it is remarkable that the survivors and the government have been able to exercise the degree of restraint they have been exhibiting.' From this perspective, Kagame is a visionary, charismatic and optimistic man; whatever violence occurred under his reign is the result of 'strategic initiatives gone wrong'.[28] The following quote from a Scandinavian senior foreign aid manager in charge of Rwanda is representative of this position: 'a strong sense of confidence and pride seemed to have led the regime to adopt what appears to be a very arrogant attitude with the donor society; it seems the regime is using the genocide as political capital in order to avoid a dialogue, let alone criticism of its policies.' Within the international human rights community, it is now common to state that Rwanda, like Israel, is skillfully using the genocide, and the general imagery of victimhood, to justify its brutal policies and deflect international scrutiny.[29] Although there are those in the international community who are not so happy with the way things are being done in Rwanda, there are total, donors fund more than 100 justice-related projects, costing more than $100 million. Donors organized the training of lawyers, judges, investigators and police; provided salary supplements to judges and prosecutors, as well as vehicles and the required fuel and maintenance; and advised on reform of administrative and court procedures; constructed buildings, libraries, prisons and living facilities.[30] NGOs assisted with confessions and with defence; bilateral and multilateral experts helped in the drafting of new laws and organigrams, etc. Rwanda has been so successful because of the international aid it has received, as well as the positive image it has gained abroad.

Conclusion

Rwanda is seen as the emerging capital for east Africa. It has had a steady 8% growth in its economy and is expected to become a middle-income country by 2020. As stated previously it is a 'darling' for international donors because of its low levels of corruption and strong political will to achieve high goals of development. Out of the four case studies, Rwanda fulfills all five independent variables in creating legislation to promote justice as well as actually implementing said legislation. While it only ranks 132 out of 182 on the Global Peace Index, this is mainly due to its involvement in the conflict in neighboring Congo. Internally it can be said that Rwanda has implemented a durable or warm peace. There is a high level of reciprocity and cooperation between Hutus and Tutsis, although there is still a high level of militarization by the mainly Tutsis military. But this military is not used internally, but externally, mainly in Congo. There are shared institutions, values, and goals by both sides, and most importantly a national sense of identity and unity. Especially within the younger generation of Rwandans, who were very small children during the genocide, and have grown up in the post- conflict phases of the country, there is a very strong sense of being 'Rwandan' rather than their ethnic identities. Because of its commitment to justice not only through formal mechanisms Rwanda has managed to create a lasting peace within its borders. This peace has been reinforced by economic development and growth. There are still many problems the Rwandan government needs to tackle, including distributing power throughout the three branches of government, external conflicts, and continued work on justice and reconciliation, it has made the most progress in the shortest amount of time.

# Northern Ireland

The 'troubles' in Northern Ireland can be traced back to Irish independence from England in 1921. While the English granted independence to most of the island, the six northern countries were to remain part of the United Kingdom because of their Protestant majority. This led to marginalization and discrimination of the catholic minority in Northern Ireland who felt more Irish than English. Most scholars cite the official start of the 'troubles' with the civil rights march in Londonderry on October 5, 1968. Catholics, using the momentum of the African-American civil rights movement, sought to end discrimination in all forms, including an end to job discrimination, public housing discrimination, voting based on property, and police discrimination. This peaceful march was met with violence by the police force, the Royal Ulster Constabulary (RUC). This led to the rebirth of the Irish Republican Army (IRA), a group committed to reuniting Ireland through any means, including military tactics, and the Ulster Protestant Volunteers (UVP) and the Ulster Volunteer Force (UVF), two groups committed to staying part of the United Kingdom. The next thirty years were filled with violent attacks by both the unionists and republicans committed against Northern Irish civilians, as well as attacks in England and Ireland. It is estimated that 3,500[31] people died during the 'troubles,' within a population of about 1.8 million Northern Irish. The end of the conflict came on April 10th, 1998 with the signing of the Good Friday agreement by the political parties of Northern Ireland including the Ulster Unionist Party, the Social Democratic and Labour Party, Sinn Féin, the Alliance Party, the Progressive Unionist

Party, the Northern Ireland Women's Coalition, the Ulster Democratic Party and Labour, as well as an agreement between the Irish and English governments.

Northern Ireland has been at peace for the past 16 years, or so most people in the international system believe. The signing of the Good Friday or Belfast Agreement, was seen as a triumph for diplomacy and the beginning of a new history for Northern Ireland. Many changes followed the agreement including a policing board, lessening of violence, and a new political structure, but one theme that was left off of the agenda was remembering the past. It was thought to be too painful, too soon to touch this delicate subject without the whole area surging into violence again, and to this day there has been no official mechanism has been put in place to address the issues of what happened for more than thirty years in Northern Ireland.

Post-Conflict

*Legal Mechanisms*

Northern Ireland faces most of these challenges and it is understandable why Stormnot is hesitant to begin such a process. Getting all the political parties to agree to a truth commission, a necessary first step, could arguably be the biggest challenge a commission would face, even before it starts. As stated by Brandon Hamber, "Most political players demand truth from those they perceive as the other side or sides, but seem unwilling to offer the truth from their side, or acknowledge and take responsibility for their actions. This is mostly due to fear that such acknowledgement (public or otherwise) will weaken their position as parties vie for power in the new dispensation and that the truth may be used against them within the context of the delicate peace that prevails"[32]. More evidence is presented on the uneasy relationship between the parties in Stormont. After his trip to South Africa Dr. Boraine points out that the political settlement in Northern Ireland has put both traditions in control, but neither one has more control than the other. In order for a truth commission to move forward, both sides would have to move beyond the double minority mindset and come together to have the necessary authority and control need to govern Northern Ireland. He brings up the important question, "can we live together if we insist on the defeat of the other side?"[33] In order for any sort of truth commission to move forward the political parties in Stormont would have to create an internal sense of reconciliation and understanding of what is best for the people of Northern Ireland.

In addition to getting Stormont to agree to a commission, Britain and Ireland would have to agree to be part of the commission as well. Because they played such central roles to the conflict itself, especially the initial causes of the conflict, their participation as well as support would be imperative in establish legitimacy for the truth commission. Once established the commission would face multiple challenges in figuring out what would be included within the mandate. The issues of amnesty and reparations have already been discussed within Northern Ireland, and both have faced heated discussion from all sides of the conflict. Especially in light of the current situation with the On the Runs, the commission would face the challenge of decided whether or not to grant amnesty to those who come forward to tell the truth about their crimes. Depending on the decision the commission makes, the issue of reconciliation whether or not to include it within the mandate or spirit of the commission, would need to be considered. Reconciliation as a concept is very challenging, but necessary if Northern Ireland wants to become an inclusive society, rather than the benign apartheid it has resorted to in the past. Reconciliation has been a complicated matter for Northern Ireland, "for some community relations practitioners, faith-based activists, academics and others, it is a common-sense term which speaks to the need in a divided society for individuals and communities to reconcile a tragic history and alternative political aspirations in a small geographical space"[34], but a truth commission might be a good vehicle to start the discussion in a public space. While there has not been a government mandated justice commission like that seen in Rwanda or South Africa, there has been less formal mechanisms put in place to address the issues of justice for the victims of the 'troubles.'

The Northern Ireland Act of 1998 calls for a Human Rights Commission to be created to "review the adequacy and effectiveness in Northern Ireland of law and practice relating to the protection of human rights,"[35] as well as "promote understanding and awareness of the importance of human rights in Northern Ireland; and for this purpose it may undertake, commission or provide financial or other assistance for—(a) research; and (b)educational activities."[36] While the Human Rights Commission has published useful information on the topic of justice it has not served as a public space for victims to tell their stories on a national scale. It has identified the need for an official justice mechanism instead of the ad hoc initiatives that have been started by governments (English and Irish) and community efforts, but these have all centered around one event, whether it be the Bloody Sunday Inquiry established by UK Prime Minister Tony Blair, or the investigations made in to the deaths of civilians by the Police Service of Northern Ireland (PSNI).[37] These random initiatives made by various actors can be attributed to the lack of formal structure put forth in the Good Friday Agreement, which only address justice as a responsibility of the criminal justice system and that the issue should be addressed at a further date. While many have filled in the gap left by the lack of a large scale, government led justice mechanism, the Northern Irish people still face many of the same issues that led to the 'troubles' in the first place.

*Power-Sharing Government Structure*

Within the Good Friday agreement a large section was devoted to the structure of Stormont, the Northern Irish Parliament. The agreement was very specific about the political parties that had to be represented with in the government structure in order to appease all sides. In the section on the Operation of the Assembly it is stated that: "At their first meeting, members of the Assembly will register a designation of identity - nationalist, unionist or other - for the purposes of measuring cross-community support in Assembly votes under the relevant provisions above.[38] The Pledge of Office for all politicians included a commitment to equality and justice: "commitment to non-violence and exclusively peaceful and democratic means; to serve all the people of Northern Ireland equally, and to act in accordance with the general obligations on government to promote equality and prevent discrimination."[39]

Safeguards were put in place to make sure that all sections of the population were adequately represented. Section 5 states:

"There will be safeguards to ensure that all sections of the community can participate and work together successfully in the operation of these institutions and that all sections of the community are protected, including:

(a) allocations of Committee Chairs, Ministers and Committee membership in proportion to party strengths;

(d) arrangements to ensure key decisions are taken on a cross-community basis;

Key decisions requiring cross-community support will be designated in advance, including election of the Chair of the Assembly, the First Minister and Deputy First Minister, standing orders and budget allocations. In other cases such decisions could be triggered by a petition of concern brought by a significant minority of Assembly members (30/108).

(e) an Equality Commission to monitor a statutory obligation to promote equality of opportunity in specified areas and parity of esteem between the two main communities, and to investigate individual complaints against public bodies."[40]

While the plan put forth by the Good Friday Agreement is admirable in its attempt to make sure that all sides of the conflict recognized and empowered, in reality this has led to a Stormont that is unable to function properly because it requires the agreement of five very different parties. The English government has dissolved the parliament twice since 1998 because of its inability to legislate over Northern Ireland, and in a study conducted by the Northern Irish government only 61% of people believe that the Executive is working in people's long-term interests and only 54% believe that the Executive is making a real difference to life in Northern Ireland.[41]

*Identity Legislation*

The Good Friday Agreement and the subsequent Northern Ireland Act of 1998 both set the majority of the legislation concerning identity within Northern Ireland. Statue 75 of the Northern Ireland Act states that it is the duty of any public authority to "promote equality of opportunity – (a) between persons of different religious belief, political opinion, racial group, age, marital status or sexual orientation." The Good Friday Agreement asks all signatures to declare their support for an equitable Northern Ireland through the Declaration of Support: "We are committed to partnership, equality and mutual respect as the basis of relationships within Northern Ireland, between North and South, and between these islands."[42]

The British-Irish Agreement which was signed in tandem with the Good Friday Agreement by the two countries stated that they would:

"(i) recognise the legitimacy of whatever choice is freely exercised by a majority of the people of Northern Ireland with regard to its status, whether they prefer to continue to support the Union with Great Britain or a sovereign united Ireland;

(vi) recognise the birthright of all the people of Northern Ireland to identify themselves and be accepted as Irish or British, or both, as they may so choose, and accordingly confirm that their right to hold both British and Irish citizenship is accepted by both Governments and would not be affected by any future change in the status of Northern Ireland."[43]

The institutionalizing of letting Northern Irish citizens formalize their identity, whether it be Irish or English was an important step in legitimizing the feelings of loyalty that both sides felt during the conflict. This was further respected through the acceptance of multiple languages and cultures within Northern Ireland through the section of the agreement entitled Rights, Safeguards and Equality of Opportunity: Economic, Social and Cultural Issues" which stated that,

> "All participants recognise the importance of respect, understanding and tolerance in relation to linguistic diversity, including in Northern Ireland, the Irish language, Ulster-Scots and the languages of the various ethnic communities, all of which are part of the cultural wealth of the island of Ireland;
>
> All participants acknowledge the sensitivity of the use of symbols and emblems for public purposes, and the need in particular in creating the new institutions to ensure that such symbols and emblems are used in a manner which promotes mutual respect rather than division. Arrangements will be made to monitor this issue and consider what action might be required."[44]

The acceptance of symbols of culture has been difficult in Northern Ireland even though it has been formalized within legislation. The issue of flags, whether the Union Jack representing England, or the Tri-Color representing Ireland, has been very prominent within the last few years, culminating in Flag protests in the winter of 2013. This issue has yet to be resolved by Stormont, but continues to divide the people of Northern Ireland and deepen the identity cleavage between the two sides.

*Civil Society*

Although a formal body has not been established in Northern Ireland to uncover the truth, it would not be fair to say that the area is just trying to forget the past. Many local initiatives have done quite a lot of work in the truth recovery field, whether it be story-telling projects, community inquires, government commissions set up for victims and policing, or church groups helping people come to terms with the events that happened during the troubles. Local initiatives are hugely important in any post-conflict country because it is through local organizations that people feel the personalization that can help them come forward with their story. Top-down approaches, like a truth commission, must work in partnership with the local initiatives, especially if the commission is an international body. Local people working towards truth recovery are the ones who understand the issues and the context in which they arise, and in an evaluation done by the Community Foundation of Northern Ireland, found that "Those with local credibility and organisational capacity are often best placed to lead the difficult conversations in past related work in diverse community and organisational settings"[45]. They are immeasurably important if any commission which to establish a holistic and shared narrative.

There are many examples of local organizations and community groups working to address questions of the past and help people find truth in the complexity of the conflict. One such organization is Community Dialogue. They uses workshops to challenge different members of the community to look at their beliefs and what they believe is the truth. In 2005 the organization published a report entitled "Dealing with the Past: From Victimhood to Survival" where they pointed out the issues that come with truth. Within the workshops they asked their members questions such as "If you support a focus on truth, how much truth will you get? How much will it alienate others if you get it?"[46] This organizations is doing the groundwork to introduce people to the idea of truth sharing. It is pushing people to think outside their comfort zones, and does not provide the answers to these complex questions. While an important initiative because it is education communities about truth, what it means, how it can be achieved, and its cost, it is only one step toward a national truth-telling mechanism such as a truth commission.

Some churches in Northern Ireland, traditionally seen as one of the markers of sectarianism, have used their power and influence to begin the truth telling process within their respective jurisdiction. Like Community Dialogue, churches are imperative in setting the foundation for the discussion about truth, but in a report done by the General Board of the Presbyterian Church, they determined that the church had a bigger role to play in this area. The report states,

> "Churches could consider modelling a truth-telling process so that if and when the time is right for a process to begin in the community there is a local model already operating on a micro scale which can be replicated in the macro setting. 'Truth' needs to be spoken publicly between the churches about the nature of their relationships and ongoing contribution to the divisions of Northern Ireland which in the telling would model the kind of truth-telling to be encouraged in the community."[47]

This report recognizes the power that the church has and how they can create an atmosphere conducive for truth.

Already there are smaller "truth commissions" occurring in the form of community inquiries, which look into the deaths of various people during the conflict. These inquiries include the Saville Inquiry about Bloody Sunday, the community hearing on the killings in the New Lodge area in Belfast, and policing inquiries including the Stalker/Sampson Inquiry, the Stevens Inquiry, the Patten Commission. These community inquires share many traits with a future truth commission- they emerged when there was doubt in the criminal justice system of prosecutions, they did not have official legal powers of discovery or the ability to compel witnesses, they usually employ international lawyers to chair the inquiry that can be removed from the emotions of the situation and are highly qualified in their field, they proved evidence and precedent for an actual legal trial (McEVOY 2006, p.63). All these inquiries are able to identify key events and then bring in international support and expertise, something that should be replicated in a truth commission.

Ex-combatants, unique to Northern Ireland perhaps, have already played a major role in the truth-telling process. Multiple organizations created by, and for ex-combatants on both sides of the conflict have promoted peace and re-evaluating the positions that loyalists and unionists have taken in regards to post-conflict reconstruction. The most important characteristic that ex-combatants promote is their leadership and their legitimacy. In a report conducted by the organization Healing Through Remembering it was found that, "Given the central role that individual members and paramilitary organisations would have to play in any successful process of truth recovery, it is precisely the leadership capacity of ex-combatants in terms of raising and engaging with a difficult debate such as this which is likely to shape the views of those constituencies."[48]

An example of a local initiative is the Women's Resources and Development Agency and their program on women and dealing with the past. This organizations works to make sure that women are included in the discussion of the past as well on the recommendations that have addressed how to deal with the past. This organizations works to make sure that women are not excluded from the new Northern Ireland, because There is a fear that "return to 'normality' could have adverse consequences for women: a reassertion of the public/private distinction, a reduction in civic engagement and a re-assertion of patriarchy. Engagement in policy areas that deal with the legacy of the past is therefore an important part of the work of the women's sector" (Women's Resource and Development Agency Mission Statement). In this regard it would be important that a Truth Commission would hear from both men and women to establish a truly shared history. To help create this shared truth, The Women in the Conflict program comprised of ten workshops across Northern Ireland and was very conscious of creating an environment where the participants felt comfortable telling their stories. The challenge for WRDA was to design workshops that allowed Community Facilitators to create an environment where women felt "comfortable and safe enough to remember their lives during the 'Troubles' and share these experiences with the other members of the group, whilst simultaneously trying to record these stories in a true, appropriate and accurate and unobtrusive manner."[49] Creating an atmosphere of acceptance and comfort is incredibly important in a truth commission because without it victims would be unlikely to come forward. International Engagement The most important international actors in post-conflict Northern Ireland have been England and Ireland because of their extremely close historical relationship to the area. Within the English justice system, inquiries have been made into their role in the violence during the 'troubles.' In 2010 the Saville Report was published to examine the British military's role in the Bloody Sunday deaths on January 30th, 1972. It found that the soldiers shot those who did not pose a threat and that "There was a serious and widespread loss of fire discipline among the soldiers of Support Company."[50]

International Assistance

Prime Minister David Cameron, in front of the House of Commons, made a statement apologizing for the role that England played in the deaths that happened on Bloody Sunday. He stated "But the conclusions of this report are absolutely clear. There is no doubt, there is nothing equivocal, and there are no ambiguities. What happened on Bloody Sunday was both unjustified and unjustifiable. It was wrong."[51] This statement was greeted with cheers from the thousands gathered around the Guildhall in Londonderry,[52] and has been seen as a step in the right direction for justice concerning this event. Further steps have been taken within the criminal justice system to try those soldiers who killed innocent civilians on Bloody Sunday.[53]

The wider European community has also played a role in Northern Ireland's path to justice. The European Court on Human Rights has served as a mechanism used to investigate the deaths of indivduals during the 'troubles'. This includes the case of McCaughey and Others v. the UK; Collette and Michael Hemsworth v. the UK, which concerned the death of the applicants' relatives at the hands of security forces in Northern Ireland. It also tried the case of Shanaghan v. the UK, which Concerned the murder of each applicant by loyalist paramilitaries, alleged collusion by the security forces and the lack of an effective investigation; the case of McKerr v. the UK and Hugh Jordan v. the UK, which Concerned the fatal shooting of each applicant by RUC officers in 1982 and 1992 respectively, the alleged "shoot to kill" policy applied by the RUC and the failure to conduct a full and public investigation; and McCann and Others v. the UK: Concerned complaints about the planning of a security operation which led to the fatal shooting of three members of the IRA during a terrorist operation in Gibraltar and the subsequent investigation into the incident.[54]

Conclusion

Since the signing of the Good Friday Agreement, Northern Ireland has fluctuated in its level of peace, but twenty years later it has not achieved a stable level of peace that is integrated and durable. While the GPI gives the Untied Kingdom as a whole a ranking of 47, this is not completely applicable to Northern Ireland. Due to deep divisions in the society, that still have not been address on a large scale, most people lead separate lives from their ideological counterparts. While there is much more integration at the government level due to the rigid nature of the peace agreement, it has not trickled down to the general population. Neighborhoods, schools, even sports teams, are still divided based on political identity throughout Northern Ireland, and although grassroots work is extensively undertaken to address justice and reconciliation needs, it has not managed to bridge the gap between factions. Yearly protests against historical marches, the recent collapse of the Haus Talks (diplomatic talks to renew the Good Friday Agreement) in 2013, the Flags Protest of 2014, and the arrests of prominent members of Sinn Fein political party, all underscore the very fragile peace that Northern Ireland is continuing to function with after the conflict. Bomb scares are still fairly common in the city center in Belfast, and although the violence is nowhere near the level it was at during 'the troubles' the fast approaching population equilibrium between Catholics and Protestants can exacerbate the already existing issues that have not been resolved. As of now Northern Ireland remains at a stable level of peace, where there is limited cooperation between Catholics and Protestants at an individual level, very little communication between sides, but there is a basic order and national stability. The outcome that most Catholics, whether nationalist or republicans, are working toward is becoming part of Ireland, whereas Protestants, whether Unionists or Loyalists, are working to stay part of the United Kingdom. While this dispute is not in question at the moment, as the population equalizes, this difference is identity goals will become an issue.

# Sri Lanka

Sri Lanka was colonized by the Portuguese in 1505, then the Dutch in 1658, and finally the British in 1796 until the island gained its independence in 1948. When the British colonized the island, they started to receive reports that spoke of "tensions between the Tamils and Singhalese because the Tamils were worried that the Singhalese had plans 'to dominate the political situation by their weight of numbers' and the Singhalese "resented the Tamils reluctance to accept their position as a minority in a Ceylonese nation"[55]. The British reinforced this propensity for education by providing a greater proportion of Christian missionary schools in the Northern provinces which created a "'structural imbalance' giving the Sri Lankan Tamils, especially the vellala caste an 'intrinsic advantage' over the

Sinhala majority and other minorities and Tamil groups with regard to higher education, colonial employment and the modern professions"[56]. The Singhalese, already feeling that they were a minority in the international context, saw this huge proportion of Tamils in the civil service as a threat, and when Sri Lanka gained independence, they used their large numbers to make sure that they gained the advantage over the Tamils.

In response to the threat perceived by the Tamil community, several organizations formed around the topic of Tamil rights, but the leading and dominant voice was the Liberation Tigers of Tamil Eelam (LTTE). The goal of the LTTE, led by Velupillai Prahbhakaran, was to create an independent country for the Tamil people and through various military and political tactics they were able to create a semi-autonomous region in the northern province of Sri Lanka for about 25 years. Classified as a terrorist group by the United States, the LTTE has "plotted many brutal attacks, including more than 200 by suicide bombers, according to the Council on Foreign Relations"[57]

The civil war officially started in 1983 because the violence against the Tamils culminated in this year. Prior to this, "elements in the Sri Lankan government encouraged or in some cases sponsored, episodes of anti-Tamil violence in 1977, 1979, 1981 and 1983."[58] The riots of 1983 began when "Sinhalese mobs were transported in Government buses and used official voter registration lists to identify and target Tamils. Thousands of deaths resulted, together with large-scale displacement, destruction of Tamil property and migration of Tamils abroad. The Government asserted that the attacks occurred in response to the LTTE's killing of 13 Sri Lankan soldiers in the northern district of Jaffna."[59]

The Sri Lankan civil war officially ended on May 19, 2009 when the army killed the leader of the LTTE, Prahbhakaran. In the last months of the war, from September 2008 to May 19, 2009 civilians living in a northern area of Sri Lanka called the Vanni were trapped between the advancing government army and the LTTE. According to the UN report,

"The Government subjected victims and survivors of the conflict to further deprivation and suffering after they left the conflict zone. Screening for suspected LTTE took place without any transparency or external scrutiny. Some of those who were separated were summarily executed, and some of the women may have been raped. Others disappeared, as recounted by their wives and relatives during the LLRC hearings. All IDPs were detained in closed camps. Massive overcrowding led to terrible conditions, breaching the basic social and economic rights of the detainees, and many lives were lost unnecessarily. Some persons in the camps were interrogated and subjected to torture. Suspected LTTE were removed to other facilities, with no contact with the outside world, under conditions that made them vulnerable to further abuses."[60]

Post-Conflict Reconstruction

*Legal Mechanisms*

The Sri Lankan government created the Lessons Learnt and Reconciliation Commission after the end of the conflict with the intention of examining what happened during the war and what needs to be done in now that it has ended. The president proclaimed that the commission will "inquire and report on the following matters that may have taken place during the period between 21st February 2002 and 19th May 2009, namely;

"(i) the facts and circumstances which led to the failure of the ceasefire agreement operationalized on 21st Febuary 2002 and the sequence of events that followed thereafter up to the 19th of May 2009;

(ii) whether any person, group or institution directly or indirectly bear responsibility in this regard;

(iii) the lessons we would learn from those events and their attendant concerns, in order to ensure that there will be no recurrence;

(iv) the methodology whereby restitution to any person affected by those events or their dependents of their heirs can be effected;

(v) the institutional, administrative and legislative measures which need to be taken in order to prevent and reccurence of such concerns in the future, and to promote further national unity and reconciliation among all communities, and to make any such other recommendations with reference to any of the matters that have been inquired into under the terms of this Warrant."[61]

The commission came to several conclusions and recommendations including those specific to the topic of justice for the victims of the war. It found that "The culture of suspicion, fear, mistrust and violence needs to be removed and opportunities and space opened up in which people can hear each other and be heard for an era of healing and peace building in the country."[62] While this recommendations calls for the space for healing and truth telling to be opened up, it does not specify how the government is to go about creating such a space. The commission also recommended that "What needs to be done for reconciliation and nation-building is that the State has to reach out to the minorities and the minorities, in turn must, re-position themselves in their role vis a vis the State and the country."[63] These are both worthwhile recommendations but after the LLRC was published, very little was done by the current regime to implement the recommendations made by its own mandated commission. Many international human rights watch dog organizations such as Amnesty International, Human Rights Watch, and the International Crisis Group stated concerns about the commission's "independence and lack of investigative powers over war crimes.[64] These concerns include the commission's failure to "properly pursue allegations of war crimes and crimes against humanity levelled against both government forces and the Liberation Tigers of Tamil Eelam (LTTE).[65] While there has been criticisms levied against the LLRC much of its content regarding recommendations for justice and reconciliation is sound, although its power to implement said recommendations is non-existent.

The Rajapaksa regime did create a National Action Plan for the Protection and Promotion of Human Rights plan to create a time line for the implementation of parts of the LLRC. In the introduction of the plan it is stated that the Plan was the "result of a Government and people deciding to take concrete action to bring about positive change . In developing the Action Plan, the Government assessed the measures in place to protect and promote human rights, identified areas that need improvement and have committed ourselves to improving the protection and promotion of human rights."[66]

Within the civil and political rights section the plan cites the government's commitment to upholding the UN International Covenant on Civil and Political Rights which states,

"Recognizing that, in accordance with the Universal Declaration of Human Rights, the ideal of free human beings enjoying civil and political freedom and freedom from fear and want can only be achieved if conditions are created whereby everyone may enjoy his civil and political rights, as well as his economic, social and cultural rights,"

Article 5: "1. Nothing in the present Covenant may be interpreted as implying for any State, group or person any right to engage in any activity or perform any act aimed at the destruction of any of the rights and freedoms recognized herein or at their limitation to a greater extent than is provided for in the present Covenant."

Article 27: "In those States in which ethnic, religious or linguistic minorities exist, persons belonging to such minorities shall not be denied the right, in community with the other members of their group, to enjoy their own culture, to profess and practice their own religion, or to use their own language." [67]

While the regime has stated its commitment to convention, in practice very little has been done to uphold these values and promises. Within the Plan though various focus areas, including justice have been created. The focus area of access to justice has multiple goals such as speedy administration of justice, appropriate provision of legal aid, implementation of official languages policies, and ensuring proper attention and ethical response to those seeking access to justice/ legal assistance.[68] `All these goals work within the existing legal structure in Sri Lanka, which has shown itself to be biased to the will of the President.[69]

*Power-Sharing Government Structures*

Because of the complete military defeat the Sri Lankan government had over the Tamil Tigers there was no peace agreement made between the two sides that called for a power sharing structure. The government system had no reason to change since they were the complete victors of the war. For this reason there are small inclusions of Tamils in the Sri Lankan government, including the Tamil National Alliance party which represents the populations of the North and East. The key tenants of the party are as follows:

The Tamils are a distinct People and from time immemorial have inhabited this island together with the Sinhalese People and others

The contiguous preponderantly Tamil Speaking Northern and Eastern provinces is the historical habitation of the Tamil Speaking Peoples

The Tamil People are entitled to the right to self-determination

Power sharing arrangements must be established in a unit of a merged Northern and Eastern Provinces based on a Federal structure, in a manner also acceptable to the Tamil Speaking Muslim people

Devolution of power on the basis of shared sovereignty shall necessarily be over land, law and order, socio-economic development including health and education, resources and fiscal powers.[70]

In September of 2013, the Tamil Provinces held their first elections since the end of the war and the TNA won the majority of the vote, and took 30 of the 36 seats which were contested on the provincial council.[71] While there is a clear support for the TNA along ethnic lines, its power with the current regime in Colombo has been extremely limited.

## Identity Legislation

The Sri Lankan Constitution is the overarching document for all legislation passed within the country has very tenants on the issues of justice and ethnicity. It states, "Every citizen is entitled to- the freedom by himself or in association with others to enjoy and promote his own culture and to use his own language."[72] The constitution also states that while Sinhala is the official language of the country, Tamil is a national language.[73] There was a proposed amendment made to the constitution in the 1970s that calls for a more inclusive document for all the minorities of Sri Lanka. It states, "Article 18 of the Constitution of the Democratic Socialist Republic of Sri Lanka is hereby amended as follows:-
> (2) Tamil shall also be an official language
> (3) English shall be the link language"[74]

Within this amendment there is also the push for devolving executive power to provincial councils-

"Subject to the provisions of the Constitution, a Provincial Council shall be established for every Province specified in the Eighth Schedule with effect from such date or dates as the President may appoint by Order published in the Gazette, different dates may be appointed in respect of different Provinces"[75]

Currently there is a big push for the regime to accept the 13th amendment as a sign of reconciliation with the northern and eastern parts of the country, but to date it has not been incorporated into the official constitution.

## Civil Society

NGOs are required to register under the National Secretariat for NGOs, which is housed under the Ministry of Defense and Urban Development. The objective of the government department is to create a conducive environment for national and international communities, coordinating the NGO sector with the government, other NGOs, and individuals, as well as making sure the NGOs are working within a the legal framework of Sri Lanka and the national policy of the country.[76] The Sri Lankan government is currently employing hostile tactics toward Sri Lankan civil society, especially those involved in issues of human rights and justice. In the Summer of 2014 the secretariat issued a circular which prohibited NGOs from "conducting press conferences, workshops, trainings for journalists and dissemination of press releases"[77] There has been widespread international criticism of this circular as well as criticism from the opposition leader, Ranil Wickremesinghe who stated that this circular was a "blatant attempt by the Government to control all non-governmental organizations, an attempt to negate the rights conferred under the Constitution and the Universal Declaration of Human Rights."[78] The Sri Lankan government has denied that this is the case, and stated in its defence that this circular was but a reminder for NGOs to "adhere to certain principles which those organizations had agreed to follow when they had been formed," and that "It is a well-known fact that certain NGOs operating in Sri Lanka had acted beyond their aims and objectives."[79] Multiple international organizations and governments, including the US are worried about the continuing pressure on Sri Lankan civil society by the regime. The US state department stated that they were "concerned by intensifying pressure on Sri Lankan civil society and human rights activists."[80]

International Engagement

There has been, and continues to be international pushes for justice within Sri Lanka. The Human Rights Council of the UN has passed in total three resolutions urging the Sri Lankan government to investigate alleged human rights violations. They have also called on the government to implement the recommendations made by its own fact finding commission- the LLRC. Navi Pillay, The U.N. High Commissioner for Human Rights concluded in her recent report after her visit to Sri Lanka in 2014, that "national mechanisms [in Sri Lanka] have consistently failed to establish the truth and achieve justice," and "an independent, international inquiry would play a positive role…where domestic mechanisms have failed."[81] In March of 2014 the Human Rights Council passed a resolution calling for investigation into the events that happened during the war, but the Sri Lankan government has vehently denied interniaotnal involvement saying that it is infringement on state sovereignty for the UN to come into the county. The government rejects conclusions by an independent U.N. Panel of Experts as lacking "credence or legitimacy."[82]

It is worth noting that the government of India remained fairly vocal on accountability for the LTTE, given its interest in determining responsibility for the assassination of then Indian Prime Minister Rajiv Gandhi by the LTTE in 1991. India has officially sought the extradition of LTTE leader Vellupillai Prabhakaran for this assassination since 1995. Here, too, the physical end of the LTTE, including of Prabhakaran, leaves little incentive for India further to influence Sri Lanka's transitional justice response.[83]

Conclusion

While Sri Lanka's post-conflict reconstruction is the youngest of the presented case studies, an analysis of the variables of transitional justice is still imperative to dissecting the type of peace in Sri Lanka. The GPI for Sri Lanka is 105, which is relatively high for the South Asian region. Because of the end of the war the GPI has risen but this only take into account the end of the war and the sharp decline in deaths, not the post-conflict justice context. Using Lund's measurements of peace, Sri Lanka is in a state of unstable peace. There is still high suspicion of all Tamils by the government, which is illustrated through their withholding of citizenship for Sri Lankan Tamil nationals, continued torture and detainment of Tamils, and very few political roles for Tamils. While these factors hold true for Lund's categorization of the type of peace for Sri Lanka, and the Tamils and Singhalese continue to see each other as the enemy, the lack of Tamil military capabilities has led to a higher level of peace, in the sense that there is no valid threat to the current regime's power. The complete and total destruction of the LTTE, as well as the heavily causalities sustained by the Tamil civilian population, has led to a mindset in which Tamils do not want to mobilize anymore. This is not a true peace, and although the country maintains much of the economic growth, prosperity, and other superficial characteristics that define a peaceful society, its lack of a balance of power allows a space for crisis and war to arise. While it does not seem likely that this will happen within this generation of Sri Lankans because of the fatigue that comes with a thirty year war, it will become a serious possibility in the future if a more durable peace is not accomplished.

## Policy Recommendations

Sri Lankan infrastructure is in place to implement justice reforms that can lead to durable peace as opposed to the compelled peace that has been put in place by the current regime. The constitution, as cited in this paper demonstrates the equality and unification that the Sri Lankan state was built upon, and now it is up to the regime and civil society to make sure that this legacy becomes active in the newly reunited state. Many policy recommendations have been made by both internal and external actors, calling upon the regime to legalize Tamil as an official language, as well as implementing the recommendations made the LLRC. While these are necessary to ensuring Sri Lanka start on the path to durable peace and eventual reconciliation, they are also completely dependent on the political will of the current regime. Other actors, such as civil society and international players can use this time to lay the foundation for justice in the form of taking testimony from survivors both inside and outside Sri Lanka, as well as following a more Northern Ireland model of creating small, informal spaces for people to discuss their experiences and share their stories. In addition, while Tamil politicians are allowed to have a role in regional government activities they should try to form people within the Muslim-Tamil community. During the war all Muslims were kicked out of the Northern Province by the LTTE and were never given back their homes. The Tamil community should implement justice mechanisms between themselves and the Muslims as a role model for how the Singhalese community should interact with the other minorities within the country. There is a lot of work to be done within Sri Lanka, and because only a short time has passed since the end of the war the opportunity to create long-term, sustainable peace, is still available.

## Epilogue

Post-conflict societies face enormous pressure and difficulties in attempting to completely rebuild states in almost all spheres. Peace is necessary for a stable state and after conflict, justice, whether immediate, or postponed, is eventually necessary to establish and maintain peace. While the international community tends to hold the simplified and quick fix solution of a formal justice mechanism, such as a commission, as the answer to most states attempting to establish transitional justice, this hypothesis rarely is the only solution to these complex and nuanced issues that these states face. As shown in this paper, sometimes the solution is multi-pronged and postponed in the name of peace. This paper also shows that there is more that the three types of peace established by Lund, and held as normative by most actors. Compelled peace, the aftermath of completely military victory, is equally important to analyze because while it is by definition 'peace' is perpetuates issues of human rights, justice, reconciliation, and long term sustainability. The relationship between peace and justice is not linear, but parabolic, in that it highest levels of peace occur without and with justice. This conceptualization of the relationship must be taken into account when proposing policy for post-conflict societies facing seemingly insurmountable problems. Domestic and international actors must look at the specific details of each country and the wider literature of transitional justice in order to fully gain and understand of what needs to be done.

# Endnotes

1. Outreach Programme on the Rwandan Genocide and the United Nations. "Rwanda: A Brief History of the Country." UN News Center. UN, n.d. Web. 14 Dec. 2013.

2. Douglass, William A. "Sacrifice as Terror: The Rwandan Genocide of 1994." *Journal of Anthropological Research* 57.1 (2001): 102-05

3. Dallaire,Romeo. Interview 52042. Visual History Achieve. USC Shoah Foundation. 2011. Web. 16 Dec. 2013

4. Corey, Allison, and Sandra Joireman. "Retributive Justice: The Gacaca Courts in Rwanda." *African Affairs* 103.410 (2004): p.73.

5. Amnesty International, 'Rwanda: Gacaca: a question of justice', December 2002, accessed December 2013

6. Corey, Allison. P.73.

7. Rwandan Government. "Justice and Reconciliation." Www.gov.rw. Rwandan Government, 2013. Web. 16 Dec. 2013.

8. UN Security Council Resolution.no. 955, 1994.

9. Straus, Scott, and Lars Waldorf. *Remaking Rwanda: State Building and Human Rights after Mass Violence*. Madison, WI: U of Wisconsin, 2011. Print. p.173

10. Ibid. p.175

11. "The Fall of the Genocidal Regime." Government of Rwanda. Accessed November 2014. Web.

12. Human Rights Watch. *Preparing for Elections: Tightening Control in the Name of Unity*. Issue brief. 2003. Print.

13. http://www.gov.rw/Speech-by-President-Paul-Kagame-at-the-20th-Commemoration-of-the-Genocide-against-the-Tutsi

14. Adamczyk, Christiane. "'Today, I Am No Mutwa Anymore': Facets of National Unity Discourse in Present-day Rwanda." *Social Anthropology* 19.2 (2011): 175-88. Web.

15. Constitution of the Republic of Rwanda and its Amendments of 2 December 2003 and of 8 December 2005 [Preamble], 4 June 2003

16. ibid, Chapter II, Article 9

17. Ibid. Title II, Chapter 1, Article 11

18. IDRC n.d.; see also AI Aug. 2004, 11; Rwanda 25 May 2006, p. 89

19. ibid

20. Amnesty International. *Safer to Stay Silent The Chilling Effect of Rwanda's Law on 'Genocide Ideology' and 'Sectarianism.'* Rep. no. AFR 47/005/2010. London: Amnesty International Publications, 2010. Print.

21. Observatory for the Protection of Human Rights Defenders. Rwanda. Rep. no. Annual Report. 2011.

22. National Unity and Reconciliation Commission, 'Report on the Evaluation of National Unity and Reconciliation', June 2002, p.5

23. Civicus. *The State of Civil Society in Rwanda in National Development*. Rep. no. A.M. N° 103/11 Du 07/09/2004.: Conseil De Concertation Des Organisations D'Appui Aux Initiatives De Base (CCOAIB), 2011. Print. p.17

24. Ngendandumwe, Jean Claude, and Jean Bosco Senyabatera. *The 2012 CSO Sustainability Index for Sub-Saharan Africa*. Rep. United States Agency for International Development, 2012. . p.118

25. ibid

26. CIVICUS, p. 37

27. Stefaan Marysse, An Ansoms, and Danny Cassimon, 'The aid "darlings" and "orphans" of the Great Lakes Region in Africa', *European Journal of Development Research* 19, 3 (2007), p. 434.

28. Uvin, Peter. "Difficult Choices in the New Post-conflict Agenda: The International Community in Rwanda after the Genocide." *Third World Quarterly* 22.2 (2001): p.179

29. ibid

30. OECD (1999a) *The Limits And Scope For The Use Of Development Assistance Incentives And Disincentives For Influencing Conflict Situations. Case Study: Rwanda* (Paris: OECD Development Assistance Committee Informal Task Force on Conflict, Peace And Development CO-Operation) (by Antonbaare, David Schearer & Peter Uvin).

31. Sutton, Malcolm. "CAIN: Sutton Index of Deaths - Menu Page." CAIN: Sutton Index of Deaths - Menu Page. CAIN Project, 2002. Web. 21 Dec. 2014.

32. Hamber, Brandon. "Conclusion: A Truth Commission for Northern Ireland?" *Past Imperfect: Dealing with the past in Northern Ireland and Societies in Transition*. Derry/Londonderry: Incore, 1998. Print. P.89.

33. Boraine, Alex. *All Truth Is Bitter:A Report of the Visit of Doctor Alex Boraine, Deputy Chairman of the South African Truth and Reconciliation Commission, to Northern Ireland*. Rep. N.p.: Community Relations Council, 1999. Print. P.20

34. McEvoy Kiran. *Making Peace with the Past: Options for Truth Recovery regarding the Conflict in and about Northern Ireland*. Rep. Belfast: Healing Through Remembering, 2006. Print.

35. Northern Ireland Act 1998, 69 (1)

36. ibid., (6)

37. *Dealing with Northern Ireland's Past: Towards a Transitional Justice Approach*. Northern Ireland Human Rights Commission, July 31, 2013.

38. Good Friday Agreement, 10 April 1998, section 6

39. Ibid, section six, pledge of office (b) and (c)

40. ibid

41. Lawther ,Steven and Evans, Kirsty . *Public Perceptions of the Executive*, Prepared for OFMD-FM,. Red Circle Communications, March 4, 2010

42. Northern Ireland Act 1998, Statue 75

43. British-Irish Agreement, Good Friday Agreement, 1998 Article I

44. Good Friday section 3, article 5

45. Gormally, Brian. D*ealing with the Past in Northern Ireland 'From Below' An Evaluation*. Rep. Belfast: Community Foundation, 2009. Print. P.5

46. Community Dialogue. "Dealing with the Past: From Victimhood to Survival | Community Dialogue." Dealing with the Past: From Victimhood to Survival | Community Dialogue., 6 Jan. 2005. Web. 21 Dec. 2014.

47. Gormally, p.5

48. McEvoy, p.68

49. Women's Resource and Development Agency. *Women and Conflict: Talking about the "Troubles" and Planning for the Future.* Rep. Belfast: Women's Resource and Development Agency, 2008. Print.p.8

50. The Rt Hon The Lord Saville of Newdigate. *Report of the The Bloody Sunday Inquiry.* Rep. London: UK Government, 2010. Print. Ch 5.4

51. "Bloody Sunday: PM David Cameron's Full Statement." BBC News. BBC, 15 June 2010. Web. 21 Dec. 2014.

52. "How Cameron's Bloody Sunday Apology Brings a Tragic Era to an End." *The Globe and Mail,* 15 June 2010. Web. 21 Dec. 2014.

53. Whitehead, Tom. "Bloody Sunday Soldiers Could Be Prosecuted with Anonymous Witnesses." *The Telegraph.* Telegraph Media Group, 13 May 2014. Web. 21 Dec. 2014.

54. European Convention on Human Rights. The United Kingdom. Rep. 2014. Print. p.13

55. Clarance, William. "Conflict and Community in Sri Lanka." *History Today* July 2002: 41-47. Web. 8 May 2013.p. 42

56. Bandarge Asoka. *The Separatist Conflict in Sri Lanka: Terrorism, Ethnicity, Political Economy.* New York: Routledge, 2009. Print. p.58

57. Pickert, Kate. "A Brief History of the Tamil Tigers." *Time* 04 Jan. 2009: n. pag. Web. 16 July 2013

58. Darusman, Marzuki, Yasmin Sooka, and Steven Ratner. *Report of the Secretart-General's Panel of Experts on Accountability in Sri Lanka.* Rep. New York: United Nations, 2011. Print. P. 7, P. 8

59. ibid

60. ibid, P.iii

61. Rajan De Silva, Chitta. *Report of the Commission of Inquiry on Lessons Learnt and Reconciliation.* Rep. Colombo:Sri Lankan Government, 2011. Print., preamble

62. Ibid, 9.174

63. Ibid, 9.178

64. "Groups Snub Sri Lanka War Inquiry." BBC News. N.p., 14 Oct. 2010. Web. 21 Dec. 2014.

65. Amnesty International. "Sri Lanka: Inquiry into Armed Conflict Fundamentally Flawed | Amnesty International." Sri Lanka: Inquiry into Armed Conflict Fundamentally Flawed | Amnesty International. N.p., 7 Sept. 2011. Web. 21 Dec. 2014.

66. Government of Sri Lanka. *National Action Plan for the Protection and Promotion of Human Rights.* Rep. N.p.: Government of Sri Lanka, 2011. Print., Introduction, p.5

67. Office of the High Commissioner for Human Rights. "International Covenant on Civil and Political Rights." International Covenant on Civil and Political Rights. United Nations, 23 Mar. 1976. Web. 21 Dec. 2014.

68. Government of Sri Lanka, P. 28-29

69. Yardley, Jim. "Sri Lanka's Parliament Tries to Impeach Chief Justice." *The New York Times,* 08 Nov. 2012. Web. 21 Dec. 2014.

70. Tamil National Alliance. "Our Stand on the Political Solution." TNA -Tamil National Alliance. N.p., 2012. Web. 21 Dec. 2014.

71. Harris, Gardiner. "Tamils Dominate Vote in Sri Lanka Province." *The New York Times,* 21 Sept. 2013. Web. 21 Dec. 2014.

72. National State Assembly, Constitution of the Democratic Socialist Republic of Sri Lanka, 1978, Ch.III Fundamental rights 14

73. Ibis, Ch. IV Language

74. Ibid, Amendment 13

75. Ibid , Chapter XVIIA- Establishment of Provincial Council ,154A. (1)

76. Government of Sri Lanka. "Objectives." National Secretariat for Non Governmental Organizations. N.p., 2014. Web.

77. CIVICUS. "ALERT: Sri Lanka: Worrying Developments for Civil Society." Media and Resources. CIVICUS, July 2014. Web

78. Special Reporter. "Govt. Circular No Attempt to Suppress NGOs – PM." *Development - Provincial. News*.lk, 11 July 2014. Web.

79. ibid

80. Psaki, Jen. "Continued Intimidation of Sri Lankan Civil Society." U.S. Department of State. U.S. Department of State, 21 Mar. 2014. Web. 21 Dec. 2014.

81. *Report of the Office of the United Nations High Commissioner for Human Rights on advice and technical assistance for the Government of Sri Lanka on promoting reconciliation and accountability in Sri Lanka*, A/HRC/25/23, p.72

82. *Comments received from the Permanent Mission of Sri Lanka on the draft report of the Office of the United Nations High Commissioner for Human Rights on promoting reconciliation and accountability in Sri Lanka* (A/HRC/25/23), A/HRC/25/G/9, ¶ 2 (24 Feb. 2013)

83. Against the grain: pursuing a transitional justice agenda in postwar Sri Lanka. Anonymous. *International Journal of Transitional Justice*5.1 (Mar 2011): 31-51.

# Bibliography

Adamczyk, Christiane. "'Today, I Am No Mutwa Anymore': Facets of National Unity Discourse in Present-day Rwanda." *Social Anthropology* 19.2 (2011): 175-88. Web.

Against the grain: pursuing a transitional justice agenda in postwar Sri Lanka Anonymous. *International Journal of Transitional Justice* 5.1 (Mar 2011): 31-51

Amnesty International, 'Rwanda: Gacaca: a question of justice', December 2002, accessed December 2013

Amnesty International. *Safer to Stay Silent The Chilling Effect of Rwanda's Laws on 'Genocide Ideology' and 'Sectarianism'.* Rep. no. AFR 47/005/2010. London: Amnesty International Publications, 2010. Print.

Amnesty International. "Sri Lanka: Inquiry into Armed Conflict Fundamentally Flawed | Amnesty International." Sri Lanka: Inquiry into Armed Conflict Fundamentally Flawed | Amnesty International. N.p., 7 Sept. 2011. Web. 21 Dec. 2014.

Arsanjani, Mahnoush H. Zeid Ra'ad Zeid Al Hussein and Marieke Wierda, "Peace V. Justice: Contradictory or Complementary" (Proceedings of the Annual Meeting (American Society of International Law), Vol. 100, 2006)

Bandarge Asoka. *The Separatist Conflict in Sri Lanka: Terrorism, Ethnicity, Political Economy.* New York: Routledge, 2009. Print.

Bass, Gary Jonathan. *Stay the Hand of Vengeance: The Politics of War Crime Tribunals* (Princeton: Princeton University Press, 2000)

Bassiouni ,Cherif. (ed.), Post-conflict Justice (2002).

Bell, Christine. 2009. Transitional justice, interdisciplinary and the state of the 'field' or 'non field'. *International Journal of Transitional Justice* 3: 5.

Bell, Christine, Colm Campbell, and Finonuala Nı´ Aola´in. 2004. "Justice discourses in transition". *Social and Legal Studies* 13(3): 305.

"Bloody Sunday: PM David Cameron's Full Statement." BBC News. BBC, 15 June 2010. Web. 21 Dec. 2014.

Boraine ,Alex. *A Country Unmasked: Inside South Africa's Truth and Reconciliation Commission* (Oxford: Oxford University Press, 2000)

Boraine, Alex. *All Truth Is Bitter:A Report of the Visit of Doctor Alex Boraine, Deputy Chairman of the South African Truth and Reconciliation Commission, to Northern Ireland.* Rep. N.p.: Community Relations Council, 1999. Print.

British-Irish Agreement, Good Friday Agreement, 1998

Bull,Hedley. *The Anarchical Society* (New York: Columbia University Press, 1977)

CIVICUS. "ALERT: Sri Lanka: Worrying Developments for Civil Society." Media and Resources. CIVICUS, July 2014. Web.

CIVICUS. The State of Civil Society in Rwanda in National Development. Rep. no. A.M. N° 103/11 Du 07/09/2004. N.p.: Conseil De Concertation Des Organisations D'Appui Aux Initiatives De Base (CCOAIB), 2011. Print.

Clarance, William. "Conflict and Community in Sri Lanka." *History Today* July 2002: 41-47. Web. 8 May 2013.p. 42

Comments received from the Permanent Mission of Sri Lanka on the draft report of the Office of the United Nations High Commissioner for Human Rights on promoting reconciliation and accountability in Sri Lanka (A/HRC/25/23), A/HRC/25/G/9, ¶ 2 (24 Feb. 2013)

Community Dialogue. "Dealing with the Past: From Victimhood to Survival | Community Dialogue." Dealing with the Past: From Victimhood to Survival | Community Dialogue. N.p., 6 Jan. 2005. Web. 21 Dec. 2014.

Constitution of the Republic of Rwanda and its Amendments of 2 December 2003 and of 8 December 2005 [Preamble], 4 June 2003

Corey, Allison, and Sandra Joireman. "Retributive Justice: The Gacaca Courts in Rwanda." *African Affairs* 103.410 (2004): p.73.

Crocker, David. "Civil Society and Transitional Justice," in *Civil Society, Democracy, and Civic Renewal*, ed. Robert Fullinwider (Lanham, MD: Rowman and Littlefield, 1999), 381-384.

Dallaire,Romeo. Interview 52042. Visual History Achieve. USC Shoah Foundation. 2011. Web. 16 Dec. 2013

Dealing with Northern Ireland's Past: Towards a Transitional Justice Approach. Northern Ireland Human Rights Commission, July 31, 2013.

Douglass, William A. "Sacrifice as Terror: The Rwandan Genocide of 1994." *Journal of Anthropological Research* 57.1 (2001): 102-05

Dyzenhaus, David. "Transitional Justice: Review Essay" (Oxford University Press: *International Journal of Constitutional Law*, 2003, v. 1 n. 1)

European Convention on Human Rights. The United Kingdom. Rep. N.p.: n.p., 2014. Print.

Freeman, Mark. *Peace vs. Justice: The Utility of Amnesties. Necessary Evils: Amnesties and the Search for Justice* (Cambridge, UK: Cambridge University Press, 2010), xx 376 pp.

Fry, Douglas. *Beyond War* (Oxford: Oxford University Press, 2007)

Good Friday Agreement, 10 April 1998

Gormally, Brian. *Dealing with the Past in Northern Ireland 'From Below' An Evaluation*. Rep. Belfast: Community Foundation, 2009. Print.

Government of Rwanda . "The Fall of the Genocidal Regime.". N.p., n.d. Web.

Government of Sri Lanka. *National Action Plan for the Protection and Promotion of Human Rights*. Rep. N.p.: Government of Sri Lanka, 2011. Print.

Government of Sri Lanka. "Objectives." National Secretariat for Non Governmental Organizations. N.p., 2014. Web.

"Groups Snub Sri Lanka War Inquiry." BBC News. N.p., 14 Oct. 2010. Web. 21 Dec. 2014.

Hamber, Brandon. "Conclusion: A Truth Commission for Northern Ireland?" *Past Imperfect: Dealing with the past in Northern Ireland and Societies in Transition*. Derry/Londonderry: INCORE, 1998. N. pag. Print.

Harris, Gardiner. "Tamils Dominate Vote in Sri Lanka Province." *The New York Times*, 21 Sept. 2013. Web. 21 Dec. 2014.

Hobbes, Thomas. *Leviathan* (Oxford: Oxford University Press, 1998 [1651]), ch. 5.

"How Cameron's Bloody Sunday Apology Brings a Tragic Era to an End." *The Globe and Mail.* N.p., 15 June 2010. Web. 21 Dec. 2014.

Human Rights Watch. *Preparing for Elections: Tightening Control in the Name of Unity.* Issue brief. N.p.: n.p., 2003. Print.

IJTJ. 2007. Editorial note. *International Journal of Transitional Justice* 1: 1.

Lawther ,Steven and Evans, Kirsty . *Public Perceptions of the Executive*, Prepared for OFMDFM,. Red Circle Communications, March 4, 2010

Lund, Michael S. *Preventing Violent Conflicts : A Strategy for Preventive Diplomacy*. Washington D.C: U.S. Institute of Peace, 1996. Print.

Mamdani, Mahmood. *When Victims become Killers: Colonialism, Nativism, and the genocide in Rwanda* ( Princeton: Princeton University Press, 2001)

McCormick, John. 2001. "Derrida on law: Or, poststructuralism gets serious." *Political Theory* 29: 395.

McEvoy, Kieran. *Making Peace with the Past: Options for Truth Recovery regarding the Conflict in and about Northern Ireland. Rep. Belfast: Healing Through Remembering*, 2006. Print.

McEvoy, K. 'Beyond the Metaphor: Political Violence, Human Rights and "New" Peacemaking Criminology' (2003) 7 *Theoretical Crim.* 319; Healing Through Remembering, Making Peace with the Past: Options for Truth Recovery in Northern Ireland (2006).

McEvoy, K. H. Mika, and K. McConnachie, *Reconstructing Justice After Conflict: A Bottom Up Perspective* (2008)

National State Assembly, Constitution of the Democratic Socialist Republic of Sri Lanka, 1978, Ch.III Fundamental rights 14

National Unity and Reconciliation Commission, '*Report on the Evaluation of National Unity and Reconciliation*', June 2002

Ngendandumwe, Jean Claude, and Jean Bosco Senyabatera. *The 2012 CSO Sustainability Index for Sub-Saharan Africa*. Rep. N.p.: United States Agency for International Development, 2012. Print.

Northern Ireland Act 1998

Observatory for the Protection of Human Rights Defenders. Rwanda. Rep. no. Annual Report. N.p.: n.p., 2011. Print.

OECD (1999a) *The Limits And Scope For The Use Of Development Assistance Incentives And Disincentives For Influencing Conflict Situations. Case Study: Rwanda* (Paris: OECD Development Assistance Committee Informal Task Force on Conflict, Peace And Development CO-Operation)(BY Antonbaare, David Schearer & Peter Uvin).

Office of the United Nations High Commissioner for Human Rights. "Advice and technical assistance for the Government of Sri Lanka on promoting reconciliation and accountability in Sri Lanka", A/HRC/25/23.

Office of the High Commissioner for Human Rights. "International Covenant on Civil and Political Rights." International Covenant on Civil and Political Rights. United Nations, 23 Mar. 1976. Web. 21 Dec. 2014.

Outreach Programme on the Rwandan Genocide and the United Nations. "Rwanda: A Brief History of the Country." UN News Center. UN, n.d. Web. 14 Dec. 2013.

Pickert, Kate. "A Brief History of the Tamil Tigers." *Time* 04 Jan. 2009: n. pag. Web. 16 July 2013

Psaki, Jen. "Continued Intimidation of Sri Lankan Civil Society." U.S. Department of State. U.S. Department of State, 21 Mar. 2014. Web. 21 Dec. 2014.

The Rt Hon The Lord Saville of Newdigate. *Report of the The Bloody Sunday Inquiry*. Rep. London: UK Government, 2010. Print.

Rwandan Government. "Justice and Reconciliation." Www.gov.rw. Rwandan Government, 2013. Web. 16 Dec. 2013.

Special Reporter. "Govt. Circular No Attempt to Suppress NGOs – PM." Development - Provincial. News.lk, 11 July 2014. Web.

Straus, Scott, and Lars Waldorf. *Remaking Rwanda: State Building and Human Rights after Mass Violence*. Madison, WI: U of Wisconsin, 2011. Print.

Stefaan Marysse, An Ansoms, and Danny Cassimon, 'The aid "darlings" and "orphans" of the Great Lakes Region in Africa', *European Journal of Development Research* 19, 3 (2007), pp. 433–58.

Sutton, Malcolm. "CAIN: Sutton Index of Deaths - Menu Page." CAIN: Sutton Index of Deaths - Menu Page. CAIN Project, 2002. Web. 21 Dec. 2014.

Tamil National Alliance. "Our Stand on the Political Solution." TNA -Tamil National Alliance. N.p., 2012. Web. 21 Dec. 2014.

Teitel, R. *Transitional Justice* (New York: Oxford University Press, 2000).

Teitel, R. 'Humanity's Law: Rule of Law for the New Global Politics (2002) 35 *Cornell International Law J.* 355-87.

Teitel, R. 'Transitional Justice Genealogy' (2003) 16 *Harvard Human Rights J.* 69 94

Turner, Catherine. 2008. "Delivering lasting peace, democracy and human rights in transition: The role of international law". *International Journal of Transitional Justice* 2: 126.

UN Security Council Resolution. Rep. no. 955. N.p.: n.p., 1994. Print.

United Nations, *The Rule of Law and Transitional Justice in Conflict and Post Conflict Societies* (2004) Available at http://daccessdds.un.org/doc/UNDOC/GEN/ N04/395/29/PDF/N0439529.pdf>

Uvin, Peter. "Difficult Choices in the New Post-conflict Agenda: The International Community in Rwanda after the Genocide." *Third World Quarterly* 22.2 (2001): 177-89. Web.

Whitehead, Tom. "Bloody Sunday Soldiers Could Be Prosecuted with Anonymous Witnesses." *The Telegraph*, 13 May 2014. Web. 21 Dec. 2014.

Yardley, Jim. "Sri Lanka's Parliament Tries to Impeach Chief Justice." *The New York Times*, 08 Nov. 2012. Web. 21 Dec. 2014.

Zimmern, Alfred. *The League of Nations and the Rule of Law* (London: Macmillan, 1936)

# 5

# Japan's Pop Culture Diplomacy:
# Is it Working?

## Leila Wang

*Popular culture has never been a conventional topic in the realm of international relations. However, in 2007, Japanese government had decided to officially include it as part of their foreign policy agenda under culture diplomacy. The aim was to make use of the popularity of Japanese pop culture to spread positive image and messages about Japan to foreign populations. Even before this, Japanese pop culture has already been branded as Japan's source of soft power, most notably by Douglas McGray. The question of whether it can really be useful as a soft power tool remains yet to be answered. Even as Japan pushes its pop culture diplomacy, relations with her neighbors, in particular China, has deteriorated over the years despite large Japanese pop culture consumption in the country. This study seeks to find out if Japanese pop culture has any tangible effects in leading to positive images of Japan in China. The data was collected from an original survey and then run through statistical analysis to obtain meaningful results. The results prove that with everything constant, there is a strong positive statistical association between consumption of Japanese pop culture and positive perceptions of Japan as a nation state. Despite limitations of the study, this provides useful empirical results for the soft power effects of pop culture, and may lay the groundwork for an extended longitudinal study which can lead to a better analysis over time of Japanese pop culture's soft power potential.*

Post-WWII Japan is known widely for its popular culture, which consists of Japanese comic books (*manga*), animated shows (anime), movies, music, art and many more. In the 80s and 90s, Japanese pop culture has seen a surge in popularity as famous icons such as Hello Kitty, Doraemon and more arose and gained popularity around the world. In a groundbreaking article in the May 2002 issue of the Foreign Policy magazine, Douglas McGray coined the term "Japan's National Cool" to describe the appeal of Japan's rich culture and its contribution to Japan's national and cultural influence. For the first time, Japanese pop culture was portrayed as a resource for promoting national image. Meanwhile, the regional context has been changing since the death of the wartime and post-war leader, Emperor Hirohito, in 1989 and the end of the Cold War in the early 1990s. The relations between Japan and its neighbors have been worsening by the day, and Japan is losing its position as a powerhouse in the Asian region. MrGray's article came at a perfect time when the Japanese government was searching for ways to improve their international standing. Pop culture, which has been traditionally seen from an economic perspective (as export), suddenly became a resource for improving national image and brand abroad. In 2007, then Japan Foreign Minister Aso Taro successfully proposed to the Diet (Japan's

Parliament) the adoption of Japanese pop culture as a diplomatic tool in their foreign policy agenda.

The use of pop culture as part of a political agenda is unconventional and fairly rare. Pop culture diplomacy is still a new concept, and little research has been done regarding its effect in terms of influence. This project seeks to contribute to this discourse by examining if there is a relationship between the consumption of Japanese pop culture and perceptions of Japan as a nation state. As highlighted in the Ministry of Foreign Affairs' Diplomatic Bluebook 2013, there is a focus on building a positive image of Japan at the general public level, forming one of the most important goals of promoting pop culture diplomacy. The proximity of China to Japan facilitates the large flow of Japanese pop culture into the former. Many young to middle-aged Chinese grew up with Japanese anime and *manga*. However, there are also strong anti-Japanese sentiments in China, especially in recent years with the surfacing of historical and territorial issues. It is hence worthwhile to study the effectiveness of Japanese pop culture in overcoming these sentiments.

## Rise of Japanese Pop Culture

With the collapse of the bubble economy and the resulting economic stagnation in early 1990s, Japan has been struggling to maintain its leadership in the changing context of the Asia Pacific region. Burdened with a declining economy, and internal political fragmentation among the different factions and parties, Japan went through a bleak period of political and economic challenges known to many as the "lost decade". During this time, ironically, Japanese pop culture began gaining popularity and prominence in several Asian countries. The economy and profit driven image of Japan with its lifetime employment and industrial policies was gradually being replaced by the image of "Cool Japan".[1] This collapse of Japan's traditional structures paved way for the rise of the youth-led pop culture and for a period of time during the 90s, there was a general craze in Asia for Japanese popular culture products, such as TV dramas, popular music, fashion, *manga* and anime.[2]

The largest Japanese pop cultural product market in Asia, and also the world, is the anime and *manga* industry. As David Leheny points out, this is the "undoubted champion in Japan's pop culture team around the world".[3] He points to the fact that some estimates put Japan as the source of about 60 percent of the world's animated TV programming and in 2003, *Focus Japan* estimates annual sales of anime-related licensed goods was at $17 billion. This does not even take into account the large black market trades of counterfeit merchandises occurring around Asia, which have been crucial to the dissemination of Japanese pop culture since it allowed for much cheaper access to the products.

The modern *manga* evolved out of post-war Japan and first began gaining international recognition with the influence of the famous *manga* artist, Tezuka Osamu. Otherwise known as the *kami-sama*[4] of *manga*, his works have included the world renowned Astro Boy (which eventually became a pop icon in itself), Black Jack, Buddha and more. He revolutionized the *manga* and anime industry, establishing practices which reduced production costs and laying the foundation for future aspiring *manga* artists. This allowed for the rise of many future favorites, such as Doraemon and Sailor Moon. Doraemon was such a hit with the Asian countries that by 1996, the 46 volume series had sold over 100 million copies.[5]

Educators and parents in Cambodia have even praised the series for its good values and behavior manners that is taught to children.[6] Now with the advance of technology and the internet, there is greater accessibility and people can read or watch *manga* and anime online without having to purchase them. Fangroups have sprung up over the years, providing their own translation, subtitles or dubbing for *manga* or anime series to distribute to other fans online. They can usually be found on online *manga* reading or anime streaming portals, providing the latest fan-translated chapters of the most popular *manga* series. Although unauthorized by the original publishers or licensers, this phenomenon has grown rapidly, providing youths all around the world who had internet an access to free popular *manga* series,[7] thus furthering the spread of this culture.

## Move Towards Pop Culture Diplomacy

The growing popularity of Japanese pop culture caught the attention of many, and in 2002, Douglas McGray published an article in *Foreign Policy* titled "Japan's Gross National Cool", coining the term and referring to Japan as "cool" for the first time.[8] In his article, he argued for the continued power and influence of Japan as a world leader due to its huge reserve of soft power gained from its increasing cultural presence, or "national cool" as he calls it. This article took the academic world by storm and Japanese pop culture was propelled to a status of national importance. Much spotlight was on it for the next couple of years where a spew of academic discourses about Japanese cultural diplomacy surfaced, and the Japanese government started taking notice of this new untapped area of power and influence.

When then Japanese Foreign Minister, Aso Taro, spoke in April 2006 to a group at the Digital Hollywood University, he brought up the importance of popular culture in Japan's cultural diplomacy, an unprecedented move in the history of Japanese politics. Speaking in the heart of Japan's pop culture center, Akihabara, Aso explained the need to take pop culture seriously as a diplomatic tool and the increasing need to use it to strengthen Japan's image abroad. He said,

> "What is the image that pops into someone's mind when they hear the name "Japan"? Is it a bright and positive image? Warm? Cool? The more these kinds of positive images pop up in a person's mind, the easier it becomes for Japan to get its views across over the long term. In other words, Japanese diplomacy is able to keep edging forward, bit by bit, and bring about better and better outcomes as a result."[9]

This argument he is making is that Japanese pop culture has the effect of instilling these positive "warm" and "cool" feelings into a person's mind. The "Japanese Dream" he calls it, evidently inspired by the "American Dream", which had for so many decades been the key contributor to the positive images attached to the US.[10] Then again in January 2007, Aso proposed to the Diet the adoption of Japanese pop culture as a diplomatic tool. It is no surprising fact that Aso was a big supporter of pop culture diplomacy, given that he himself had been an avid *manga* reader.[11] His speech about the global reach of Japanese pop culture is not too far-fetched as well. With the rapid spread of Japanese pop culture in the 1980s and 90s, people all around the world, especially in the Asian region, were exposed to and enthralled by the vibrant nature of Japanese pop cultural products. Japanese pop icons, such as Astro Boy, Hello Kitty, Pokemon and Doraemon, still hold a special place in the hearts of many, even now. However, as Lam points out, 'being "cool", "fun" and "hip" have now become serious business for the Japanese state".[12]

True to his words, Aso led the move into harnessing the power of pop culture as cultural diplomacy. As the Foreign Minister, he established in May 2007 the "International *Manga* Award" to award *manga* foreign *manga* artists who contribute to the promotion of *manga* culture overseas. This was the first official policy that deals with pop culture diplomacy, and it paved the way for MOFA to be more involved in the spread of pop culture. In the same year, MOFA also sponsored the Foreign Minister's Prize to the best costume-player in the "World Cosplay Summit", the biggest annual Cosplay event in Japan which attracts Cosplay contestants from all around world. In 2008, MOFA began its "Anime Ambassador" project in hopes of promoting Japan as a nation through the medium of anime. The first ambassador to be assigned was the Doraemon, the beloved robo-cat that is still popular all around Asia even now.[13]

## Japanese Pop Culture in China

Situated in the heart of East Asia, Japan is one of the key players in the region, along with its neighbor, China. The two countries share close proximity, being separated only by the East China Sea. As a result, it is not surprising that Japanese pop culture products would be widely disseminated and consumed in China. However, it was not until 27 years after the Second World War that China and Japan officially normalized country relations in 1972. Even then, it was only in 1979 that Japanese pop culture could be legally imported into and sold in China.[14] The Chinese government's strict restrictions on foreign imports made it even harder for Japanese pop culture products to find its place into the Chinese market. In fact, the Chinese government set an annual quota of only 20 foreign movies allowed broadcast the country, many of which are taken by American Hollywood films.[15]

This did not deter the Chinese population, however, which craved for the seemingly affluent and exciting lifestyles depicted in the Japanese pop culture products.[16] They began to turn to pirated or illegal sources. This was especially appealing to the young Chinese students who did not have a steady income flow. Pirated sources were much cheaper than the licensed ones, and they were rampant, found everywhere in stores and on the streets. For a cheap price, the students were able to get their fill of Japanese pop culture. Scholar Yoshiko Nakano called it "digital fast food" explaining that it was "pervasive, fast, cheap, often predictable, but filling."[17] In fact the Japan's Copyright Research and Information Center estimated around 3.18 billion pirated disks of Japanese games, music, anime, drama and movies circulating in China during years 2000 and 2001. This astonishing number shows that vast volumes of consumption of Japanese pop culture are through underground means, hence official figures may be underestimating the true consumption of Japanese pop culture in China.

Although this may result in losses for the Japanese production companies, the availability of these pirated products allowed the rapid spread of Japanese pop culture in China, hence generating more interest and demand. It is not a far-fetched claim to say that China is a large consumer of Japanese pop culture products. In fact, according to Cooper-Chen

(2010), there were estimated roughly 500 million consumers of Japanese anime and *manga* in China, more than one-third of the population, and the market was worth 14.6 billion USD.[18] Many of them consume Japanese pop culture on a regular basis, prompting the term *harizu*[19] used to describe this subculture population.

# Sino-Japanese relations

The strained Sino-Japanese relationship, however, continued even with Chinese consumption of Japanese pop culture. Being the two great powers in the region, the two countries have often gone head to head with each other on several issues. Furthermore, China and Japan has a long history of hostile relations and have engaged in several wars in the modern era. This history between them has fuelled the tensions between the two countries and exacerbated conflicts and disagreements. At the turn of the last century, China had part of its territory colonized by Japan after their defeat in the first Sino-Japanese war. Then, in 1937, Japan invaded China again, resulting in the infamous Nanjing Massacre shortly after their soldiers reached the city in December.[20] Japan's acts of atrocities in the war left a deep scar in China's history. The best-selling author Iris Chang, who wrote the famous book titled *Rape of Nanking,* placed the number of Chinese casualties at around 300,000, and the number of Chinese women raped at 20,000-80,000.[21] The memory of the war remains strong in the minds of the Chinese people. This remains a hugely contentious point in Sino-Japanese history, and is a constant source of bad relations between China and Japan.

Disagreements between China and Japan about war apologies, textbook content and the Yasukuni Shrine visits by high profile Japanese officials have further exacerbated this historical tension. Award winning journalist Nicholas Kristof argued that Japan's failure to apologize satisfactorily for its war crimes contributed to regional tensions, especially between Japan and China.[22] China shares the same thoughts, believing that Japan has not yet addressed their crimes nor express remorse and seek forgiveness. Japan on the other hand, felt that they have already apologized and given enough reparations via their generous Official Development Aid to China.[23] The Japanese people have been feeling the "apology fatigue", frustrated that there still condemnations from China despite numerous apologies.[24] Furthermore, many of the younger generations in Japan do not feel personally responsible for the war, hence become exasperated due to the repeated apologies.[25] While official statements from the Japanese government have been made expressing remorse for the war, they were often limited in scope and do little to address all the concerns in the region. Previous prime minister Junichiro Koizumi actually made at least 2 comprehensive apologies, referencing Japan's colonial rule and aggression, and the atrocities that Asia had suffered under Japan's imperialism. However, Koizumi's annual visits to the controversial Yasukuni shrine largely discounted his credibility in the eyes of the Chinese people.[26] In fact, his term as prime minister had been widely criticized for leading to the worst Sino-Japanese relations in decades.[27]

The textbook controversies were a result of the two countries disagreeing on what should be included in history textbooks taught in school. The Japanese government vets history textbooks to be taught in schools and suggests edits before approving of their use. China argues that Japan downplays its responsibilities for the various war crimes while glorifying their war sacrifices and tried to reason their decision to go to war in those textbooks. Despite China and many other countries' loud protests, the Japanese government still went ahead and approved several of such textbooks in 2005, once again straining Sino-Japanese relations.

Japan's high-profile visits to Yasukuni Shrine has been a constant source of antagonism ever since the move to enshrine 15 class A war criminals, including war general Hideki Tojo, in 1978.[28] China and many other countries view these visits as honoring the war criminals who had committed crimes against humanity, hence were vehemently opposed to the visits. While many others have stopped[29] or refrained from visiting the shrine, former Prime Minister Koizumi had been undeterred, visiting to pay respects every year during his term.[30] The resulting effect was extremely debilitating to Sino-Japanese relations, as China strongly criticized Koizumi's actions. In fact, in a survey done from 2002-2006, the percentage of Chinese who cited history issues as the reason they do not feel close to Japan rose from 64% at the start of Koizumi's career to more than 90% by the end.[31]

Another pertinent issue in Sino-Japanese relations is territorial disputes, in particular the Senkaku/Diaoyu Islands controversies. These islands were not clearly defined in the normalization agreement between China and Japan in 1972. Previously not a source of contention, they only came into the spotlight when oil and natural gases were discovered within its water boundaries in 1969.[32] It was not until the 2000s that China and Japan started staking serious claims on the islands, resulting in near skirmishes and near-violent outbreaks. In 2012, the Sino-Japanese tensions reached an all-time high with Japan purchasing the islands from a private owner and effecting nationalizing them.[33] These disputes are further reinforced by the animosity due to history issues, resulting in high tensions between the two countries. Anti-Japanese sentiments have risen to unprecedented levels in China, cumulating in protests and demonstrations, sometimes turning violent.[34]

Can pop culture diplomacy have a soft power effect on foreign populations? China still consumes huge amounts of Japanese pop culture, as stated earlier, hence it is a relevant and useful case to study. Furthermore, China has profound and deep-seated hostile relations with Japan and, strong anti-Japanese sentiments among its people. In fact, an annual study by the Genron-NPO found that China and Japan's impression of each other had moved towards being unfavorable rapidly over the last decade. (See Graph 1 below) Can pop culture exhibit soft power effects under such dire circumstances? China presents itself as a hard case to answer this question. The results produced by a research into the soft power effects of Japanese pop culture in China may therefore go further to show the effects of soft power, if any.

## China and Japan's impression of each other

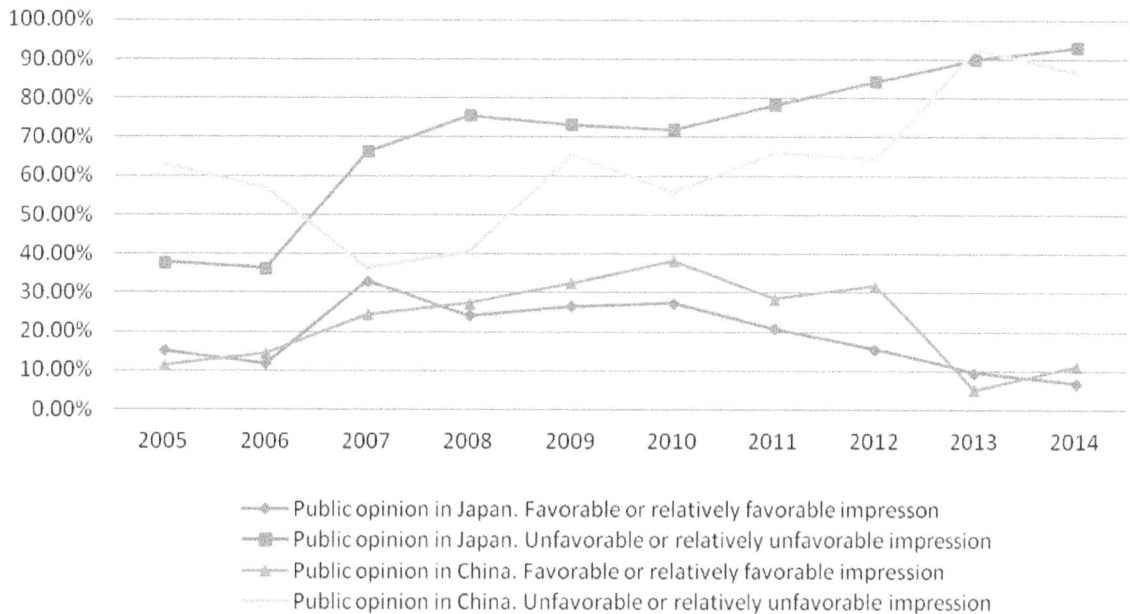

Graph 1. *China and Japan's impressions of each other*[35]

## Literature Review

The Japanese government has endorsed pop culture diplomacy because they see the potential in pop culture to influence foreign populations and create a better image of Japan in their eyes. This is a display of soft power, as McGray (2002) had pointed out in his article. In order to understand the efficacy of pop culture as a soft power tool, there is a need to explore the concept of power first.

Power is one of the most important core concepts in the field of IR, and like many others, a highly contentious topic. The understanding and definition of power is neither universal nor static. Over the years, the concept of power has been debated and developed by many scholars, leading to a variant of definitions and extensions. Most distinctly, power is being categorized into two broad categories: coercive power (hard power) and non-coercive power (soft power). While early studies of this topic have started off with an almost exclusive emphasis on the coercive aspect, the idea of non-material power has been referenced at times by some scholars. Hans Morgenthau, for example, identified national character, morale, quality of diplomacy and government as intangible sources of power.[36] Peter Bachrach and Morton Baratz made popular the concept of the two faces of power which listed agenda-setting as the second face of power, alluding to the importance of the influence of ideas.[37] More recently, Steven Luke, political theorist, built upon this article, coming up with three dimensions of power, in which the third dimension refers to the power to manipulate interests.[38] Even before all this, prominent realist scholar E. H. Carr had made claim that "power over opinion" was part of international power, as with military and economic power.[39] It is really in the past few decades however, that the debate has overwhelmingly moved towards the importance and potential of non-coercive power. This is no doubt driven by the official terming of the word "soft power" and the subsequent expansion of the concept by scholar Joseph Nye. Since then, literature has explored the concept closely, focusing on how it is supposed to work, and why it does or does not work in real life.

Earlier interpretations of power present a view in which power is relational and a zero-sum game. Robert Dahl defined power as "A has power over B to the extent that he can get B to do something that B would not otherwise do."[40] This definition has rung true for many scholars throughout this field, and each sought to add a new dimension to this definition. Some emphasized the idea of threat, or "negative sanction" as P. M. Blau put it, in getting the other party to do the deed.[41] This describes the coercive side of power as it is with the actual or intended punishment that others will be subjected to under your influence. In order for the coercive power to work, the entity in power must possess some kind of ability to impose the punishment. That is the tangible power resources which can include military might or economic prowess. Realist scholars especially endorse this view as it falls in line with their belief system which place strong emphasis in the importance of material power to individuals and states (Carr 1964, Krauthammer 2006, Mearsheimer 2001, Morgenthau 1967, Waltz 1979). They were the main proponents of defining power as using those "material resources to compel another state to do something it does not want to do."[42] This view rapidly manifested during the Cold War era, when bipolarity and superpower competition saw the world place strong emphasis on the creation and accumulation of material sources of power.

With the fall of the Soviet Union and the collapse of the bipolar system of the end of the 1980s, more scholars began to explore newer and less conventional ways of thinking about power. In 1990, Joseph Nye, in his groundbreaking book *Bound to Lead*, coined the term soft power to name the concept of attractive power. Nye defined the concept of "soft power" in the context of the end of the Cold War. The US was seen as the "victors", with the American ideals emerging triumph against the "fall of communism" (symbolic fall of Soviet Union). Nye argues that in the new world order, the US was, and could continue to be dominant in the international realm with less focus on the tangible coercive sources of powers. Emphasis should no longer be only on using coercive power as there was no clear "enemy" to coerce. The US also lost their bargaining chip for countries to ally on their side.[43] It has to now find ways to convince other states to "want what it wants" through attraction.[44]

Eventually, as the concept took form and became widely discussed, Nye broadened its scope to make it more applicable to countries other than the US. In his 2004 book *Soft Power: The Means to Success in World Politics*, also his most cited work to date, Nye tried to develop a more universal conceptualization of soft power. He defined soft power as "getting people to want the outcomes you want [by] co-opt[ing] people rather than coerc[ing] them" and via "power of attraction and seduction."[45] Soft power is seen by Nye as relational to hard power as they are both "aspects of the ability to achieve one's purpose by affecting the behavior of others."[46] He placed soft power and hard power resources and their corresponding behaviors on a spectrum. Hard power and soft power are not two different absolutes, in fact, the "distinction between them is one of degree."[47] Nye shows this relationship in a diagram in his book, which has a spectrum of behavior from command at one end through coercion (force and sanctins) and inducement (payments and bribes), which are defined as hard power, and then agenda setting (instutions) and attraction (values, culture, politics) to cooperation, which is the soft power end of the spectrum.[48]

Nye identifies three resources upon which soft power rests: a country's culture, political ideals and policies. Culture is "the set of values and practices that create meaning for a society" and can be further broken down into "high culture" (e.g. literature, traditional art) which appeals to the elites, and "popular culture" which appeals to the masses.[49] When those values are shared and appreciated by others (i.e. universal values), it is easier for the country to obtain their desired outcome, due to the "relationships of attraction".[50] The political ideals or values a government supports can influence the perceptions of others.[51] This is also somewhat related to government policies (domestic and foreign) as it will affect and manifest in what the government decides to do. Championing for a good cause can elevate the position of a country in others' perceptions, and in a country with a clear and streamlined foreign policy, their actions should reflect their values.

Nye is careful to emphasize the distinction between resources and behavior. A country's soft power resources may not always, if at all, lead to behavior outcomes which are in favor of it. Hence, having the soft power resources may not necessarily mean having soft *power*. The context is highly important in determining the effectiveness of a power resource.[52] In essence, to find out if a soft power resource really leads to favorable behavior outcomes (i.e. does actually have soft *power*), one will have to investigate each case individually and separately.

This concept of soft power became very popular with scholars and policy makers alike. Within years, major governments around the world have begun talking about "soft power" and incorporating it into their foreign policy agenda.[53] With the success and popularity of this concept, scholars began to debate the usefulness of applying it to the real world. Soft power is by nature an elusive topic due to its focus on intangible resources and effects (such as perceptions). Despite best efforts to conceptualize and operationalize it, soft power is still often subjected to misuse and criticisms, hence impeding progress in its research groundwork. As a result, scholars have constantly tried to refine the concept in their own way to make it more accurate and applicable to the real world. This concept thus should not be taken as set in stone; instead it is fluid and evolving to better fit universal explanations.

There has been wide acceptance of Nye's definition and framework of soft power and most scholars do not dispute this working definition. (Ding and Saunders, 2006; Gallarotti 2011; Gill and Huang 2006; Vuving 2009; Wang and Lu 2008) One exception has been Guen Lee, who had redefined soft power in his own terms so as to make it easier to operationalize and grasp. Most other discourses about soft power occur from the use and application of theory. Scholars argue that the theory is frequently misunderstood and misused, hence leading to false conceptualizations and interpretations of the concept (Blanchard & Lu 2012; Berger 2010). Some also mentioned that due to the "fuzzy" nature of the concept, it was difficult to operationalize soft power and really test for solid evidence that it exists (Womack 2005; Smith-Windsor 2000; Feguson 2003). On the extreme end of the spectrum, there are people who deny the existence of soft power or who insist on the importance of hard power over everything else (Mattern 2005; Womack 2005).

Guen Lee (2009) found that Nye's soft power framework had some shortcomings as it was mainly conceptual and does not reveal the power conversion mechanisms. In a bid to try and theorize the power conversion process from soft power resource to soft power, Lee redefined the concept of soft power, where instead of differentiating soft power between the nature of the power (coercive vs. non-coercive), he differentiated it between the types of resources use.[54] In other words, the non-material soft resources are used to exert soft power, while the material hard resources are used to exert hard power. In this way, both soft and hard power can be either coercive or non-coercive, depending on the context of the situation.

Lee raised an important point about the shortcoming of Nye's framework, which is the focus on the producer of power instead of the outcome. Military might may also attract the admiration of another state, and in such case, it will be difficult to say whether that is hard power or soft power. However, his theory is problematic as it radically changed the meaning of the word "soft power" and seems to be another theory entirely instead of building off of Nye's. At the core of Nye's definition of soft power is the idea of attraction. The reason why it is coined "soft" is because there is no element of threat or fear involved, and countries willingly behave the way they do. Hence, to claim that soft power should be both coercive and co-optive is taking away the very core meaning of the theory. It may be better to differentiate soft and hard power along the lines of coercion and co-option, then identify that certain resources have both soft and hard power capabilities.

Much of the literature on soft power actually addresses this problem that Lee has identified. While staying true to the definition of Nye's soft power, scholars such as Jean-Marc Blanchard and Fujia Lu have pointed out the serious limitation of current understandings of soft power, which is that the attraction of certain components of resources may be in the in the eyes of the beholder.[55] This signals that literature have tended to look at soft power from the producers' point of view and naturally will see its attractiveness. However, this fails to take into account the reaction the particular resource of soft power tool have evoke in other countries. To put simply, power resources does not always translate to power; what one country viewed as an attractive may not come across as so in another country's perspective. Blanchard and Lu argues that soft power needs to be conceptualized together with the target audience, hence context must be taken into account. Thomas Berger also echoes this in his analysis of Japan's soft power. He says that soft power is a relational concept and has to e understood in relation to the desired outcome. Only when there is actually a positive effect from the resources, can one safely say that soft power is present.

This brings us to another problem often brought up in the soft power literature, that is the difficulty of operationalizing the concept of soft power. Soft power is notorious for being intangible and elusive, making it highly difficult to detect and wield properly. This also makes it very hard to analyze accurately and obtain concrete results. Brantly Womack had called this the "analytical fuzziness" of soft power and points out the confusion this concept causes. The issue here is that the vagueness of soft power makes it seem like anything that attracts can be considered soft power.[56] Brooke Smiths-

Windsor claims that soft power "risks being convoluted to the point of practical uselessness."[57] Nye also referenced to Niall Ferguson, who had dismissed soft power saying that "it's, well, soft", alluding to the lack of concreteness of the concept.[58] The problem lies in the fact that there are no boundaries for what can be considered attractive. Therefore, soft power can only be tested on a case by case scenario, and each test must be tailored to suit the soft power and the context in which it is testing. While this may be tedious, it does not take away the usefulness or validity of the concept. Just because it is difficult to detect does not mean soft power's effect is negligible The only way to thread around this obstacle is to constantly develop better scientific methods test for soft power while controlling for various possible intervening variables.

Among all these, there are also scholars who are extremely skeptical of the existence of soft power and believe that hard power is more important than anything else. Womack questions whether or not soft power is separate from hard power at all and he suggests that soft power is merely an illusion, a "halo of hard power".[59] He argues that soft power is merely a welcomed side effect, peripheral to hard power decisions which affect foreign policy directly. Janice Bially Mattern also argues that soft power's attraction is constructed through "representative force" in that the audience is forced to submit to the speaker's viewpoint. Hence, she argues that soft power is merely an extension of hard power.[60] It is important to note though, that Nye's concept of soft power attraction does not involve coercion or the perception of coercion. The receiving party should be *willingly* submitting to the "attractiveness" of the wielding party, and hence there should not be any perceived force involved. Furthermore, soft power is meant to work together with hard power, they are not mutually exclusive. Womack's point about soft power being a peripheral to hard power may be true for some countries, but it does not take away the soft power effects or its ability to attract and influence other states. A state may choose to build up mainly on hard power, but that should not stop them from being able to build up their soft power potential as well. Hence, states may exploit their soft power resources as another form of influence they could wield.

Douglas McGray's *Foreign Policy* article in 2002 explored the soft power potential of Japan's pop culture.[61] Following that, there was a budding interest among soft power scholars about the popularity of Japanese pop culture. Since soft power is the power of attraction, one way to measure soft power is to measure how much the target audience is attracted to your source of soft power, this can be done so through opinion polling.[62] The few academic works on Japanese pop culture, however, often offer a more negative view of Japanese pop culture's soft power effectiveness, especially towards neighbors China and South Korea, both of which have had tensions and conflict-ridden histories with Japan. The overwhelming argument is that the tense relations between Japan and its neighbors had impeded on the effectiveness of Japanese pop culture. Even though the Chinese and South Koreans consume Japanese pop culture products readily, they are not so positive about feelings towards Japan (Lam 2007; Otmazgin 2008). In the people's minds, Japanese pop culture is separated from Japan as a nation state. Enjoying Japanese pop culture does not necessarily equate to better image of Japan (Iwabuchi 2002; Nakano 2008). The literature usually offer extensive accounts on the history of Japanese pop culture dissemination and the various tools and events the Japanese government used to promote pop culture. Many went on to list the potential limitations of pop culture diplomacy, but few tried to analyze and prove (or disprove) the effectiveness of pop culture diplomacy from the perspective of the receiver.

The problem of soft power being seen too often from the perspective of the producer manifests. The consensus seems to be that pop culture faced too many limitations and does not really help country relations especially in the face of political tensions. However, studies are rarely empirical and conclusions tend to overly focus on qualitative reasoning and the theoretical aspect of things. While they offer many deep and interesting insights into the topic, they do not offer any concrete evidence to support their claims. This makes it difficult to draw any conclusions about this already elusive concept, and any conclusions drawn can only be said to be speculation without enough real-world backing.

A recent empirical study into the efficacy of Japanese pop culture as soft power was done by Richard Harris, graduate student at Georgetown University. He attempted to find out the effect of the consumption of Japanese pop culture on how Japan is viewed by people in China and South Korea by using data from a 2008 Chicago Council of Global Affairs public opinion poll. Harris' study provided some interesting insights and results in which he tested for effects of different variables in affecting the perception of Japan so as to test for intervening variables. Through his analysis, he found a strong statistically significant relationship between consumption of Japanese pop culture and, age and feelings towards Japan. Due to the possibility of endogeneity, he concluded that three possible relationships may occur: consumption of Japanese pop culture increases feelings toward Japan, people who like Japan tend to consume more Japanese pop culture, or both exists. Effects are predicted to be stronger for the younger generation.[63] While his study is the most comprehensive empirical study to date about this topic, it inadvertently faces limitations. First, he is using data from a general public opinion poll which was not designed especially for such a study, as a result, the some questions and options given may be crude and not phrased ideally. Furthermore, the study is limited to the variables listed in the poll, hence preventing him from testing for other possible intervening variables, such as the general media consumption. My research will attempt to build on his and address many of those limitations to improve validity of the results.

# Methodology

The goal of this research is to find out how effective Japanese pop culture is in helping Japan improve its image among the Chinese public. Japanese pop culture is attractive, as evident from its strong presence and high levels of consumption in Asia. The question is does it contribute to Japan's soft power at all? Can it have a tangible effect? Given the existing limitations in measurement methods, the best way to go about attempting to answer this is through survey. However, with survey research of the general public, there is no way to test for and establish the relationship between Japanese pop culture and actual political outcomes. The vast variety of intervening factors renders it impossible with the resources I have access to. Hence my study only goes so far as to test for the relationship between Japanese pop culture and public perceptions. The purpose will be to test for causal effects of Japanese pop culture on foreign perceptions. Further research will have to be done to explore whether actual causal mechanisms are in place, and whether public perception can affect elite decision making at the state level or not.

The paper chooses to focus on China as its population consumes substantial amounts of Japanese pop culture, and it is a harder case with the strong anti-Japanese sentiments as discussed earlier, hence results can go further in explaining any soft power effects. While South Korea may also present as a viable research subject, I am limited by language barriers. Future studies on South Korea may be done and compared against this study to obtain useful information.

In constructing the model of this study, the researcher has identified the independent variable to be the consumption of Japanese pop culture, and the dependent variable to be the image of Japan as a nation state. Using a well-tailored survey, the researcher will directly ask respondents questions pertaining to the identified variables to obtain results which are useful to the research question. The data obtained in this paper will be cross-sectional.

The hypothesis of this study is that higher consumption of Japanese pop culture will more likely lead to positive perception of Japan. High consumption of Japanese pop culture suggests that it is attractive to the consumers; therefore it should have soft power capabilities and be able to lead to a better image of Japan in their eyes.

In addition to the independent variable, consumption of Japanese pop culture, there are likely to be many confounding variables that affects perception as well. In order to minimize the omitted variable bias, they have to be included. The proposed confounding factors are: age, education, urbanicity, whether they have traveled to Japan before, and whether they know/have met a Japanese person, their impression of Japanese pop culture, frequency of consumption of media, knowledge of foreign affairs. They are listed below in Table 2 with explanations of why they may interfere with the results of this study.

*Table 2. List of confounding variables and explanation for their inclusion.[67]*

| Confounding Variable | Explanation |
|---|---|
| Age | The younger generation tends to have better perception of Japan as they have less personal experiences and memories regarding historical events, hence are less likely to feel passionately about the animosity arising from those events. The younger generation also tends to be more involved in popular trends, hence consuming more pop culture products. This variable is measured on a ratio scale, and respondents were asked for their specific age. |
| Education | People with higher education tend to have better perception of Japan. They tend to have better analytical skills and are more likely to understand the history of Japan in a nuanced way. Hence, they will be more likely to see issues from both sides and have a balanced view of Japan as a nation state. This variable is measured on an ordinal scale, and respondents were asked to choose their current or previous level of education obtained from the following list: uneducated, elementary school, middle school, high school, some associate degree, some college degree, graduate school or higher, others (specify). |

| Confounding Variable | Explanation |
|---|---|
| Urbanicity | People who grew up in more urban areas have better perception of Japan as they are likely to have more exposure to international elements (including Japanese pop culture). This variable is measured on an ordinal scale, and respondents were asked to pick the province they grew up in. The provinces are then categorized into urban or rural based on whether the city proportion of urban population is larger than the national proportion of urban population of 52.57% or not.[64] If bigger, it is considered urban; if smaller, it is considered rural. |
| Traveled to Japan before or not | People who have traveled to Japan are expected to hold more understanding of and familiarity to Japan since they have personally been to and seen the country and the people. The mere-exposure effect, a psychological concept developed most prominently by Robert Zajonc, states that the objective exposure of an individual to something increases the preference for that particular object.[65] Hence people who have traveled to Japan before should have better perceptions of Japan. Furthermore, people who have traveled to Japan may have done so because they enjoy consuming Japanese pop culture, hence they should have better perceptions according to the hypothesis. This variable is measured on a nominal scale, and respondents were asked to state whether they have traveled to Japan or not. |
| Know/ have met a Japanese person before or not | People who know or have met a Japanese person tend to hold more understanding of and familiarity to Japanese people in general. According to Zajonc's further research about mere-exposure effect, there is evidence that it applies in person perception as well.[66] Hence, they are likely to have positive perceptions of the Japanese people and be more sympathetic toward Japan since they can identify that person with their home country. They will have better perceptions of Japan. This variable is measured on a nominal scale, and respondents were asked to state whether they know a Japanese person or not. |
| Impression of Japanese pop culture | People who have better impression of Japanese pop culture, whether they consume it or not, will tend to have better perception of Japan as a nation state. They will identify Japanese pop culture with the country of origin (since the survey question asks specifically about Japanese pop culture), hence if they feel positively for Japanese pop culture, they will likely think the same of the country that produces it. This variable is measured on an ordinal scale, and respondents were asked to choose from the following list: very negative, negative, positive, very positive. |

| Confounding Variable | Explanation |
|---|---|
| Media consumption | Media, especially the internet, TV and magazines, is one of the most salient channels for the distribution of pop culture. Therefore, it is expected that with more consumption of media, the more consumption of Japanese pop culture products, and hence, according to the hypothesis, better perceptions of Japan. This variable is measured on an ordinal scale, and respondents were asked to choose the number of hours they spend on media consumption each week from the following list: 0-5 hours, 5-10 hours, 10-15 hours, 15-20 hours, above 20 hours. |
| Knowledge of current affairs | It is expected that people with better knowledge of foreign affairs will tend to have a more nuanced view of Sino-Japan relations. They will be more likely to view issues from both sides and have a more balanced view of Japan as a nation state. This variable is measured on a ordinal scale, and respondents were asked to choose how often they pay attention to the news from the following list: once a day, once every 2-3 days, once a week, once every 2 weeks, once a month, once every 3 months, do not pay attention to the news. |

1        Urban proportion data taken from National Bureau of Statistics of China. "Population and Its Composition" *China Statistics Yearbook 2013*. (China Statistics Press: 2013). Web.
2        Zajonc, Robert B. "Mere Exposure: A Gateway to the Sublimal." *Current Directions in Psychological Science*. 10, no 6. (Dec 2001): 225
3        Zajonc, Robert B. and Moreland, Richard L. "Exposure Effects in Person Perception: Familiarity, Similarity, and Attraction." *Journal of Experimental Social Psychology*. 18 (1982): 395

A random sample of about 350 respondents was taken and questions will be used to measure consumption, perceptions and each of the confounding factors (see appendix). The model that the hypothesis supports is as such:

$$Y = \beta_1 X + \beta_2 V_1 + \beta_2 V_2 + \ldots + \beta_{K+1} V_K + \varepsilon$$

Where:

$Y$ = measure of perception of Japan as a nation state

$X$ = measure of frequency of consumption of Japanese pop culture

$V_1 \ldots V_k$ = confounding variables

$\beta_1 \ldots \beta_2$ = effect that the corresponding variable has on perceptions

$\varepsilon$ = estimated error

The survey will be conducted online via a professional Chinese survey research platform called SOJUMP.[68] I will first run using Stata the independent variable and the confounding variables through a bivariate analysis for the dependent variable to check which variables are statistically significant and should be included in the model. Then, I will run the significant variables through regression analysis for the dependent variable using the Clarify program on the Stata to check the results and significance of the model, the independent variable and the confounding variables. I will also use the program to further obtain results to predict the change in perceptions of Japan as a nation state with the change in consumption of Japanese pop culture.

## Results

In order to assess the perception of Japan as a nation state, the survey asked respondents to choose from very positive, positive, negative and very negative to describe their impression of Japan as a nation state. An ordinal scale (very negative, negative, positive, very positive) was chosen for this question as perception is an intangible idea, and it is easier for respondents to translate into relative concepts of positive and negative instead of numbers. The result was that most respondents fell in the middle two options of positive or negative, with negative impressions slightly more than positive impressions. The results can be seen in Graph 2 below:

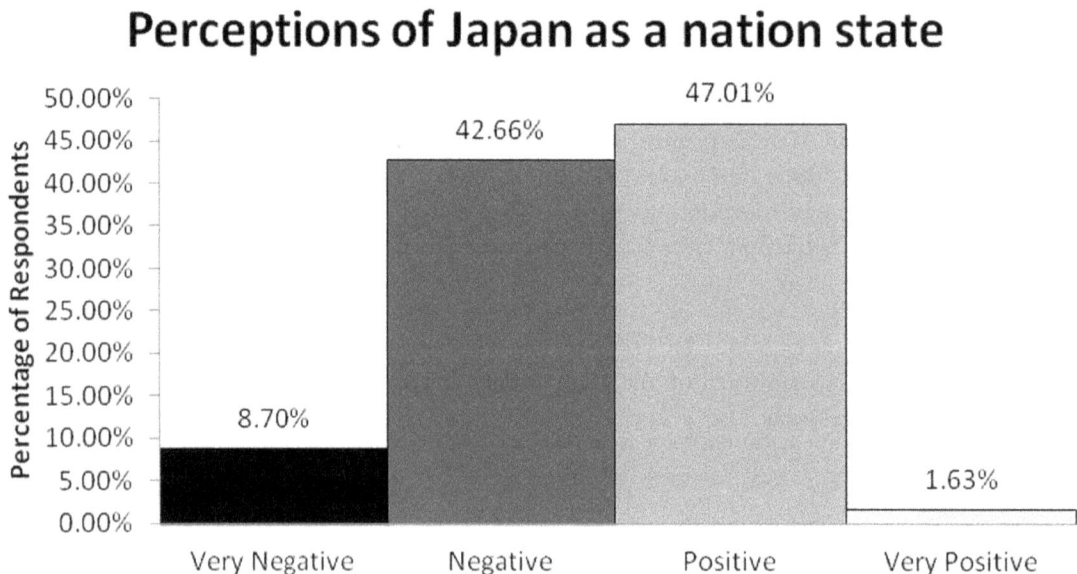

*Graph 2. Perceptions of Japan as a nation state*

This falls within expectation that a larger proportion of the Chinese people will have negative perception of Japan as a nation state given Sino-Japanese tensions and the strong anti-Japanese sentiments in China.

The independent variable of consumption of Japanese pop culture was measured on a interval scale. Respondents were asked to choose a range for how many hours they spend on average per week on the consumption of Japanese pop culture products. They were given the options: no time at all, 0-2 hours, 2-5 hours, 5-10 hours, 10-15 hours, 15-20 hours, above 20 hours. The results are plotted on Graph 3 below:

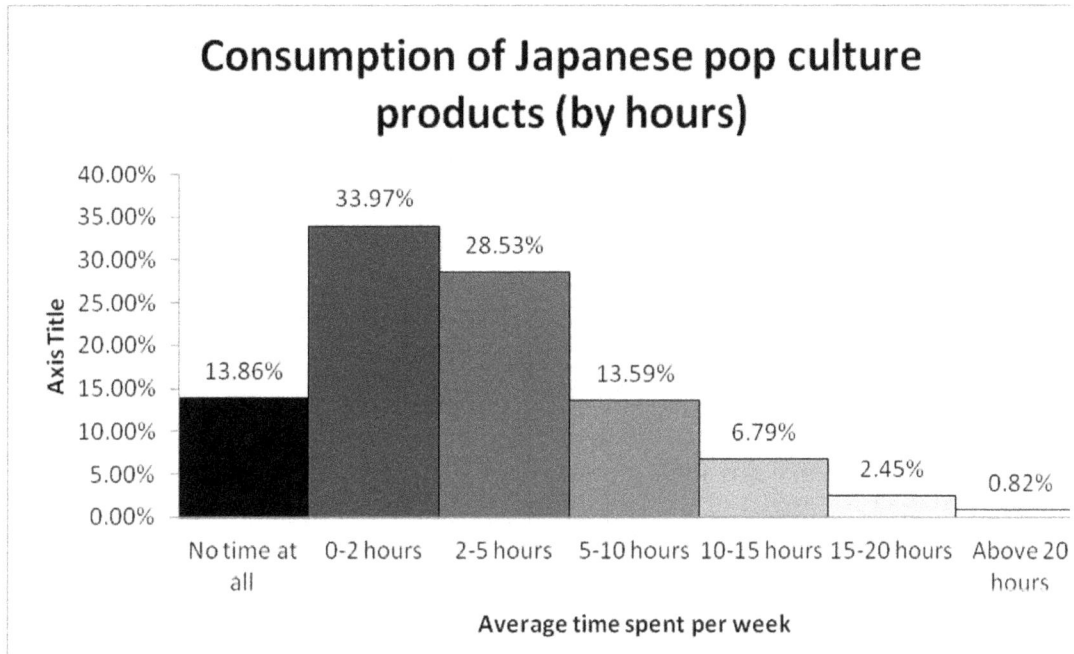

## Consumption of Japanese pop culture products (by hours)

*Graph 3. Consumption of Japanese pop culture products*

Most respondents gave between 0-5 hours as their estimated time spent per week. There is a surprisingly substantial portion of people who claimed that they do not spend time at all on Japanese pop culture products.

## Statistical Analysis

Bivariate Analysis

Before running the regression model, it is recommended to look at the relationship between the dependent variable of perceptions of Japan as a nation state and the independent and confounding variables. That way we can see which variables are significant in explaining the perceptions of Japan as a nation state and should be included in the model for regression analysis. Therefore, I ran all the independent and all the confounding variables though a bivariate analysis for the perceptions of Japan as a nation state.

The chi-square test is used for all the variables except age as it tests the relationships between two categorical variables. Age was collected as a continuous variable, hence the Student's t-test is used to determine whether there were differences in age between the two categories of the dichotomous transformation of the dependent variable.. For many of the variables, the Fisher's exact test is also used because some cells in the cross tabulation had expected frequencies of less than 5, hence it is recommended to obtain more robust results. There was a need to collapse some of the categories since the the Fisher's exact test cannot be computed for large tables. Perception of Japan as a nation state was collapsed into negative and positive. Education was collapsed into three categories: high school or below, associate or bachelor degree and postgraduate degree. Consumption of Japanese pop culture was collapsed into 5 categories: no time at all, 0-2 hours, 2-5 hours, 5-10 hours, above 10 hours. The results can be seen in Table 3 below:

| Variables | $N$ | Perception of Japan as a nation state | | |
| --- | --- | --- | --- | --- |
| | | Negative (n=189) | Positive (n=179) | p-value* |
| Total responses | 368 | 51.36 | 48.64 | |
| Consumption of Japanese pop culture | | | | .000² |
| No time at all | 51 | 90.20 | 9.80 | |
| 0-2 hours | 125 | 60.80 | 39.20 | |
| 2-5 hours | 105 | 40.00 | 60.00 | |
| 5-10 hours | 50 | 34.00 | 66.00 | |
| Above 10 hours | 37 | 21.62 | 78.38 | |
| Age in years (Mean, (SD)) | 368 | 31.22 (6.79) | 29.99 (5.96) | .068¹ |
| Education | | | | .799² |
| High School or below | 12 | 58.34 | 41.67 | |
| Assoc./Bachelor degree | 323 | 51.39 | 48.61 | |
| Postgraduate degree | 33 | 48.48 | 51.51 | |
| Urbanicity | | | | .000² |
| Rural | 131 | 65.65 | 34.35 | |
| Urban | 237 | 43.46 | 56.54 | |

| Traveled to Japan before or not | | | | .000[2] |
|---|---|---|---|---|
| No | 235 | 62.55 | 37.45 | |
| Yes | 133 | 31.58 | 68.42 | |
| | | | | |
| Know/have met a Japanese person or not | | | | .000[2] |
| No | 134 | 71.64 | 28.36 | |
| Yes | 234 | 39.74 | 60.26 | |
| | | | | |
| Impression of Japanese pop culture | | | | .000[2] |
| Very Negative | 13 | 100.00 | 0.00 | |
| Negative | 53 | 94.34 | 5.66 | |
| Positive | 266 | 45.86 | 54.14 | |
| Very Positive | 36 | 11.11 | 88.89 | |
| | | | | |
| Media Consumption | | | | .553[2] |
| No time at all | 4 | 100.00 | 0.00 | |
| 0-2 hours | 32 | 56.25 | 43.75 | |
| 2-5 hours | 58 | 51.72 | 48.28 | |
| 5-10 hours | 62 | 53.23 | 46.77 | |
| 10-15 hours | 66 | 53.03 | 46.97 | |
| 15-20 hours | 50 | 48.00 | 52.00 | |
| Above 20 hours | 96 | 46.88 | 53.12 | |
| | | | | |
| Attention to news (knowledge of current affairs) | | | | .542[2] |
| Do not pay attention | 1 | 100.00 | 0.00 | |
| Once a month | 3 | 100.00 | 0.00 | |
| Once every 2 weeks | 4 | 50.00 | 50.00 | |
| Once a week | 17 | 58.82 | 41.18 | |
| Once every 2-3 days | 73 | 47.95 | 52.05 | |
| Once a day | 270 | 51.11 | 48.89 | |

* p-values corresponding to the Chi-square test; [1] p-value corresponding to the t-test; [2] p-value corresponding to the Fisher's exact test

Table 3. Bivariate Analysis for the perceptions of Japan as a nation state

The consumption of Japanese pop culture is the independent variable and the predictor variable which this study is interested in. There is a distinct difference between respondents who consume more pop culture and those who consume less. As seen in the table, a significantly larger proportion of respondents who spend less time on consuming Japanese pop culture had negative perceptions of Japan as a nation state. That proportion decreased with the increase in time spent on consumption of Japanese pop culture. Hence, the more hours a respondent spends on consuming Japanese pop culture, the more likely they will have positive perceptions of Japan as a nation state. There is also strong statistical significance with the fisher's exact p-value at .000. Hence, our predictor variable is significant at describing changes in the independent variable.

For the confounding variable age, the mean age of respondents who answered positive perceptions is lower than that of negative perceptions. There is no significance at the 5% level, however there is statistical significance at the 10% level with p-value being .068. Hence, this variable should be included in the model as it can potentially explain changes in the dependent variable.

For the confounding variable education, there is a distinct pattern and trend of more proportion of respondents feeling positive about Japan with increase in education. However the relationship is not statistically significant since the Fisher's exact p-value is .799. Hence this variable should not be included in the model.

For the confounding variable urbanicity, there is a distinct difference between respondents who grew up in rural provinces and those who grew up in urban provinces. A larger portion of those who grew up in rural provinces had negative perceptions of Japan as a nation state, while a larger portion of those who grew up in urban provinces had positive perceptions of Japan as a nation state. There is strong statistical significance with fisher's exact p-value at .000. Hence this variable should be included in the model.

For the confounding variable of whether the respondent has traveled to Japan before or not, there appears to be a distinct difference between those who have and those who have not. A larger portion of those who have traveled to Japan had positive perceptions, while a larger portion of those who have not traveled to Japan had negative perceptions. There is strong statistical significance with the fisher's exact p-value at .000. Hence this variable should be included in the model.

For the confounding variable of whether the respondent knows/has met a Japanese person before, there appears to be a distinct difference between those who do and those who do not. A larger portion of those who know a Japanese person had positive perceptions, while a larger portion of those who do not know a Japanese person had negative perceptions. There is strong statistical significance with the fisher's exact p-value at .000. Hence this variable should be included in the model.

For the confounding variable impression of Japanese pop culture, there appears to be a distinct difference between those who had positive impressions and those who had negative impressions. A larger portion of those who had positive impressions of Japanese pop culture had positive perceptions of Japan as a nation state, while a larger portion of those who do had negative impressions of Japanese pop culture had negative perceptions of Japan as a nation state. There is strong statistical significance with the fisher's exact p-value at .000. Hence this variable should be included in the model.

For the confounding variable media consumption, the general pattern is that a larger proportion of respondents had positive perceptions of Japan as a nation state with increase in media consumption. However, there is one outlier where the proportion actually decreased from the 2-5 hours to 5-10 hours intervals. The relationship is not statistically significant since fisher's exact p-value is .553. Hence this variable should not be included in the model.

For the confounding variable knowledge of current affairs, although the general trend is that the proportion of respondents who had positive perceptions increases with increased attention to news, there seem to be no clear pattern indicating this is the case from every point to the next. In fact, there is not statistical significance since fisher's exact p-value is .542. Hence this variable should not be included in the model.

Logistic Regression Analysis

The results from the bivariate analysis show that the following confounding variables should be included in the regression model: age, urbanicity, whether the respondent has traveled to Japan or not, whether respondent know a Japanese person or not, and impression of Japanese pop culture. The next step is to use Clarify to run the logistic regression for perceptions of Japan on consumption of Japanese pop culture and the significant confounding variables. The results are summarized in Table 4 shown below:

| Variable | Odds Ratio | Coefficient | Standard Error | z | $P > |z|$ |
|---|---|---|---|---|---|
| Consumption of Japanese pop culture | 1.611 | .477 | .127 | 3.74* | .000 |
| Age | .994 | -.006 | .022 | -.28 | .782 |
| Urbanicity | 1.870 | .626 | .272 | 2.30** | .021 |
| Traveled to Japan before | 2.182 | .780 | .313 | 2.50** | .013 |
| Know a Japanese person | 1.698 | .530 | .313 | 1.69* | .091 |
| Impression of Japanese pop culture | 11.278 | 2.423 | .415 | 5.83** | .000 |
| Constant | .000 | -8.821 | 1.502 | -5.87** | .000 |

Table 4. Logistic Regression for perception of Japan on consumption of Japanese pop culture and significant confounding variables. * significant at p<0.10 level; **significant at p<0.05 level; (1) The model itself is significant with p-value = .000

The predictor variable, consumption of Japanese pop culture, is shown to be very significant to the model as it has a p-value of .000. The odds ratio is also > 1 at 1.611, signaling that it has good association with the dependent variable of perceptions of Japan as a nation state. People with higher consumption of Japanese pop culture will likely have positive perceptions of Japan.

Age is surprisingly found to be not significant with a high p-value of .782. It also does not have association with the dependent variable since the odds ratio is >1 at .994, hence suggesting that it does not have any effect on the changes in perceptions of Japan as a nation state.

For the other confounding variables, all are found to be significant to the model and have good association with perceptions of Japan as a nation state. Urbanicity is found to be significant at the 5% level with a p-value of .021. It has odds ratio >1 at 1.870, which means it has good association with the dependent variable. People from urban provinces are more likely to have a positive perceptions of Japan.

Whether the respondent has traveled to Japan before is also significant at the 5% level with p=value being .013. The odds ratio are 2.182, hence there is strong association between this and perceptions of Japan. People who have traveled to Japan are more likely to have positive perceptions of Japan.

Whether the respondent knows a Japanese person or not is not significant at the 5% level, but significant at the 10% level with a p-value of .091. Nevertheless, the odds ratio of 1.698 is >1, showing good association with perceptions of Japan. People who know a Japanese person are more likely to have positive perceptions of Japan.

Finally, the impression of Japanese pop culture is not only significant with a p-value at .000, but it also has the strongest association with perceptions of Japan of all the variables, with odds ratio at 11.278. People who have positive impressions of Japanese pop culture are very likely to have positive perceptions of Japan.

## Predicted Probability of Positive Perception

In order to see the effect of the predictor variable on the dependent variable (i.e. consumption of Japanese pop culture on perceptions of Japan as a nation state), we can look at the different predicted values for the dependent variable and how it changes with change in the predictor variable. All significant confounding variables must be kept constant to minimize interference and omitted variable bias which may skew the results. It is recommended that the confounding variable be set to their mean values for control. The mean value of each confounding variable is shown in Table 5 below:

| Significant Confounding Variable | Mean Value |
|---|---|
| Urbanicity | .6440217 |
| Traveled to Japan before | .361413 |
| Know a Japanese person | .6358696 |
| Impression of Japanese pop culture | 2.883152 |

*Table 5. Mean values of significant confounding variables*

Keeping those at mean, we can now see the predicted probability of positive perceptions of Japan at different levels of consumption. The results are presented in Graph 4 below:

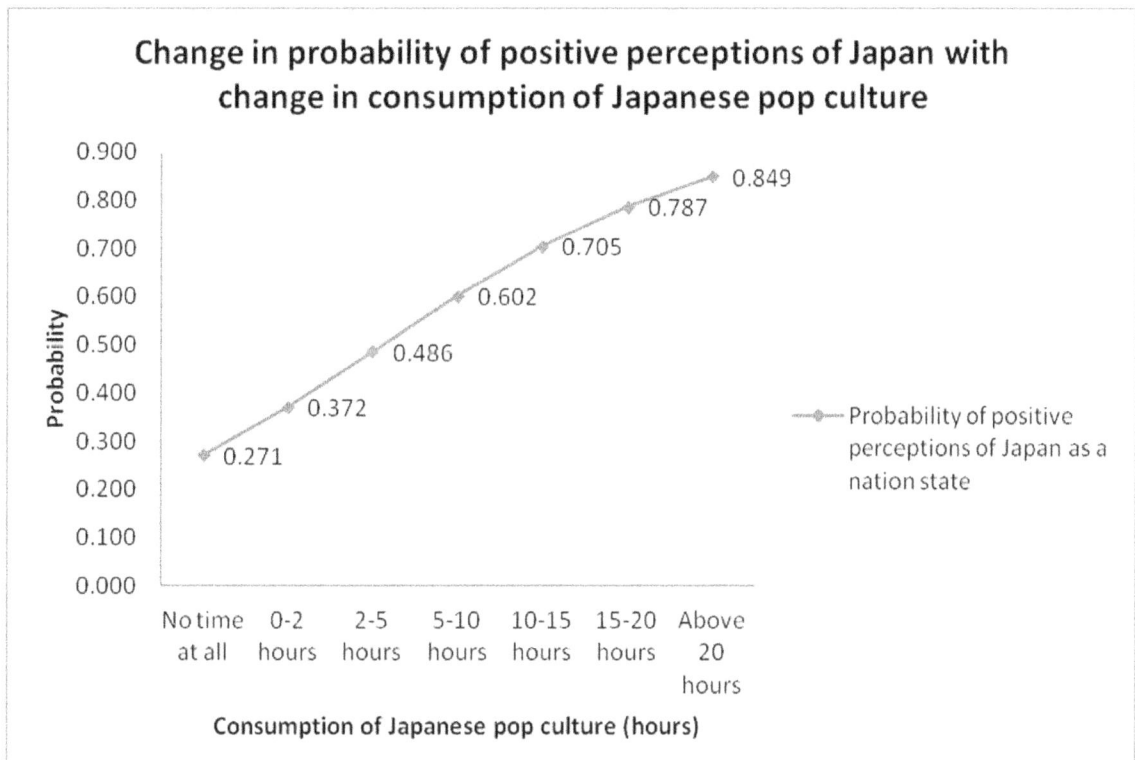

*Graph 4. Changes in probability of positive perceptions of Japan*

As shown clearly on the graph, the probability of having positive perceptions of Japan as a nation state increases steadily with the increase in consumption of Japanese pop culture. For people who do not consume Japanese pop culture at all, there is only a 27% chance that they will have positive perceptions of Japan. Meanwhile for people who consume Japanese pop culture over 20 hours per week, they have an 85% chance of having positive perceptions of Japan, an extremely high probability.

## Interpretation of Results

The results were in support of the hypothesis, with the model itself having strong significance. With everything held constant, people who consume more Japanese culture tend to be more likely to have positive perceptions of Japan as a nation state. Some confounding variables will affect this. In general, people who are from urban provinces, have traveled to Japan before, have known a Japanese person or have a good impression of Japanese pop culture tend to have positive perceptions about Japan.

It was surprising that some of the proposed confounding variables turned out to be not significant in explaining the perceptions of Japan. This is especially so for age, as it runs contrary to many scholars' belief that pop culture is generally consumed by younger people. It also differs from Harris' study which had shown strong significance in age in affecting perceptions.[69] The different outcome of my study may be an inherent problem of the online survey method, where most respondents will be expected to be younger since they will have to understand how to use the computer to be able to respond to the survey. Of the 368 respondents to my survey, 41 were in the 18-24 age group, 255 in the 25-34 age group, 56 in the 35-44 age group, 15 in the 45-54 age group and only one person above 54 years old. Hence, the results are heavily concentrated in one particular age group, the 25-34, and thus making it difficult for the results to show any variations in responses due to age.

Another surprising result was media consumption, where it was not only insignificant, but there were not even patterns that show that higher media consumption will more likely result in positive perceptions. This may be because the media is all encompassing of not just pop culture, but also things like news source, traditional culture, education and more. Hence it becomes difficult to establish any patterns unless we know exactly what type of media content each respondent consumes.

It was found that knowledge of current affairs is not a significant explanatory variable for perceptions, and there is no pattern supporting the predicted effect that more knowledge will more likely lead to positive perceptions. This may be because in China, media is tightly controlled and mostly state-owned, hence the people may not be getting a balanced and fair breakdown of current affairs. Furthermore, this question was a subjective question as it required the respondents to judge their attention to news themselves. There may be a social desirability bias as respondents may want to seem like they are well-informed and keep in touch with the world. Therefore, the results may be inflated. This can be circumvented the future with additional questions or tests to gauge the respondents' real knowledge of current affairs.

The results may be surprising considering how Sino-Japanese relations have actually deteriorated over the last few years. A possible explanation is that consumption of pop culture does increase probability of positive perceptions, but its positive effects cannot mitigate all of the hostilities arising from other events. Hence, it can be said that if Japanese pop culture was not present in China, the hostilities will be even worse. In addition, random events may occur which can cause sudden short-term spikes in negative feelings. For example, since Japan's nationalization of the Senkaku/Diaoyu islands in late 2012, the unfavorable ratings in China have spiked in year 2013 (please refer to Graph 1 above).[70] The high unfavorable ratings had continued into 2014 after Prime Minister Shinzo Abe visited the controversial Yasukuni Shrine in December 2013, a first high profile visit since 2005.[71] In such cases, the soft power effects of Japanese pop culture may be overpowered by the high running tensions among the two countries.

# Limitations

There are some limitations to this study which may hinder or bias the results. First, as with most statistical analysis, this model only proves association, it does not prove causation. Even though higher consumption of Japanese pop culture may be associated with higher probability of positive perceptions, the model is not able to tell whether it is really the independent variable which drives the change in the dependent variable and not another omitted variable. While several confounding variables were included in the analysis to reduce the omitted variable bias, there is no way of telling whether there are other significant confounding variable except by including them in and running the analysis. Therefore we are bounded by the current progress of research in this field and our own knowledge which informs us of the possible confounding variables to include. We are also bounded by the limited resources available, since there could be many confounding variables but it will not be feasible to test for all of them in one survey without any bias.

There is also the possibility that the independent variable and dependent variable suffer from an endogeneity problem. People may start consuming more Japanese pop culture due to already present positive perceptions about Japan. There is little way to overcome this other than more advanced research methods in the future. Even then, this is not a rejection of the hypothesis that higher consumption of Japanese pop culture result in high probability of positive perceptions. Therefore, there is still a problem of having to find out if the relationship between the two variables is cyclical. This may prove to be not feasible given the current research limitations.

The limitation with online surveys is that the sample collected may not be a good representation of the population. First, this means that the respondent must have access to the internet and a medium, such as a computer or a phone with internet capabilities. This could already be alienating parts of the Chinese population. Furthermore, the population of people who most frequently use the internet tend to be young, hence the sample maybe skewed towards the younger populations.

This problem may be mitigated by the fact that Japan's pop culture diplomacy is targeted towards the younger audiences.[72] Since the government is really trying to instill a positive image of Japan in the minds of the younger generations, it may not be worthwhile to look at the effect of pop culture diplomacy on the older generations.

Another limitation is the cross-sectional nature of this study, as mentioned before. This survey measures the consumption and perceptions at one point in time, hence may not take into account how the two variables can change over time and also the effect of significant events, such as Japan's nationalization of the Senkaku/Diaoyu islands in 2012. Results taken during different times may be vastly different due to the surrounding circumstance.

Longitudinal data from surveys done over a period of time may be more desirable in this case. However, time remains a prohibitive factor which prevents the collection of substantive longitudinal data. This may be overcome eventually if there is more time and resources for the project to be expanded into the future and continue collecting similar data overtime.

# Implication

As mentioned earlier, this study goes only as far as to test for the causal effects of consumption of Japanese pop culture on foreign perceptions. In China's case, it can be seen that increased consumption of Japanese pop culture does increase the probability of positive perceptions of Japan. This is so even with the hostile relations between the two countries and the anti-Japanese sentiments in China. The results therefore go further in showing the soft power effects of pop culture, and there seems to be a real tangible effect on perceptions.

Further research will be needed to test for the actual causal mechanism in place which link increased consumption of Japanese pop culture to the increased probability of positive perceptions. This will be useful in explaining exactly how consumption of Japanese pop culture help increase the probability of positive perceptions.

The results show that Japanese pop culture does have strong associations with positive perceptions of Japan. It exhibits soft power traits in this study and seem to positively influence perceptions. Yet it remains to be seen whether perceptions actually have an impact on political decision making or not. Positive perceptions by the masses may not actually translate into actual country policy or behavior. Merely having soft power effects will not be enough to justify its usefulness as a political or diplomatic tool. Future research can be done to try and prove any relationship between perception and government-level outcome.

Furthermore, pop culture is something that is difficult to wield. It is usually consumed and enjoyed by people out of their own choice. Even if the Japanese government poured resources into trying to spread its pop culture, it may not always translate into tangible results, or increased consumption. In order to fully examine the Japanese government's pop culture diplomacy and its effectiveness, studies will also have to be done into the current use of pop culture diplomacy funds and the resulting effects. Such studies will be extremely useful in informing how the government may harness pop culture to achieve their foreign policy agenda.

Meanwhile, all these unanswered questions should not deter the government from continuing its pop culture diplomacy. To conduct research to obtain concrete evidence of Japanese pop culture's soft power abilities may be extremely costly and time-consuming. Advanced research methods will have to be used to determine actual casuality, and subsequent research on the relationships between perception and government policy and decision making will have to be conducted. Even without foolproof evidence to justify pop culture's usefulness as a soft power tool, the Chinese market remains lucrative for Japanese pop culture exports due to the high consumption. The presence of a large underground market of Japanese pop culture products in China also alludes to the high demand for

Japanese pop culture products in China. The demand is already in place, the Japanese government does not have to put in extra resources to create demand. They can ride on this high demand to continue "attracting" the Chinese people and trying to instill good images of Japan in their minds.

That said, it is also important for the Japanese government to evaluate their other policies towards China. Some scholars have noted the ongoing issues of history and territorial disputes as sources of high tension which negates any good relations achieved via other means, for example pop culture diplomacy. Japan will have to pair pop culture diplomacy with other appropriate foreign policy actions in order to truly build good relations with China and other neighboring countries.

## Conclusion

My study has shown that there is a relationship between increased consumption of Japanese pop culture and increased probability of positive perception of Japan as a nation state among the Chinese people. In showing this, the study also found four confounding variables which are significant in explaining changes to perception as well. They are urbanicity, whether respondents have been to Japan or not, whether respondents know a Japanese person or not and their impression of Japanese pop culture.

While there are remains many limitations to this study, some can be overcome by more access to resources and improved research methods. Furthermore, this self-administered survey designed solely for the purpose of answering the research question can be used as a template for further research in the future. This way, results over time can be collected and compared on a longitudinal scale.

While this study does not explore the actual soft power outcomes of pop culture diplomacy, it still provides important empirical results to show soft power effects of Japanese pop culture. From this, one can conclude that Japanese pop culture does have potential as a soft power resource since it attracts foreign populations to have positive image about Japan. This can be a first step in trying to study the soft power abilities of pop culture.

The uncertainties involved do not mean that it is not advisable for the Japanese government to pursue pop culture diplomacy. With the large demand in China, the government does not have to invest resources to create demand. Their pop culture diplomacy initiatives can benefit from this Chinese interest in Japanese pop culture. This can also become a good source of export for their pop culture products, if anything.

In the midst of this, the Japanese government continues strengthening its culture diplomacy towards China, establishing The China Center in 2006 to facilitate exchanges among Chinese and Japanese youths, and inviting pop culture enthusiasts to participate in events and annual conventions in Japan.[73, 74] More recently, the newly launched Cool Japan Fund announced that they will be investing 50 billion yen out of their budget of 60 billion yen into a project in China to open a department store selling Japanese products.[75, 76] This will be one of the largest pop culture diplomacy investments

Japan has ever made, and it takes up almost the entire budget, pointing to the seriousness of Japan in promoting pop culture diplomacy in China.

In the end, the target markets of most pop culture products are the younger generations. With technology advancing at a rapid rate and the world becoming more open, Chinese youths will inadvertently be more aware and exposed to information and foreign imports, including Japanese pop culture. This may have more of an impact on them than previous generations, and it may show as they grow up and take on positions of power and influence. With Japan's pop culture diplomacy just taking off and gaining traction, the full potential of pop culture as a soft power tool may remain yet to be seen. Only time and further research can tell.

# Appendix 1

<u>Survey Questionnaire (translated from Chinese by the author):</u>
[Page 1]

**Japanese pop culture products may refer to: TV programs, movies, comic books (*manga*), animation (anime), popular music, games, fashion, literature etc.

1) What is your age?
2) What is your gender?
   a. Male
   b. Female
3) What is your highest level of education attained or in the process of attaining?
   a. Not-educated
   b. Primary School
   c. Middle School
   d. High School
   e. Some Associate degree
   f. Some Bachelor's degree
   g. Some Master's degree or above
4) Where did you grow up? (pick from a list of provinces)
5) What is your impression of Japan?
   a. Strongly positive
   b. Positive
   c. Negative
   d. Strongly negative

[Page 2]

6) Have you ever visited Japan?
   a. Yes
   b. No
7) Have you personally met or known a Japanese person?
   a. Yes
   b. No
8) What do you first think of when you think of Japan? Please choose the top three
   a. Popular culture
   b. Weak economy
   c. Senkaku/Diaoyu islands
   d. Technologically advanced country
   e. Joint Communiqué of the Government of Japan and the Government of the PRC
   f. Strong economy
   g. Sino-Japanese war
   h. American ally

    i.   Meiji Restoration

    j.   Yasukuni Shrine

9) What are some words you associate with Japan? Please choose 3 and rank them.

    a.   richly colorful

    b.   intelligent

    c.   respectfully polite

    d.   friendly

    e.   cultured

    f.   unique

    g.   powerful

    h.   advanced

    i.   withdrawn/gloomy

    j.   passive

    k.   stubborn

    l.   narrow-minded

    m.  hypocritical

    n.   treacherous

    o.   aggressive/violent

    p.   murderer

[Page 3]

10) Have you ever consumed Japanese pop culture products?

    a.   Yes; I still do now

    b.   Yes; in the past

    c.   No; but I am open to trying

    d.   No; and I do not want to

11) Which products have you consumed?

    a.   Japanese TV programs

    b.   Japanese movies

    c.   Japanese *manga*

    d.   Japanese anime

    e.   Japanese popular music

    f.   Japanese video games

    g.   Japanese fashion

    h.   Japanese literature

    i.   Never consumed

    j.   Others: please specify_____

12) Please indicate one Japanese pop culture product you consume by the specific product name and type. (i.e. [Product type] Product name, e.g. [Anime] Naruto)

13) On average; how many hours a week do you spend on consuming Japanese pop culture products?

    a.   No time at all

    b.   0-2 hours

    c.   2-5 hours

    d.   5-10 hours

    e.   10-15 hours

    f.   15-20 hours

    g.   20 hours and above

14) Which Japanese pop culture product do you like best? Please choose top 3.

    a.   Japanese TV programs

    b.   Japanese movies

    c.   Japanese *manga*

    d.   Japanese anime

    e.   Japanese popular music

    f.   Japanese video games

    g.   Japanese fashion

    h.   Japanese literature

    i.   Never consumed

    j.   Others: please specify_____

15) What are some words you associate with Japanese pop culture? Please choose 3 and rank them.

    a.   richly colorful

    b.   intelligent

    c.   respectfully polite

    d.   friendly

    e.   cultured

    f.   unique

    g.   powerful

    h.   advanced

    i.   withdrawn/gloomy

    j.   passive

    k.   stubborn

    l.   narrow-minded

    m.   hypocritical

    n.   treacherous

    o.   aggressive/violent

    p.   murderer

16) What is your impression of Japanese pop culture?

    a.   Strongly positive

    b.   Positive

    c.   Negative

    d.   Strongly negative

17) What do you think of Sino-Japanese relations?

    a.   Very good

    b.   Good

    c.   Neutral

    d.   Bad

e. Very bad

[Page 4]

18) Please read the statements below and choose the extent to which you agree with them. (Strongly agree; agree; neutral; disagree; strongly disagree; N/A if the sentence does not apply to you)
   a. Even though I like Japanese pop culture, I do not like Japan.
   b. My favorite idol comes from Japan
   c. I envy the Japanese way of life
   d. I think that there is nothing unique/special about Japanese pop culture
   e. I prefer other pop culture to Japanese pop culture (e.g. American pop culture, Korean pop culture etc)
   f. Most of my understanding of Japan comes from Japanese pop culture
   g. I sometimes wish I can become a character in Japanese dramas, *manga* or anime
   h. I think that Japanese pop culture is childish/immature
   i. For the accuracy of this survey, please select disagree for this question
   j. When I consume Japanese pop culture, I do not think of the negative aspects of Japan
   k. Even though I like Japanese pop culture, I cannot forgive Japan for their war crimes
   l. I have or wish to have Japanese friends
   m. I do not trust Japanese people
   n. I wish I were Japanese
   o. As Chinese people, we should reject Japanese pop culture

[Page 5]

19) What is your attitude toward future Sino-Japanese relations?
   a. Strongly positive
   b. Positive
   c. Negative
   d. Strongly negative
20) On average; how many hours a week do you spend on media? (including serving the internet, gaming, watching TV, listening to the radio, reading magazines etc)
   a. No time at all
   b. 0-2 hours
   c. 2-5 hours
   d. 5-10 hours
   e. 10-15 hours
   f. 15-20 hours
   g. 20 hours and above
21) On average, how often do you pay attention to the news?
   a. Once a day
   b. Once every 2-3 days
   c. Once a week

d. Once every 2 weeks
e. Once a month
f. Once every 3 months
g. Do not pay attention to the news

# Works Cited

Aso, Taro. "A New Look at Cultural Diplomacy: A Call to Japan's Cultural Practitioners". Speech at Digital Hollywood University, (Tokyo, April 28 2006)

Bachrach, Peter and Baratz, Morton. "Two Faces of Power," *The American Political Science Review*, 56, No. 4 (1962): 947-952

Barnett, Michael and Duvall, Raymond. "Power in International Relations," *International Organization* 59, no. 1 (2005): 39-75

BBC News. "Scarred by history: The Rape of Nanjing." BBC News. (Apr 11, 2005) Web. Last-Accessed Dec 13, 2014. <http://news.bbc.co.uk/2/hi/asia-pacific/223038.stm>

Blanchard, Jean-Marc F. and Lu, Fujia. "Thinking Hard About Soft Power: A Review and Critique of the Literature on China and Soft Power," *Asian Perspective* 36, (2012): 569

Blau, P. M. *Exchange and Power in Social Life* (New York: John Wiley, 1967)

Carr, E. H. *The Twenty Years' Crisis, 1919-1939: An Introduction to the Study of International Relations* (New York: Harper & Row, 1964)

Chua, Beng Huat. "East Asian Pop Culture: Mapping the Contours," *Structure, Audience and Soft Power in East Asian Pop Culture*, (Hong Kong: Hong Kong University Press, 2012): 9-30.

Cooper-Chen, A. M. *Cartoon Cultures: The Globalization of Japanese Popular Media.* (New York: Peter Lang Publishing Inc. 2010)

Dailot-Bul, Michal. "Japan Brand Strategy: The Taming of 'Cool Japan' and the Challenges of Cultural Planning in a Postmodern Age," *Social Science Japan Journal* 12, No. 2 (Oct 30 2009): 247-266.

Ding, S. and Saunders, Robert A. "Talking Up China An Analysis of China's Rising, Cultural Power, and Global Promotion of the Chinese Language." *East Asia* 23, no. 2 (June 2006): 3–33

Ferguson, Niall. "Think Again: Power" *Foreign Policy* 134 (2003): 21

Fujita, Junko. "Japan Is Cool Again, According To Japan's New 'Cool Japan Fund'." *Business Insider.* (Nov 24, 2013) Web. Last Accessed Nov 30, 2014. Web.
<http://www.businessinsider.com/cool-japan-fund-2013-11>

Gill, B. and Huang, Yanzhong. "Sources and Limits of Chinese 'Soft Power.'" *Survival* 48, no. 2 (2006): 17–36.

Gallarotti, Giulio M. "Soft Power: What it is, Why it's Important, and the Conditions Under Which it Cen Be Effectively Used" *Division II Faculty Publications* 57, (2011)

Harris, Richard. *Ambassador Doraemon: Japan's Pop Culture Diplomacy in China and South Korea.* MPP Thesis, Georgetown University. 2012

Jiji. "Cool Japan Fund aids sales in China." *The Japan Times.* (Apr 25, 2014). Web. Last Accessed Nov 30, 2014. Web.
<http://www.japantimes.co.jp/news/2014/04/25/business/cool-japan-fund-aids-sales-in-china/#.VJT1-V4AKA>

Jun, Hongo. "The blunt, blue-blooded Aso is back." *Japantimes.co.jp.* (Jan 22, 2013). Web. Last Accessed Dec 19, 2014.<http://www.japantimes.co.jp/news/2013/01/22/reference/the-blunt-blue-blooded-aso-is-back/#.VJR3pmcAKA>

Krauthammer, Charles. "How Do You Think We Catch the Bad Guys?" *Time* 167, No. 2 (2006): 35

Kristof, Nicholas. "The Problem of Memory." *Foreign Affairs*, Vol. 77, No. 6 (1998)

Kyodo News Agency. "Abe Cabinet says deal with China preventing Yasukuni visit 'does not exist'" *The Japan Times* (Nov 5, 2014) Web.

Kyodo News Agency. "Yasukuni Shrine remains opposed to enshrining war criminals at separate site." *The Japan Times* (Aug 11, 2014) Web. Last accessed Dec 18, 2014. <http://www.japantimes.co.jp/news/2014/08/11/national/yasukuni-remains-opposed-to-enshrining-war-criminals-at-separate-site/#.VJTnDl4AKA>

Lam, Peng Er. "Japan's Deteriorating ties with China: The Koizumi Factor." *China: An International Journal*, 3, no. 2, (2005): 275-291

Lam, Peng Er. "Japan's Quest for 'Soft Power': Attraction and Limitation," *East Asia: An International Quarterly* 24, no. 4 (2007): 349-363.

Lee, Guen. "A theory of soft power and Korea's soft power strategy" *The Korean Journal of Defense Analysis*, 21, no. 2 (June 2009): 209-210

Leheny, David. "A Narrow Place to Cross Swords: Soft Power and the Politics of Japanese Popular Culture in East Asia," *Beyond Japan: The Dynamics of East Asian Regionalism*, Ed. Katzensten, Peter J., Ed. Shiraishi, Takashi, (New York: Cornell University Press, 2006): 214

Lukes, Steven. *Power: A Radical View: 2nd Ed* (London: McMillan, 2005): original 1974.

Mattern, Janice Bially. "Why 'Soft Power' Isn't So Soft: Representational Force and the Sociolinguistic Construction of Attraction in World Politics" *Millennium – Journal of International Studies* 33, No. 3 (2005): 586

McGray, Douglas. "Japan's Gross National Cool," *Foreign Policy*, No. 130 (May/June 2002): 44 54

Mearsheimer, John J. *The Tragedy of Great Power Politics* (New York: W.W. Norton & Company, 2001)

MOFA. "Pop-Culture Diplomacy". *mofa.go.jp.* Web. Last Accessed Sept 26, 2014 <http://www.mofa.go.jp/policy/culture/exchange/pop/>

MOFA. "World Cosplay Summit". *mofa.go.jp.* Web. Last Accessed Dec 19, 2014. <http://www.mofa.go.jp/policy/culture/page5e_000021.html>

Moore, Gregory. "History, Nationalism and Face in Sino-Japanese Relations." *Journal of Chinese Political Science*, no. 15. (2010): 283-306

Morgenthau, H. J. *Politics among Nations: The Struggle for Power and Peace* (New York: Alfred A. Knopf, 1967)

Nagashima, Daniel. "Japan's Militarist Past: Reconciliation in East Asia?" *Yale Journal of International Affairs*. Vol. 2, Issue 1. Fall/Winter 2006.

National Bureau of Statistics of China. "Population and Its Composition" *China Statistics Yearbook 2013*. China Statistics Press. 2013. Web <http://www.stats.gov.cn/tjsj/ndsj/2013/indexeh.htm>

Nakano, Yoshiko. "Shared Memories: Japanese Pop Culture in China," *Soft Power Superpowers: Cultural and National Assets of Japan and the United States*. Ed. Watanabe, Yasushi, Ed. McConnell, David L, (New York: M.E. Sharpe, Inc., 2008): 111-127.

Nye, Joseph S. *Bound to Lead. The Changing Nature of American Power* (New York: BasicBooks, 1990)

Nye, Joseph S. *Soft Power: The Means to Success in World Politics* (New York: PublicAffairs, 2004)

Otmazgin, Nissim Kadosh. *Regionalizing Culture: The Political Economy of Japanese Popular Culture in Asia.* (University of Hawaii Press: Oct 2013)

Ryall, Julian. "Japan agrees to buy disputed Senkaku islands." *The Telegraph.* (Sept 5, 2012) Web. Last Accessed Dec 19, 2014.

<http://www.telegraph.co.uk/news/worldnews/asia/japan/9521793/Japan-agrees-to-buy-disputed-Senkaku-islands.html>

Shiraishi, Saya S. "Doraemon Goes Abroad" *Japan Pop! Inside the World of Japanese Popular Culture,* Ed. Craig, Timothy J, (New York: M.E. Sharpe, Inc. 2000): 287-308.

Smith-Windsor, Brooke A. "Hard Power, Soft Power Reconsidered," *Canadian Military Journal* (Autumn 2000): 53

Tang, Didi. "Anti-Japan protest in China turn violent." *The Independent.* (Sept 15, 2012). Web. Last accessed Dec 19, 2014.

<http://www.independent.co.uk/news/world/asia/antijapan-protests-in-china-turn-violent-8142028.html>

The Genron NPO; China Daily. "The 10th Japan-China Public Opinion Poll: Analysis Report on the Comparative Data". The Genron NPO. (Sept 9th 2014) Web. Last Accessed Dec 20, 2 0 1 4 http://www.genron-npo.net/en/pp/docs/10th_Japan-China_poll.pdf>

The Japan Foundation. "Arts and Culture Exchange." *Japan Foundation Worldwide.* (2009/2010) Web. < https://www.jpf.go.jp/e/about/outline/ar/2009/pdf/ar2009-08.pdf>

Vuving, Alexander L. "How Soft Power Works." Paper presented at the annual meeting of American Political Science Association (Toronto, Sept 2009)

Waltz, K. N. *Theory of International Politics* (New York: Random House, 1979)

Wang, H. and Lu, Yeh-Chung. "The Conception of Soft Power and Its Policy Implications: A Comparative Study of China and Taiwan." *Journal of Contemporary China* 17, no. 56 (August 2008): 425–447.

Womack, Brantly. "Dancing Alone: A Hard Look at Soft Power," *The Asia-Pacific Journal: Japan Focus* (2005). Web access <http://www.japanfocus.org/-Brantly-Womack/1975>

Zajonc, Robert B. "Mere Exposure: A Gateway to the Sublimal." *Current Directions in Psychological Science.* 10, no 6. (Dec 2001): 224-228

Zajonc, Robert B. and Moreland, Richard L. "Exposure Effects in Person Perception: Familiarity,Similarity, and Attraction." *Journal of Experimental Social Psychology.* 18 (1982): 395-415

# Endnotes

1.  Daliot-Bul, Michal. "Japan Brand Strategy: The Taming of 'Cool Japan' and the Challenges of Cultural Planning in a Postmodern Age". *Social Science Japan Journal*. 12, No. 2 (Oct 30, 2009): 247-266.

2.  Manga is the Japanese name for Japanese comics. Anime is a generic name for Japanese animation production.

3.  Leheny, David. "A Narrow Place to Cross Swords: Soft Power and the Politics of Japanese Popular Culture in East Asia," *Beyond Japan: The Dynamics of East Asian Regionalism*. Ed. Katzensten, Peter J., Ed. Shiraishi, Takashi. (New York: Cornell University Press, 2006) 214.

4.  Kami-sama means "God" in Japanese

5.  Shiraishi, Saya S. "Doraemon Goes Abroad" *Japan Pop! Inside the World of Japanese Popular Culture*. Ed. Craig, Timothy J. (New York: M.E. Sharpe, Inc. 2000) 287-308.

6.  Ibid.

7.  See mangafox. http://mangafox.me/

8.  McGray, Douglas. "Japan's Gross National Cool". *Foreign Policy*, No. 130 (May/June 2002): 44-54

9.  Aso, Taro. "A New Look at Cultural Diplomacy: A Call to Japan's Cultural Practitioners". Speech at Digital Hollywood University. (Tokyo, April 28 2006)

10.  Ibid.

11.  Jun, Hongo. "The blunt, blue-blooded Aso is back." Japantimes.co.jp. (Jan 22, 2013)

12.  Lam, Peng Er. "Japan's Quest for 'Soft Power': Attraction and Limitation" *East Asia: An International Quarterly* 24, no. 4 (2007): 349-363

13.  MOFA. "Pop-Culture Diplomacy". mofa.go.jp.

14.  Ibid. 88

15.  Otmazgin, Nissim Kadosh. "Popular Culture and the East Asian Region." *Regionalizing Culture: The Political Economy of Japanese Popular Culture in Asia*. (University of Hawaii Press: Oct 2013) 38

16.  Nakano, Yoshiko. "Shared Memories: Japanese Pop Culture in China." *Soft Power Superpowers: Cultural and National Assets of Japan and the United States* (New York: M.E. Sharpe, Inc., 2008) 116

17.  Ibid. 117

18.  Cooper-Chen, A. M. *Cartoon Cultures: The Globalization of Japanese Popular Media*. (New York: Peter Lang Publishing Inc. 2010) 87

19.  Harizu, a Chinese slang term which translates to a population of people who enjoy and pursues Japanese culture.

20.  "Scarred by history: The Rape of Nanjing." BBC News. (Apr 11, 2005) Web.

21.  Moore, Gregory. "History, Nationalism and Face in Sino-Japanese Relations." *Journal of Chinese Political Science*, no. 15. (2010): 289

22.  Kristof, Nicholas. "The Problem of Memory." *Foreign Affairs*, Vol. 77, No. 6 (1998): 38–39.

23.  Moore. "History, Nationalism and Face in Sino-Japanese Relations." 291

24.  Nagashima, Daniel. "Japan's Militarist Past: Reconciliation in East Asia?" *Yale Journal of International Affairs*. Vol. 2, Issue 1. Fall/Winter 2006.

25.  Lam, Peng Er. "Japan's Deteriorating ties with China: The Koizumi Factor." *China: An International Journal*, Vol 3 no. 2, (2005): 276

26.  Moore. "History, Nationalism and Face in Sino-Japanese Relations." 290-293

27. Lam, Peng Er. "The Koizumi Factor." 275

28. Kyodo News Agency. "Yasukuni Shrine remains opposed to enshrining war criminals at separate site." *The Japan Times* (Aug 11, 2014) Web.

29. People who have stopped visiting the shrine include former prime ministers Yasuhiro Nakasone and Ryutaro Hashimoto.

30. Moore. "History, Nationalism and Face in Sino-Japanese Relations." 293

31. Ibid. 291

32. Ibid. 294

33. Ryall, Julian. "Japan agrees to buy disputed Senkaku islands." *The Telegraph.* (Sept 5, 2012) Web.

34. Tang, Didi. "Anti-Japan protest in China turn violent." *The Independent.* (Sept 15, 2012). Web.

35. Source: The Genron NPO; *China Daily.* "The 10th Japan-China Public Opinion Poll: Analysis Report on the Comparative Data". The Genron NPO. 2014.

36. H. J. Morgenthau, *Politics among Nations: The Struggle for Power and Peace* (New York: Alfred A. Knopf, 1967), 158

37. Peter Bachrach and Morton Baratz, "Two Faces of Power." *The American Political Science Review.* 56, No. 4 (1962): 947-952

38. Steven Lukes, *Power: A Radical View.* 2nd Ed (London: McMillan, 2005): original 1974.

39. E. H. Carr, *The Twenty Years' Crisis, 1919-1939: An Introduction to the Study of International Relations* (New York: Harper & Row, 1964), 108

40. Dahl. (1950) 202-3

41. P. M. Blau, *Exchange and Power in Social Life* (New York: John Wiley, 1967) 117

42. Michael Barnett and Raymond Duvall, "Power in International Relations," *International Organization* 59, no. 1 (2005): 40

43. i.e. By forcing states to choose between siding with their "liberal democratic world order" or with the "communists"

44. Joseph S. Nye, *Bound to Lead. The Changing Nature of American Power* (New York: Basic Books, 1990), 76

45. Joseph S. Nye, *Soft Power: The Means to Success in World Politics* (New York: PublicAffairs, 2004), 5

46. Ibid. 7

47. Ibid.

48. Ibid. 8

49. Ibid. 11

50. Ibid.

51. Ibid. 14

52. Ibid. 12

53. Ibid.

54. Guen Lee, "A theory of soft power and Korea's soft power strategy" *The Korean Journal of Defense Analysis*, 21, no. 2 (June 2009): 209-210

55. Jean-Marc F. Blanchard & Fujia Lu, "Thinking Hard About Soft Power: A Review and Critique of the Literature on China and Soft Power," *Asian Perspective* 36, (2012): 569

56. Brantly Womack, "Dancing Alone: A Hard Look at Soft Power," *The Asia-Pacific Journal: Japan Focus* (2005).

57.　Brooke A. Smith-Windsor, "Hard Power, Soft Power Reconsidered," *Canadian Military Journal* (Autumn 2000): 53

58.　Niall Ferguson, "Think Again: Power" *Foreign Policy* 134 (2003): 21

59.　Womack. (2005)

60.　Janice Bially Mattern, "Why 'Soft Power' Isn't So Soft: Representational Force and the Sociolinguistic Construction of Attraction in World Politics" *Millennium – Journal of International Studies* 33, No. 3 (2005): 586

61.　Douglas McGray, "Japan's Gross National Cool," *Foreign Policy*, No. 130 (May/June 2002): 44-54

62.　Nye (2004), 14

63.　Harris, Richard. *Ambassador Doraemon: Japan's Pop Culture Diplomacy in China and South Korea.* MPP Thesis, Georgetown University . 2012

64.　Urban proportion data taken from National Bureau of Statistics of China. "Population and Its Composition" *China Statistics Yearbook 2013.* (China Statistics Press: 2013). Web.

65.　Zajonc, Robert B. "Mere Exposure: A Gateway to the Sublimal." *Current Directions in Psychological Science.* 10, no 6. (Dec 2001): 225

66.　Zajonc, Robert B. and Moreland, Richard L. "Exposure Effects in Person Perception: Familiarity, Similarity, and Attraction." *Journal of Experimental Social Psychology.* 18 (1982): 395

67.　Please see Appendix 1 for more the comprehensive list of survey questions

68.　See http://www.sojump.com/

69.　Harris. "Ambassador Doraemon." 2012

70.　Ryall. "Japan agrees to buy disputed Senkaku islands."

71.　Kyodo News Agency. "Abe Cabinet says deal with China preventing Yasukuni visit 'does not exist'" *The Japan Times* (Nov 5, 2014) Web.

72.　MOFA. "Pop-culture Diplomacy."

73.　The Japan Foundation. "Arts and Culture Exchange." *Japan Foundation Worldwide.* (2009/2010) Web.

74.　MOFA. "World Cosplay Summit". mofa.go.jp. Web.

75.　Jiji. "Cool Japan Fund aids sales in China." *The Japan Times.* (Apr 25, 2014). Web.

76.　Fujita, Junko. "Japan Is Cool Again, According To Japan's New 'Cool Japan Fund'." *Business Insider.* (Nov 24, 2013) Web.

# 6

# International Pressures and Multi-National Corporations in the Extractive Industry

## Owen (Yun) Wang[1]

*This thesis examines and compares the varying effectiveness different types of international pressures have in changing the behaviors of Multi-National Corporations in the Extractive Industry (EMNC). Articles and reports are collected and analyzed to construct the pressures from International actors and the reactions by the EMNCs. The pressures are categorized into four major types – Activist Pressure, Economic Pressure, Legal Pressure and Political Pressure; Reactions by the EMNCs are evaluated for effectiveness, in hope to observe a correlation between a specific pressure and a specific level of effectiveness. The findings of this research supports the hypothesis where the political pressure is said to have a strong influence on company's decision making. Among the other types of pressure, there is a clear indication that legal pressure can be the most effective. The strength of activist pressure, however, remains questionable and discredited.*

It was 1998. Talisman Energy, a global resource exploration and production company based in Canada, was brought onto trial in the United States, by a coalition of Non-Governmental Organizations (NGOs) and religious groups. Talisman was accused of fueling the on-going Second Sudanese Civil War by supplying and funding the Khartoum Government's repressive activities. In pursuit of profit it was alleged, Talisman was indirectly responsible for severe human right abuses, which included the enslavement of women and children. Under international pressure, Talisman Energy retreated from Sudan.[2]

History repeats many similar instances. From the beginning of global trade, Multinational Corporations (MNCs) have willfully undertaken irresponsible actions against international norms of basic human-rights, in pursuit of high profit-margins. With globalization on the rise, the number of MNCs in the extractive industries (EMNCs) has increased dramatically along with reports of their abuse of human-rights.[34] To name a few; Talisman in Sudan, Anvil in the Congo; and Shell in Nigeria. Recognizing the need for better regulations, Kofi Annan, the then-Secretary General of the United Nation (UN), held the first Global Compact Leaders' Summit in 2004.[5] The UN hopes to intensify worldwide focus and increase momentum tackling this particular problem of contemporary global society. In facing the many examples of MNCs' ignoring regulations and assisting with violations of the rights of indigenous people in their areas of operation, broad action is urgently needed to address the absence of any effective process to protect the people from such harm. These concerns led the

UN Sub-Committee on the Promotion and Protection of Human-rights to approve the "Norms on the Responsibilities of Transnational Corporations and Other Business Enterprises with Regard to Human-rights"[6].

To further the understanding of the available tools and their relative effectiveness in countering businesses' violations of human-rights, one must ask - What mechanisms are effective in changing the behavior of the extractive MNC when they violate human-rights? There are four candidates highlighted by four relevant schools of thought; NGO pressure, legal pressure, economic pressure and political pressure.

One school investigates the roles of activists in NGOs and voluntary alliances. As human-rights beliefs became mainstream, the effectiveness of activist pressures including global Naming and Shaming also grew[7]. Today, Naming and Shaming is one of the major mechanisms suggested by these scholars. Pressured globally, the company or state in question may change their behavior and adopt better protection for human and political rights. In the context of this study, the mechanism would imply that activists bring the violations of EMNCs to global recognition, and so help alter the behavior of those EMNCs.

The "legalist" focuses on the concept and application of jurisdictions through such mechanisms as U.S alien tort statutes to alter EMNC behavior. It emphasizes the international legal system's role in changing corporate behavior. Attempts to discipline entities include mandatory and enforceable human-rights-related rules and responsibilities. Recognizing the difficulties and ambiguities in the concepts and applications of the jurisdictions, scholars here argue that law empowers opposition forces to call recalcitrant entities to account through criminal proceedings. By applying this mechanism, the EMNC is likely to change its behavior once it is subjected legal pressure with its rigid, regulatory code of law.

The third school of thought emphasizes the importance of economic incentives and how a changing profit and loss calculations would affect EMNC's decisions. Therefore, this school pays detailed attention to international sanctions and other methods that may affect the profitability of the EMNC in question as a method of changing its behaviors. According to the views of economic rationalists, the priority for company is to maximize profit for their stockholders. Therefore, human-rights incentives should not be of concern to the decision makers unless the profitability of the operations are affected. Altering profitability will change the behavior of the entities in question if the international community can adopt mechanisms such as sanctions to affect the decisions of EMNCs.

Despite their different theoretical approaches, however, these three mechanisms boil down to financial pressures. By Naming and Shaming a company, activists are either seeking to turn customers away from the products of that company, or trying to halt the operation of that company. Both types of activist pressure materialize in financial losses. Similarly, legal methods entail the possibility of large settlements and litigation costs. As for rationalist mechanism, it is a direct interpretation of financial pressure. Fundamentally speaking, the three mechanisms, through divergent methods, affect the intrinsic value of the MNC, since MNC itself can be considered as a financial entity. Political pressure, on the other hand, does not rely on financial pressure. It relies on realists' definition of power, and will be examined here separately.-

This study seeks to discover which of the mechanisms is most effective in changing corporate behaviors. It also seeks to show the mechanisms' *relative* strengths. With these findings, the international community may have a better understanding of how to manage a human-rights friendly extractive industry more effectively. It will evaluate the effectiveness of pressures from international communities to change EMNCs behaviors as well as the responses of the EMNC to these specific pressures.

This study sets the types of pressure as independent variables, with the change by MNC as dependent variables in order to discover the correlation between the types of pressure and the company's responses. With sufficient empirical data, the study produces a relative likelihood for a specific type of pressure, or a level/form of financial incentive to be effective. The likelihood was then ranked to see the comparison among the mechanisms. Evidence gathered by the study suggest that *none of the pressures suggested by the three non-political mechanisms are uniquely effective. Among the three non-political mechanisms, legal mechanism ranks highest, and activist mechanisms takes the lowest rank.*

In fact, the study indicates that *state to state and state to company political pressures are the most effective types of pressure.* Also, *among the mechanisms that entail potential financial losses to the EMNCs, a higher magnitude of financial loss does not always correlate to higher consistency in changing EMNCs' behaviors.* These findings lead to another preliminary conclusion – *EMNCs formulate their decisions not only on financial grounds, but also political grounds.*

## Literature Review

A large body of literature documenting the power of international activists and NGOs has demonstrated that their organizations and networks are capable of doing great things, from lobbying to standard-setting to monitoring compliance to shaming violators. Paul Wapner (1995)[8] laid out a conceptual roadmap on the dimensions of activist work.

He noted that NGOs are not simply transnational pressure groups, they are, rather, political actors. Activists work to change conditions without pressuring their subjects by the power of traditional political or military methods. Their activity creates, and takes place in a realm called "global civil society" - an arena of social engagement between the individual and the state at the level of politics. It is based on a complex network of economic, social and cultural practices, constructed upon friendship, family, the market, societal norms as well as voluntary affiliations. It is in utilizing, targeting and creating these institutions and processes that activists try to assert their power over errant MNCs.

Wapner argues that while activists' efforts may not produce action from states and other entities, they should not be viewed simply as cultural or societal interests, rather, they involve manipulating strategies for shaping collective life, and are, in all perspectives, power politics. According to the study, two such strategies become apparent.

The first strategy is simply to bring hidden instances of violations to the attention of wider audiences, enabling the public to witness said abuse. Secondly, in order to demonstrate how serious certain situations are, activists may take personal risks to highlight their degree of commitment as well as the dreadfulness of the scenario. Essentially, these two strategies aim to change the way the vast international audience sees the world, instead of directly challenging and changing the behavior of the ones responsible for the abuses.

However, the powers of NGO activism is limited. Ultimately, the rights to govern, for any entity, per se, rests on the claim to a monopoly of legitimate coercive power.[9] Civic power has no such force and cannot be wielded in such a manner. It depends on constitutive employment of persuasive power, where people change their practices through persuasion by civic actors – it is the creation of voluntary and customary practices into a mechanism that governs public affairs. Therefore, this type of civic power may not have sufficient political weight to change policies directly, unlike hard power, which may govern by right of coercive power- a big chip on the bargaining table.

Nevertheless, Keck and Sikkink argued that international activism is crucial in the earlier stages of norm emergences and adoption, and can break the cycle of history by opening new ways to bring alternative visions to the international debate.[10]

Building on Wapner's construct, Emilie M. Hafner – Burton (2008)[11] evaluated a commonly adopted mechanism to enforce international human-rights and norms on more powerful actors, which is within the confined political powers of international activists. She suggested that "Naming and Shaming"- the collective action by a coalition of non-governmental organizations, news media and communities to publicize instances of violation, as well as to urge reform, is one of the most prominent mechanisms when it comes to activist actions. However, she has demonstrated that, contrary to what the activists would love to believe, Naming and Shaming is a double-edged blade. Cases have shown that, based on the rational decisions of the aggressor, the relative weighing of tempering the violation and the use of political terror may change the results of Naming and Shaming. Also, Holly Alison Duckworth and Rosemond Ann Moore illustrated the effectiveness of a publicity-based approach on the matter of enhancing Corporate Social Responsibility (CSR). They believe that teaching people how to think in a more socially responsible way will result in gradual, careful, mindful improvements, and this improvement can urge managers and stakeholders to assess and prioritize the risk of behaving irresponsibly as well as corrective actions that needs to be taken to mitigate the risk. [12]

Under what conditions, then, are mechanisms by activists effective in the enforcing of human right norms? Susan Burgeman (2001) laid out five such conditions, each necessary and not sufficient.[13] The first condition is the evolution of international human-rights regime. Since the end of World War II, in the normative domain of international politics, institutionalized human-rights norms resulted in the evolution of a recognition of the appropriateness of outside intervention to enforce compliance for a higher good. Only when decision makers begin to incorporate human-rights regimes into their concepts of identity, or interest, may they operate within the norms of this regime. The second condition is whether or not a powerful political unit has an interest in the cooperation with and in the providing of norm enforcement. Political will, positions and relative strengths of participating and targeting political units are important factors in determining whether the norm can be mobilized. The third condition relies on the level of continuous pressure from activist networks. The network of activists, as they strengthen their outreach through activities including publicity campaigns, lobbying, petitions and protests, provide other political units with both the material and the incentives to join the effort. Without such consistent and impactful pressures, decision-makers have little motivation to incorporate the norm into their actions, given that the effectiveness of international NGO in promoting human-rights is based on the action and the abilities of the decision makers of targeted entity. The fourth condition focuses on the decision makers of the targeted entity, whether if they are both concerned with improving the entity's international reputation, and are capable of controlling the violating forces. The last condition refers to local activists and the proximity of the targeted entity's political power. The local activists must be in place to relay information to international allies and be vocal in making their concerns part of the international agenda. Taking these together, Burgerman argues, the conditions will, by interaction, produce results within the international community in response to systematic violations of human-rights, which may then lead to higher degrees of compliance.

Given that the most proactive, self-motivated elements are activists, they must start the norm-enforcing chain – and this is where the mechanism suggested by Burton comes to light. Activists have been successful by Naming and Shaming to place human-rights issues on the international agenda, generating publicity about instances of abuses as well as constructing issues and concepts. Recognizing their importance, some scholars of CSR have adopted the argument made by the activist literature, and have suggested some mechanisms and frameworks.

In defending the legitimacy of transferring the arguments above into the realm of CSR, Wesley states that the acquisition of government-like powers by corporations also got them to assume the responsibilities of governments. He says that this approach is distinctive in that the scope and nature of the human-rights obligations assigned to corporations is congruent to the scope and nature of human-rights obligations of states. It gives human-rights a global character and reach that locating human-rights obligations solely in the nation state cannot achieve. Activist mechanisms that may change the behavior of states also have the potential to change that of MNCs. While connecting the human-rights obligations of corporations to widely endorsed international standards.[14] Naming and Shaming should also be more effective when applied on MNCs, in comparison to when applied to countries, given MNC's relatively limited power, simpler decision making process and clearer objectives.

John Ruggie also avidly supported this line of thinking. After outlining the shortcomings of more legalistic approaches, he envisioned a path forward showing a new regulatory dynamic where public and private governance systems each come to add distinct value and compensate for one another's weaknesses and shortcomings. These initiatives would, with time, evolve into a more comprehensive and effective global regime.[15] Capitalizing on this view, the U.N. Guiding Principles on Business and Human-rights were created. With regard to the underlying principles, it relies heavily upon states' duties to protect, corporate's responsibility to respect and actor's access to all remedies.

Depending on the intended audiences, Naming and Shaming can be further divided into two types. The first type is where activists focus their resources onto a selected group of individuals who have high decision-making power within the company. For example, shareholders. These acts of Naming and Shaming do not intend to bring the masses into condemning the MNC, rather, they act to change the decision makers' perception of the situations. The second category is where activists try to have as broad a reach as possible to the general public. By spreading the knowledge of the MNC's potential involvement in controversies, financial pressure is created where potential customers may be turned away from using the company's product. In turn, this may pressure the company to change its actions in search of a better brand image.

Therefore, from this literature we find the first hypothesis:

*H1: Naming and Shaming by international activists will produce a positive change in EMNC's policy regarding its human-rights violation.*

The exterritorial judiciary literature has different expectations than the activist literature. Legal scholars argue that regulations and normative constructions without legal compliance and enforcement mechanisms are rarely effective in long-term behavioral change, based as they are upon the foundations constructed by philosophies of human-rights within International Law (IL).

Mark W. Janis's work "An Introduction to International Law" is highly regarded for its straightforward presentation of the basics of International Law. In it, Janis recorded the theoretical background of IL, saying it is rooted in the detailed peace treaties and alliances between Jews, Romans, Syrians and Spartans. The Romans, in specific, developed a "jus gentium" – which was interpreted as a law "common to all men", serving the purpose of a code of conduct above the national level.[16] The Dutch jurist Hugo Grotius's 1625 classic "The Law of War and Peace" is widely acknowledged as the foundation of modern laws of nations.[17] It is English philosopher Jeremy Bentham, in 1789, whom reframed these concepts, and constructed the concept of "International Law"[18]. Although the enforcement and definition of International Law is in constant flux and division, it does influence the behavior of political units to a certain extent. John Austin, a famous critic of jurisprudence, acknowledged that international legal rules were effective. On the other hand, he made the point that international law being weaker than positive law enacted by sovereign states internally, due to the lack of an international authority to enforce it[19] – which brings the question of whether international law is actually "law", or merely "morality", in the sense that it urges individuals and nations to act in a way that is responsible to others yet is without a strict method of enforcement.

Martti Koskenniemi addressed this dilemma of IL being between morality and law. The author discovered that the concept of International Law is fighting a "battle on two fronts". On one hand, it tries to distinguish itself from laws of a sovereign state and, by that, to ensure the normativity of IL. On the other hand, it attempts to ensure concreteness as a code of conduct to distance itself from natural morality.[20] Hence, to show that IL is, in fact, a concept that exists in reality, its normativity as well as concreteness needs to be demonstrated. In attacking the validity of IL, two criticisms have been advanced to deny the "realness" of international law. The first argues that international laws are too political and dependent on state policies, making it not "international"; the second group claims that the law is not enforceable, and thereby does not satisfy the necessary concreteness of being "law".

Be it from a state's extraterritorial legality, or from a voluntary alliance, International Law, whether protecting human-rights or other rights, according the critics, should not be valid, and cannot hold political actors legally responsible in the realm of reality.

Todd Howland posits that states can and do hold legal responsibility to protect and promote the rights of individuals not under their sovereignty. He claims that the bureaucratic and political concerns on the common rights of individuals actually hides the reality of human-rights obligations, mainly because when thinking about the concept in this manner, the political forces do not consider themselves to be constrained by laws common to all – and to take the commonness away from International Law is to defeat its purpose of universal applicability.[21] Hence, a state may avoid its legal responsibility by claiming humanitarian purpose. To further his arguments, Howland dives into the essence of Human-rights law. He notes that, during the Vienna World Conference on Human-rights, leaders of states have reach the agreement that "Human-rights and fundamental freedom are the birthright of all human beings; their protection and promotion is the first responsibility of Governments"[22], inferring that more than one government can be concerned with the right of a particular individual, and that human-rights are universal, and most importantly, indivisible. With the responsibilities of political units confirmed, Howland advances his argument that many actors (States, multinational organizations and NGOs) are "parts of a joint enterprise of bringing sustainable peace and the respect of the full spectrum of human-rights to (troubled instances), there should be shared responsibility and accountability. Not only general principles of law, but general principles of international law supports this position."[23]

Examining the linkage between international law and CSR, Esther M.J. Schouten demonstrated that CSR of international businesses can be defined in terms of human-rights responsibilities, and in turn, regulated by international law.[24] As indicated by Amnesty International, noted Schouten, the recent increase of corporation power has led to the perception that they can influence human-rights situations in a country negatively or positively. This potential effect of MNCs on the human-rights of individuals, then, made them possible nominees to be accountable to the international human-rights law. However, the current standpoint on whether international human-rights law should be applied onto MNCs is still in a flux. As Tomuschat indicates: "It is true that, particularly in developing countries, transnational corporations bear a heavy moral responsibility because of their economic power, which may occasionally exceed that of the host state. But on the level of positive law, little if anything has materialized"[25]. Acknowledging the debate of whether MNCs are subjected to any international legal regimes, Ilias Banketas examined their international legal personality. The conclusion is that the international legal personality of non-State entities must be based on precise legal capacity drawn from customary law or binding treaties. Duties and obligations must be not only directly and clearly addressed to the particular non-State entity, but enforcement mechanisms must also be available.[26] A common mechanism that is used to hold MNCs accountable is the use of legal statues such as the "Alien Tort Claims Act" (ATCA) of U.S – where MNCs are brought onto trial in a state other than its host, often due to the lack of effective human-rights law.[27] This mechanism remedies the shortcoming of international law lacking an enforcing actor, while still valid normatively given the Tort's universality. Even as ATCA are existential, expensive and limited, the mere fact that such a method is present makes a difference in the decision making of MNCs. A company can also be sued in its state of operation, as well as the state of the company's headquarters.

Furthering the development of International Law into the CSR realm, then, supporters of a stricter international legal regime believe that punishment and the enforcement of codes of conducts are an invaluable pillar to the enhancement of human-rights when involving MNCs. Corporations are legal entities socially constructed within the legal framework of the global society, and have the power to harm or benefit individuals in the process of value creation. Therefore, they should be held and regulated by and within the paradigm of applicable law. Robert McCorquodale[28] examines the subject from this legal perspective. He notes that regulations without a legal compliance mechanism are rarely effective in terms of long-term behavioral change. In his overview, he briefly described the functionality of legal regulations including ECOSOC Norms, OECD and the like. Questioning the extent to which State Law or Corporate Law may be effective in handling such cases, his article analyzed examples of failed international human right cases. McCorquodale's conclusion suggests that it is essential to develop an effective legal regulation in the realms of CSR. Similarly, Jesse Dillard et al, in the article "Human-rights within an ethic of Accountability"[29] proposed that in light of the asymmetries of power created within the market-based system, societies must design the accompanying reporting and evaluation criteria in regards to recognizing, respecting, and advancing human-rights. Articulations of what constitutes an abuse of human-rights on the part of the corporation must be specified and incorporated into the regulatory regimes, whereas it is the society's responsibility to create the relevant principles and rights in order to hold corporate management accountable for human-rights responsibilities.

The options companies have in facing CSR, according to Keith Michael Hearit, come down to the conclusion that it is possible for an organization to act in a socially responsible manner without being pressured by legal liability.[30] It could be done by distinguishing between the public and private communication. However, if the company has caused some serious harm, it is necessary to have codes of conduct to hold the company and its officers accountable, so it gives incentive for the officers to reflect on the misdeeds, the victims, the media attention, and the possibility that good PR will lessen the possibility of a lawsuit. This process will in turn facilitate CSR.

However, Matthew W. Seeger and Steven J Hipfel noted that legal obligations, although often the minimal moral standard, sometimes become positioned as the organization's maximum obligation, so impeding the ability of the organization to act in an ethically appropriate way.[31]

They pointed out that although codes of conduct may be used to maintain a set of normative moral standards, moral principles, ethical framework and legal codes have different realms and meanings, and so are unique in their own traditions, domains and forms, even as they sometimes intersect. Morality is the larger framework of values and beliefs one lives by, while ethics are general provisions, norms and standards for judging good versus bad. Laws, on the other hand, mandate and prohibit a range of conduct, but are, arguably, minimal standards designed largely to maintain basic social order. Hence it could be argued that Legal codes would fail as a source of ethical behavior and moral conduct. Taking this into consideration, Seeger and Hipfel suggest that detailed legal structures regarding responsibilities, while sometimes desirable, may ultimately limit the corporation's flexibility and ability to be responsive to the dynamic and competing values of stakeholders, especially too tightly written. A social responsibility model of the law and an organizational responsiveness approach, therefore, are the most appropriate way to facilitate Corporate Social Responsibility.

Dean Ritz argues that law, by its existence, produces inequality in human society. The argument appeals to the ideals of human equality before law and universal participation in the political community, and the ability of the privileged few to make laws which will result in inequality. [32] CSR should, by this line of thought, realign and drive towards two ends. First, empowering human communities to resist corporate rights claims that deny the rights of human beings by increasing the power and efficiency of democratic processes. Second, reduce the constitutional rights granted to corporations. Similarly, 12 top managers from various industries criticized the legal approach on the grounds that the existence of a legal punishment makes managers evaluate damages not on moral grounds, but on an external, neutral and distant judge, hence, muddying managers' views of responsibility which could lead to inaction through fear of being designated responsible. [33] Furthermore, Ruggie noted that the International Law Commission finds that the predominant trend in international legalization in recent decades is toward the "fragmentation of international law" into separate and autonomous spheres of law, and that no hierarchical metasystem is realistically available to resolve the problem of incompatible provisions and overlapping jurisdictions - a purely legal mechanism for international CSR causes would thus meet complications. Ruggie concludes that although international law has an important role to play in constructing a better functioning global regime to govern business and human-rights, promoting an overarching global legal framework for corporate accountability was not a productive objective for his mandate, as the foundations were lacking, the issues too complex, and the states too conflicted. [34]

Based on the difference in jurisdictions, three major types of pressure can be derived from the legal mechanism. A company can be brought to trial by the legal codes of its home state, in which case the strength of the pressure is based on the regulatory ability of its home state. It can also face trial in the state where its actions are scrutinized, where the outcome will depend on the capabilities of its host government's legal framework. The third type of jurisdiction comes independent of home and host state, it relies on codes of law by third-parties, an example being U.S.'s Alien Tort Statute.

From this literature, a second hypothesis can be drawn:

*H2: EMNCs will change their behavior and comply with human-rights norms when facing litigation.*

The third body of thought relies on the framework of economic rationalism. Differing in emphasis from the previous two, it focuses on the decision-making at the business level. The word "rational" does not mean 'sensible' or 'not absurd', rather, it originates from the rationalist philosophy of being guided by reason instead of emotions. [35] Economic Rationalism holds that market mechanisms should determine all economic transactions, hence, decisions will be made based on market incentives, instead of human-rights or other types of normative pressures. As summarized by Max Weber, economic rationalism is "a term of art to describe an economic system based not on custom or tradition, but on deliberate and systematic adjustment of economic means to the attainment of the objective of pecuniary profit." [36] Hence, companies would react to changes in their ability to earn profit, instead of other pressures. As Jedrzej George Frynas has recorded[37], instabilities and outside pressures are not effective in changing MNC's questionable operations and investments if the operation is still profitable. Sanctions, large settlement fees and stock plunges or trade barriers can bring effective change in the decisions of MNCs.

The development of economic rationalism runs parallel to the progress of economic theories. As the western world shifted away from feudalism (1500 onward) – when economic decisions were largely dictated by religious organizations,[38] an "objective and passionless"[39] school of thought called Mercantilism emerged. Mercantilists measured the wealth of nations based on their stock of commodities such as gold, and advocated trade policies that would increase the wealth of the nation.[40] Looking deeper into market mechanisms and individual incentives, Adam Smith, in 1776, published a work-"The Wealth of Nations" that was regarded as the beginning of classical economics. The so-called Smithsonian attacked Mercantilists and argued for a different theoretical foundation of measuring a nation's wealth.[41] By 1871, the Marginalist revolution had generated a distinction from the then-conventional classical economic theories and came to be regarded as the harbinger of neoclassical economics.[42] In the view of neoclassical economists, the partners in trade would only endeavor to obtain maximum satisfaction for their wants. This will be satisfied only through the two partners maximizing their utility and rarity obtained in the transaction.[43] At this stage of the development of economic theories, the rationalist framework has deeply taken its root. It became, by then, commonly assumed that economic actors act in their "passionless"[44] economic interest, nothing more and nothing less.

As a scholar of economics drawing from earlier theories, Milton Friedman holds that the essence of a competitive, utility maximizing market lies, precisely, in its impersonal character, and that the most important social responsibility for the businessman is to maximize profits for stock holders. Friedman further claims contributions to charitable activities by corporations are inappropriate in a free-enterprise society, given that it is up to the morality and responsibility of the shareholders to make gifts to the society, not that of the companies.[45] Hence, it is not in the duty of a MNC to choose human-rights measures against profit maximization. Carroll, A.B, provides a stakeholder interpretation[46] which extends to Friedman's approach and reasons that there is a natural fit between the idea of corporate social responsibility and an organization's stakeholders. It should be the shareholder's morality that ensures CSR developments rather than corporate volunteerism. However, David Vogel attacked Friedman on the grounds that the world Friedman researched has become obsolete, in fact, many modern management theories emphasize that the firms flourish financially and image wise when acting in a socially responsible manner. [47] By showing the world Friedman and his followers envisioned contains flaws, Vogel effectively cast doubt on this school of thought - whether it is possible for a firm to act according to CSR while maximizing their profit potential.

James Arnt Aune, another critic of Friedman's approach described Friedman's argument as an ideological distortion.[48] He claims that Friedman assumes an individualist and utilitarian ethical standard without proper support, while refusing to engage in conversation on the possibility that the economy is embedded in society and culture and that his antisocial responsibility argument fails by privileging short-term over long-term wealth enhancement. Also, Aune mentioned that at the time

Milton's works were written, the major concerns related to CSR included environmental and racial issues. However, the challenges and needs of CSR has changed from those days long passed.

Paolo D' Anselmi also criticized Friedman's approach based on the idea that it has too narrow a focus, only on the shareholders, in making decisions that will affect a pool of participants.[49] Sumantha Ghoshal argued that liberal management theories, including Friedman's various publications, do not reflect a more broad and realistic notion of human nature.[50] His objections to Friedman were grounded in Friedman's self-fulfilling prophecy in which corporate governance was founded on the principle of defending shareholders. Once distrust is institutionalized and self-seeking behavior is assumed to be the norm, then inevitably we will find such bad behavior. Ghoshal placed the blame on Friedman for insisting that the role of ethics in human behavior be left out of economics in favor of strict reliance on self-interest.

Considering economic rationalism in the decision making of EMNCs, the third hypothesis can be constructed:

*H3: Economic punishment including rising cost of production, sanctions, stock plunge or boycott will produce a positive change in EMNC's policy regarding its human-rights violation.*[51]

The forgoing literature, albeit with varying focuses, has each provided the theoretical background and rationales for types of international pressure that can be applied by activists to EMNCs to produce change. They share a liberal foundation that assumes that the institutions, international actors, as well as human-rights regimes are valid factors to be considered in international politics; and that these non-state forces are capable of enforcing a change in the activities of political units that can affect security in their regions.

However, the rich realist literature of International Relations suggests otherwise. The pioneers of realism like Morgenthau[52] and Waltz[53] emphasize the power and interests of, and only of, sovereign states. Variances in domestic politics and societies, as well as the values and beliefs of non-state actors have been put to the side.[54] The assumption is that, since the international environment exercises extensive pressure on its members, non-state factors' influences are only peripheral.[55] International institutions and regimes, according to realists, do not effectively ensure co-operation, and when they do they may only do so marginally. The stability of the international system is purely based on states' micro motives and unintended behaviors. As Anthony Patey has acknowledged, political pressure from governments on corporate behavior is common, and that human-rights pressure seems more effective when "transmitted through a government with both little existing economic interest in the country and the ability to influence the targeted company"[56]. Hence, unless a state has an interest in intervening, policies of political units can hardly be altered.

From this perspective, a null-hypothesis to H1~3 can be drawn:

*H4: Non-political pressures will not induce significant changes in the behaviors of abusing EMNCs, unless a strong political unit (state) has an interest in supporting and backing the pressure.*

If H1~3 fails to show consistent and meaningful correlations, the effects of non-political international pressures on changing EMNC behavior will be nil, and a conclusion of the ineffectiveness of the will be proved.

The fact that each school of thought has provided specialized information on a specific mechanism hints at their limitations. Each focuses exclusively on one type of international pressure, with little mention of the others. Without comparison to alternate possibilities, scholars of CSR will not be able to prove the effectiveness of mechanisms suggested by each literature, and will fail in evaluations on a broader level. Observing this particular deficiency in the realm of CSR, this study looked across the realms of literatures and aims to discover relationships among these theories.

## Methodology

With the four hypotheses formulated, the existence of mechanisms suggested by each hypothesis in a particular case has been treated as the independent variable, a collection of such instances (international pressure) and EMNC reactions, the dependent variable, for the cases were established. Evidence for this has been gathered from news articles, historical sources (books, archives) and NGO reports. Then, the mechanisms were evaluated with a reaction from the EMNC[57]. The responses of EMNCs specifically to that international pressure were evaluated, based on the outcome achieved for its effectiveness.

As briefly mentioned, the Extractive industry has a unique set of pressures for each of the mechanism suggested as hypothesis. Under the activist mechanism, protestors may choose to Name and Shame the company to a broad audience basis, or to choose to focus on a specific group of individuals that have high decision making power. Under the economic mechanism, the activists may pursue small-end weak pressures, or large-end state sanctions. Under the Legal mechanism, litigators may utilize the company's home state's courts, the host state's (where the company is operating) as well as international third party's legal means. As to political pressures, a government may issue verbal warnings and hold meetings with companies in question where the topic would be the company's transgressions.

Organizing the types of pressures, we reach the following diagram. From left to right: Category of Mechanisms, Types of Mechanisms, and Types of pressures.

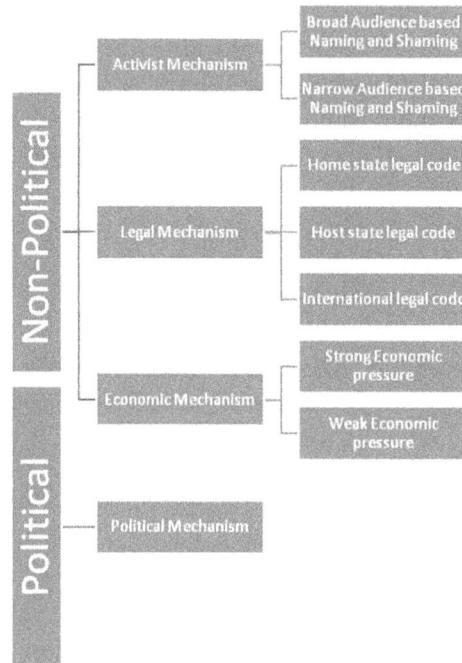

The goal of the case studies is to gain information on *relative* strength of a type of pressure within a given instance in comparison to another. By comparing the reaction of MNCs to pressures, a ranking of the effectiveness of the mechanisms can be established, and this will be done both within each case and across cases. Given sufficient instances, a correlation of the types of international pressure and their relative effectiveness can be established. The effectiveness of these pressures can then be aggregated to represent the effectiveness of a mechanism. In each instance, a pressure is paired up with a response exclusively to that pressure. Using a company's response to specific instances, the problem of one pressures affecting decision making on another pressure can be limited. The first goal of the study will examine the dynamics between the magnitude of potential financial damage from the non-political pressures and their effectiveness; the second goal of the case study will be grouped according to types of pressures as to compare the relative strength of specific pressure. The third goal will be looking at the dynamics of instances within a case, and will be organized by cases.

Given the above objectives and specifications, the Cases will include the following:[58]

Shell in Nigeria: Royal Dutch Shell of Nigeria has a long history of working with the Nigerian government to oppress opposition to its presence in the region. Requested by Shell, and with Shell's financing and assistance, Nigerian Soldiers brutally cracked down on a movement by the Ogoni people against Shell's operations during early '90s. Numerous human-rights organizations, from Greenpeace to academics pressured Shell. There are also plans for the boycotting and sanctioning Nigerian oil by several states. Furthermore, attorneys sued Shell for human-rights violations against the Ogoni. After 13 years of litigation, the cases ended in a $15.5 million settlement for the plaintiff.

Anvil in Congo: In 2004, the Australian-Canadian company, operating a large mine near Kilwa, was accused of providing logistic support to the Congolese military, assisting them in the looting and murder of villagers. More than 70 innocent people were killed, with many more injured by the troops. In 2006, three employees of Anvil were accused of complicity by the ICC. In 2010, supported by rights organizations, an association of citizens from Democratic Republic of Congo (DRC) filed suit in Quebec against Anvil. Superior Court Judge Benoit Emery issued a landmark ruling that the case could go ahead – giving the victims hope that they might finally see justice done.

Talisman Energy in Sudan: In 2001, a coalition of religious organizations and individuals filed a suit in the U.S. federal court against Talisman. The allegation states the company's complicity in the Sudanese Governments human-rights abuses against non-Muslim Sudanese living in the area of Talisman's operations. According to the plaintiffs, the Sudanese government involved itself with acts of ethnic cleansing including massive civilian displacement, extrajudicial killings, torture, rape and burning of villages, religious properties and farms, and that these abuses amounted to genocide. The court, however, dismissed the plaintiff's claims based on insufficient evidence.

Unocal in Burma: In the early '90s, a few Western and Asian oil companies, including Unocal, entered into partnership with Burma's brutal, repressive military regime to build the Yadana and Yetagun pipelines. As the pipeline area is inhabited by the Karen, Mon and Tavoy peoples, the project brought forced village relocation, forced labor as well as and fatalities attributable to the Burmese State Law and Restoration Council (SLORC) troops, resulting in daunting privations against the livelihood of the people and environmental degradation in its areas of operation. A U.S. law suit (Doe v. Unocal) was filed on behalf of the victims. There was also a boycott on Unocal-funded 76 gas stations. In 1997, Unocal sold its stake in 76 to Tosco Oil Company, ending the boycott.

## Case Study

Broad Basis Naming and Shaming

In June of 2005, Australian Broadcast Corp's Four Corners program aired a documentary focused on Democratic Republic of Congo's violent responses to rebel activities in the village of Kilwa, where Anvil has its biggest copper mines. Armed rebels took over the location in October 2004, and forced Anvil to end operations. Being a major television producer, ABC's programs are viewed all over the world, making it an act of Naming and Shaming with broad reach. The program accused Anvil of providing vehicles and financial aid to transport the 62nd Brigade of the Congolese Army. The documentary also provided eye-witness accounts of the troop's killings,[59] revealing more than 100 villagers killed, with at least 28 by "summary execution". [60] Recognizing the potential crimes to humanity done by Anvil, Richard Meeran of Slater and Gordan, a human-rights lawyer, claimed that he will be urging the Australian Federal Police to investigate Anvil's operations in Congo.

In response, Bill Turner, Anvil's chief executive, claimed that Anvil had no part in the killing.[61] Acknowledging that its planes did made up to four trips to the regional capital to bring in between 80-100 troops, Turner condemned the program's allegations as being "deplorable and without foundation." He said that Anvil had no knowledge of what was planned by the military operation, and was not complicit or involved with the military action in any way. "The fact that Anvil may influence the military action, or should be seen as complicit in the military action, is nonsense", said Turner.[62] Commenting on the military actions, Turner noted that "we (Anvil) were not part of this, this was a military action conducted by the legitimate army of the legitimate government of the country." When asked about the usage of Anvil vehicles, Turner said "So what?"[63]

In this instance, Anvil is complicit in the actions of the Congolese military. Although it did not directly participate in the killing of villagers, it did not question the government's intentions for the vehicles, and was cooperating with the military. The Naming and Shaming by ABC did not change the behavior of Anvil. After being scrutinized in the media, Anvil did not criticize the government, nor did it adopt policies to better examine potential military use of company vehicles. Instead, it defended its action by saying it is innocent of any wrong doing. Anvil also defended the rights-violating government by claiming it to be the legitimate army of the legitimate government of the country. Hence, the effort to broadly name and shame Anvil in this instance was not effective.

In May of 2001, Amnesty International (AI), called on Talisman Energy of Sudan to do more to safeguard human-rights in Sudan. It publicly criticized Talisman by noting that its annual yearly report do not adequately address the issue of the human-rights impact of the company's operations in Sudan. According to Amnesty International's statement on the armed conflict between government of Sudan forces, armed oppositions and various local militias, civilians were forcibly displaced and unlawfully killed – all near Talisman's operation areas. As a world-renowned NGO, Amnesty International has a very broad reach, hence, this act of Naming and Shaming is categorized as broad reach. AI claims that Talisman's report, although focused on the investments in social and developmental investments made by the company in the area of its operations, underplayed serious violations related to Talisman, and so, does not accurately reflect the overall human-rights situation. Furthermore, acknowledging Talisman's exploration in a new oil concession in a significant new oilfield in Kaikang, AI fears that the development may lead to more human-rights violations. It is discovered that, in order to secure oilfields, the Sudanese government adopted a scorched-earth policy, including massive displacement of civilians within Sudan. Utilizing oil revenues, the Sudanese government expanded its military budget and further fueled the civil war. AI urged Talisman to consider the human-rights situations more, and adopt a better policy to improve the dire situation in Sudan.[64]

In response, Talisman denied its role in the violation of human-rights in its areas of operations. "None of this happened within our concession area." Said Barry Nelson, a spokesman for Talisman. Furthermore, Nelson noted that during the time Talisman operated in Sudan, there has not been civilian displacement. Facing reports by Amnesty International, Nelson says that some people may have been displaced around the pipeline, but that Talisman has a compensation process for such cases. In defending the non-defense, military usage of Talisman's airstrip to hit rebel armies, Nelson claims that it is due to the rebels' pre-emptive targeting of oil fields. "There has to be defense, clearly, they have to defend us".[65]

In this instance, Talisman is complicit, and benefitting from the questionable actions of the Sudanese government. It would be harder for Talisman to operate its oil fields if the villagers were not evacuated from the areas. It is also, as discovered by the AI report, helping the Sudanese government by providing funding to the military. This instance of Naming and Shaming by Amnesty International did not result in Talisman's pursuit of a different path. Acknowledging the report, Talisman did not openly urge the Sudanese government to better its human-rights measures, neither did it plan to reduce its stake in risky areas. Instead, Talisman defended its position by shaping an image of being innocent of violations and being a victim of the conflict. Given the above factors, it is reasonable to say that this Naming and Shaming effort of Amnesty International was not effective in changing the behaviors of Talisman.

In February of 1996, Amnesty International undertook a campaign in Washington, DC, to urge Shell to use its considerable influence to improve human-rights in Nigeria. The campaign followed the execution of Nigerian human-rights activist Ken Saro Wiwa and eight others. AI placed its campaign ads as taillight displays on buses traveling on Capitol Hill and in downtown Washington.[66] Again, Amnesty International is a very active NGO with a broad reach. The strategy they've pursued is also a move to gain the attention of a broad audience. The message on the bus reads: "Nine hanged in Nigeria. Are Shell's hands clean? Call 1-800-Amnesty for more information. Amnesty International USA. Keep the light on Human-rights." According to William F.Schultz of AI, while Shell's United States company itself is not involved in operations in the Niger Delta, it could influence its parent company, Royal Dutch Shell, to take an active role and protect human-rights. He also noted that among the oil companies operating in Nigeria, Shell has the largest share, and was the main target of peaceful protests led by Ken Saro-Wiwa, who was ultimately charged with instigating a riot that resulted in the death of four.[67] There was not a report of Shell's response, neither did Shell show any change in action, or revised policies in the proximate period.

In this instance, then, the broad-based effort of Naming and Shaming did not produce any apparent substantive effect on Shell's decision making. Both before and after, Shell is complicit in the violating government's actions. The Naming and Shaming did not bring the effects it hoped to bring, which is to have Shell to take active role and protect human-rights in the region. Shell simply ignored the negative press. Hence, the pressure here is ineffective in changing the behavior of Shell.

In March of 1997, the World Council of Churches (WCC) published a report entitled "Ogoni: the Struggle Continues." documenting the oppression of people in Nigeria's Ogoniland. WCC has roughly 500 million members across the globe. Hence, it is reasonable to code this instance of Naming and Shaming as one intended for a broad audience. Written by Dr. Deborah Robinson of WCC's Program to combat racism, the report contains detailed background on the economic and political situation in Nigeria, a history of the military, its dictatorship, and an extensive review of the role of the oil industry in Nigeria's political economy. The report also describes the Nigerian military's efforts to suppress peaceful protests, and has first-hand accounts of beating, torture and intimidation. Also reported are accounts of the environmental devastation oil production has brought on the people of the Niger Delta, including evidences of oil spill, the dumping of oil into waterways, continual flaring of waste gases and hazardous above-ground oil pipes that cross the region.[68] WCC, with the report, claimed that criticism targeting Shell is justified, and urged Shell to cleanup existing oil spills and use its influence with the government to ensure protection of human-rights there.[69]

Two months later, during Shell's annual meeting, shareholders voted against a resolution calling for greater attention to environmental and human-rights policies. The voters say that they have received the protestors' messages, but would not submit to an independent external review of its environmental or social programs.[70]

In this instance, therefore, the act of Naming and Shaming to a broad audience by WCC, in the hope of having Shell clean up its oil spills and influence the Nigerian government to ensure protection of human-rights did not achieve its intended purpose. Shell, although acknowledging the suggestions, did not adopt any substantial programs or policies that could have a positive impact on the environmental and human-rights situation in Nigeria. Considering these factors, WCC's initiative was ineffective in changing the behavior of Shell.

In April of 2001, a delegation of Canadian church leaders called for an international withdrawal of investment in Sudan until a peace treaty is signed to end the bloody civil war. Reverend Bill Phipps, former moderator of the United Church of Canada, criticized Talisman for using its revenues to fuel the civil war and "the calculated slaughter of defenseless people being driven from their land". Given that the intention of this action is to educate international audiences, and that a delegation of churches has a broad audience, this act of Naming and Shaming will be coded as broad basis. "Canada and the International community must declare a moratorium on all aspects of oil development in Sudan, including Talisman operations." Said Phipps[71]. By publicly criticizing Talisman's role in Sudan, the United Church of Canada is hoping to pressure Talisman into halting its operations in the contested region, leading to less revenue to the Sudanese government, which could, in turn, reduce the amount of bloodshed in the civil war.

On the same day that the Church coalition made their announcement, Talisman released a report on the company's controversial role in Sudan, announcing its $806 million acquisition in the region.[72] The report lays out Talisman's operating principle in the areas of human-rights, ethical business conduct and stakeholder participation. It also detailed the steps the company has taken to uphold human-rights principles. "We hope this report will be received as an honest effort to respond to concerns about our investments in Sudan." Said Jim Buckee, CEO of Talisman. However, the report was criticized for omitting important discussion of key issues revolving around the impact of Talisman's oil developments on the conflict as a whole and the population displacement. Also, Gary Kenny of Inter-Church Coalition on Africa pointed out that the principles Talisman has adopted are based on the International Code of Ethics for Canadian Business-which itself is an inadequate and problematic.[73] There were no further responses recorded after this from Talisman to the plea of the church coalition.

In this instance, the coalition of churches hoped to change Talisman's complicit actions in

Sudan, from those which fuel the civil war. They adopted a method of Naming and Shaming to a broad audience in order to pressure Talisman into following their recommendations. However, as its responses indicated, Talisman did not comply with the churches' plea. Instead, it sought to defend itself by citing its own report of innocence. Talisman did not pull out of the questionable areas, neither did it address the accusations of its revenue fueling the war with records indicating otherwise. Therefore, this instance of Naming and Shaming was not effective in changing the behaviors of Talisman.

Organizing the instances of broad reach-based Naming and Shaming pressure, we get this table:

| Pressure | Potential Financial Loss if MNC ignore the pressure | Response | Effectiveness |
|---|---|---|---|
| Television Broadcasting Documentary | Low (some customer gets discouraged from consuming MNC's good.) | Company defended its actions and the legitimacy of the violating government | Low |
| Called on the company to adopt a better policy on human-rights situations | Low (some customer gets discouraged from consuming MNC's good.) | Company denied the accusations, and claimed its innocence | Low |
| Post advertisements on buses in Washington D.C. USA. | Low (some customer gets discouraged from consuming MNC's good.) | No response | Low |
| Urged the company to clean up its oil spills and to ensure the protection of human right in the contested area | Low (some customer gets discouraged from consuming MNC's good.) | Shareholders voted against adopting a human-rights friendly set of policies | Low |
| Calling on company to withdraw investments from contested areas | Low (some customer gets discouraged from consuming MNC's good.) | Company defended itself by publishing a report which omitted important issues | Low |

Narrow basis Naming and Shaming

In April of 2006, a group of over 500 miners protested at Anvil mining's KuIu copper mine in the Democratic Republic of Congo. Reports say that the protestors gathered due to the killing of 30-year-old miner Kayembe Mukoj. He was killed while being removed from Anvil's property. Conflicting reports on the cause of his death say he drowned in a river while fleeing and the others say they saw Anvil security guard throw the man down a well. The protest grew as 1000 people walked through the town, according to witnesses. Angry protestors burned down a guest house owned by the company and killed two Anvil staff members, an Anvil cook and a contracted security guard. Sources indicate that the protestors dispersed when local police fired live rounds into the crowd. In the midst of gunfire, two protestors were shot to death.[74] The protestors in this instance, although violent, protested against a single entity, Anvil's operation site. The subject matter of the protest might have been to seek justice for the deceased Kayembe Mukoj. This act of protest, therefore, can be categorized as one of a narrowly focused activist pressure.

In response to the death of Kayembe Mukoj, Anvil said that it tried to remove illegal artisanal miners from its land for months, but that it has no problem with those who have permits from the government to mine in the area. Also, the contracted security company denied its involvement with the death of Kayembe Mukoj. After the protest, however, Anvil quickly notified the UN mission in Congo, as well as the DRC government. The mine was shut down immediately and its staff flew to safe locations. A month later, the mine was reopened. In its release, Anvil announced that it is "extremely upset that these deaths have occurred and is making every effort to assist the affected families and to protect its staff." Furthermore, the company says that it will invest close to $1 million in social programs this year, with 10% of earnings going to the local community. [75] Therefore, Anvil is trying to show the international and local community that despite the bloody protest, it is trying to compensate the locals by assisting the affected families, as well as investing more money to help the local population.

In this instance of the protesters seeking justice and compensation. They have adopted a very conventional, albeit violent, method of protest that focuses on the local Anvil facility. One may argue that there is no clear intention when it comes to angry mobs targeting specific collectives, but given that the protestor focused their anger toward the unfair treatment and the possible unlawful killing, their objective will be achieved if Anvil compensates the loss, and improves the human-rights situations in the area. In its response, Anvil did say it will make every effort to assist the affected families. It also promised to invest in the local welfare, as well as using mining revenues to benefit people in the region. However, despite its short-term promises, Anvil failed to deal with long-term risks. It did not address the root of the problem, which could fuel incidents of similar nature. The company is merely compensating for the harms it has done, instead of actively lobbying the government or ending its operations in contested areas. Therefore, the act of protest by the miners was of medium effectiveness. It did bring the company to some responsible reactions, but did not produce long-term changes in the company's policies.

In May 1995, a group of protestors, including representatives from Greenpeace, arrived at

Unocal's annual shareholder in Sugar Land, Texas. The protestors hammered away at company officials, insisting Unocal pull out of military-controlled Burma. Protestors held up banners reading "Unocal Supports Slave Labor in Burma", and "Save Burmese Rainforests/ No Deals with Dictators" went up along U.S. 59, the main highway leading up to the shareholder meeting. By targeting the shareholders of Unocal, the protestors were aiming at a narrowly defined audience basis consisting of a key group of individuals. Their intentions were clear – to inform the shareholders of Unocal's violations of human-rights in Burma, and potentially, when shareholders start to challenge the decisions of Unocal, to pressure Unocal into exiting the contested areas of operations. The protestors claim that by doing business with the Burmese government, Unocal is funding the country's military regime, and its State Law and Order Restoration Council (SLORC) thereby, invalidating the results of a 1990 democratic election. By publicizing the plight of Burmese citizens being relocated to make way for the pipeline and railways and being forced to work in slave labor camps, the protestors argue that the longer Unocal works with SLORC, the more it helps the ruthless military government cling to office.

In response, Richard Stegemeier, Chairman of Unocal, claimed the accusations to be "outrageous". He said that "we have not observed, ourselves, any human-rights violations in the area in which we work." When asked to help development human-rights measures in the area, Stegemeier said "We are, by necessity, apolitical" and that there is only so much a U.S. company working in foreign land can do. After the protestor-infested meeting, Stegemeier jokingly said to the mayor of Sugarland "Mr. Mayor, we may go back to Los Angeles next year." Indicating that Unocal intends to avoid encountering protestors.[76] There are no further recorded responses from Unocal to this situation.

Here we see an act of pressure focused on a narrow audience by protestors intended to change Unocal's behavior from compliance with the Burmese government in violating human-rights to leaving the contested areas. The response from Unocal showed that Unocal did not take activists' actions into consideration. Unocal defended its actions by saying that it is apolitical and powerless against the Burmese government. Furthermore, not only did the protest fail to bring meaningful changes in the company, it pushed the company away from human-rights initiatives, evidenced by Stegemeier's escapist comments. Considering the above factors, this act of Naming and Shaming to a narrow audience was ineffective in changing the course of actions of Unocal.

In May 1997, about 30 demonstrators from Nigerian Advocacy Group for Democracy (NAGD) chanted in front of Paulson's Shell on Massachusetts Avenue in Cambridge, England, as Shell shareholders met to vote on a proposal that would allow third party auditors to monitor Shell's environmental practices in Nigeria. Maureen Idehen of NAGD claims that "we're saying no to environmental degradation and to corporate irresponsibility." The group is giving out information on the roles Shell played in the arrest and execution of environmentalists and playwright Ken Saro-Wiwa and eight other activists who opposed the way Shell conducted business in Ogoniland of Nigeria. The protestors, by exposing Shell's violations in Nigeria, hope to pressure Shell Shareholders into voting for the proposition that would bind Shell to outside monitors. Given that the target audience of the Naming and Shaming is a select group of key individuals, this instance will be categorized as one of narrow basis.[77] The vote, however, did not yield the results that the protestors intended. The proposal was defeated by an 8 to 1 ratio. There was no recorded response from Shell on this particular pressure after the vote.

In this instance, Naming and Shaming Shell to a selected group of individuals did not produce the kind of result the activists hoped for, to have Shell change its course from compliance with and creation of a tougher set of policies overseeing its actions in the region. Instead, even as they are informed of Shell's irresponsible actions in the area, merely 10% voted for the enactment of such measures, leaving Shell's policy virtually unchanged. Therefore, this instance of activist pressure was not effective in changing Shell's course of actions.

In June 1996, shareholders of Unocal complained loudly at Unocal's annual meeting in Brea, California. Half a dozen shareholders in an audience of 400 vocally and persistently raised the issue of human-rights violations in Burma and Unocal's involvement. "We are profoundly troubled by the horrendous human-rights violations in Burma as reported to us by our own missionaries in the field." Said Rev. Joseph P. La Mar, of a Catholic foreign mission society. The activist shareholders also used their ballot proposal to call for Unocal to add social criteria to its international code of conduct.[78] With an intention to have Unocal adopt a better set of policies to embrace human right issues, the activists, in this instance, hoped to achieve their objective by presenting information and concerns on Unocal's role in Burma to a selected, narrowly defined audience base whom may have the power to change the course of Unocal's actions. Therefore, it is reasonable to categorize this as narrow basis activist pressure.

In response, Roger Beach, Chairman of Unocal, defended operations in Burma by noting that "we are convinced the Yadana project will bring many long-term benefits to the people of Myanmar and help move the country into modern world. I visited Burma six weeks ago…and let me assure you that there is no conscripted labor working on (Unocal's) project. In fact, we are tremendously impressed with the positive impact the Yadana Project is already having on the people who live near the pipeline route." Also, the ballot urged by activist shareholders was defeated by a majority of the shareholders.[79]

In this instance, as the factors indicate, the activists did not achieve their intended result. The acts of focusing protests on a group of decision-makers did not make the decision makers vote differently. Instead of following the calls of protestors, the chairman of Unocal actively defended Unocal's role in Burma by noting potential long-term benefits it can create, rather than tackling the immediate human-rights problems head-on. Other shareholders were not influenced by the calls of activists, and did not turn Unocal from committing potential violations in Burma to actively seeking better human-rights measures by adding a social criteria to Unocal's programs. For these reasons, Naming and Shaming was not effective in changing Unocal's behavior.

Organizing the data, the following table can be established:

| Pressure | Potential Financial Loss if MNC ignores the pressure | Response | Effectiveness |
|---|---|---|---|
| Violently protest against the company at the site of operation | Medium (temporary halting of operations) | Compensate the affected family, promise to invest more in community | Medium |
| Protest at shareholder meeting | Low (Small possibility of shareholders voting to adopt costly codes of conducts) | Company verbally defended its actions, no change in conduct | Low |
| Protest at shareholder meeting | Low (Small possibility of shareholders voting to adopt costly human-rights programs) | No response | Low |
| Protest at shareholder meeting | Low (Small possibility of shareholders voting to adopt costly policies) | Shareholders voted against adopting a human-rights friendly policies | Low |

Weak Economic Pressure

In 1995, a local Nigerian democracy pressure group aligned with South African President Nelson Mandela's ruling African National Congress called for a two-day, worldwide boycott of Shell products. According to a statement released by the ANC, "The boycott is a reminder of Shell's failure to use its economic power to put pressure on the military regime to democratize Nigeria."[80] And, the ANC "urged holiday makers to simply drive past Shell filling stations. In this way they will be able to show their commitment to the creation of democracy in Nigeria and send a clear message to Shell about the responsibilities that they cannot escape."[81] This boycott, although sponsored by powerful figures with global reach, cannot be said to have great strength, given the relatively short boycott. In response, Shell took out full-page advertisements in major newspapers to defend its role in Nigeria.[82]

In this instance, then, ANC hoped to put pressure on Shell by boycotting its product for two days. It was not effective in changing Shell's course of actions, as indicated by Shell's defending of its position through a public relations campaign.

Also in '95, the Berkeley City Council voted to boycott products of companies doing business in Burma, due to its ruthless military government.[83] With a population of 112,580, Berkeley is not a major metropolitan city. A boycott in Berkeley, alone, is weak, compared to other boycotts. Acknowledging its relative weakness, Council woman Betty Olds said that "it (the boycott) is more symbolic than anything." In response, Unocal defended itself by arguing that it is helping to develop Myanmar's economy and thus its people's quality of life. "We have nothing to hide" said a spokesperson of Unocal.[84]

In this instance, the initial pressure put on Unocal, by boycotting its products on a small-scale, did not change Unocal's behavior. Instead, Unocal verbally defended its operations, referring to the benefits it can bring to the region, ignoring its compliance with and support of Burma's military regime. This level of economic pressure, therefore, was not effective in Changing Unocal's actions.

In November of 1995, the environmental group Greenpeace urged Canadians to boycott Shell gas stations for a day to protest the execution of nine minority-rights activists in Nigeria. Although the boycott called on all of Canada, it was only intended for one day, therefore, was limited in its economic strength.[85] Shell Canada's spokeswomen Jan Rowley defended the company's position by noting that "Shell Canada has no involvement with the government of Nigeria, nor does it have any operations in Nigeria. A boycott of Shell Canada service stations will only serve to hurt Shell Canada retailers – Canadians".[86]

In this instance, therefore, the boycott by Greenpeace of Shell services states did not bring a meaningful outcome. Instead of trying to remedy the human-rights problems, Shell Canada avoided responsibly by hiding in its management structure, relying on the argument that there is nothing they can do to help. Hence, this act of economic pressure was not effective in changing Shell's decision making.

In December of 1995, a 560,000-member environmental organization, The Sierra Club, called for a boycott of Shell Oil Co, asking members to not purchase Shell products, and to cut up their Shell Credit Cards to protest environmental and human-rights damages in Nigeria. The Sierra Club announced that they will not stop the boycott until Shell cleans up pollution in Nigeria, agrees that its continued operation will conform to U.S. environmental standards and has "paid fair compensation" to Nigerians adversely affected by their activities. Given that the club's membership is relatively low compared to Shell's global market, it is reasonable to consider this as weak economic pressure. In response, Shell's U.S. subsidiary noted that "Most of the correspondence (of the boycotts) is from individuals who are not Shell customers and there has been no impact on our business." It also adds that, as an American subsidiary, it has nothing to do with production of Nigerian crude.[87]

This instance indicates that the Sierra Club's attempt to use boycott to pressure Shell's decision making did not achieve its intended result of having Shell clean up their pollution or conform to a better environmental standards, or to pay fair compensation to the affected. Instead of conforming to Sierra Club's demands, Shell defended itself, again, by noting the limitation of its power over a subsidiary. Hence, this act of economic pressure was not effective in Changing Shell's course of actions.

Organizing the above dataset, we have:

| Pressure | Potential Financial Loss if MNC ignore the pressure | Response | Effectiveness |
|---|---|---|---|
| Two-day Worldwide Boycott | Medium (Earning significantly lower profit for two days.) | Company uses advertisement to defend its position | Low |
| City-wide Boycott | Medium (Earning lower profit for a long period of time) | Company denied any wrongdoings, and notes their value in the contested area | Low |
| One-day National Boycott | Medium (Earning significantly lower profit for one day.) | Company denied accusations, citing organizational structure | Low |
| Membership-wide Boycott | Low (Earning slightly lower profit for a long period of time.) | Company denied accusations, citing organizational structure | Low |

Strong Economic Pressure

In 1995, a project of Shell and its joint-venture partners, Elf of France, Agip of Italy and the Nigerian National Petroleum Company, was aiming at constructing a $ 2.5 billion liquefied natural gas plant at the mouth of the Niger River. Due to mounting pressures from supporting nations, the World Bank would not fund a $100 million loan for this project. Without the funding, the project would stop. Shell desperately needed to go ahead because gas reserves would last long after the oil runs out. Gas is presently burnt from the well at a rate of 1.1 billion cubic feet a day, and, if the project was built, gas will be shipped to France, Spain and Italy.[88] By denying Shell this huge profit opportunity, World Bank is presenting Shell with a significantly strong economic incentive.

In defending itself to its lender, Shell described allegations of its responsibility for environmental devastation in Nigeria as false. It also blamed locals for sabotaging facilities in order to create oil spills, as well as activist campaigners distorting the facts.[89] There were no further recorded responses from

Shell in regard to this economic pressure.

In this instance, the pressure was effective in halting Shell's productions in the areas, thereby reducing the chances that Shell might pollute, or violate the human safety in the area. However, it was not effective in changing Shell's overall attitude regarding its violations against Nigeria's environment and residents. In fact, the economic pressure did achieve, although not with the consensus of Shell, what activists who urged this act had hoped. Shell halted its potential operations, but did not bring Shell to actively clean-up and pay compensation. Considering these factors, this pressure was of medium effectiveness in changing Shell's conducts.

In 1996, A U.S. Senate Appropriations panel approved severe trade and investment sanctions against Burma until there is a freely elected government in place. The measure stops any U.S. citizen or company from investing in Burma, and stops any further US assistance. U.S. representatives on international financial institutions would be directed to oppose loans for Burma, and the Burmese would face a potential limited on visas to U.S.[90] This act of economic pressure, considering its reach and strength, is rather strong, when compared to other economic pressures. Unocal, since it is a U.S. company, will not be able to receive any future U.S. investments until Burma holds a democratic election. Owning 28 % of a $1 billion pipeline project, Unocal would face disastrous consequences as the sanctions are enforced. In defending their position, David Garcia, a spokesperson for Unocal said "We intend to operate in a very democratic fashion. We can lead by example." Unocal never left its Burma operations.

In this instance, then, the economic pressures did not bring changes to Unocal's actions. Even as the pressure was relative strong and potentially devastating, Unocal did not back out of its operations in Burma, neither did it gave verbal promises of its intention to better human-rights measures in Burma. Unocal defended itself by noting the positive effects it has had in the contested area. Considering these factors, it is reasonable to say that this case of economic pressure was not effective in Changing Unocal's behavior.

In February of 2000, the U.S. government imposed sanctions against a Sudanese government oil pipeline project that is partly owned by Calgary-based Talisman Energy.[91] According to the rulings, America citizens or companies can no longer engage in trade or financial transactions with Sudan's Sudapet Ltd, or with Great Nile Petroleum Operation Company Ltd, where Talisman owns a quarter of the company. Furthermore, any assets of the venture in the U.S. or under U.S.'s company's control, such as banks, are immediately frozen.[92] Following the sanctions, the U.S. House of Representatives, in June of 2001, passed a bill that would bar companies active in Sudan from U.S.'s capital markets, invalidating Talisman's New York Stock Exchange listing.[93] This act of economic pressure is relative strong, when compared to other economic pressures. The fact that it bans U.S. investment is sufficiently devastating to companies traded internationally.

By August of 2001, Talisman Energy had cleared its way to exit Sudanese operations. Jim Buckee, CEO of Talisman, said that the key strategy driver was a "very large upscale in Malaysia." When asked about the role U.S.'s sanction played in the making of the decision to retreat, Buckee said:

"I don't think anybody could afford not to have access to US capital markets. No asset is worth more than that."[94]

In this instance, therefore, the economic pressure U.S. government imposed on Talisman did effectively change the company's actions, which went from being complicit with the violating government to leaving its contested operations. With its operations ended, Talisman will not assist the Sudanese government in threatening the human-rights of those who are against the government. Considering these factors, it is safe to say that this particular economic pressure is relatively effective.

| Pressure | Potential Financial Loss if MNC ignore the pressure | Response | Effectiveness |
|---|---|---|---|
| Cancelling a business loan to the company | High (Inability to start a high profit-margin project.) | Company halted its operations, defended its position by claiming the accusations to be false | Medium |
| Sanction, preventing U.S. entities to invest in the contested regions | High (Severe Loss of investments.) | Company defended its actions, and stayed in operation | Low |
| Sanction, preventing U.S. entities investment in the contested regions, delist company from NYSE, frozen all company accounts controlled by the U.S. | High (Severe loss of investments, Stock delisted, frozen accounts.) | Company ended its operation in contested area | High |

Home Nation Court

In 2008, four fishers filed a legal suit in Dutch court, accusing Royal Dutch Shell of its pipes polluting their fish ponds in 2005. The case has proved to be landmark case, as it is the first time a Dutch company has been brought before its home court to answer charges of environmental damage caused abroad.[95] According to Friday Akpan, one of the fish farmers, Shell's local subsidiary was liable for damages because sabotage was done by simply by opening the over-ground valves with a wrench, an act that Shell Nigeria could have prevented.[96] Channa Samkalden, the lawyer for the farmers, argued that Shell has violated its legal obligations since "it knew for a long time that the pipeline was damaged but didn't do anything." The farmers demand Royal Dutch Shell to clean up the mess, repair and maintain defective pipelines to prevent further damage and pay out compensation. Shell, on the other hand, defended itself on the grounds that "The spills that happened in the year between 2004 and 2007 all happened as the consequence of illegal theft and sabotage."[97]

In 2013, the court decided to dismiss the claims for compensations against Royal Dutch Shell, with a fifth of compensation payable to the farmers. The court has ruled that the oil spills weren't caused by poor maintenances by Shell's Nigeria subsidiary, but by sabotage from third parties, and that Nigerian laws meant that only Shell's local subsidiary was liable. Nevertheless, the court ruled Shell's Nigerian subsidiary was to pay compensation, since it "would, and should have prevented the sabotage of its pipelines that caused the spill by installing a concrete plug on abandoned oil wells.[98] Allard Castelein, Shell's vice-president for the environment, said that the company was happy with the ruling. Mr. Akpan, representing the fish farmers, also welcomed the judgment, which he said would help repay substantial debts he'd been left with when the ponds were destroyed.[99]

In this instance of legal pressure from the company's home court, the activists hoped to pressure Shell into cleaning up its spills, repair broken pipes and pay compensations. The legal suit, however, did not lead to a win for the activists. Despite Shell's escape from legal charges, it was ordered to pay compensation. Considering these factors, this instance of legal pressure is evaluated as of medium effectiveness.

In 2003, an allegation filed by 15 Myanmar refugees, in 1996, against the El Segundo-based oil company Unocal Corp. A three-judge panel of the U.S. 9th Circuit Court of Appeals found that there was sufficient evidence for Unocal to stand trial on charges of complicity in human-rights abuse allegedly committed by soldiers in Myanmar who were guarding a pipeline partly owned by Unocal.[100] Unocal's argues that the Alien Tort Act, which the prosecutors relies upon in bringing Unocal onto the courtroom, does not grant overseas victims of atrocities access to American courts, and is misapplied.[101] In 2004, a judge kept the lawsuit alive and ruled that Unocal could and should be held liable for the alleged enslavement of local residents.[102]The allegation includes human-rights abuses in violations of international law, including forced labor, rape and murder.[103]The court is set to take place in June of 2005.

In 2004, Unocal reported that it reached an out-of-court settlement with the plaintiffs regarding the allegations. According to analysts, a "reasonable financial settlement" was most certainly the case. Unocal has firmly contested the claims linking it to human-rights abuse, as well as the inapplicability of Alien Tort in this case.[104] In its announcement, Unocal noted that the settlement will compensate 14 anonymous villagers who first sued Unocal in 1996, as well as provide funds to improve living conditions, health care and education in the region of its pipelines.[105]

In this instance, then, although the plaintiffs failed to hold Unocal criminally accountable, but compensations and improvements were achieved. Under the legal pressure, Unocal did change its behavior from ignorance to compliance, compensation and improving the local human-rights situations. Considering these factors, the legal pressure in this instance will be evaluated as effective.

Organizing the Data, we have:

| Pressure | Potential Financial Loss if MNC ignore the pressure | Result | Effectiveness |
|---|---|---|---|
| Sued in home nation | Medium (a large legal fine, criminal proceedings, possible charges.) | Company compensates the plaintiffs, not charged, declines charges | medium |
| Sued in home nation | Medium (a large legal fine, criminal proceedings, possible charges.) | Company compensates the plaintiffs, not charged, declines charges, improve human-rights in the regions around its pipelines | High |

Host Nation Court

In 2000, a River State High Court in Port Harcourt of Nigeria has ordered Royal Dutch Shell to pay $40 million directly to Ejama Ebubu community, in compensation for an oil spill happened in Ogoniland 30 years ago. Shell claimed no responsibility for the damage, arguing that during the time of the spill, the company had left the Niger Delta region due to the 1967 Nigerian/Biafran Civil War, when the spill happened. Shell further claims that "the highly-publicized spill at Ebubu near Ogoni was a legacy of the civil war when a retreating army cut a main pipeline and set the crude oil on fire in the late 1960s, Nevertheless, SPDC has purchased the land at Ebubu and undertook periodic clean-up as oil seeps the surface.[106] Shell said it will appeal the fine. With the rulings on appeal, the fine has been delayed. There has yet to be a report on Shell's payment, or none thereof regarding this incident.

In this instance, as one observes, the pressure from Nigeria's legal system did not achieve its intended purpose, which is to have Shell make the payment, and to use that payment in compensating the damage done to the Ebubu community. Shell, by appealing and denying its environmental damage, has so far successfully delayed payment. Considering these factors, the legal pressure in this instance will be evaluated as ineffective in changing corporate behavior.

In 2006, Anvil Mining Limited confirmed that one if its subsidiaries, Anvil Mining Congo sarl, received notification from the Military prosecutor of the Ministry of National Defence and Military Justice of the Democratic Republic of Congo, asking it to turn in three Anvil employees at the time of the Kilwa incident. They were accused of knowingly, and voluntarily omitting the withdrawal of vehicles commandeered by the 62nd Military Brigade, in during a counter-offensive to recapture the town of Kilwa on October 15, 2004. By doing so, they knowingly facilitied the commission of war crimes by Colonal Ilunga Ademar. In response, Anvil claims that the allegations are unfounded and without merit.[107] According to Reuters, a court document, signed by military prosecutor Eddy Nzambi, accuses the three Anvil staff of facilitating crimes including summary execution, rape and looting.[108]

In July of 2006 and January of 2007, however, Anvil is seen increasing its ventures in Congo's Kinsevere-Nambulwa copper –cobalt Joint Venture.[109] In June of 2006, the military court cleared Anvil and its employees of any involvement in the violation of human-rights during the Kilwa incident. Anvil welcomed the decision.[110]

In this instance, the legal pressure did not achieve what it was originally planned to achieve – to have Anvil answer for its human-rights violations, and to bring the violators to justice. Instead, not only did Anvil walk away from the court a free company, it also increased its investment in the region, furthering its complicity with a shady regime, as well as operating in risky areas of operation. Observing these factors, this instance of legal pressure will be evaluated as ineffective. Organizing the data, we have:

| Pressure | Potential Financial Loss if MNC ignore the pressure | Result | Effectiveness |
|---|---|---|---|
| Sued in host nation | Medium (a large legal fine, criminal proceedings, possible charges.) | Company appealed, and delayed court progress | low |
| Sued in host nation | Medium (a large legal fine, criminal proceedings, possible charges.) | Company boosted its stake in the contested areas, cleared from charges. | low |

International Court

In 2001, U.S. Supreme Court allowed Royal Dutch Shell to be sued in New York for allegedly instigating the torture and murder of leaders of human-rights movements by the former Nigerian military government, and for taking land for development without paying adequate compensation.

The suit was filed in 1996 in federal court in Manhattan by the families of Mr. Saro-Wiwa and other activists. The allegation were filed under U.S. Alien Tort Statute, which allows lawsuits against companies accused of involvement in human-rights violations anywhere in the world.[111]

In June of 2009, Shell announced its agreement with the plaintiff to settle the suit. The out-of-court settlement includes a $15.5 million compensation, with a $5 million trust fund for the families of environmental activists. By paying the compensation, Shell claims that it believes that the settlement is the beginning of a reconciliation process. Insisting on denying guilt of violating the human-rights of the Ogoni people, Shell claims they believe the right way forward is to focus on the future of the Ogoni people, instead of clearing Shell's name in court.[112]

Here, the legal pressure that activists put on Shell was successful in bring Shell's compensation, and their promise to focus on improving Ogoni community's welfare. Instead of ignoring and avoiding responsibility, Shell fulfilled its responsibility and paid fair amount of compensation. With these factors in consideration, this act of legal pressure, when compared to other instances, was rather effective.

In 2001, a class-action law suit filed in United States against Talisman Energy Inc. alleged that the company's complicity in human-rights abuses in Sudan. Carey D'Avino and Stephen Whinston, prominent U.S. lawyers, representing four Sudanese, argue that Talisman assisted human-rights abuses by the northern-based Islamic government against Christians and Animist populations in the South. The lawyers claimed that revenue from a Sudanese oil project, in which Talisman is a 25-percent partner, provides funds for the government's war efforts. The law suit is being launched under the U.S Alien Tort Claims Act, and was filed under a class-action complaint.[113] The Supreme Court allowed the suit in March of 2001, in which the suit officially alleged that the Nigerian Shell affiliate recruited the police and military to attack local villages and suppress organized opposition, as well as provided money, weapons and logistical support to the Nigerian military.[114] In its claim, the plaintiffs, the Presbyterian Church of Sudan sought damage for victims of Talisman's actions. The damage may exceed $1 billion.

In 2005, Denise Cote, a District Judge in New York, declined to certify the case as a class-action on behalf to the plaintiffs. Without that certification, the court will not proceed to the trial, dealing a fatal blow to the suit. Talisman announced that they were pleased with the result, denied the allegations and argued that its presence in the region was a force for good.[115] In this instance, then, the legal pressure did not achieve its intended purpose of having Talisman pay compensation to the victims. Instead of paying compensation, Talisman avoided it, and denied its crimes in the region. Considering these factors, the legal pressure in this case is evaluated as not effective.

In March of 2012, lawyers representing 11,000 Nigerians made a claim against Royal Dutch Shell at the U.K High Court. The lawsuit against Shell related to two oil spills in 2008, which caused damage to 49,000 fisherman and farmers of the Bodo community. The claim alleges that the oil spill had a devastating effect on the local land, mangroves and waterways and this has been so bad that the local fishing industry has ground to a halt.[116]Shell admitted that 400 barrels of oil in total were spilled in Bodo in 2008 as a result of operational failures, and a cleanup was completed in 2008. It also noted that since then, more oil has been spilled due to sabotage and theft.[117] Shell also announced that the oil spills "are deeply regrettable operational accidents, and they absolutely should have not happened. We (Shell) want to fairly compensate those who have been genuinely affected as quickly as possible, and cleanup all areas where oil has been spilled."[118]

In June of 2014, the U.K. based London Technological and Construction Court delivered judgment on preliminary issues raised in the legal action. The decision on preliminary issues has resolved a range of contentious issues, and planned for a full trial to take place in 2015.[119] The judgment found Shell to be responsible for taking reasonable step toward the safety of its pipelines, including measures of leak detection, as well as surveillance equipment and anti-tamper equipment. Shell, in response to the potential of a full-on legal disaster, has negotiated the amount of out-of-court compensation with the plaintiffs, but no decisions has been made yet.[120]

| Pressure | Potential Financial Loss if MNC ignore the pressure | Result | Effectiveness |
|---|---|---|---|
| Sued in United States | Medium (a large legal fine, criminal proceedings, possible charges.) | Company paid compensation in out-of-court settlement, set up trust fund for the victims, promised to improve the victim's community | High |
| Sued in United States | Medium (a large legal fine, criminal proceedings, possible charges.) | Class action was denied, Company won in court | Low |
| Sued in United Kingdom | Medium (a large legal fine, criminal proceedings, possible charges.) | Company suggested out-of-court settlement of compensation and cleanups in the region | High |

Although this case is still developing, by analyzing Shell's announcements, it is reasonable to say that it is willing and prepared to pay compensation, and to clean up the oil spill. The legal suit put on Shell has seen the company move from ignoring the oil spill to preparing to pay compensation and do cleanup. Considering these factors, this case of legal pressure would be evaluated as effective.

## Political Pressure

In March of 1999, Canada's Foreign Affairs Minister Lloyd Axworthy put pressure on Talisman, accusing the company of fueling the civil war in the region. Axworthy told a seminar attendees that he spoke to officials of Talisman and reminded them of the strategic place they occupy in Sudan, and their need to abide by the International Code of Conduct for Canadian Business, which calls for businesses to demonstrate ethical leadership and to do business throughout world in the same way they operate in Canada. "We should begin looking at how we can work directly on problems (in Sudan) like child slavery and social breakdown,"[121] said Axworthy to Talisman. In this case, the government of Canada is asserting pressure on Talisman in order to have it adopt a better set of policies that may improve the human-rights scene in Sudan. Given that there are no major economic or legal measures involved, this act of pressure can be seen as purely from political powers.

Jim Buckee, CEO of Talisman, said after the meeting with Axworthy that Talisman was prepared to sign Canada's code of ethics for companies abroad. "All of our discussions with Foreign Affairs have been very positive in terms of Talisman using whatever influence it has in Sudan and in participating with Foreign Affair in the peace process." Said Talisman spokesman David Mann.[122]In December 1999, Talisman announced its official adoption of the code of conduct. "Our board was pleased to adopt the International Code, which is in compliance with our long-standing policies of business conduct," said Jim Buckee.[123] "Talisman is committed to maintaining high standards of ethics everywhere it does business. We have also made substantial progress in meeting the other requests made by Mr. Axworthy and continue to support the efforts of the government of Canada towards peace in Sudan." With the adoption of the code of conduct, Talisman will also abide by provisions of the U.S. Foreign Corrupt Practices Act and the Canadian Corruption of Foreign Officials Act. The company will also start an education program for all employees, which requires employees to complete annual compliance certificates.[124]

In this instance, the pressure Canada's government asserted on Talisman was successful in changing Talisman's policies. The intention was to pressure Talisman to sign the Code of Conduct, and it's achieved that through having government officials meet with the decision-makers of Talisman. As a result of this act of political pressure, Talisman adopted a better human-rights measure. Considering these factors, this instance of political pressure was effective.

In November of 1995, South Africa's President Nelson Mandela called in Shell South Africa executives to complain that the oil group wasn't doing enough to exert pressure on the ruthless Nigerian regime. President Mandela questioned, very strongly, Shell's planned investment in a $3.6 billion LNG project.[125]Using forceful language, Mandela described Nigerian military leadership under General Sani Abacha as an "illegitimate, barbaric, arrogant dictatorship which has murdered activists using kangaroo courts and false evidence." He also warned Shell that he would take actions against the company in South Africa.[126] By warning Shell, President Mandela utilized his political power likely to move Shell away from a position of complicity with the Nigerian regime to one of influencing the human-rights situation in Nigeria in a positive way.

Shortly after President Mandela's announcements, John Drake, head of Shell South Africa sent a confidential letter to Mandela. In the letter, Shell offered to help set up a new private sector forum in Nigeria, with South Africa's oversight and support. It also offered access to a South African parliamentary delegation to inspect its oil and gas installations in Nigeria. When asked about whether Shell will be re-opening the operations in Ogoniland, Shell commented: "We will not return without the support of the whole community."[127] Shell never resumed its operations in Ogoniland, and eventually pulled out.

In this instance, South Africa's President Mandela successfully used his political power to influence Shell's behavior. With Shell agreeing to have better human-rights measures, as well as promising to not return to Ogoniland until the community supports its return, Mandela's demands and criticisms are mostly satisfied. Considering these factors, this instance of political pressure was effective in changing the company's behavior.

Organizing the data, we have:

| Pressure | Result | Effectiveness |
|---|---|---|
| Government official held meeting with Company leadership, urging to adopt codes of conducts | Company adopted codes of conducts | High |
| President of South Africa openly criticized and warned the company, urge better human-rights measures | Company adopt better human-rights measures, promised to not restart operations in the contested regions until community approves | High |

## Conclusion

As previously mentioned, this study has three main goals: 1) To identify, among three non-political pressures, the correlation between the magnitude of potential financial loss vis-à-vis the effectiveness of the pressure. 2) To rank the effectiveness of pressure. 3) To observe the dynamics of pressure within a case. The following table combines the data gathered in cases as an attempt to organize and analyze the cases. From left to right, the table first details the type of overarching mechanism, activist, legal, economic or political. The following column details the overall effectiveness of the overarching mechanism. The next column divides the mechanisms into types of pressure, the next one records the effectiveness of the pressure. Moving on to the right, it further divides the types of pressure into individual cases. The next two columns record the cases' potential financial loss as well as effectiveness. From right to left, the effectiveness aggregates and becomes the basis of evaluation for the next level.

For example, the effectiveness of each instance of Broad Basis activist pressure will form the rating for Broad Basis. The rating of Broad Basis will then combine with the rating of Narrow Basis, produced in the same fashion, to provide foundation for the rating for Activist mechanism. The column for potential financial loss is utilized to evaluate the relationship between magnitude of financial pressure and effectiveness of outcomes.

| Mechanism | Overall Effectiveness | Type of Pressure | Type effectiveness | Potential Financial Loss | Effectiveness |
|---|---|---|---|---|---|
| Activist | Medium Low | Broad Basis | Low | Low | Low |
| | | | | Low | Low |
| | | | | Low | Low |
| | | | | Low | Low |
| | | | | Low | Low |
| | | Narrow Basis | Medium Low | Medium | Medium |
| | | | | Low | Low |
| | | | | Low | Low |
| | | | | Low | Low |
| Economic | Medium-Low | Weak | Low | Medium | Low |
| | | | | Medium | Low |
| | | | | Medium | Low |
| | | | | Low | Low |
| | | Strong | Medium | High | Medium |
| | | | | High | Low |
| | | | | High | High |
| Legal | Medium | Home Nation | Medium-High | Medium | Medium |
| | | | | Medium | High |
| | | Host Nation | Low | Medium | Low |
| | | | | Medium | Low |
| | | International Court | Medium-High | Medium | High |
| | | | | Medium | Low |
| | | | | Medium | High |
| Political | High | Political warning | High | N/A | High |
| | | | | N/A | High |

Let's now use the information to answer our questions. Generally speaking, among the three mechanisms that have financial impact, higher potential of loss does lead to a higher likelihood of positive change in an MNC's decision making. Legal mechanism, on the other hand, may lead to high effectiveness with medium financial impact. This hints that EMNCs do not base their strategies only on financial grounds, as different outcomes happen on similar levels of potential financial loss. Overall, the aggregated data shows that Political mechanism has the highest effectiveness, followed in order of effectiveness by Legal, Economic and Activist mechanisms. Also, if ranked by the type of pressure, political warning ranks as the most effective, followed in order of effectiveness by legal pressure in company's home state, legal pressure in international courts, strong economic pressure, narrow basis activist pressures (ranked from high to low) and, equally ranked as lowest, host nation legal pressure, weak economic pressure and broad basis Naming and Shaming. The data supports the fourth hypothesis, where the political support is said to have a strong influence on company's decision making. Among the three non-political mechanisms, there is a clear indication that legal mechanisms can be the most effective. The strength of activist pressure, however, remains questionable and discredited.

Observing the above dynamics, one may come to the realization that the decision making process of EMNCs is not purely financial. Although financial impact does affect the likelihood for a company to respond responsibly, the highest potential financial loss fails to outperform legal and political mechanisms in terms of producing consistent positive responses. These findings indicate that EMNCs make their decisions both financially and politically.

Moving to the dynamics within cases, the following table is organized to reflect the order in which pressures took place in respective EMNCs. The column on the left is the year when said pressure took place. Columns to the right represent different companies. Instances of pressures are then categorized based on their year and the company it was intended for, with its effectiveness recorded next to it.

When looking at cases holistically, and chronologically, the distribution of effectiveness does not seem to have a strongly consistent pattern. Although, generally speaking, the earlier stages of development are filled with activist and economic pressures, there are instances with political actors interfering much earlier in the process, and instances of legal action preceding other types of pressure. The implication of this random distribution implies that a more effective pressure does not necessarily have to be adopted later than a less effective pressure, contrary to what many believe. It also means that the effectiveness of pressures do not need to be aggregated to reach high effectiveness. Activists, therefore, need to focus their resources and energy on the most effective types of pressure, like political pressure, home state legal pressure and International legal pressure.

There are three major limitations of this study. The first is its inability to look into company's decision making, as this type of information is not available to me. With no insight into the actual effects a specific pressure has on the decision maker's judgment, the study can't achieve absolute certainty of the effectiveness of a specific pressure. To remedy the lack of depth, then, this study has shown as many instances as the time and length allow, aiming to see a correlation among cases – This leads to the

| Year | Unocal | | Anvil | | Talisman | | Shell | |
|---|---|---|---|---|---|---|---|---|
| 1995 | Weak Economic | Low | Weak Economic Political Pressure | | Low / Strong Economic / Medium / High | | Weak Economic | Low |
| 1996 | Narrow Activist / Strong Economic | Low / Low | | | | | | |
| | Narrow Activist | Low | | | | | | |
| 1997 | | | Narrow Activist | Low | | | Broad Activist | Low |
| 1999 | | | | | Political Pressure | High | | |
| 2000 | | | | | Strong Economic | High | | |
| 2001 | Broad Activist / Broad Activist | | Low / Low | | International Court | Low | International Court | High |
| 2003 | Home State Court | High | | | | | | |
| 2005 | | | Broad Activist | Low | | | | |
| 2006 | Host State Court / Low | | Narrow Activist | Medium | | | Home State Court | Low |
| 2008 | | | | | | | Home State Court | Low |
| 2012 | | | | | | | International Court | High |

second limitation. If, with infinite amount of time and length to collect data on of more cases, this paper would serve to better expose evidence in support of its conclusions. The third limitation is from the types of source I've chosen. By relying on university library portals, the study has a built-in bias in that all the instances recorded in this paper come from news agencies and research institutions. I was not able to record an instance where activist interests were non-existent, given that all of the recording can be treated as a form of Naming and Shaming.

According to Keck and Sikknik, Transnational Advocacy Networks (TAN) in both domestic and international politics have the effect of issue-creating and agenda-setting, influencing state's discursive positions, changing institutional procedures, changing policy and influencing state behavior.[128] TAN can be seen as a type of activist mechanism, as they often adopt Naming and Shaming as their method to set agendas. Since the result of this study indicates that state pressure is the most effective type of pressure in changing a company's behavior, an important question arises –Would EMNC's activities come to the attention of the State without activist? If there isn't any TAN to raise the issue, will states act to address the company in question? The true effectiveness of Naming and Shaming may be different than how it was captured in this study, depending on whether state pressure functioned differently in cases where TAN was absent.

Given these limitations for this research, future studies might look more deeply into the mindset of the decision makers, in order to give specification to the actual corporate behavioral effects while under a given type of pressure. Also, future studies might spend more time and resources in collecting additional instances that broaden the sample base, and so create more reliability in the dataset. Last but not least, future studies could do more field research, collect first-hand data in cases that have not reach the eyes of the media, to see the essential value of activist pressures.

## Epilogue

Who are the true victims? The people? Or, the MNC?

It is easy for a study like this to achieve an intended purpose - to find the most effective method for the international community to pressure a company to do something that might improve the livelihood of people within its region of operations. It is easy to develop a tool to remedy the problems, but it becomes much more complex when we seek the root of the problem. It is often complicated, when trying to put absolute judgment on exactly who is to blame and then to determine the best way to address the problems.

In the international market, MNCs are confined by a daunting "race to the bottom" construct. Generally speaking, western companies adhere to a higher human-rights standard. However, they might be forced to lower their bar just to stay competitive in the world market, given that less scrupulous MNCs from other parts of the world do not devote as many resources to social development, in order to lower their costs. Since higher production costs would make them less price-competitive, all MNCs may be forced to pay bribes, comply with questionable actions of host governments, or cut costs in social programs. The construct, therefore, dictated that the MNCs cut costs whenever possible. By this, the MNCs do not have an option but to comply, if they wish to keep operating.

But why does the Extractive industry, in particular, face more severe violations than other industries? I believe that it is because it is relatively easy for a MNC to cut costs thru methods that may have negative impacts on human-rights. Due to the unique qualities of many of the regions EMNCs operate in, many irresponsible actions are allowed, if not, encouraged by host governments. The market and legal systems in many of the states and regions are not as well developed as their counterparts in more advanced regions of the world. The rights of its people were not well-protected to begin with. For example, the Ogoni people will be oppressed by Nigerian government regardless of Shell's involvement. These factors render the Extractive industry more vulnerable to irresponsible acts, and it is not in the power of MNCs to change problematic regimes.

With these hard-to-move, powerful constructs pinning opposition to the wall, it is not practical to expect that any NGO, or business, or national government, by itself, can shake the foundation of the problem of EMNCS' human-rights violations. From a business perspective, then, it is of necessity for firms to carefully analyze and study the region's social and political situation. The existence of businesses in a region, I believe, is beneficial to the development of infrastructure, through adoption and use of legal codes, public projects or through the safety and security that might and should be provided to its local people. Hence, commerce is helping peace as long as rights violations are strongly curtailed and eliminated early, with due diligence paid to the given state's political risks.

# Endnotes

1.  I would like to thank Professor Robert English, Professor Nina Rathbun and Professor Douglas Becker for their unrelenting support and patience as advisors to this project. I would also like to thank my classmates, for without their support and encouragement, I may not have the endurance to complete the project. Last but not least, I would like to thank Robert Robinson, my step-father, for patiently editing.

2.  For an overview of the case, please refer to Talisman lawsuit (re Sudan). (n.d.). Retrieved October 8, 2014, from http://business-humanrights.org/en/talisman-lawsuit-re-sudan#c9318

3.  For example, Visser, W. (2010). *The World Guide to CSR a Country-by-Country Analysis of Corporate Sustainability and Responsibility*. Sheffield, U.K.: Greenleaf Pub.

4.  Also for examples and overviews of instances of violations, please refer to UN Global compact's database: https://www.unglobalcompact.org/Issues/conflict_prevention/meetings_and_workshops/Reg_stability.html

5.  Here are the details regarding the meeting, and key announcements: The Global Compact Leaders' Summit - 24 June 2004, UN Headquarters. (2004, June 24). Retrieved October 8, 2014, from https://www.unglobalcompact.org/NewsandEvents/event_archives/global_compact_leaders_summit.html

6.  For the document itself, Norms on the Responsibilities of Transnational Corporations and Other Business Enterprises with Regard to Human-rights. (2003, August 13). Retrieved October 8, 2014, from http://www1.umn.edu/humanrts/business/norms-Aug2003.html, for the approval: Sub-Commission resolution 2003/16. (2003, August 13). Retrieved October 8, 2014, from http://www1.umn.edu/humanrts/business/res2003-16.html.

7.  Burgerman, S. (2001). *Moral Victories: How Activists Provoke Multilateral Action*. Ithaca: Cornell University Press.

8.  Politics Beyond the State: Environmental Activism and World Civic Politics, Paul Wapner, *World Politics*, Vol. 47, No. 3 (Apr., 1995), pp. 311-340

9.  Weber, M. (1965). *Politics as a Vocation*. Philadelphia: Fortress Press.

10.  Keck, M., & Sikkink, K. (1998). *Activists Beyond Borders: Advocacy networks in international politics*. Ithaca, N.Y.: Cornell University Press.

11 Sticks and Stones: Naming and Shaming the Human-rights Enforcement Problem *International Organization*, 2008, vol. 62, issue 04, pages 689-716, *http://econpapers.repec.org/article/cupintorg/v_3a62_3ay_3a2008_3ai_3a04_3ap_3a689-716_5f08.htm*

12.  Duckworth, H., & Moore, R. (2010). *Social Responsibility: Failure Mode Effects and Analysis*. Boca Raton, FL: CRC Press/Taylor & Francis.

13.  Burgerman, S. *Moral Victories*.

14.  Cragg, W. (2010). Business and Human-rights: A Principle and Value-Based Analysis. *The Oxford Handbook of Business Ethics*.

15.  Ruggie, J. (2013). *Just Business: Multinational Corporations and Human-rights*. New York: W.W Norton& Company.

16.  Janis, M. (1999). *An Introduction to International Law* (3rd ed.). Gaithersburg [Md.: Aspen Law & Business.

17.  Hugo Grotius, *The Rights of War and Peace*, edited and with an Introduction by Richard Tuck, from the Edition by Jean Barbeyrac (Indianapolis: Liberty Fund, 2005). 3 vols. Wednesday, Oc-

tober 08, 2014.

    18. Bentham, J. (2007). *An Introduction to the Principles of Morals and Legislation* (Dover ed.). Mineola, N.Y.: Dover Publications.

    19. Austin, John, *Lectures on Jurisprudence and the Philosophy of Positive Law* (St. Clair Shores, MI: Scholarly Press, 1977)

    20. Koskenniemi, M. (2005). *From Apology to Utopia the Structure of International Legal Argument.* Cambridge, UK: Cambridge University Press.

    21. Howland, T. (2007). The Multi-State Responsibility for Extraterritorial Violations of Economic Social and Cultural Rights. *Denver Journal of International Law & Policy; Summer/Fall2007, Vol. 35*(Issue 3/4), P389

    22. The World Conference on Human-rights and the Vienna Declaration and Programme of Action. (n.d.). *International Journal of Refugee Law,* 597-600.

    23. Howland, T. (2007). The Multi-State Responsibility for Extraterritorial Violations of Economic Social and Cultural Rights. *Denver Journal of International Law & Policy;Summer/Fall2007, Vol. 35*(Issue 3/4)

    24. Esther M.J. Schouten, (2007) "Defining the corporate social responsibility of business from international law", *Managerial Law,* Vol. 49 Iss: 1/2, pp.16 - 36

    25. Tomuschat, C. (2008). *Human-rights Between Idealism and Realism* (2nd ed.). Oxford: Oxford University Press.

    26. Bantekas, I. (2004). *Corporate Social Responsibility in International Law.* Boston University International Law Journal 22.

    27. 28 U.S. Code § 1350 - Alien's action for tort. (n.d.). Retrieved October 8, 2014, from http://www.law.cornell.edu/uscode/text/28/1350.

    28. McCorquodale, R. (2012). Corporate Social Responsibility and International Human-rights Law. *Journal of Business Ethics,* 385-400.

    29. Dillard, J., Haynes, K., & Murray, A. (2013). *Corporate Social Responsibility: A Research Handbook.* London: Routledge.

    30. Hearit, K. (2007). Corporate Deception and Fraud: The Case for an Ethical Apologia. *The Debate Over Corporate Social Responsibility,* P. 167-176.

    31. Seeger, M, Hipfel, S. (2007). Legal versus Ethical Arguments: Contexts for Corporate Social Responsibilty. *The Debate Over Corporate Social Responsibility,* P. 155-165.

    32. Ritz, D (2007). Can Corporate Personhood be Socially Responsible? *The Debate Over Corporate Social Responsibility,* P. 190-203.

    33. Cambourg, P. (2006). *Corporate accountability and trust: Thoughts from 12 top managers.* Paris: Mazars

    34. Ruggie, J. *Just Business.*

    35. Gates, D., & Steane, P. (n.d.). Historical origins and development of economic rationalism.*Journal of Management History,* 330-358.

    36. Weber, M. (1958). *The Protestant Ethic and the Spirit of Capitalism* ([Student's ed.). New York: Scribner.

    37. Frynas, J. (n.d.). Political Instability And Business: Focus On Shell In Nigeria. *Third World Quarterly,* 457-478.

    38. Tawney, R.H. (1938), *Religion and the Rise of Capitalism,* Penguin, West Drayton.

    39. Coleman, W. and Hagger, A. (2001), *Exasperating Calculators: the Rage Over Economic Rationalism and the Campaign Against Australian Economists,* Macleay Press, Sydney

40. De Malynes, G. (1622), *The Maintenance of Free Trade*, William Shefford, London, available at: www.efm.bris.u/het/malynes/malynes.txt

41. Johnson, H.G. (1971), "The Keynesian Revolution and the Monetarist Counter-revolution", *Amercian Economic Review*, Vol. 61, pp. 1-14

42. Berstein, M.A. (2003), "American economists and the marginalist revolution: notes on the intellectual and social context of professionalization", *Journal of Historical Sociology*, Vol. 16 No. 1, pp. 135-80

43. Ibid

44. Tawney, R.H. (1938), *Religion and the Rise of Capitalism*, Penguin, West Drayton

45. Friedman, M., & Leube, K. (1987). *The Essence of Friedman*. Stanford, Calif.: Hoover Institution Press.

46. The Pyramid of corporate social responsibility, Business and Society. (1991). *Business Horizons, Volume 34*(Issue 4), 39-48.

47. Vogel, D. (2006). *The market for Virtue: The Potential and Limits of Corporate Social Responsibility* (Paperback ed.). Washington, D.C.: Brookings Institution Press.

48. Aune, J. (2007). How to Read Milton Friedman: Corporate social responsibility and today's capitalisms. *The Debate over Corporate Social Responsibility.*, P. 207-218.

49. Anselmi, P. (2011). *Values and Stakeholders in an Era of Social Responsibility: Cut-throat Competition?* Houndmills, Basingstoke, Hampshire: Palgrave Macmillan.

50. Ghoshal, S., & Birkinshaw, J. (2005). *Sumantra Ghoshal on Management: A Force for Good.* New York: FT Prentice Hall/Pearson Education.

51. It is important to note that activists play a critical role in bringing the EMNC onto the courtroom, as well as boycotts. To distinguish the hypothesis, this study focuses on the mechanism chosen by the activist. Activist may choose to use Naming and Shaming, legal suits as well as organized boycotts. Since the rationale of these three mechanisms comes from different theoretical backgrounds, they will be treated as "not H1", even if initiated by activists. In other words, activism alone cannot satisfy H1. Activist must adopt non-legalist, non-economic mechanisms to be included as H1.

52. Morgenthau, H. (1975), *World Politics and the Politics of Oil*, in G. Eppen (ed.), Energy: The Policy Issue, Chicago: University of Chicago Press.

53. Waltz, K. (1979), *Theory of International Politics*, New York: McGraw-Hill

54. Jervis, R. (1994), "Hans Morgenthau, Realism, and the Scientific Study of International Politics", *Social Research*, 61(4), 853-77

55. Bağce, E. (2003). Was Realism and State Really Sacked by Capitalism. *METU Studies in Development*, 139-161.

56. Patey, Luke Anthony, "State Rules: Oil Companies and Armed Conflict in Sudan,*" Third World Quarterly*, 2007, Volume 28, Issue 5, pp 997-1016.

57. That is, the reaction in between mechanism 1 and mechanism 2 will be treated as the effect of mechanism 1. If there is no reaction caused by mechanism 1, it is concluded that mechanism 1 has no significant effect. Often times, however, in a news article or report, the writer already linked the pressure and reaction. They will summarize the events before a change of behavior, and they will note the most likely mechanism that has caused the change. There are, also, reports of failed attempts of certain pressure, therefore, this sort of articles will be used to show the ineffectiveness of that article. The limitation of this study is in the limitation of the articles available to public sources.

58. The Shell, Anvil and Talisman cases contain all three mechanisms, they are good cases to test the absolute strength of a certain mechanism, Also, they contain many instances pressures of

various strength, through which we may observe the effect of a variance of strength on the reaction. There is, also, significantly more analysis written for these cases.

59.  Leyden, Fleur, ABC documentary on Congo hits Anvil, *The Courier- Mail,* page 39, News Digital Media, Jun 8, 2005

60.  Shaw, Meaghan, Mining firm implicated in massacre, *The Age*, page 4, Fairfax Digital, Jun 7, 2005

61 Aust miner denies role in deaths, *Papua New Guinea Post*, page 23, News Digital Media, Jun 7, 2005

62.  Leyden, Fleur, ABC documentary on Congo hits Anvil, *The Courier- Mail*, page 39, News Digital Media, Jun 8, 2005

63. Fed: Aust mining company says it played no part in Congo deaths, AAP General News Wire, page 1, Australian Associated Press Pty limited, Jun 6, 2005

64.  Amnesty International Sudan -- Talisman Energy must do more to protect human-rights, M2 Presswire, page 1,  M2 Communiactions, May 1, 2001

65.  Begos, Kevin, Oil Company Denies Role in Sudan Strife; Exploration Fuels Civil War, Activists Report, *Winston-Salem Journal,* page 10, Media General, Inc, April 24, 2002

66.  Amnesty International's Ad Campaign Questions Shell's Role In Nigeria, *Sun Reporter*, Volume 52, Issue 7, page 4, Feb 15, 1996

67.  Ibid.

68.  WCC report documents oppression of people in Nigeria's Ogoniland, *New York Amsterdam News*, page 2, March 29, 1997

69.  Church Group Attacks Nigeria, Shell for Problems in Oil Region, *Chicago Tribune*, page 8, Tribune Publishing Company LLC, January 7, 1997

70.  Ibrahim, Youssef M, Shell Shareholders Reject A Human-rights Initiative, *New York Times*, page D4, May 15, 1997

71.  Church leaders want Talisman out of Sudan, *Daily Commercial News and Construction Record* 74.76, A15, April 18, 2001

72.  Frank, Charles, Talisman again feeling the heat over Sudan Churches slam company, but there's more to the issue than meets the eye [Final Edition], *Calgary Herald*, E1, April 12, 2001

73.  Nguyen, Lily, Talisman review of Sudan venture assailed Doesn't answer human-rights concerns, critics say, *The Globe and Mail*, B6, April 11, 2001

74.  Vaccaro, Anthony, Bloodshed in the Congo, *The Northern Miner,* Volume 92, Issue 11, page 1, Business Information Group, May 5, 2006

75.  Ibid

76.  Ibid

77.  Shell Based for Nigeria Investment, The Associated Press, Sun Sentinel, 8D, Tribune Publishing Company, May 15, 1996

78.  Taylor, Cathy, Unocal's role in Myanmar brings protest [MORNING Edition], *Orange County Register*, C01, June 4, 1996

79.  Ibid

80.  ANC-Aligned Group Calls for Shell Boycott Over Nigeria Project, *Wall Street Journal*, page 4, December 20, 1995

81.  Taxi forum says no to boycott of Shell, M2 Presswire, page 1, Normans Media Ltd, December 20, 1995

82.  ANC-Aligned Group Calls for Shell Boycott Over Nigeria Project , *Wall Street Journal*,

page 4, December 20, 1995

    83.  Schevitz, Tanya, Berkeley boycotts Burma It's mostly symbolic, co-sponsor admits [FOURTH Edition], *San Francisco Examiner,* A 7, March 1, 1995

    84.  Iritani, Evelyn, Feeling the Heat Unocal Defends Myanmar Gas Pipeline Deal [Home Edition], *Los Angeles Times,* page 1, February 20, 1995

    85.  Evenson, Brad, Nigerian dissident calls for Shell boycott, *The Ottawa Citizen,* A13, August 23, 1996

    86.  One-day Shell boycott urged by Greenpeace - Canadian Press, *Times – Colonist,* page 1, November 16, 1995

    87. Woodyard, Chris, Sierra Club calling for boycott of Shell over Nigeria, *Houston Chronicle,* page 1, December 8, 1995

    88.  Mortished, Carl, Boycott threatens Shell gas project;Nigeria;Business, *The Times,* page 1, November 13, 1995

    89.  Ibid

    90.  Senate panel approves sanctions against Burma, *Wall Street Journal,* B3, June 19, 1996

    91.  Morton, Peter, Cattaneo, Claudia, Alberts, Sheldon, U.S. imposes sanctions on Talisman Sudan project Contrast with Canada [National Edition], *National Post,* A.1, February 17, 2000

    92.  U.S. sanctions Talisman, oil companies over Sudan, *Examiner,* 14, February 17, 2000

    93.  Sudan Talisman packs up its troubles, *Petroleum Economist,* page 37, August, 2001

    94.  Ibid

    95.  Shell's 'Unique' Civil Legal Suit in the Netherlands, International Newsstand, Allafrica.com, Al Bawaba (Middle East) Ltd., October 17, 2012.

    96.  Varma, Subodh, Shell held responsible for oil pollution in Nigeria by Dutch court, *The Times of India,* February 1, 2013.

    97.  Shell on Trial in Netherlands Over Pollution in Nigeria, International Newsstand, Allafrica.com, Al Bawaba (Middle East) Ltd., October 12, 2012.

    98.  Williams, Selina, Apparent Win for Shell in Nigeria Spill Cases, Wall Street Journal Online, Dow Jones and Company Inc., January 30, 2013.

    99.  Cluskey, Peter, Dutch court says Shell partly responsible for Nigeria spills, *Irish Times,* page 17, January 31, 2013.

    100.  Tam, Pui-Wing, Hearing Set in Case Alleging Unocal Brutality, *Wall Street Journal,* A8, June 10, 2003

    101.  Kravets, David, Unocal battles atrocity lawsuit [HOME Edition], *Daily Breeze,* C1, June 18, 2003

    102.  Chavez, Paul, Judge allows human-rights lawsuit against Unocal to proceed, Associated Press, page 1, September 15, 2004

    103.  Bruno, Kenny, Cheverie, John, Burmese villagers face Unocal in US court. *The Bangkok Post,* page 1, September 28, 2002

    104.  Alden, Edward, Arnold, Martin, Cameron, Doug, Unocal pays out in Burma abuse case [London 1st Ed.], *Financial Times,* page 12, December 14, 2004

    105.  Chavez, Paul, Unocal to pay villagers, fund improvements to settle rights case, Associated Press, page 1, December 14, 2004

    106.  Nigeria Court Fines Shell $40 Million for 1970 Spill, Environment News Service, June 2, 2000

    107.  Anvil Mining Congo receives notification from Congolese Military Court in relation to

the Kilwa incident in October 2004, Canada Newswire, page 1, PR Newswire Association LLC, October 18, 2006

108. Lewis, David, Congo wants Anvil staffers tried in war crimes case, *The Globe and Mail*, B15, October 17, 2006

109. Moore, Lynn, Anvil to boost stake in Congo venture [Final Edition], *The Gazette*, B3, January 11, 2007

110. Anvil and its Employees Acquitted in Kilwa Incident, Canada Newswire, page 1, PR Newswire Association LLC., June 28, 2007

111. Vicini, James, Nigerian tribe can sue Shell in US, court says [FINAL Edition], *The Scotsman*, page 13, March 27, 2001

112. Balduaf, Scott, Cheers in Nigeria after Shell agrees to pay $15.5 million, *The Christian Science Monitor*, page 6, June 9, 2009

113. Nguyen, Uly, Suit filed in U.S. against Talisman, The Globe and Mail, B3, *The Globe and Mail*, November 9, 2001

114. U.S. trial is granted in Nigeria case Slain activists opposed Shell exploration, *Houston Chronicle*, page 4, March 27, 2001

115. Harding, Jon, Cattane, Claudia, Talisman wins latest Sudan ruling Calgary energy firm accused in war crimes case, *National Post*, A7, March 29, 2005

116. Croft, Jane, Nigerians to launch action against Shell in UK court, *The Financial Times*, page 16, March 23, 2012

117. Shirbon, Estelle, Shell sued over Nigerian pipeline spills, *Calgary Herald*, D4, March 24, 2012

118. Community Fights Shell in UK Court Hearing, International Newsstand, Allafrica.com, Al Bawaba (Middle East) Ltd., April 30, 2014

119. UK Court to Deliver Preliminary Judgment On Suit Against Shell, International Newsstand, Allafrica.com, Al Bawaba (Middle East) Ltd., June 19, 2014

120. Shell Risks Fresh Compensation Claims After UK Court Ruling, International Newsstand, Allafrica.com, Al Bawaba (Middle East) Ltd., June 24, 2014

121. Harvey, Bob, Feds pressure Talisman Oil Axworthy screens firm's role in Sudan, *The Windsor Star*, A10, March 18, 1999

122. Tricky, Mike, Talisman, Axworthy move closer on Sudan [Final Edition], *Sault Star*, A5, November 5, 1999

123. Laverty, Gene, Talisman adopts ethics code [Final Edition], *Calgary Herald*, D2, December 11, 1999

124. Talisman Adopts International Code of Ethics for Canadian Business, PR Newswire, page 1, PR Newswire Association LLC, December 10, 1999

125. Mandela faults Shell leaders about Nigeria, *Dallas Morning News*, 9A, November 21, 1995

126. Mandela presses for tougher measures against Nigeria [Final Edition], *Kingston Whig*, page 22, November 27, 1995

127. Ghazi, Polly, Worried Shell seeks Mandela's support Oil giant defends Nigerian links, *The Guardian*, page 22, December 3, 1995

128. Keck, M., & Sikkink, K. (1998). *Activists beyond borders: Advocacy networks in international politics*. Ithaca, N.Y.: Cornell University Press.

# References

## Literature Review

28 U.S. Code § 1350 Alien's action for tort. (n.d.). Retrieved October 8, 2014, from http://www.law.cornell.edu/uscode/text/28/1350.

Anselmi, P. (2011). *Values and stakeholders in an era of social responsibility: Cutthroat competition?* Houndmills, Basingstoke, Hampshire: Palgrave Macmillan.

Aune, J. (2007). *How to read Milton Friedman: Corporate social responsibility and today's capitalisms.* The Debate over Corporate Social Responsibility, P. 207218.

Austin, John, *Lectures on Jurisprudence and the Philosophy of Positive Law* (St. Clair Shores, MI: Scholarly Press, 1977)

Bantekas, I. (2004). Corporate Social Responsibility in International Law. *Boston University International Law Journal 22.*

Bağce, E. (2003). Was realism and state really sacked by capitalism? *METU Studies in Development*, 139161.

Bentham, J. (2007). *An introduction to the principles of morals and legislation* (Dover ed.). Mineola, N.Y.: Dover Publications.

Berstein, M.A. (2003), "American economists and the marginalist revolution: notes on the intellectual and social context of professionalization", *Journal of Historical Sociology*, Vol. 16 No. 1, pp. 13580

Burgerman, S. (2001). *Moral victories: How activists provoke multilateral action.* Ithaca: Cornell University Press.

Cambourg, P. (2006). *Corporate accountability and trust: Thoughts from 12 top managers.* Paris: Mazars..

Coleman, W. and Hagger, A. (2001), *Exasperating Calculators: the Rage over Economic Rationalism and the Campaign Against Australian Economists*, Macleay Press, Sydney

Cragg, W. (2010). *Business and Human-rights: A Principle and Value-Based Analysis.* The Oxford Handbook of Business Ethics.

De Malynes, G. (1622), The Maintenance of Free Trade, William Shefford, London, available at: www.efm.bris.u/het/malynes/malynes.txt

Dillard, J., Haynes, K., & Murray, A. (2013). *Corporate social responsibility: A research handbook.* London: Routledge.

Duckworth, H., & Moore, R. (2010). S*ocial responsibility: Failure mode effects and analysis.* Boca Raton, FL: CRC Press/Taylor & Francis.

Esther M.J. Schouten, (2007) "Defining the corporate social responsibility of business from international law", *Managerial Law*, Vol. 49 Iss: 1/2, pp.16 36

Friedman, M., & Leube, K. (1987). *The essence of Friedman.* Stanford, Calif.: Hoover Institution Press.

Frynas, J. (n.d.). Political Instability And Business: Focus On Shell In Nigeria. *Third World Quarterly*, 457478.

Gates, D., & Steane, P. (n.d.). Historical origins and development of economic rationalism. *Journal of Management History*, 330358.

Ghoshal, S., & Birkinshaw, J. (2005). *Sumantra Ghoshal on management: A force for good*. New York: FT Prentice Hall/Pearson Education.

Hearit, K. (2007). *Corporate Deception and Fraud: The Case for an Ethical Apologia*. The Debate over Corporate Social Responsibility, P. 167176.

Howland, T. (2007). The MultiState Responsibility for Extraterritorial Violations of Economic Social and Cultural Rights. *Denver Journal of International Law & Policy*; Summer/Fall 2007, Vol. 35(Issue 3/4)

Hugo Grotius, *The Rights of War and Peace*, edited and with an Introduction by Richard Tuck, from the Edition by Jean Barbeyrac (Indianapolis: Liberty Fund, 2005). 3 vols. October 08, 2014.

Janis, M. (1999). *An introduction to international law* (3rd ed.). Gaithersburg [Md.: Aspen Law & Business.

Jervis, R. (1994), "Hans Morgenthau, Realism, and the Scientific Study of International Politics", *Social Research*, 61(4), 85377

Johnson, H.G. (1971), "The Keynesian revolution and the monetarist counterrevolution", *Amercian Economic Review*, Vol. 61, pp. 114

Keck, M., & Sikkink, K. (1998). *Activists beyond borders: Advocacy networks in international politics*. Ithaca, N.Y.: Cornell University Press.

Koskenniemi, M. (2005). *From apology to Utopia the structure of international legal argument*. Cambridge, UK: Cambridge University Press.

McCorquodale, R. (2012). Corporate Social Responsibility and International Humanrights Law. *Journal of Business Ethics*, 385400.

Morgenthau, H. (1975), *World Politics and the Politics of Oil, in G. Eppen (ed.), Energy: The Policy Issue*, Chicago: University of Chicago Press.

Patey, Luke Anthony, State Rules: Oil Companies and Armed Conflict in Sudan, *Third World Quarterly*, 2007, Volume 28, Issue 5, pp 9971016.

Ritz, D (2007). *Can Corporate Personhood be Socially Responsible?* The Debate over Corporate Social Responsibility, P. 190203.

Ruggie, J. (2013). *Just business: Multinational corporations and human-rights*. New York: W.W Norton& Company.

Seeger, M, Hipfel, S. (2007). *Legal versus Ethical Arguments: Contexts for Corporate Social Responsibilty*. The Debate over Corporate Social Responsibility, P. 155165.

Sticks and Stones: Naming and Shaming the Human-rights Enforcement Problem International Organization, 2008, vol. 62, issue 04, pages 689-716,   , http://econpapers.repec.org/article/cupintorg/v_3a62_3ay_3a2008_3ai_3a04_3ap_3a689-716_5f08.htm

Tawney, R.H. (1938), *Religion and the Rise of Capitalism*, Penguin, West Drayton

*The Pyramid of corporate social responsibility, Business and Society.* (1991). Business Horizons, Volume 34(Issue 4), 3948.

The World Conference on Humanrights and the Vienna Declaration and Programme of Action. (n.d.). International Journal of Refugee Law, 597600.

Tomuschat, C. (2008). *Humanrights between idealism and realism* (2nd ed.). Oxford: Oxford University Press.

Vogel, D. (2006). *The market for virtue: The potential and limits of corporate social responsibility* (Paperback ed.). Washington, D.C.: Brookings Institution Press.

Waltz, K. (1979), *Theory of International Politics*, New York: McGrawHill

Wapner, Paul (1995) Politics Beyond the State: Environmental Activism and World Civic Politics, Paul Wapner, *World Politics*, Vol. 47, No. 3 (Apr., 1995), pp. 311-340

Weber, M. (1958). *The Protestant ethic and the spirit of capitalism* ([Student's ed.). New York: Scribner.

Weber, M. (1965). *Politics as a vocation*. Philadelphia: Fortress Press.

# Case Study

Alden, Edward, Arnold, Martin, Cameron, Doug, Unocal pays out in Burma abuse case [London, 1st ed], *Financial Times*, page 12, December 14, 2004

Amnesty International Sudan  Talisman Energy must do more to protect humanrights, M2 Presswire, page 1, M2 Communications, May 1, 2001

Amnesty International's Ad Campaign Questions Shell's Role in Nigeria, *Sun Reporter*, Volume 52, Issue 7, page 4, Feb 15, 1996

ANC Aligned Group Calls for Shell Boycott over Nigeria Project, *Wall Street Journal*, page 4, December 20, 1995

Anvil and its Employees Acquitted in Kilwa Incident, Canada Newswire, page 1, PR Newswire Association LLC., June 28, 2007

Anvil Mining Congo receives notification from Congolese Military Court in relation to the Kilwa incident in October 2004, Canada Newswire, page 1, PR Newswire Association LLC, October 18, 2006

Aust miner denies role in deaths, Papua New Guinea Post, page 23, News Digital Media, June 7, 2005

Balduaf, Scott, Cheers in Nigeria after Shell agrees to pay $15.5 million, *The Christian Science Monitor*, page 6, June 9, 2009

Begos, Kevin, Oil Company Denies Role in Sudan Strife; Exploration Fuels Civil War, Activists Report, *WinstonSalem Journal*, page 10, April 24, 2002

Bruno, Kenny, Cheverie, John, Burmese villagers face Unocal in US court. *The Bangkok Post*, page 1, September 28, 2002

Chavez, Paul, Judge allows humanrights lawsuit against Unocal to proceed, Associated Press, page 1, September 15, 2004

Chavez, Paul, Unocal to pay villagers, fund improvements to settle rights case, Associated Press, page 1, December 14, 2004

Church Group Attacks Nigeria, Shell for Problems in Oil Region, *Chicago Tribune*, page 8, January 7, 1997

Church leaders want Talisman out of Sudan, *Daily Commercial News and Construction Record* 74.76, A15, April 18, 2001

Cluskey, Peter, Dutch court says Shell partly responsible for Nigeria spills, *Irish Times*, page 17, January 31, 2013

Community Fights Shell in UK Court Hearing, International Newsstand, Allafrica.com, Al Bawaba (Middle East) Ltd., April 30, 2014

Croft, Jane, Nigerians to launch action against Shell in UK court, *The Financial Times*, page 16, March 23, 2012

Evenson, Brad, Nigerian dissident calls for Shell boycott, *The Ottawa Citizen*, A13, August 23, 1996

Fed: Aust mining company says it played no part in Congo deaths, AAP General News Wire, page 1, Australian Associated Press Pty limited, June 6, 2005

Frank, Charles, Talisman again feeling the heat over Sudan Churches Slam Company, but there's more to the issue than meets the eye [Final Edition], *Calgary Herald*, E1, April 12, 2001

Ghazi, Polly, Worried Shell seeks Mandela's support Oil giant defends Nigerian links, *The Guardian*, page 22, December 3, 1995

Harding, Jon, Cattane, Claudia, Talisman wins latest Sudan ruling Calgary energy firm accused in war crimes case, *National Post*, A7, March 29, 2005

Harvey, Bob, Feds pressure Talisman Oil Axworthy screens firm's role in Sudan, *The Windsor Star*, A10, March 18, 1999

Ibrahim, Youssef M, Shell Shareholders Reject A Humanrights Initiative, *New Yrok Times*, page D4, May 15, 1997

Iritani, Evelyn, Feeling the Heat Unocal Defends Myanmar Gas Pipeline Deal [Home Edition], *Los Angeles Times*, page 1, February 20, 1995

Kravets, David, Unocal battles atrocity lawsuit [HOME Edition], *Daily Breeze*, C1, June 18, 2003

Laverty, Gene, Talisman adopts ethics code [Final Edition], *Calgary Herald*, D2, December 11, 1999

Lewis, David, Congo wants Anvil staffers tried in war crimes case, *The Globe and Mail*, B15, October 17, 2006

Leyden, Fleur, ABC documentary on Congo hits Anvil, *The Courier Mail*, page 39, June 8, 2005

Mandela faults Shell leaders about Nigeria, *Dallas Morning News*, 9A, November 21, 1995

Mandela presses for tougher measures against Nigeria [Final Edition], *Kingston Whig*, page 22, November 27, 1995

Moore, Lynn, Anvil to boost stake in Congo venture [Final Edition], *The Gazette*, B3, January 11, 2007

Mortished, Carl, Boycott threatens Shell gas project; Nigeria; Business, *The Times*, page 1, November 13, 1995

Morton, Peter, Cattaneo, Claudia, Alberts, Sheldon, U.S. imposes sanctions on Talisman Sudan project Contrast with Canada [National Edition], *National Post*, A.1, February 17, 2000

Nguyen, Lily, Talisman review of Sudan venture assailed doesn't answer humanrights concerns, critics say, *The Globe and Mail*, B6, April 11, 2001

Nguyen, Uly, Suit filed in U.S. against Talisman, *The Globe and Mail*, B3, November 9, 2001

Nigeria Court Fines Shell $40 Million for 1970 Spill, Environment News Service, June 2, 2000

Oneday Shell boycott urged by Greenpeace Canadian Press, *Times – Colonist*, page 1, November 16, 1995

Schevitz, Tanya, Berkeley boycotts Burma It's mostly symbolic, cosponsor admits [Fourth Edition], *San Francisco Examiner*, A 7, March 1, 1995

Senate panel approves sanctions against Burma, *Wall Street Journal*, B3, June 19, 1996

Shaw, Meaghan, Mining firm implicated in massacre, *The Age*, page 4, Fairfax Digital, June 7, 2005

Shells Based for Nigeria Investment, the Associated Press, *Sun Sentinel*, 8D, May 15, 1996

Shell on Trial in Netherlands Over Pollution in Nigeria, International Newsstand, Allafrica. com, Al Bawaba (Middle East) Ltd., October 12, 2012.

Shell Risks Fresh Compensation Claims After UK Court Ruling, International Newsstand, Allafrica.com, Al Bawaba (Middle East) Ltd., June 24, 2014

Shell's 'Unique' Civil Legal Suit in the Netherlands, International Newsstand, Allafrica.com, Al Bawaba (Middle East) Ltd., October 17, 2012.

Shirbon, Estelle, Shell sued over Nigerian pipeline spills, *Calgary Herald*, D4, March 24, 2012

Sudan Talisman packs up its troubles, *Petroleum Economist*, page 37, August, 2001

Talisman Adopts International Code of Ethics for Canadian Business, PR Newswire, page 1, December 10, 1999

Tam, PuiWing, Hearing Set in Case Alleging Unocal Brutality, *Wall Street Journal*, A8, June 10, 2003

Taxi forum says no to boycott of Shell, M2 Presswire, page 1, Normans Media Ltd, December 20, 1995

Taylor, Cathy, Unocal's role in Myanmar brings protest [MORNING Edition], *Orange County Register*, C01, June 4, 1996

Tricky, Mike, Talisman, Axworthy move closer on Sudan [Final Edition], *Sault Star*, A5, November 5, 1999

U.S. sanctions Talisman, oil companies over Sudan, *Examiner*, 14, February 17, 2000

U.S. trial is granted in Nigeria case Slain activists opposed Shell exploration, *Houston Chronicle*, page 4, March 27, 2001

UK Court to Deliver Preliminary Judgment On Suit Against Shell, International Newsstand, Allafrica.com, Al Bawaba (Middle East) Ltd., June 19, 2014

Vaccaro, Anthony, Bloodshed in the Congo, *The Northern Miner*, Volume 92, Issue 11, page 1, May 5, 2006

Varma, Subodh, Shell held responsible for oil pollution in Nigeria by Dutch court, The *Times of India*, February 1, 2013

Vicini, James, Nigerian tribe can sue Shell in US, court says [FINAL Edition], *The Scotsman*, page 13, March 27, 2001

WCC report documents oppression of people in Nigeria's Ogoniland, *New York Amsterdam News*, page 2, March 29, 1997

Williams, Selina, Apparent Win for Shell in Nigeria Spill Cases, *Wall Street Journal* Online, January 30, 2013

Woodyard, Chris, Sierra Club calling for boycott of Shell over Nigeria, *Houston Chronicle*, page 1, December 8, 1995

www.ingramcontent.com/pod-product-compliance
Lightning Source LLC
Chambersburg PA
CBHW080326270326
41927CB00014B/3111